DICTIONARY OF RUSSIAN LITERATURE

DICTIONARY OF
RUSSIAN LITERATURE

by WILLIAM E. HARKINS

GREENWOOD PRESS, PUBLISHERS
WESTPORT, CONNECTICUT

The Library of Congress cataloged this book as follows:

Harkins, William Edward.
    Dictionary of Russian literature, by William E. Harkins.
Westport, Conn., Greenwood Press ₍1971, c1956₎

    vi, 439 p.   23 cm.

1. Russian literature—Dictionaries.   I. Title.

PG2940.H3   1971   891.7′09   75-139135
ISBN 0-8371-5751-X   MARC

Library of Congress   71

Copyright 1956 by Philosophical Library, Inc.

Originally published in 1956 by Philosophical Library,
New York

Reprinted with the permission of Philosophical Library

Reprinted by Greenwood Press,
a division of Williamhouse-Regency Inc.

First Greenwood Reprinting 1971
Second Greenwood Reprinting 1976

Library of Congress Catalog Card Number 75-139135

ISBN 0-8371-5751-X

Printed in the United States of America

PREFACE

The present work seeks to provide in a compact form essential information on the entire field of Russian literature, as well as much information on literary criticism, journalism, philosophy, theater, and related subjects.

Russian tradition has tended to obliterate the distinction between social and political criticism on one hand, and literary criticism on the other, and even, to an extent, the distinction between philosophy as such and literature. I believe that this tradition will help to justify the inclusion of many philosophers, as well as writers on political and social questions.

A number of short articles on historical topics have been included for the value they may have for readers of Russian literature who require background information on Russian history. In every case the reflection of these events in literature has also been mentioned.

While the present work does not aim at presenting a discursive history of Russian literature, the reader may obtain a continuous account of the historical development of literature in Russia by reading the following articles in succession: Literature, Old Russian; Classicism; Sentimentalism; Pre-Romanticism; Romanticism; Parnassian Poets; Realism; Symbolism; and Literature, Soviet. Other major subject entries include: Drama and Theater; Philosophy; Folk Literature; Criticism and Criticism, Soviet.

Although the book is primarily intended as a reference work, I have not refrained entirely from critical judgment, particularly in the case of the more important writers. I sincerely trust that readers will accept these comments as helpful suggestions rather than *ex cathedra* pronouncements.

The present work treats only literature of the Great Russian people, and Ukrainian and Belo-Russian literatures have not been included. A few leading Ukrainian and Belo-Russian writers are listed and identified as such, however, to prevent any possible misunderstanding. In regard to the old Russian period, I consider writing of the Kievan period (tenth to thirteenth centuries) to be the common heritage of all three East Slavic peoples: Great Russian, Ukrainian and Belo-Russian. In support of this view I would point out that it is in Northeast (Great) Russia, to a large extent, that Kievan literature has survived.

I wish to express my sincere thanks to Mrs. Martha Bradshaw Manheim for her article on "Drama and Theater"; to Professor George Kline for his article on "Philosophy"; to Professor Rufus W. Mathewson, Jr. for "Literature, Soviet"; and to Professor Edward J. Brown for "Criticism, Soviet." All other articles are my own responsibility. Thanks are also due to Miss Rose Raskin, to Professor Leon Stilman and to Professor George Kline for their friendly and helpful criticism of certain articles. Sincere appreciation is also expressed for Mr. Richard Witz's aid in matters of style.

Cross-references may be indicated either in parentheses (see . . .), or simply by spelling the cross-referenced entry in capitals: e.g., PUSHKIN. The titles of published English translations are given only when they deviate significantly from a literal translation of the original Russian titles.

Every care has been taken to insure the accuracy of facts, but in a work of this nature certain errors will no doubt be found. Any comment concerning mistakes will be welcome; such communications should be directed to me in care of the publishers.

WILLIAM E. HARKINS

New York, N. Y.

DICTIONARY OF RUSSIAN LITERATURE

A

Ablesimov, Alexander Onisimovich (1748-83), a writer of comic operas, the most famous of which is *The Miller as Wizard, Cheat and Matchmaker* (1779), a light, gay comedy, based partly on folklore motifs, and concerned with the problems of love and matchmaking. The music was selected from Russian folk songs by Ablesimov himself.

Acmeism, a movement in Russian poetry founded in 1912 by Nikolay GUMILYOV and Sergey GORODETSKI as a reaction against SYMBOLISM. The nickname of "Acmeism" was accepted by the members of the Poets' Guild (as it was officially called) as a warrant of the perfection and achievement for which they were striving. The Acmeists objected to the mysticism of much of symbolist poetry, and, particularly, to the vagueness of its imagery. They also opposed the symbolists' use of images as symbols of unseen metaphysical realities, and called for a return to the use of clear, precise and concrete imagery. Gumilyov declared that he wanted to admire a rose for its beauty, not because it symbolized mystical love. In place of the suggestiveness of symbolist poetry, the Acmeists substituted an emphasis on naming, and for them the use of correct names was much of the essence of poetry. In many of their works, particularly those of Akhmatova, verbs are almost lacking. The Acmeists, and especially GUMILYOV, also emphasized the expression of the virile, the direct and the heroic in their attitude toward life. They applied the name "Adamism" to this tendency in their movement.

Besides Gumilyov and Gorodetski, the school included Anna Akhmatova (see Gorenko) and Osip MANDELSTAM. As an organized movement it lasted from 1912 only until the First World War.

Adamism. See Acmeism.

(1)

Aesopic language, the name given in Russian criticism to the language of oppositional political writing, disguised in literary form for the purpose of passing the CENSORSHIP. Such writing makes extensive use of circumlocution and topical hints at current political happenings; it may also be cast in a generalized form, such as the fable. The reader is supposed to read between the lines or give the particular application suggested by current events. Such devices were most used in the nineteenth century; present-day Soviet critics are better able to detect them. The great master of Aesopic language in Russian literature is SALTYKOV, who himself first used the term in this sense.

Afinogenov, Alexander Nikolayevich (1904-41), a Soviet playwright. He specialized in melodramas about Soviet and foreign life, filled with labor struggles, spies and sabotage. His play *Fear* (1930) became one of the most famous Soviet plays, though it hardly rises above the level of the sensational. It describes how an old Soviet scientist is led by saboteurs to oppose the Soviet regime, but ends by repenting of his error. The play's theme, that fear inspires opposition to Soviet progress, never really becomes credible. *Distant Point* (1935) is less melodramatic, though its thesis—that every Soviet village should be on the alert for defense —is still a sensational one. Afinogenov's final play, *On the Eve* (1941), depicts the German attack on the Soviet Union. It was completed only a month before the writer himself was killed in a German air-raid on Moscow.

Akhmatova, Anna. See Gorenko, A. A.

Aksakov, Ivan Sergeyevich (1823-86), a Russian poet and publicist of the second half of the nineteenth century. The son of the writer S. T. AKSAKOV, he was, along with his brother, K. S. AKSAKOV, one of the younger leaders of the Russian SLAVOPHILES. Outspoken and captious in his criticism of Russian life and politics, he insisted on his right to speak freely, and, in spite of his conservatism, he was often in difficulty with the authorities. Besides articles on political and social questions, Aksakov wrote poetry, for the most part in his younger years, the 1840's and 1850's. He is a didactic poet whose main theme is the civic duty of the individual. He calls for work and discipline that Russian society may progress, and criticizes the inaction of the Russian intellectuals. His unfinished narrative poem of peasant life, *The*

Tramp (1852), had conisderable influence on NEKRASOV's long poem, *Who Can Live Happy in Russia?* Aksakov also wrote on literary questions, and his work includes a noteworthy biography of the poet TYUTCHEV (1874).

Aksakov, Konstantin Sergeyevich (1817-60), a Russian critic and thinker of the mid-nineteenth century. The son of the writer S. T. AKSAKOV, Konstantin, like his brother, I. S. AKSAKOV, was one of the younger leaders of the SLAVOPHILES. In his political writings he strongly idealized the Russian peasant commune as a voluntary association for self-government. The egoism of the individual was swallowed up by his association in this communal society, Aksakov held. He contrasted this "voluntary" social organization to the Western European concept of the state, governed by laws and bureaucratic apparatus, rather than by conscience and inner impulse.

Aksakov wrote literary criticism, in which he accused Russian writers of lacking an organic tie with the people. He also produced original poetry and plays of lesser significance.

Aksakov, Sergey Timofeyevich (1791-1859), a leading Russian prose writer of the mid-nineteenth century. The descendant of a family of gentry, he graduated from the University of Kazan in 1807, and entered the civil service. After an interval spent on his estates, he settled in Moscow in 1826, where he served as a censor and later as a school director. He retired from the service in 1839. In 1832 he had met the writer GOGOL, whose close friend he became. Gogol encouraged him to continue writing (Aksakov's early attempts had been without success). He began his *Family Chronicle* in 1840, but it was published as a whole only in 1856. For some years he wrote books on hunting and fishing, but returned to more serious literature when the eventual publication of his *Family Chronicle* established him as one of the leading writers of the day.

Aksakov's works mix fiction with personal reminiscences of his childhood on a provincial estate. His greatest merit is the delicacy and sensitivity of his recollections, their objectivity, and the intuitive understanding of the child for himself and his elders. He also had a keen and nostalgic feeling for nature and the landscape of the open steppe country of the Volga region, where he had lived as a child.

Aksakov's *Family Chronicle* (1856) is more fictional than most of his works, describing the life of his grandparents and parents before his birth. His grandparents were landowners who had settled on the borderland steppes. The vivid portrayal of the patriarchal figure of the grandfather, called Stepan Bagrov, as well as the accurate depiction of estate life in the eighteenth century, are the most striking features of the book. Aksakov, no liberal, was not greatly disturbed by the sometimes cruel and tyrannical behavior of the landowners toward their serfs, but he did not attempt to disguise it. The book thus served as political ammunition for both the conservatives and the radicals. The novel was published together with Aksakov's *Recollections* of childhood.

The Childhood of Bagrov the Grandson (1858) continued Aksakov's youthful reminiscences, this time in semi-fictional form. It is a peaceful and uneventful narrative, notable for its evocation of a contented, nostalgic atmosphere and its sensitive description of a child's development, rather than for any story interest as such.

Aksakov also left a collection of *Literary and Theatrical Reminiscences* from the period 1810-30, as well as his *Recollections of Gogol*. The latter work, the product of his close friendship with that writer, is of great value for understanding Gogol's complex psychology.

Aksakov's conservative idealization of Russian manorial life placed him close to the Russian SLAVOPHILES. His sons, K. S. and I. S. AKSAKOV, were destined to play leading roles in the Slavophile Movement.

Albov, Mikhail Nilovich (1851-1911), a story writer of the late nineteenth century. His serious tales recall DOSTOYEVSKI'S novels both in their manner and their depiction of pathological states of mind. He also wrote humorous stories.

Aldanov, Mark. See Landau, M. A.

Alexeyev, Konstantin (Stanislavski). See Drama and Theater.

Aliger, Margarita Iosifovna (1915-   ), Soviet poet. Her early poetry was influenced by Anna Akhmatova (see Gorenko). She became popular for her war poetry. Her best-known poem, the narrative *Zoya* (1942), tells of the heroic death of a Young Communist girl tortured and executed by the Germans. Since the war she has been concerned with the theme of reconstruction. Her more intimate and lyric verse gives her the right to be considered one of the most promising of the younger Soviet poets.

Alphabet. The Russian alphabet *(azbuka)* is derived from the alphabet of the OLD CHURCH SLAVONIC language, known as the Cyrillic alphabet after its supposed inventor, St. Cyril, apostle to the Moravian Slavs in the ninth century. Probably Cyril himself was not the inventor of the Cyrillic alphabet, however, but of the Glagolitic, an abstruse alphabet of obscure origin which soon lost favor, presumably because of its difficulty. So-called Cyrillic, modelled to a large extent on the Greek alphabet, then replaced it. The Cyrillic alphabet is still used in approximately its original form for the Church writings of the Orthodox Slavs, including the Russians. It was introduced into Russia some time after her CHRISTIANIZATION (988 or 989). From the Cyrillic alphabet there have developed the modern Russian, Ukrainian, Belo-Russian, Bulgarian and Serbian alphabets.

Under the direction of PETER THE GREAT, the modern Russian secular alphabet, the so-called "civil alphabet," was introduced in 1708. It is based on the original Cyrillic alphabet, but has a smaller number of letters and a less ornate form. Four characters were subsequently dropped as superfluous in 1918, while one, the "hard sign," was restricted in its use. The present alphabet consists of thirty-two letters. It is relatively phonetic, though it does not indicate word stress, an important element in pronunciation.

Andreyev, Leonid Nikolayevich (1871-1919), a Russian writer of the early twentieth century. He was the son of a land surveyor of the Province of Oryol. He studied law at the University of Petersburg, painting portraits in order to support himself. Gloomy and neurotic, he made several attempts at suicide during his student years, and left the university for a time. But in 1893 he enrolled again at the University of Moscow, and in 1897 took his degree in law. His practice consisted of a single case only, which he lost. He turned to newspaper reporting; his articles on court trial gave him material for stories, which he published in the Oryol papers. In 1898 he began to gain wider recognition, and came to the attention of Gorki (see Peshkov), who encouraged him and helped to publish his work. Andreyev's first stories were realistic, often on moral themes. But soon he added more sensational subjects, such as sex and horror, to his repertoire. He was tremendously popular, wrote rapidly, and earned a large fortune in royalties, much of which he dissipated in luxurious living. Ever in search of a more shocking and sensational manner, he drew further away from Realism, and cultivated a modernist style influenced by the Symbolists (see Symbolism). But his "modernism" was largely second-hand and derivative, and his talent, stimulated by drugs, waned rapidly. The First World War revived his activity as one of the few Russian writers who believed in the war, and he waged a vigorous anti-German propaganda campaign. In 1917, finding himself outside Russia (he lived in a villa in Finland, which was now independent), he took a violently anti-Bolshevik attitude in his writing. He died two years later.

Andreyev was a writer of great inventiveness who largely failed to develop his capabilities. He rarely rose above the level of a talented writer of sensational horror tales, in which his literary techniques, borrowed from many and various sources, were chosen with little sense of their taste or purposefulness. Poe, Maeterlinck, Przybyszewski, TOLSTOY and DOSTOYEVSKI were important influences on his work. At arousing a sense of horror Andreyev was skilled enough, at least for the readers of his own generation. But his attempts to inspire a feeling of "metaphysical horror," at which he aimed, largely failed, for his philosophical resources were too meagre. "Andreyev tries to scare us," Tolstoy said, "but I am not afraid."

Philosophically, Andreyev was an atheist and pessimist, without faith in life; for him the fundamental realities are death and sex. All else, even life itself, tends to become illusion, and is depicted as such in his stories. He specializes in blurring the outlines of reality; in his work opposites such as life and death, consciousness and unconsciousness, dream and waking, sanity and insanity —all tend to merge so that we cannot distinguish one from the other. Thus, in the story *Thought* (1902), a man murders a friend while feigning insanity, and is then put into an asylum to discover that he actually is insane.

Andreyev's early realistic stories were written under the strong influence of TOLSTOY. *In the Fog* (1902) is a powerful, if crude story of a young boy who contracts syphilis from a prostitute, and ends by killing both her and himself. *The Governor* (1906) and

Seven That Were Hanged (1908) are later works in this somewhat more restrained Tolstoyan manner. The first is the story of
an old official who orders the execution of revolutionary terrorists,
knowing full well that they will take reprisals and assassinate
him. The second is the story of seven revolutionaries, condemned
to death for an assassination which they have plotted. They are
portrayed with considerable sympathy. The tale was written in
an unsuccessful attempt to placate the radicals, with whom
Andreyev had broken, partly because of a play, *King Hunger*
(1907), which he had written depicting the corruption of all
classes of modern society, including the workers.

The Red Laugh (1904), a pacifist tale published during the
Russo-Japanese War, is typical of Andreyev's stories of unrestrained horror. It depicts, in non-realistic and stylized terms, how
a soldier goes mad after he comes to know the "red laugh" of the
madness and horror of war. The tale's principal merit is that it is
one of the first literary works to show war as a cause of madness.
But Andreyev is no psychologist, and the hero's insanity is described only in the most stereotyped terms. Similarly, *Lazarus*
(1906) is an attempt to depict the horror of death and its corroding power in life; the Biblical Lazarus is used by Andreyev as a
man who has seen death and who communicates its horror to the
living. *Judas Iscariot* (1907) is another story on a Biblical theme.
In it Judas betrays Christ as an inevitable first step in Christ's
Passion, and kills himself in order to join Christ in his kingdom.

Andreyev's later writing and, in particular, his dramas, became
more anti-realistic and symbolic in manner. *The Life of Man*
(1906) is a morality play in which the characters are pure
abstractions: Man, His Wife, Their Son, etc. "Someone in Gray,"
i.e., Fate, reads the chronicle of Man's life and at the end snuffs
out the candle. *He Who Gets Slapped* (1914) has been very
popular both in Russia and abroad. It depicts a circus, a milieu
chosen to symbolize life; the clown who is beaten to make others
laugh is Everyman.

Though Andreyev was sensationally popular during the first
decade of the twentieth century, his popularity waned very rapidly after 1910. As a result, his later influence was quite restricted,
though one can find traces of it in the work of Pilnyak (see
Vogau), GLADKOV and one or two other Soviet writers. An-

dreyev's chief importance is historical. Perhaps no other writer was so in tune with the disillusionment of the Russian intelligentsia of his day, particularly after the failure of the REVOLUTION of 1905.

Andreyevski, Sergey Arkadievich (1847-1920), a critic and writer of the late nineteenth century. By profession he was an advocate. His poetry is not important, but he wrote significant critical studies of Poe, DOSTOYEVSKI, BARATYNSKI (whom he "rediscovered" for our time), TURGENEV and LERMONTOV.

Annals. See Chronicles.

Annenkov, Pavel Vasilyevich (1812-87), a critic of the mid-nineteenth century. At one time the close friend of GOGOL, he left important recollections of that writer, as well as of BELINSKI, HERZEN and others. His study, *Pushkin in the Age of Alexander* (1874), is a classic in the field. In the 1850's and 1860's Annenkov broke away from the civic tradition of BELINSKI in criticism and advocated a doctrine of art for art's sake.

Annenski, Innokenti Fyodorovich (1856-1909), a poet of the early twentieth century. Annenski was professor of Greek literature at the Tsar's Lycée at Tsarskoye Selo and a leading classical scholar. He translated Euripides into Russian, as well as some of the French Parnassian and Symbolist poets. His first volume of lyrics, *Quiet Songs,* appeared in 1904, under the curious pseudonym of Nik. T-O (*nikto,* Russian for "no one"). His masterpiece was his second collection, *The Cypress Chest,* published posthumously in 1910.

Annenski's lyrics are refined, formally perfect and concise, so much so that the structure of the verse is rather elliptic and difficult to understand. The cryptic quality of his work has made him a "poet's poet," whose work is largely unread by the general public. His favorite theme is the weariness and futility of life, which can be surmounted only through love or through art. His lack of mysticism and clarity of expression were rare traits in a poet who was the contemporary of the symbolists (see Symbolism), and these qualities were influential on the younger Acmeists (see Acmeism). Indeed, Annenski was the teacher of both GUMILYOV and Akhmatova (see Gorenko).

Apocrypha. See Literature, Old Russian.

Apukhtin, Alexey Nikolayevich (1841-93), a poet of the late nineteenth century. His poetry expressed in conventional, almost salon verse his nostalgia for lost youth and its pleasures. He also wrote songs in gypsy style. Some of his poems were set to music by his childhood friend, Tchaikovski, and by Mussorgski.

Artsybashev, Mikhail Petrovich (1878-1927), a writer of the early twentieth century. After publishing some stories about the 1905 REVOLUTION, he turned to themes of free love and sex, so popular in Russian literature at this period. His novel *Sanin* (1907) was famous for its advocacy of free love and gratification of individual desires. Its philosophy was influenced by Nietzsche, or, more correctly, by a popular vulgarization of Nietzsche. Artsybashev is against culture, which he regards as a thin veneer imperfectly concealing the primitive sexual drive beneath. His other main theme is death, which for him is, together with sex, the only reality. His novel *At the Brink* (1911-12) depicts intellectuals who alternate between sexual desire and a longing for death; many of them end by committing suicide. Artsybashev's plays were better written than his novels, but their themes were equally crude and negative.

Artsybashev was expelled from the Soviet Union in 1923, and became a journalist abroad.

Arzamas, the name of a literary circle founded in 1815, which supported the new literary and stylistic reforms of KARAMZIN, opposing the "Slavonic" party of SHISHKOV. The group included the poets ZHUKOVSKI, BATYUSHKOV, VYAZEMSKI, PUSHKIN and others. The main activity of the circle was the composition and reading of parodies of the Slavonicized style of their opponents. It was disbanded in 1818. (See Shishkov, Old Church Slavonic.)

Aseyev, Nikolay Nikolayevich (1889-   ), a Russian futurist poet (see Futurism), the friend and follower of MAYAKOVSKI. He entered literature in 1914 as a Bohemian extremist who attempted to shock by his use of vulgar images, such as his famous phrase, "The world is an ugly mug." In the Soviet period his work became more restrained and conventional. His principal poems are *Semyon Proskakov* (1926), a romantic picture of the Civil War, and *Mayakovski Begins* (1940), a long portrait of that poet's life.

Atava, S. See Terpigorev, S. N.

Averbakh, Leopold Leonidovich (1903-?), Soviet critic and politician. A prominent member of the group of proletarian writers called OCTOBER, Averbakh rose to a leading position in the Russian Association of Proletarian Writers (see RAPP). In 1929 the Party allowed RAPP to assume control of Soviet literature. Averbakh has been accused of using his position as unofficial head of RAPP for personal advantage, and even to pay off old scores. In April, 1932, RAPP was dissolved, and the "dictatorship" of Averbakh came to an end. He disappeared completely from the literary scene, and his subsequent fate is unknown.

Averchenko, Arkadi Timofeyevich (1881-1925), a humorist of the early twentieth century, editor of the humorous magazine, *The Satyricon*. His stories are often hilarious, based on an extravagant humor of comical situations. They make fun of the banality of middle-class, philistine life. After the Civil War Averchenko emigrated and settled in Prague, where he wrote stories directed against the Soviet regime.

Avvakum, Archpriest (ca. 1621-82), leader of the sect of Old Believers, which originated during the religious SCHISM of the middle of the seventeenth century. Avvakum was a parish priest who attracted attention by his religious zeal and puritanical strictness. For his opposition to the reforms made by Patriarch Nikon in the Church ritual (see Schism), Avvakum was exiled in 1653 to Siberia, where he served as priest to a band of troops who were engaged in the conquest of the eastern province of Dauria. Recalled in 1662, he accepted the Nikonian reforms, but soon attacked them anew, and was exiled to the far north. A Church council of 1666-67 defrocked and imprisoned him; in his subterranean prison he wrote a large number of works of devotional and inspirational literature for his followers of the Old Believers' sect. In 1682 he was burned at the stake.

As a writer Avvakum is most famous for his *Life* (written 1672-75), the first extensive autobiographical work in Russian literature. It is noteworthy for its directness and frankness; Avvakum succeeds in escaping from the vicious circle of high-style OLD CHURCH SLAVONIC and the rhetorical repetitiousness of earlier Church literature. He writes in the vernacular Russian, and does not hesitate to use colorful, even vulgar, expressions. A record of the tortures and privations of his many years of exile and imprisonment, the work reveals a strong personality reminiscent of the Old Testament prophets in zeal and dignity, as well as not infrequent obstinacy, self-righteousness, and opposition to new ideas. A keen observer of reality, Avvakum was able to break away from the bookish subject matter traditional in earlier writing, and to depict contemporary life. Though in his *Life* he created a new form of expression, his influence was necessarily restricted, for he was opposed both by the official Church and by the advocates of Western enlightenment. Thus he has remained an isolated figure, though there is little doubt that he deserves to be ranked among the greatest Russian writers.

Azhayev, Vasili Nikolayevich (1915-   ), Soviet novelist. His popular novel, *Far from Moscow* (1948), describes the construction of an oil pipeline in the far north during World War II.

B

Babayevski, Semyon Petrovich (1909-   ), Soviet novelist. His collection of stories, *Tales of the Kuban* (1940), concerns collective farms and the struggle to develop responsibility for communal property among the farmers. *The Cavalier of the Gold Star* (1947) and its sequel, *Light over the Land* (1949), treat post-war reconstruction in the collectives.

Babel, Isaak Emanuilovich (1894-1938?), a story writer of the early Soviet period. He was born in a Jewish middle-class family in Odessa. He first published in 1915, when Gorki, who encouraged him, printed two of his stories in his *Annals*. They were highly erotic, and proceedings were taken against Babel for pornography. During the Civil War he joined the Bolsheviks, and in 1920 served as a political commissar in Budyonny's famous cavalry army. In 1923 he returned to literature, and began to publish short sketches of the Civil War, which he subsequently collected in 1926 under the title of *Konarmia* ("Red Cavalry"). The next year he published a collection of *Odessa Tales* (1927) about Jewish life in the Black Sea port city.

The stories of Babel's *Konarmia* were fantastically popular during the 1920's, and went through many editions. At first the critics received them favorably, and only gradually was it realized that Babel's stories showed a certain lack of enthusiasm for the justice of the Red cause. He published little in the 1930's; his last article, a tribute to Gorki, appeared in 1938. Babel disappeared about that time, and was evidently arrested and taken to a concentration camp; report has it that he was executed. The cause of his arrest is not known.

Babel's best work is found in the volume of short tales, *Konarmia* (1926), or "Red Cavalry," as it is known in English translation. These stories show Babel, not unlike his contemporaries

Pilnyak (see Vogau) and Vsevolod IVANOV, fascinated by the violence and brutality of war. He sees the Civil War as a collection of malevolent ironies; he is attracted to the irrational aspects of life, to its ironic paradoxes, its surface color and picturesqueness. He is not interested in psychological analysis, for it is action which interests him, not its cause. Life in his descriptions remains profoundly irrational. Like Pilnyak and Ivanov, Babel is an ornamentalist (see Ornamentalism), and in this respect a follower of REMIZOV. His stories are told in SKAZ—colloquial narrative with much use of dialect elements and slang. Compositionally, with their sharp ironic *pointes,* they show the influence of Maupassant.

The stories of the collection are pictures of horrifying, uncomprehended violence. *The Letter* tells how a son kills his father, a White, and then reports the fact with brutal relish to his mother. *Berestechko* describes the looting and killing which accompany the Red capture of a Polish town; after the carnage is over the Red commander announces to the terrified populace that they are now "liberated." There is little doubt that *Konarmia* constitutes a powerful expression of what for Babel is the essential pointlessness of the Civil War. Budyonny himself criticized the collection as too negative and brutal.

Babel's *Odessa Tales* (1927) are colorful in their strong autobiographic notes and their descriptions of the exotic way of life of the Odessa Jews. The story *Benya Krik* (1926) introduces a fascinating character, a legendary Jewish gangster who lords it over the Odessa underworld and terrorizes the police.

Bagritski, Eduard. See Dzyubin.

Bahdanovich, Maxim (1891-1917), a leading Belo-Russian poet (see Preface).

Bakunin, Mikhail Alexandrovich (1814-76), a Russian radical thinker of the mid-nineteenth century, one of the founders of modern political anarchism. The son of a well-to-do nobleman, he was educated in cadet school in St. Petersburg, and entered military service. But he soon gave up this career and went to Moscow, where he joined the philosophic circle of STANKEVICH, and where he engaged in radical journalistic activity. Going abroad in the 1840's, he took part in the German revolutions of 1848-49, for which he was arrested by the Austrian government and extradited to Russia. From 1851 to 1857 he was in prison; there he wrote a confession of his political "errors," and obtained a commutation of his sentence to exile in Siberia. He escaped from exile in 1861, returning to Europe by way of America. The rest of his life he devoted to revolutionary activity. He and his followers joined the First International, and attempted to convert its membership to anarchism, but they came into violent conflict with the Marxists, and were expelled in 1872.

Bakunin advocated a program of "anarchism, collectivization and atheism" as a solution for man's political and social problems. He had no use for reform, and maintained that revolution was the only weapon of progress. It was Bakunin who gave modern anarchism its collectivist spirit and much of its violent tone, in spite of attempts by later anarchists such as KROPOTKIN to moderate its character. (See Philosophy.)

Ballads. See Folk songs; *Bylina.*

Balmont, Konstantin Dmitrievich (1867-1943), a poet of the late nineteenth and early twentieth century. He is one of the first poets of the new movement of SYMBOLISM, but one whose modernist and symbolist tendencies were relatively superficial. The chief quality of his poetry was its wealth of sound. He knew how to play on certain sounds, such as the mellifluous consonants or the sibilants, to produce verse of unparalleled richness. Poe and Shelley were important models for this poetry. The opulent sound effects of Balmont's verse made him fantastically popular, the most popular of the Symbolists in his own day.

Balmont's important collections were *Under Northern Skies* (1894), *Buildings on Fire* (1900) and *Let Us Be As the Sun* (1903). His poems are vast cosmic pictures of the cold brilliance of the far north, the radiance of the sun, the tempestuousness of storm and sea. These cosmic forces appear as symbols, sometimes of the poet's egotistic desire to pose as a Nietzschean superman, but his ideas and symbolisms are usually banal and puerile. Balmont translated a great deal, especially from English poetry; his translations include versions of Poe, Shelley, Whitman, Wilde and others. They are very popular, but are almost all bad, since he translated foreign poets too freely and in the same ornate and prettified style of his own verse.

Balmont joined the Social Democratic (Marxist) Party and

eagerly greeted the 1905 REVOLUTION. As a result he was forced to leave Russia in 1907. His travels to distant lands, such as Mexico, South Africa and the Pacific Islands, resulted in exotic descriptions of these regions, something new in Russian poetry. After the Revolution of 1918 he left Russia again, this time as an anti-Bolshevik. He settled in France, fell into poverty and neglect, and died insane.

Baltrushaitis, Jurgis (Yuri Kazimirovich; 1873-1945), a symbolist poet of Lithuanian origin, after the Revolution of 1917 Lithuanian minister to the U.S.S.R. He translated Ibsen, Hauptmann and D'Annunzio into Russian. His own poetry is metaphysical, concerned with the theme of man's isolation in the universe.

Barantsevich, Kazimir Stanislavovich (1851-1927), a minor writer of the late nineteenth century. He described the poverty of poor intellectuals of St. Petersburg in a number of rather sentimental stories and novels.

Baratynski (or Boratynski), Yevgeni Abramovich (1800-44), a contemporary of PUSHKIN and, next to him, the leading member of the great poetic generation which matured during the 1820's. Educated in the Corps of Pages as a cadet, he was expelled for theft and reduced to the ranks as a private soldier. Encouraged by DELVIG, he began to write and publish poetry. In 1820 he was transferred to Finland and spent six years there. Finally receiving a commission, he was able to resign from the army and retire to his estate near Moscow. In 1843 he travelled to France and Italy, where he died in Naples the following year.

Baratynski is the most original of the younger poets who formed the so-called "PUSHKIN PLEIAD." His poetic style resembles PUSHKIN's in its conciseness and expressiveness, and shows an even greater precision. Like his greater contemporary, he was still much of a classicist in form and style, if a romanticist in his attitude toward life. He borrowed the new form of the narrative poem from Pushkin, but employed it with originality. His *Eda* (1824-25) is the story of the seduction of a poor Finnish girl by a Russian officer; the poem contains fine descriptions of the Finnish landscape. *The Ball* (1828) concerns the jealousy and suicide of a society lady deserted by her lover. *The Gipsy Girl* (1842) is perhaps his most famous work, in which the heroine inadvertently poisons her faithless lover, supposing that she has given him a love philter.

Baratynski is at his best as an elegist, though in his youth he also wrote light-hearted verse of an Anacreontic character. At the end of the 1820's his poetry became more philosophical, and pessimistic in tone. He feels that man is growing away from nature and, hence, from his own happiness. He writes of death, autumn, eternal recurrence, the sorrows and contradictions of life. The end of all is death, which the poet finally accepts as the only escape, save for that of artistic creation. Such poems are his *The Last Death* (1827), *Death* (1833) and *Autumn* (1837).

Batyushkov, Konstantin Nikolayevich (1787-1855), a leading Russian poet of the beginning of the nineteenth century. He served in the army and civil service, and took part in three campaigns against Napoleon. Subject to attacks of melancholy, he became permanently insane in 1821.

Batyushkov, like his contemporary, ZHUKOVSKI, was a follower of KARAMZIN and a leader in the new trends of early nineteenth-century literature which served to introduce PRE-ROMANTICISM to Russia. But his work is more classical in its inspiration and spirit than Zhukovski's, and more pagan. Its main themes are Epicurean enjoyment of life, erotic passion and sensualism, with overtones of melancholy and disillusionment. Latin, French and Italian poets are his masters, particularly Parny, Tasso and Petrarch. He sought to make Russian poetry equal Italian in its smoothness and melody, and his style is extremely fluent and sweet. Though active in literature between 1805 and 1821, his output is small, consisting mostly of elegies, lyric songs and epigrams. Well known are his elegies, *The Shade of a Friend* (1814) and *The Dying Tasso* (1817). His *Greek Anthology* (1817-18) helped to acquaint Russian readers with Greek classical poetry. Batyushkov is an important predecessor of PUSHKIN.

Bedny, Demian. See Pridvorov, Ye. A.

Beklemishev, Yuri Solomonovich (1908-41), a Soviet novelist who wrote under the pseudonym of Yuri Krymov. His first novel, *The Tanker Derbent* (1938), portrays life and work on a Soviet oil tanker, with much emphasis on competition and Stakhanovite methods. The author was killed at the front in World War II.

Belinski, Maxim. See Yasinski, Y. Y.

Belinski, Vissarion Grigoryevich (1811-48), a leading Russian literary critic, political thinker and philosopher of the 1830's and 1840's. The son of a poor ship's doctor, he entered the University of Moscow in 1829, studying literature, but was expelled after three years, and never took his degree. One cause of his expulsion seems to have been the fact that he had written a play sharply critical of serfdom. His education was largely self-acquired. Though his philosophy was a development of German idealism, particularly of Fichte, Hegel, and later Feuerbach, he could not read German, and knew these philosophers only from translations and from conversations with his friends.

Belinski made his debut as a literary critic in 1833, in NADEZHDIN's journal, *The Telescope*. His early articles, called *Literary Musings*, were characterized by a striking lack of reverence for traditional judgments in literature, combined with a strong admiration for writers of a liberal and progressive cast. His enthusiastic, pugnacious manner soon earned him the nickname of the "frenzied Vissarion." In 1836 *The Telescope* was suppressed, and Belinski found himself without work. He supported himself by tutoring, compiling a Russian grammar, and publishing a newspaper, which, however, soon failed. In 1839 he went to St. Petersburg to become the chief critic of the *Fatherland Notes*. Underpaid, he remained with that journal until 1846, when NEKRASOV invited him to become the critic of *The Contemporary*. Suffering from tuberculosis, he went abroad for his health the following year. There, free of the censorship, he wrote his famous letter to GOGOL, in which he attacked his former literary idol for what he imagined was Gogol's sudden defection to the camp of reaction. The letter, though forbidden in Russia, became famous among the radicals as a testament of Belinski's progressive beliefs. In 1848 Belinski returned to Russia, where he died shortly after. The police were already suspicious of his activities, and in all probability it was only his early death which saved him from martyrdom at their hands.

Belinski's role as a political thinker, philosopher and critic is of the first importance. Historically his work marks the end of the complete domination of Russian literature by the aristocracy, and the emergence of a new class of writers and critics, the so-called *RAZNOCHINTSY*, or classless intelligentsia. Belinski's ideas changed rapidly, and it is difficult to give a unified account of his thought. He demanded that literature express ideas, by which he meant, to a large extent, positive social tendencies. Literature, he believed, should be practical and progressive. His other chief criterion was that literature be natural in its expression. Naturalism for him presumably meant fidelity to life, or realism, although Belinski, writing in a romanticist age, did not of course anticipate the development of the Russian Realist Movement; in his view, the greatest Russian "naturalist" was GOGOL, who was scarcely a realist in the historical sense or, indeed, in any other. Presumably, by naturalism Belinski meant a kind of inner fidelity or truth to life. But in his later writing he definitely excluded the fantastic, and also made it plain that a naturalistic literature should devote at least proportionate attention to the mass of the people. In these last respects his conception of naturalism was of great influence on the developing movement of nineteenth-century REALISM.

In his critical estimates of his contemporaries, Belinski was almost infallible. GOGOL and, to an extent, LERMONTOV were praised by him as the greatest Russian writers. But he underestimated the value of earlier nineteenth-century literature, though he did stress the historical significance of PUSHKIN as the first writer, in his view, to create a distinctly Russian national literature. His judgments of foreign literatures were more fallible; his favorite contemporary writer outside Russia was George Sand. He rejected Russian eighteenth-century literature as too imitative and insufficiently national; for the same reason, paradoxically, he denied the value of Russian folk literature, which he regarded as deprived of spontaneity by the peasants' condition of serfdom.

Belinski's political and philosophical thought, like his criticism, is complicated by the progressive development of his ideas. He successively underwent the influence of the German philosophers Schelling, Fichte, Hegel and Feuerbach. His debut in literature was marked by a period of conservative Hegelianism, in which, influenced by Hegel's proposition that "all that is, is rational," he accepted tsarist absolutism and reaction as part of a rational cosmic order. But he soon threw over conservativism, partly because of his own innate idealism, partly because of the influence of Feuerbach and of his own socialist friends, such as HERZEN,

among the Russian WESTERNERS. He became a Utopian Socialist, with a faith in the inevitability of human progress. An atheist
in his final period, he rejected the Russian Orthodox Church, and
even asserted in his famous letter to Gogol that the Russian
people were profoundly atheistic.

Belinski's influence was of first importance in the further development of Russian criticism, which, since his day, has generally
tended to emphasize moral, social and political values at the
expense of purely esthetic ones. Thus his influence has had both
a salutary and a harmful effect: it has helped to infuse Russian
literature with that spirit of moral questioning and ethical sensitivity which is one of its chief distinctions; on the other hand, it
encouraged neglect of esthetic values and of such essentials as
form and craftsmanship. Belinski's diffuse style demonstrated his
own indifference to such considerations, and had a deleterious
influence in the subsequent development of journalistic criticism
in Russia.

Belinski's chief followers were the "civic critics" of the 1860's,
CHERNYSHEVSKI, DOBROLYUBOV and PISAREV. They car-
ried even further the demand that literature express progressive
social and political ideals, as well as the contempt for esthetic
standards and the tendency to substitute sermons on literary
texts for real critical analysis. In the Soviet Union today, Belinski
is revered as the greatest nineteenth-century Russian critic and
as one of the leaders of the nineteenth-century revolutionary
movement. (See Criticism.)

Belo-Russian literature. See Preface.

Bely, Andrey. See Bugayev, B. N.

Benediktov, Vladimir Grigoryevich (1807-73), a poet of the 1830's.
He followed a career as a civil servant in the Ministry of Finance.
His poetry is primarily erotic, full of conceits and extended metaphors, brilliant, even flashy in technique, and polished but pompous in style. Popular with sentimental readers of the day, he is
today largely forgotten, though his work had some influence on
the SYMBOLISTS. Benediktov was satirized in the figure of
KOZMA PRUTKOV, an imaginary poet created by Count A. K.
TOLSTOY and the Brothers ZHEMCHUZHNIKOV.

Berdyayev, Nikolay Alexandrovich (1874-1948), a leading twentieth-century religious philosopher. In his youth Berdyayev was

a Marxist socialist; in 1898 he was arrested and exiled to Vologda. Philosophically he sought at this period to combine Marxism with Neo-Kantianism. But after the turn of the century he gave up Marxism and turned to a kind of religious romanticism. He joined with S. N. BULGAKOV, who had undergone a similar spiritual change, in publishing the new journal, *Problems of Life* (1903), and in contributing to the collection *Signposts* (1909; see Struve). In 1922 he was expelled from Russia along with many other non-Marxist thinkers. In Berlin he founded a Religious and Philosophical Academy, which was moved to Paris in 1925; in Paris he also edited the journal *The Way* and headed a religious and philosophical publishing house, the Y.M.C.A. Press.

Berdyayev is the best-known of the so-called "Russian Orthodox" philosophers in the West. But it is hardly correct to regard him as an Orthodox thinker; actually his thought is in many respects independent of Orthodox tradition. At the center of his philosophy is the problem of freedom. For him freedom exists before God, as the Divine Nothing, or *Ungrund,* a conception which he took from the German mystic, Boehme. God himself arises from the *Ungrund,* and in turn creates men from it. Man, as the child of both God and of non-being, thus has free will apart from God. God is neither omnipotent nor omniscient, for his power is limited by non-being and by human freedom. But, besides his heritage of irrational freedom from non-being, man may attain rational freedom and, finally, freedom in the love of God. Evil arises when man attempts to set himself up in place of God. Evil brings with it "objectivization," that is, it occasions the development of nature (as opposed to spirit), with its laws and physical properties. Man becomes preoccupied with objectivized nature, and forgets the spirit and God. Though nature is thus viewed by Berdyayev as evil and the result of separation from God, still it is no mere illusion; man's spirit creates it as a reality which is the consequence of the spirit's falling away from God.

Though Berdyayev regards human society and the political order from an anarchic point of view, still redemption and salvation are communal and universal, in his view, not individual. One man cannot accept salvation when he knows that others are eternally damned. Hence Berdyayev stresses the communality of all believers. He finds Christian legalism and its emphasis on the torments of hell a disguised sadism, propagated by man, not by God.

Berdyayev has written an excellent study of DOSTOYEVSKI and the problem of freedom, as well as biographies of KHOMYA-KOV and LEONTIEV.

Bergholz, Olga Fyodorovna (1910-), a Soviet poet. Her early poetry was influenced by Anna Akhmatova (see Gorenko). During the war she published her *Leningrad Notebook* (1942), a collection of war poems, and a long poem, *The Epic of Leningrad* (1942), about that city's heroic defense. More recently she has published *On Stalingrad Soil* (1952), lyric reminiscences of the defense of Stalingrad. Her best poetry is lyrical and intimate, with great pathos.

Bestuzhev, Alexander Alexandrovich (1797-1837), a romantic novelist and poet of the early nineteenth century. His novels and tales were published under the pseudonym of A. Marlinski. While an officer in the guards, he joined the secret conspiracy of the Decembrists (see Decembrist Movement). Together with the poet RYLEYEV, he edited the Decembrist almanac, *The Polar Star*. For his share in the Decembrist Uprising of 1825, he was exiled to the Caucasus as a private soldier. There he was able to continue his literary activity. He was killed in a battle with the Circassians in 1837.

Bestuzhev specialized in writing romantic novels and tales, which are spoiled, unfortunately, by their pompous rhetoric and blasé Byronic heroes. His dialogue is brilliant and witty, however, and his plots lively and full of action. The novels *Ammalat-Bek* (1832), perhaps his finest, and *Mullah-Nur* (1835-36) are set against the exotic background of the Caucasus. Bestuzhev's great contemporary LERMONTOV owed much to him, particularly in the depiction of fashionable society and of the Caucasian landscape.

Bezymenski, Alexander Ilyich (1898-), a Soviet poet and playwright. He entered literature in 1918, and during the 1920's became one of the leading proletarian poets, as well as an active member of OCTOBER and later of RAPP. A follower of MAYA-KOVSKI, Bezymenski used crude diction and a coarse, declamatory style, but without Mayakovski's inspiration. He repeats Mayakovski's superficial optimism, but with little of his complexity. Life for Bezymenski is joyous and optimistic; one has only to be a Communist. Membership in the Party is a favorite subject of his early collections of verse, such as *October Dawns* (1920) and *How Life Smells* (1924). Along with Bedny (see Pridvorov), Bezymenski became a kind of "official" Soviet poet laureate, though he was sometimes criticized for his coarseness. During the 1930's he abandoned his "modernist" techniques, and his subsequent poems are in quite conventional metres. World War II inspired the collection, *Note-book from the Front* (1946), poems on the heroism of Red Army soldiers. *Verses of Wrath* (1949) are satirical poems directed against Britain and America.

Blok, Alexander Alexandrovich (1880-1921), a leading Russian symbolist writer and the greatest Russian poet of the twentieth century. His father, who was partly German by origin, was Professor of Public Law at the University of Warsaw. The parents were divorced soon after the son's birth, and Alexander lived with his mother in Petersburg and on the family estate near Moscow. He entered the University of Petersburg in 1898; by this time he had begun to write poetry, but did not publish anything. He was graduated from the university in 1906, taking his degree in philology. Meanwhile he had married the daughter of D. I. Mendelev, the famous chemist, in 1903. Their marriage was at first a happy one, and some part of Blok's mystical adoration of Sophia, the feminine principle of Divine Wisdom, he bestowed upon his wife. Discovered by MEREZHKOVSKI the same year, he published a few poems in the journal *The New Way,* and the following year his first collection in book form, called *Verses about the Beautiful Lady,* appeared. He was soon recognized as a leading symbolist poet, the greatest of the young mystical poets who were followers of Vladimir SOLOVYOV.

But the harmony of Blok's mystical vision dissolved rapidly after 1903. More and more he gave way to despair, and increasingly he sought escape in debauchery. The Revolution of 1905 aroused his enthusiasm for a short while, and he took part in radical demonstrations. But the failure of 1905 disillusioned him, as it did most Russian intellectuals. Unlike the majority of his fellows, however, Blok greeted the 1917 Revolution with fresh enthusiasm, and made common cause with the Bolsheviks. His great poem, *The Twelve* (1918), celebrates his fervent acceptance of the October Revolution. But his new-born enthusiasm soon waned, and he wrote nothing after January, 1918. He relapsed into a state of chronic melancholy, and died three years later.

Blok was the greatest and most inspired of the Russian symbolist poets. His work is more natural, less calculated and less affected than the poetry of such symbolists as BRYUSOV or Bely. It springs from spontaneous feeling and perception rather than great intellect, and is rich in symbolic and suggestive imagery. But Blok's greatest achievement is the musicality of his verse; it is among the most musical in all Russian poetry. A favorite form which inspired him is the gypsy song: its cabaret themes and melancholy accents appealed to him especially in his middle period, and he was responsible for rediscovering the gypsy songs of the nineteenth-century poet, Apollon GRIGORIEV. Blok is also a great rhythmic innovator, and he contributed to the variety of Russian metrical forms both by varying existing ones and by introducing newer and freer rhythms. He made extensive use of the free "folk" rhythm of the *dolnik,* an irregular, purely tonic form with a varying number of syllables (see Prosody).

Blok's first period, extending from 1898 to the end of 1903, is one of exalted harmony of mystical belief, of the ecstatic vision of Sophia, the feminine hypostasis of Divine Wisdom. The cult of mystical worship of Sophia originated with the philosopher-poet Vladimir SOLOVYOV, and Blok, who had come under Solovyov's influence, shared it with his friends Andrey Bely (see Bugayev) and Sergey Solovyov, nephew of Vladimir Solovyov. In Blok's poetry of this period Sophia appears in various incarnations as the Beautiful Lady, the Eternally Young One, the Mistress of the Universe, the Mysterious Maiden, etc. For him Sophia is the "Eternal Feminine," and his mystical love, though spiritualized, is also a passionate and erotic one. This early poetry is his most harmonious and musical. But it lacks concrete interest; it is too pure and refined.

Towards the end of the year 1903 Blok lost his mystical vision, and his serenity gave way to despair and terror. Demons and apparitions begin to haunt his poetry, and the Unknown Woman, a prostitute whose identity the poet cannot discern, replaces the Beautiful Lady as the chief symbolic figure. The loneliness and ugliness of the city; the coldness and fierceness of snowstorms; drink; taverns and the love of gypsies and prostitutes become favorite subjects of this new poetry, contained in such collections as *Earth's Bubbles* (1905) and *The City* (1906). In the most famous poem of this period, *The Unknown Woman* (1906), the poet observes a courtesan who comes every night to a suburban restaurant to mingle with the drunken revellers. Blok later wrote a play under the same title about this enigmatic figure. In another early verse play, *The Puppet Show* (1907), he pokes savage fun at his own earlier mystic dreams and visions.

After the failure of the Revolution of 1905, Blok gave way more and more to gloom and despair. But a new positive faith slowly emerges, a powerful, irrational love of Russia, which he feels in spite of—almost because of—Russia's backward and contradictory nature. The feminine image of Russia comes to be identified with the Unknown Woman, the prostitutes and gypsies of the earlier poems. This new love of his homeland is expressed in the great cycle, *The Field of Kulikovo* (1908), about the victory of the Russians over the Tartars in 1380; these poems use motifs from the Old Russian Prose poem, the ZADONSHCHINA. The most characteristic expression of Blok's new faith is found in a brief poem to Russia written in 1914, in which he enumerates the sins and stupidities of his motherland, but concludes with a declaration of his love for her.

Blok began a long narrative poem, *Retaliation,* in 1910, but never completed it. He planned it as a synthetic picture of Russian history during the period of the reign of Alexander III and the 1905 REVOLUTION. It would have included three cantoes, one for each of three generations of heroes. The fate of the grandson, who represents Blok himself, is never resolved.

Blok's undoubted masterpiece is *The Twelve* (1918), a poem on the October REVOLUTION. It is completely unique in his poetry, with its use of the frequently vulgar tone and the free rhythms of the contemporary *chastushka,* or popular rhymed quatrain (see Folk Songs). *The Twelve* is composed of a number of short sections which differ rhythmically and stylistically. The effect is in the poem's rhythm, language, and in the brilliant imagery of cold and snow. The work opens with a series of images of the defeated old order: a fat bourgeois with his face muffled in his collar, a priest, a tattered sign proclaiming "All power for the Constituent Assembly!" and, towards the end, a mangy mongrel dog. The heroes, twelve Red guardsmen, march along, quarrelling and shooting. They kill a prostitute who passes by, the faithless mistress of one of their group. As they march on through the frost and blinding snow, Christ appears at their head, as if to lead them. Blok's use of Christ as a symbol is far from clear, and obviously highly personal; he declared, even, that the image did not entirely satisfy him, but that it had to be there. Apparently Christ serves to consecrate the revolutionary activity of the Red guardsmen (whose number—twelve—recalls Christ's disciples). Christ may also symbolize the victory of the Revolution over the Russian Empire, in which Blok saw the heir of the Roman Empire, in its own day conquered by the revolutionary force of Christianity. *The Twelve* shows the influence of the ideas of Ivanov-Razumnik and the Socialist Revolutionary SCYTH-IANS; indeed, Blok embraced the 1917 Revolution because he believed that it would purify Russia through suffering and give her a new spiritual birth.

The poem called *The Scythians*, also written and published early in 1918, likewise shows the influence of the Scythian movement. The poem depicts the Russian people as "Scythians," "Asiatics," who will be the friends or the conquerors of the West as the latter chooses. The poem was written as a threat to the Allies, then contemplating intervention in the Russian Civil War. A powerful piece of invective, it has served as a disturbing prophecy of events which may still be to come.

In spite of Blok's stature as a poet, his influence has not been great. This may have been due in part to his morbidity and pessimism, as well as to the deeply personal spirit of his poetry. Something of the melodiousness of his verse, though on a much simpler scale, was acquired by YESENIN. The anti-symbolist trends of the period after 1910, culminating in the new schools of ACMEISM, FUTURISM and IMAGISM, helped to weaken any influence he might have had. By the early Soviet period the cultural atmosphere had so changed that Blok's mystical serenity and his despair alike already seemed moods from a far distant past. Though Blok has been honored in the Soviet Union as a great poet who accepted the Revolution, still Soviet critics have little use for his mysticism and gloom. Like MAYAKOVSKI, he is necessary to the Soviet regime as an example of a great poet who came to prominence before the REVOLUTION of 1917 and who promptly accepted that Revolution and made common cause with the Bolsheviks. The fact that he, somewhat like Gorki and Maya-kovski, accepted the Revolution because of a highly personal interpretation of its significance, has been overlooked.

Boborykin, Pyotr Dmitrievich (1836-1921), a novelist of the late nineteenth and early twentieth century. Influenced by TUR-GENEV and the French naturalists, he attempted in such novels as *On the Wane* (1890) to depict the ideological development of the Russian intelligentsia throughout the final decades of the nineteenth century. He also sought to portray the whole social history of contemporary Russia and the rise of capitalism, as in the novels *Businessmen* (1872) and *Kitay-Gorod* (1882). His works are relatively unique in Russian literature in that they express few ideas, but merely seek to give an objective picture of society and its development. Besides his countless novels, he wrote a number of realistic plays on similar themes. Like his naturalistic models, Boborykin's novels and tales are weak in construction and crowded with unnecessary details.

Bobrov, Semyon Sergeyevich (1767?-1810), a poet and literary theoretician of the late eighteenth and early nineteenth century, an adherent of the "Slavonic" party of SHISHKOV. Bobrov's poetry is remarkable chiefly for its rich and fanciful diction, much of which he himself invented.

Bogatyr, Russian name for one of the heroes of the *byliny,* or heroic folk songs (see *Bylina*).

Bogdanov, A. (pseudonym of Alexander Alexandrovich Malinovski, 1873-1928), a Marxist philosopher and political leader of the late nineteenth and early twentieth century. Under the influence of Mach and Avenarius he attempted to modify Marxism by denying any sharp opposition of psychic and material being; the spiritual and the physical for him are simply different aspects of the same experience. This position was severely criticized by LENIN. Bog-danov later replaced Marx's emphasis on dialectic development with that of deliberate organization of nature by man, which he called "tektology": spontaneous processes of change in nature and

society must be replaced, in his view, by man's active intervention. (See Philosophy.)

Bogdanov attempted the systematic creation and encouragement of a new proletarian literature. He was the leading spirit
behind the PROLETKULT ("Proletarian Culture"), an organization founded in 1917 for training proletarian writers and encouraging the development of a distinctively proletarian culture.
Bogdanov's insistence that this organization should be independent of State and Party antagonized LENIN and TROTSKI,
and his demand for the independence of proletarian culture was
officially regarded as a heresy; in 1920 the Proletkult was put
under state control, and soon after was liquidated.

Bogdanov also wrote several science-fiction novels.

Bogdanovich, Ippolit Fyodorovich (1743-1803), an eighteenth-
century poet and translator from French. His *Dushenka* ("Little
Psyche," 1783) is a free reworking of La Fontaine's *Les amours
de Psyché et de Cupidon,* which, in turn, was an adaptation of
Apuleius' *Golden Ass.* Its originality depends partly on the introduction of motifs from Russian folklore into the classical narrative. Its verse is light and polished, and the poem was extremely
popular during the early nineteenth century.

Bogdanovich, Maxim. See Bahdanovich.

Books. See Manuscripts; Printing.

Boratynski. See Baratynski.

Bronstein, L. D. See Trotski.

Bryusov, Valeri Yakovlevich (1873-1924), a leading Symbolist poet.
The son of a wealthy merchant, he received an excellent education, which included study at Moscow University, and was one
of the best educated men of his day. His poetry was strongly
influenced by the French Symbolists, Baudelaire and Verlaine.
His youthful poems imitated the French Symbolists, and provoked ridicule among his readers. Only by 1906 did he begin to
receive wide recognition. In 1904 he founded a review, *The
Scales* (1904-09), which was the most important literary publication of the Symbolists and, indeed, of the whole period. Bryusov
became the acknowledged leader of the Moscow Symbolists, as
well as one of the leading critics and verse theorizers of the day.
He translated widely, including the French Symbolists, Armenian
poets, and the first complete version of Poe's poetry in Russian.

He was also a scholar of real merit, and before his death undertook the editorship of a collected edition of the works of PUSH-
KIN, which, however, was never completed.

After the Revolution of 1917, Bryusov joined the Bolsheviks.
He had previously taken little part in politics, but was violently
opposed to the tsarist regime. He was made head of the Soviet
Russian censorship, but proved unreliable and was soon replaced.
He also gave instruction in the art of poetry to young Soviet
poets. Since he was, during his final years, a party member and
official, he is the only Symbolist poet, besides BLOK, whose
poetry receives the stamp of approval of the Soviet regime today.
But this approval is largely formal, for the Communists have little
real enthusiasm for Bryusov's "decadent" verse and must content
themselves with extravagant admiration of his few flat patriotic
poems.

Bryusov entered literature with a group of lyrics published in
the first volume of the almanac, *Russian Symbolists*, which he
helped to edit and publish privately in 1894. This collection may
be said to mark the formal beginning of the Symbolist movement
in Russia. His more important volumes of verse are *Urbi et Orbi*
(1903) and *Stephanos* (1905). Many of his poems are on classical
themes, which he treats with cold sensuality, great erudition and
a delight in heroic action. Bryusov's verse is saturated with opulent sound effects and dazzling imagery. Erotic love is a favorite
subject, often presented in its perverse aspects or as a kind of
impassioned mystic ritual. Another favorite subject, paradoxically
(in view of Bryusov's cult of antiquity), is the modern city, and
he is perhaps the first major poet of the city in Russian literature;
for him the city serves as another source of the mysterious and
exotic. His poem, *The Pale Horse* (1903-04), symbolizes the city
and modern civilization in the image of the "pale horse" of the
Apocalypse. The destruction of modern civilization, half feared,
half welcomed by Bryusov, is another of his themes.

Bryusov's prose is close to his poetry, with the same opulence
of sound and imagery, the same eroticism and interest in the
perverse. The wonders of the supernatural and fantasies of the
future are other themes, as well as pictures of the classic world.
His tales are strongly influenced by the fantastic stories of Poe.
His best novel, *The Fire Angel* (1907), is a story of witchcraft in

Germany during the time of Luther. *The Republic of the Southern Cross* is perhaps his most famous tale. It tells how a totalitarian state is threatened with extinction by a mysterious epidemic, a subject which seems to belie Bryusov's avowed Communist sympathies, and which the Soviets have tried to forget.

Buchinskaya, Nadezhda Alexandrovna (1876-1952), a poet and humorist of the early twentieth century, who wrote under the pen-name of Teffi. Her poetry combines erotic themes with eastern exoticism. Her tales are lightly humorous and delicate, in the style of CHEKHOV. After the Revolution of 1917 she emigrated, and her later writings present satiric portraits of the life of Russian émigrés.

Budantsev, Sergey Fyodorovich (1896-   ), a Soviet novelist and dramatist. His first significant work, *The Revolt* (1923), is a novel of the Civil War depicting the suppression of a local Socialist Revolutionary insurrection by the Reds. *A Tale of the Sufferings of Mind* (1931) describes a scientist's estrangement from life and his attempts at suicide; at the last minute he is saved, in part by his scientific curiosity, which gives him a new interest in life.

Bugayev, Boris Nikolayevich (1880-1934), a leading symbolist writer, who published under the pseudonym of Andrey Bely ("white"). He early met the great religious philosopher, Vladimir SOLOVYOV, and came under his influence. Bely studied philosophy and mathematics at the University of Moscow, at the same time beginning to write extravagant and decadent poetry, the first of which appeared in 1902 under the unusual title of *Symphony (Second Dramatic)*. Bely's poetry was ridiculed by the critics, and never became very popular. In spite of ridicule he continued to publish both poetry and prose. In 1913 he and his wife became disciples of Rudolf Steiner, the anthroposophist, and they spent four years in Germany with Steiner. Meanwhile Bely came under the influence of the SCYTHIANS, and greeted the REVOLUTION of 1917 as a terrible ordeal which would nevertheless purify Russia. His poem *Christ Is Risen* (1918) carries a confusing mystical identification of the Revolution with Christ, in which it resembles BLOK's *The Twelve*. But Bely soon rejected Bolshevism, and began to hope for a mystical rebirth of Russian spiritual culture. In 1921 he emigrated, but returned in 1923 and remained in the Soviet Union until his death.

Bely is a difficult writer, mystical in his thought and often obscure. Never very popular, he is a "writer's writer," who influenced the style of many of the novelists of the 1920's with his ORNAMENTALISM. Bely's style, both in his poetry and prose, is highly mannered, with an intricate musical system of interwoven themes and motifs. The poetry is often in free verse, but is rhythmical, and even "symphonic"; Bely uses as a genre title the term "symphony." At the same time he experiments with words by coining neologisms and by the "autonomous" use of free linguistic formations, the coining of new word hybrids from existing roots, and the interchanging of parts of speech, so that verbs are formed from nouns and adjectives, etc. In *Kotik Letayev* (1918) this tendency reaches its height, and in its many-leveled use of language, stream of consciousness narrative and deliberate mixing of planes of narration the novel reminds one of Joyce, though it is independent of his influence.

Bely's symbolism and his use of language are related to his mystical philosophy. He shuns reality as such, and his treatment of it is satirical, or fantastic as he attempts to replace reality with a grotesque or comic world of his own imagination. For him the cosmos is disordered and unstable, and as such terrifying to man. To protect himself man employs reason, which, by interpolating the law of causality in nature, forcibly reduces it to order. But reason is cold and inadequate for comprehension of the spiritual values of life. The fear of chaos and the weakness of man's reason are frequent themes in Bely's writing, and his fictional works inevitably end with the destruction of the rational and stable by the insecure and chaotic. But through the symbol, which for Bely is a mythic image achieved by mystic experience, the gap between ego and non-ego, consciousness and being can be bridged. The task of art is the creation of such mythic symbols, and thus art has a philosophic, even a religious function.

The Silver Dove, Bely's first and least obscure novel, was published in 1910. Strongly influenced by GOGOL, it treats the theme of the contrast of East and West in the Russian cultural tradition. The hero, a poet steeped in classical and western culture, remains unsatisfied with his learning, and joins a sect of peasants called White Doves who practise mystical erotic rites. For a time he finds enjoyment with them, but later seeks to return to his former life. Terrified that he may divulge their secrets, the sectarians murder him.

Petersburg (1913) shows the influence of DOSTOYEVSKI as well as GOGOL, particularly of Dostoyevski's early Petersburg tales and grotesque characterizations of madness. Petersburg appears as a place where Western rationalism mixes with a substratum of Asiatic "feeling." The story concerns the struggle of reactionary officials and nihilist revolutionaries; the action centers around a concealed bomb, masked as a can of sardines and due to explode within twenty-four hours.

Kotik Letayev (1918) is Bely's most original work. It is autobiographical; its main theme is the progressive development of a child's conception of the external world. The author uses certain prenatal memories in accordance with the anthroposophical belief that the child inherits experiences of the race. The novel is remarkable in that the narrative structure as well as the language is broken down and "reassembled" in a system of contrapuntal references which suggest the gradual organization of the child's experience; the story itself emerges from chaos, as it were. By contrast, the sequel, *The Crime of Nikolay Letayev* (1921), is thoroughly conventional; it is the story of his parents' rivalry for control of the writer's education. Bely's later novels, *The Memoirs of a Crank* (1923), *Moscow* (1926), and *Masks* (1930-32), carry his ornamentalist and polyphonic tendencies even further.

Bely's four volumes of memoirs (*Recollections of Alexander Blok*, 1922; *On the Border of Two Centuries*, 1929; *The Beginning of a Century*, 1932, and *Between Two Revolutions*, 1933) are valuable for the record they give of the ideological history of the intelligentsia and the evolution of the Symbolist Movement (see Symbolism). Bely is also an important literary critic, as well as an original theorist on Russian prosody.

Bulgakov, Mikhail Afanasievich (1891-1940), a Soviet novelist and playwright. He was graduated from the Medical Faculty of Kiev University in 1916, but never practised. His first important novel, *The White Guard* (1924), depicts the successive occupation of the Ukraine by the Germans, by the forces of Petlyura, and finally by the Bolsheviks. The work is unique in Soviet literature in that its heroes are White officers, and are portrayed sympathetically. Bulgakov dramatized the novel as *Days of the Turbins*

(1926). One of the best constructed of Soviet plays, its success was spectacular. Because of the play's doubtful ideology, however, the government soon stopped its performance.

By contrast with the realism of *The White Guard,* Bulgakov's early collection of tales, *Deviltry* (1925), is fantastic and satiric. The stories are criticisms, at least implicit, of the Soviet regime. The longest of them, *The Fatal Eggs,* tells how a professor, engaged in genetic experiments on poultry, treats a shipment of the eggs of crocodiles, ostriches and anacondas sent to him by mistake through the error of a government bureau. The monsters which hatch out lay waste the area and threaten the future of the whole Soviet Union; the country is saved only by an early frost which destroys them and their eggs.

Another story in this collection is *The Adventures of Chichikov* (the title which the tsarist censorship had forced on GOGOL's *Dead Souls).* Chichikov, Gogol's rascally hero, is transplanted to the Soviet Union, where he finds life exactly the same: dirt and filth are everywhere, and there is no end of opportunity for the exercise of his knavish talents.

Bulgakov also wrote several satirical plays. *The Crimson Island* (1928) is a direct attack on the Soviet censorship. Towards the end of his career official opposition forced him to restrict his writing to dramatizations of the works of other writers, such as his *Dead Souls* (1932); or to write plays on the lives of famous writers: *Molière* (1936), and *Pushkin* (1943).

Bulgakov, Sergey Nikolayevich (1871-1944), a leading religious philosopher of the twentieth century. In his youth Bulgakov was a Marxist economist, but beginning in 1901 he underwent a spiritual crisis which resulted in his conversion to Orthodoxy. Along with BERDYAYEV, he contributed to the liberal and anti-Marxist collection *Signposts* (1909; see Struve, P. B.). In 1918 he was ordained a priest. In 1922, with Berdyayev and other anti-Marxist philosophers, he was expelled from the Soviet Union. He went to Prague and later to Paris, where he continued to publish until his death.

Bulgakov's religious philosophy was strongly influenced by SOLOVYOV, especially by the concept of Sophia, the femininely conceived principle of Divine Wisdom. In Bulgakov's thought Sophia is identified with the world-soul, the world of eternal ideas, which stands between Absolute Deity and the cosmos as a mediator, sharing the nature of both. Sophia is the Eternal Feminine, which, as receptive to God's creativity, is thus the "principle of the world." The world itself, impregnated with the eternal ideas of Sophia, is in process of merging with Sophia. Evil results, in Bulgakov's view, from the intrusion of "nothingness" into the cosmos as a chaotic force. Salvation has been achieved for man by Christ's passion; Bulgakov believes that all men will eventually be redeemed, arguing that it is impossible that men should suffer forever for finite and particular sins.

Bulgarin, Faddey Venediktovich (1789-1859), a Russian writer and journalist of Polish origin. Bulgarin was notorious as a spy and informer for the secret police during the reign of Nicholas I. His paper, *The Northern Bee*, represented the interests of the government and the conservative nobility; in it he attacked progressive writers such as PUSHKIN, LERMONTOV and BELINSKI. Published by him from 1825 to 1857, it was for a long time the only private newspaper in Russia, as well as the only private periodical authorized by the government to publish political news. Bulgarin also wrote didactic novels and historical fiction, in which history was distorted to serve official purposes.

Bunin, Ivan Alexeyevich (1870-1953), a leading writer of the late nineteenth and twentieth century. He came from an old, impoverished family of landowning gentry. Bunin left school at the age of fifteen, and in 1888 published his first poetry. In 1892 he printed his first collection of stories. He travelled much in the Mediterranean and the Orient, and his stories about these countries created a new exoticism in Russian literature. In 1918 he emigrated, settling in France. He continued to write in emigration, and remained an uncompromising enemy of the Soviet Union until his death. In 1933 he received the Nobel Prize for literature; he is the only Russian writer to receive this honor.

Though Bunin was perhaps the finest lyric poet of the pre-Symbolist romanticists, his poetry is less important than his prose. He is a Parnassian, the chief subject of whose lyrics are impressions of nature. Though he continued publishing poetry long after the turn of the century, he ignored the modernist movement of SYMBOLISM completely.

Bunin's prose is in many ways an extension of his poetry. Indeed, it is at times more opulent, more lyrical, even, than his rather dry verse, though at other times it is quite sparse and bare. The lyricism of certain of his stories depends on the poetic quality of imagery, often exotic, and of moods, often nostalgic. Bunin's lyricism is in the tradition of AKSAKOV, of TURGENEV's stories of young love, of CHEKHOV's *The Steppe* and of GONCHAROV's "Dream of Oblomov." Another of Bunin's gifts is that of understatement; his effects are often so delicate and subtle that he can be described as a "writers' writer." These understated effects are buried in a matrix of terse, bare writing, or of beautiful but monotonous, nostalgic mood painting.

Bunin has two types of tales: the one, starkly naturalistic and bare in style, such as his novel, which he calls an "epic," *The Village* (1909-10); the poetry here is largely that of understatement. The other manner, as in *The Dreams of Chang* (1916), is rather more opulent and exotic. Bunin tends to prefer the former style for Russian subjects, the latter for foreign ones, but this is far from universal, and it is just its terseness which makes *The Gentleman from San Francisco* a masterpiece.

Bunin's manner is exceptional for the period in which he began to write. But his content, his constant preoccupation with the themes of love and death, as well as his strongly esthetic attitude, show his relation to his contemporaries, the Symbolists. Philosophically, Bunin is a hedonist who believes that the joys of life must be seized before old age and death intervene. But sexual love has its dark side for him as well as its joyous one, and the lover readily comes to desire his own death and to identify love and death, as in the story called *The Elagin Affair* (1927).

The Village (1909-10) is Bunin's most naturalistic and gloomy work, a sordid picture of the Russian village after the decay of the landowning gentry, with the peasants living in anarchy, squalor and drunkenness. Two brothers, shopkeepers, are the protagonists: one practical, the other a dreamer; in the end both conclude that life is not worth living.

Sukhodol ("Dry Valley," 1911) is a tale with a similar theme. As later with the semi-autobiographical *Life of Arseniev* (1927; English translation as "The Well of Days"), the subject is the disintegration of the life of the gentry, exemplified by the decay of a noble family; insanity and poverty are the symptoms of this decay.

The Gentleman from San Francisco (1915) is Bunin's masterpiece. It belongs to the tradition of Lev TOLSTOY's writings on death, particularly *The Death of Ivan Ilyich*. Both Tolstoy and Bunin use a terse economy of means to increase the horror and emphasize the irony of death. Bunin's American millionaire has spent all his life piling up money; now, in a belated attempt to enjoy life, he takes a trip around the world, but dies as soon as he reaches the isle of pleasure, Capri.

Not long before his death, Bunin published an interesting collection of *Reminiscences* (1950; English translation as "Memories and Portraits") about Russian writers, including CHEKHOV, Gorki (see Peshkov) and A. N. TOLSTOY. Unfortunately, Bunin's distaste for everything Soviet often blinded him to the talent of Soviet writers.

Bunin is quite alone in the stream of Russian literature. His gift of lyrical understatement, and, above all, his almost complete lack of philosophical ideas, make him quite exceptional. His influence has been limited; FEDIN is the only important Soviet writer who shows its traces.

Burlyuk, David Davidovich (1882-   ), a futurist poet (see Futurism), the teacher of MAYAKOVSKI. After the 1917 Revolution he left the Soviet Union for the United States, where he has become well-known as a painter.

Butkov, Yakov Petrovich (ca. 1815-56), a mid-nineteenth century writer of stories. Of middle-class origin, he lacked formal education. He was a follower of GOGOL, and his tales, collected in the volume of *Petersburg Summits* (1845-46), describe the poverty-stricken life of petty civil servants, treated both humorously and sympathetically.

Bylina (pl. *byliny*), a special type of epic folk song, often loosely connected with some historical movement or event, and embellished with much fantasy or hyperbole. The name *bylina* ("what happened") is a purely scholarly term which came into use in the 1830's; *starina* ("what is old") is the name actually used by the folk. The songs relate the deeds of the *bogatyrs*, heroes who gather at the court of Prince Vladimir in Kiev, where they feast, and from where they set out to repel invasion, conquer new lands, hunt game, or combat fantastic giants and monsters. Today the *byliny* are the exclusive property of the folk (peasantry), and are largely restricted to the far north of European Russia and some parts of Siberia. Since folk literature is constantly developing and changing, it is improper to regard the *byliny* as works of an older literature, though this mistake is often made. At best it can be said that they preserve certain archaic features.

Historical events are reflected in the subjects of the *byliny*, though vaguely and inaccurately. A number of subjects date from the earliest period of Russian history (ninth to thirteenth centuries), such as Russia's Christianization (symbolized as a battle with a dragon), the struggle with the nomad Polovcians, the career of the magician Prince Vseslav of Polotsk (reflected in the song about the *bogatyr* Volkh Vseslavevich), and others. These subjects suggest that the epic song form is at least as old as the dawn of Russian history, and probably much older. A large number of *byliny* treat the Tartar invasion in the thirteenth century, though most of these give the victory to the Russians, suggesting that earlier tragic songs relating the Russian defeat were altered either through wishful thinking or after the final Russian victory over the Tartars. Ivan the Terrible (1533-84) appears in several songs as a stern, awesome ruler. In the sixteenth and seventeenth centuries older epic songs were reworked in approximately the form in which we have them today. Since then new *byliny* have been rare; the form was partially supplanted by the newer historical song, a shorter, less fantastic narrative which gives the impression of greater fidelity to truth. (See Folk songs.)

Most of the *byliny*, whatever the historical period from which they derive, are set against one background, the court of Prince Vladimir Svyatoslavich (978-1015) at Kiev. This produces anachronisms, as when the Tartar invasion of the thirteenth century occurs in the reign of Vladimir. It is clear that this setting is only a cliché detail which became more or less obligatory for new songs, so that it is possible to speak of a Kievan cycle of *byliny*.

The principal heroes of the Kiev cycle are Ilya Muromets, Dobrynya Nikitich and Alyosha Popovich. The latter two are known to us from history, Dobrynya as the uncle of Prince Vladimir (in the songs he appears as his nephew), Alyosha as a Rostov hero of the early thirteenth century. Ilya is not mentioned in historical sources, but he is referred to in both the Scandinavian *Thidreksaga* of the thirteenth century and the Middle High German poem of the same century, the *Ortnit*. His appellative name of Muromets ("from Murom") may actually be a corruption of "Norman." This suggests that Ilya was originally a Scandinavian (Varangian) leader active in Russia. On this basis he has sometimes been identified with the Varangian ruler Oleg (879-912), but this is doubtful. In Ilya's case we are in no position, therefore, to judge the historical authenticity of the numerous tales about him, and most of them, such as the story of his combat with the Tartars or the fantastic pagan giant Idolishche ("the great idol"), probably have nothing to do with him as a historical personage. This is also true of most of the subjects about Dobrynya Nikitich, but several of these do suggest their connection with the historical Dobrynya. Vladimir's uncle Dobrynya actually served as his matchmaker, as he does in one of the songs. The historical Dobrynya undertook a campaign to put down paganism in Novgorod, and this fact seems to be reflected in the *bylina* account of Dobrynya's struggle with the dragon, a well-known medieval symbol of paganism. Alyosha Popovich is mentioned in the chronicles as killed in the battle with the Tartars on the River Kalka in 1223; so he perishes (or rather, is turned to stone) in the *bylina* account of that battle.

A certain number of *byliny* are not connected with Kiev or Vladimir. These include a group set in the northwest Russian trading city of Novgorod. The principal heroes are Sadko, a dulcimer player who wins a fabulous fortune and becomes a merchant (reflecting Novgorodian trading interests), and Vasili Buslayev, a giant who cannot restrain his boisterous brashness and energy. He probably reflects lower-class opposition to the rule of the city by its merchant oligarchy. Both these *bogatyrs* are mentioned in Novgorod historical sources, but we know almost nothing about them as historical personages.

Byliny are of two kinds: heroic, in which deeds of valor are described, and romances, which deal with love, infidelity, intrigue, magic or fabulous wealth. The latter group is by far the smaller, and the subject of romantic or chivalric love almost absent. Russia did not undergo the influence of Western European chivalry, of course. A popular hero of the romances is Churilo Plenkovich, renowned not for valor but for great wealth, good looks and elegant dress. He is killed by an outraged husband who discovers him in his wife's bed. Dyuk Stepanovich is another *bogatyr* noted for fantastic wealth. He is represented as coming from India, but it is supposed that his great wealth actually reflects the rise of the West Russian province of Galicia in the twelfth and thirteenth centuries, when Galicia gained an ascendancy over Kiev.

The *byliny* are sung today, or rather chanted, by specialist singers, called *skaziteli* ("narrators"). These are often artisans, sometimes blind, who perform as amateurs. There is no accompaniment. The songs vary in length from 100 lines or less to 1,000 or more, depending on the skill of the singer. Details of plot are relatively fixed, but the narrator has great freedom in his choice of words and embellishing details. There is a tendency for the verse to pass into prose in some areas (e.g., the Ukraine) and with less skilled narrators. Where it is preserved, the verse is a free line with a constant number of stresses and relative freedom in the number and position of unstressed syllables. This freer form may have developed from an older, more rigid metrical form. Rhyme is only sporadic; the chief poetic device, besides repetition of words, phrases and plot motifs, is parallel syntactic construction of lines. Similes involving nature are also common. Fixed epithets (e.g., *"brave* youth," *"white* hands," *"swift* feet") are frequent, almost obligatory with many nouns, even when they may contradict the sense of the tale.

Byliny were recorded in manuscript as early as the sixteenth and seventeenth centuries, probably because of the shrinking of the territory in which they were still performed. Scholarly collection and study began early in the nineteenth century, and many excellent collections (Kireyevski, Rybnikov, Gilferding, Markov, the Brothers Sokolov, etc.) have been made. The form persists among the folk until today, but it is evidently dying out with the spread of literacy and modern civilization.

Scholarly interpretation of the *byliny* has varied with the passing of time. Mid-nineteenth century Russian scholars such as Buslayev and Orest Miller, influenced by the German Mythological School, considered them, along with folk tales, to be dramatizations of the cosmic struggle of the forces of light and darkness, or as representations of other mythic themes. In the 1860's this view yielded to that of the Diffusionist School, influenced by Theodor Benfey, according to which the subjects of the *byliny* were merely a series of migrant plots, passing from people to people. Towards the end of the nineteenth century the Historical School was founded by Vsevolod Miller. It concentrated on the study of historical details preserved in the *byliny*. The Formalist School of the 1920's (see Formalism) stressed the use of poetic devices and formulas. All these schools have contributed something of value to an overall comprehension of the songs. In accordance with the principles of so-called Vulgar Sociology (see Criticism), Soviet scholars at first neglected the *byliny* because of the view that they were originally the work of professional singers in the pay of the ruling classes. Today this attitude has been rejected, and it is now considered that they are creations of the whole Russian people. Though it is true that the peasantry has preserved the songs and even altered them, it is doubtful if the folk is responsible for their original composition; ultimately they were probably the work of professionals, probably analogous to the minstrels and troubadours of the West.

Byliny have had some influence on modern Russian literature, especially in poetic reworkings by LERMONTOV, MEY, A. K. TOLSTOY, and others. Outstanding is Rimsky-Korsakov's opera *Sadko*, a retelling of the songs about that hero.

C

Cadets. See Revolution of 1905.

Catherine the Great (Catherine II, 1729-96; reigned 1762-96).
Famed as a liberal and enlightened despot, Catherine's liberalism
was actually characteristic only of the first few years of her reign;
after the Pugachov Uprising of 1773-75 she lost enthusiasm for
reform. Though she came to the throne with plans for improving
the lot of the serfs, her reign actually increased the privileges of
the nobility and confirmed them in their rights over the peasants.

A person of considerable culture, Catherine corresponded with
Voltaire, Diderot, D'Alembert and Grimm. Her Russian writings,
though not equal to her French letters and memoirs, are quite
creditable, considering that Russian was not her native language.
She wrote satires, comedies, comic operas and didactic fairy tales.
The main targets of her satires were provincialism, backwardness,
faddish imitation of the superficial aspects of Western culture,
and FREEMASONRY, popular among the Russian nobility towards the end of the century.

Catherine was a patron of literature and the arts. In 1769 she
encouraged the development of satirical journals by founding her
own, called *Omnium-gatherum (Vsyakaya vsyachina)*, to which
she herself contributed. Other journals soon appeared, including
those of NOVIKOV, but, instead of confining their attacks to such
harmless targets as prejudice and provincialism, as Catherine
wished, they turned to serious social and political satire. In 1774
she closed down all the satirical journals.

After the French Revolution, Catherine became reactionary,
and herself directed a wave of repression against liberal writers,
resulting in the arrest and imprisonment of NOVIKOV and
RADISHCHEV.

Censorship. In one form or another, the control of literature by State or by Church has been practised throughout Russian history. Indexes of heretical books were circulated from the beginnings of Russian literature (see Literature, Old Russian). Formal, preliminary censorship of all printed materials was instituted only in 1796, however, under CATHERINE THE GREAT, while the first detailed statute on censorship appeared only in 1804 under Alexander I. Censorship was fairly liberal under Alexander, though the law of 1804 suggested that the censor should not only suppress harmful writings, but should also further the "true enlightenment of minds and improvement of morals."

During the reign of Nicholas I (1825-55), censorship became extremely severe, partly as a consequence of the Uprising of 1825 (see Decembrist Movement) and the Polish Uprising of 1830. The government prohibited not only opinions which were unfavorable to it, but even those which were favorable; it viewed such writings as tacit implications that the public had some right, after all, to criticize the government's actions. Preliminary censorship did not constitute any guarantee of security for the writer; he could be arrested or a journal suppressed even after the censor's approval of the material in question had been received. Thus POLEVOY's paper, *The Moscow Telegraph,* was shut down in 1834 for its critical review of a play by KUKOLNIK, a hyperpatriotic drama which had been well received by the court. Many of the journals of the 1830's were arbitrarily suppressed in this fashion, and the government even became reluctant to grant permission to publish new journals. Censorship was not only political at this time, but extended to all types of thought which contradicted (or even ignored) the official philosophy of "Orthodoxy, Aristocracy, and Nationalism." Thus, GOGOL was forced to change the title of his great novel, *Dead Souls* (the title means simply "dead serfs"); the censor objected to this title, observing that the human soul is immortal, and cannot die.

In spite of its severity, the censorship suffered from the rigidity of its own point of view, and liberal opinion could not be silenced completely. Many works circulated in manuscript, while writers developed a neutral style of allusion, known as "AESOPIC LANGUAGE," for circumventing the censorship.

The somewhat more liberal atmosphere of the reign of Alexander II (1855-81) brought belated relief. In 1865 preliminary censorship was abolished for longer works and for most periodicals. This did not free writers from the possibility of legal prosecution for their work, nor did it stop the banning of books, but it did facilitate the task of writing; before this time works had often been cut to ribbons by the shears of overly vigilant censors. Confiscation then became the most frequent type of control exercised over literature. By the end of the century censorship and other forms of control had eased greatly. A government manifesto of 1905 (see Revolution of 1905) guaranteed complete freedom of speech and press, but controls were soon restored in the wave of reaction which followed the 1905 Revolution.

Under the Soviet regime, preliminary censorship still exists, and is vested in the office known as Glavlit. But it has lost much of its pivotal importance. Other types of controls, such as government or Party supervision of the media of publication, the theaters and the dramatic repertory, are obviously more effective. The formation of an official Union of Soviet Writers, to which all writers must belong and from which they may be expelled, obviously serves as a control, and has actually been used as such in the case of ZOSHCHENKO, Akhmatova (see Gorenko) and others. Preliminary censorship can only remove material which is objectionable; Soviet critics and leaders insist that literature actively and positively propagate those principles on which the Soviet system is founded. (See Literature, Soviet; Criticism, Soviet; Socialist Realism.)

Chaadayev, Pyotr Yakovlevich (ca. 1793-1856), a leading Russian philosopher of the early nineteenth century. In the 1820's he underwent a religious conversion to mystical Christianity, with pro-Catholic leanings. In 1829 he wrote a series of philosophical letters, which he circulated in a French manuscript. The first of these was published in 1836 in Russian by NADEZHDIN in his journal, *The Telescope*. It was a profound criticism of Russian history as viewed from the standpoint of Western Catholicism. Russia, for Chaadayev, had not yet entered the arena of history because she did not belong to a single, universal Church. Hence her culture was inferior to that of the West, which he saw as great because, for him, it was inspired by a divine providentialism.

Chaadayev's *Letter* created a sensation on its appearance, for its negative appraisal of Russia's past directly contradicted the official view. *The Telescope* was closed down by the police, while the author himself was officially declared insane and confined to his house. Later these repressions were lifted on the condition that he write no more. Chaadayev thus became a martyr to police persecution, one of the most celebrated in the history of Russian letters. He is significant as a predecessor of the Russian WESTERNERS.

Chapygin, Alexey Pavlovich (1870-1937), a Soviet historical novelist. He began to publish early in the twentieth century with gloomy pictures of the poverty of city life. His principal novel was his ambitious *Stepan Razin* (1926-27), about the Cossack rebel of the seventeenth century and his uprising. The details of the novel are accurate, but the motives behind Razin's rebellion seem too modern. *Roving People* (1935), a sequel to *Stepan Razin,* concerns the Old Believers (see Schism).

Charot, Mikhas, pseudonym of M. Kudzolko (1896-?), a leading Belo-Russian writer (see Preface).

Chastushki. See Folk songs.

Chekhov, Anton Pavlovich (1860-1904), a leading Russian writer of the late nineteenth and early twentieth century. He was born in Taganrog, on the Sea of Azov, the grandson of a serf who had bought his freedom. His father was a small shopkeeper, and Anton was forced to toil in his shop from early childhood. His family was able to send him to school, however, and eventually to high school. In 1876 Chekhov's family went to Moscow to seek employment after the failure of the father's business; Anton remained in Taganrog, where he completed high school in 1879. He rejoined his family in Moscow the same year and enrolled in the University, in the Faculty of Medicine. To help support himself and his family, he began to contribute humorous sketches and tales to the comic papers, under a number of ridiculous pseudonyms, such as "Antosha Chekhonte," "My Brother's Brother," "A Man without a Spleen," and others. He was successful from the very start, and published almost everything he wrote. Most of it was hack work, but in 1886 he was able to publish a volume of his better tales, called *Motley Stories.* SUVORIN, publisher of the conservative *New Times,* invited Chekhov to contribute to his paper. This offer freed Chekhov of the necessity to do hack work and permitted him to develop his own style; it also began a long friendship with Suvorin. Once he was an established writer, Chekhov turned to more serious stories, though he never deserted the comic manner entirely. He took his medical degree in 1884, but never practised medicine professionally, though he sometimes treated needy cases. But his interest in medicine had influence on his work. He regarded himself both as an impartial, objective, almost "scientific" observer of society, and as a warm humanitarian, pointing out the better future which he believed science would give man.

In 1887 Chekhov produced his first full-length play, *Ivanov*. It had considerable success, and he now devoted himself more and more to the theater as well as to his stories. In 1890 he made a trip to Sakhalin to study the notorious prison conditions there. The trip resulted in a volume of reportage called *Sakhalin Island* (1893). From 1891 to 1897 Chekhov lived on an estate he bought at Melikhovo, near Moscow. He took part in famine relief during the year 1891-92, and sometimes joined in local civic activity. In 1897 developing tuberculosis forced him to leave Melikhovo, and he spent most of his late years at Yalta in the Crimea, or at French and German health resorts. He became politically more liberal in his final years, and broke with his publisher, Suvorin, over the Dreyfus Affair. When in 1902 the government annulled the election of Gorki (see Peshkov) to the Academy of Sciences, Chekhov joined KOROLENKO in resigning in protest.

During these final years Chekhov was close to the newly founded Moscow Art Theater (see Drama and Theater), and his last plays, *The Three Sisters* (1901) and *The Cherry Orchard* (1903), were written specifically for that theater. In 1901 Chekhov married the actress who had played the role of Masha in *The Three Sisters*, Olga Knipper. Their relationship was largely platonic, for she continued her stage career, while he lived at health resorts. In June, 1904, he died in Badenweiler, Germany.

Chekhov's early stories written for the comic papers are poorly known to English readers, who persist in regarding him as a gloomy writer. Many of the comic stories are celebrated in Russian, and some Russian readers know Chekhov exclusively in this genre. These short anecdotes and sketches are exaggerated and farcical, sometimes vulgar and silly. There is often real humor in them, however, though it may be untranslatable, as in the story called *A Horsey Name* (1885). A general, ill with toothache, tries to discover the name of a healer who can work magical cures, but of whom it is known only that he lives in a certain town and has a "horsey" name. The remainder of the story is nothing but a catalog of names which suggest horses, supplied by the whole of the general's household. These comic stories are sometimes redeemed by excellent craftsmanship; in them Chekhov learned the trick of concentration, economy of effect and singleness of point. *The Chorus Girl* (1886) is one of the finest of these early stories, and shows much of the compact construction and polish of the later tales. It describes a comic duel between a man's wife and his mistress, which takes place while he is hidden in the next room. Though the chorus girl comes off morally superior, the guilty husband can appreciate only what he fancies is the nobility of his wife.

The transition from the early comic manner to the later serious stories is a gradual one. The stories of what might be called the "middle" period, from 1886 to 1889, are often humorous, but conform to a new pattern, that of "laughter through tears." Such a story is *A Joke* (1886), in which a young man sledding with a girl whispers several times to her that he loves her, but then pretends that he has said nothing. Much later, in a typically Chekhovian mood ending, he regrets having joked in this silly fashion and let life slip through his fingers. Another example is *Grief* (1886), in which a poor old cabman whose son has just died tries unsuccessfully to interest people in his sorrow, and finally ends by telling it to his own horse. A third example of the formula is *Vanka* (1886), about a little orphan boy, apprenticed by his grandfather to an artisan who treats him cruelly. Vanka writes to his grandfather and begs him to come and take him home, seals the letter, addresses it, in his simplicity, to "grandfather in the village," and drops it in the mailbox.

The stories of this period comprise a tremendous range of styles and subjects, so that it is difficult to generalize concerning them. In them we see depicted representatives of all Russian social classes and many professions. Chekhov is, in fact, the broadest of the great Russian writers in his treatment of different social strata, and the totality of his stories add up to a great picture of much of Russian society of his day.

There are even stories about children, in which Chekhov shows an amazing intuitive understanding of the workings of a child's mind. The most famous, perhaps, is the story called *Sleepy* (1888). A young girl who toils and slaves as a maidservant is kept awake night after night by the cries of the baby whom she must rock to keep quiet. Finally she succumbs to exhaustion, and, as if hypnotized, takes a knife, slits the infant's throat and drops into a deathlike sleep. There are also stories about animals, such as *Kashtanka* (1887), which tells of a dog who cannot respect the vaudeville comedian who treats her well, and deserts him for her former master, who had ill-used her.

Perhaps the favorite subject of these stories is the boredom and triviality of life, especially as lived by intellectual neurotics. Chekhov's characters are often melancholy and moody; they lack the resources of personality necessary to find life rewarding. This is true of most of the characters of his later plays, and of many of the stories of his middle and later periods, such as *Enemies* (1887), *Lady N.'s Story* (1887), or later, *A Dreary Story* (1889), *A Woman's Kingdom* (1894), *Ariadne* (1895), and many others. In *The Kiss* (1887), another story of "laughter through tears," an officer is unexpectedly kissed by a pretty girl who mistakes him in the dark for her lover. But this humorous, anecdotal occurrence is not the point of the story; rather it is only a kind of spring, releasing a crowd of memories and reflections in the mind of the officer; in the end he is left with the realization that his life is lonely and unhappy. This device of a trivial or commonplace event which suddenly releases a train of reflections, usually melancholy ones, is a method typically Chekhovian.

Chekhov was not, of course, exclusively concerned with subjects such as boredom and futility, as the great scope of his hundreds of stories testifies. But melancholy, gloomy themes recur in his work again and again. He himself was relatively cheerful in life, as well as hard working, and denied any special sympathy for his apathetic, frustrated heroes. One reason for his preference for such moods and characters may have been their suitability to the epoch itself. It was a period of rapid social and economic change, when it was difficult to know the direction which social movement was taking. The pathos of a class in disintegration—the decay of the landowning aristocracy—contributes to this sense of futility; man feels that society is changing, but no new class emerges to take the aristocracy's place of political and cultural leadership. Instead there are only the vulgar parvenus of the new capitalism, whom Chekhov often depicts as villains. It would be an exaggeration, of course, to find the whole explanation of such themes in the epoch; part of it must lie in Chekhov's personality, with its extreme sensitivity and sympathy. Chekhov may also have been struck by the suitability of such themes for treatment in the form of the lyric short story with muted *pointe*, a form which he came to prefer. And a great deal of the explanation doubtless lies in the common mood of futility characteristic of the fin de siècle.

As Chekhov's style matured, he came to place less and less attention on plot and narrative as such. In his stories plot is very often reduced to a mere situation which serves as an excuse for the release of moods and feelings. This is the case in *Dreams* (1886), in which a tramp, arrested for vagrancy, dreams of finding a life of ease and plenty in Siberia. His dream is punctured, however, when the guard escorting him observes that he is too weak to travel such a distance. In such a story feelings themselves are the chief content of the narrative. A unity of mood, or of development of mood, holds these stories together and gives them unique force and cohesion. The moods may be happy or unhappy, but generally they are vague, spontaneous, often irrational, sometimes even with little apparent relation to the events of the tale as such. Chekhov's stories have been described as "slices of life," but such a characterization is misleading, for in this presentation of mood arising from a seemingly trivial event Chekhov seeks to define the essence of a character in terms of his leading emotion, rather than merely depicting a naturalistic scene.

Chekhov's characters, stripped of their emotions and moods, are weakly depicted and difficult to remember; their only really memorable trait is their apathy.

In some of Chekhov's stories feeling is carried to the lyrical extreme of a pure poetry of mood. Such is the long story, *The Steppe* (1888), in which the lyricism of a child's monotonous journey over the endless steppe creates a powerful poetic effect of nostalgia and quiet melancholy.

Chekhov wrote comparatively few stories after 1889, but almost all are masterpieces. Again it is difficult to generalize, but the favorite theme of the earlier stories, that of the boredom and futility in life, is repeated in many of these later tales. One of them is even called *A Dreary Story* (1889); it describes how an old professor comes to the realization that he can no longer expect anything of life. The main theme of these tales, and of the later dramas, is that of mutual isolation and the incommunicability of deep human feelings. In the dramas this reaches such a point that the characters indulge in outpourings of feelings which are essentially monologues; they seem neither to be speaking nor listening to one another.

A number of Chekhov's last stories, like the later plays, have the theme of the slow rotting of human energies and talents. This is the case in *The Teacher of Literature* (1894), in which an ambitious young man wakes to discover that he has achieved nothing, and that life has passed him by. This lament for lost youth or lost hopes and ambitions is the commonest outpouring of grief in Chekhov; it finds early expression in the vaudeville monologue called *A Swan Song* (1887-88). His characters are the victims of an inner corrosion, an eating away of ambitions, energies, talents, and, most important, of the ability to love. Part of this inner corrosion is due to neurotic egotism and self-preoccupation. But part is also caused simply by the passage of time; time itself permits a gradual corroding to take place without our knowledge. We are made aware of the process only by chance circumstances, which release trains of self-awareness, but only when it is too late.

There is a considerable element of satire in Chekhov's work, and in private he expressed strong disapproval of his neurotic and apathetic heroes. Still Chekhov was perhaps the most humane and tolerant writer in all Russian literature. He bestows such warmth and sympathy on his characters that it is impossible not to pity them in their melancholy and futility. Frequently he makes fun of them, but his laughter is almost as humane as his sympathy. An example of this is the story called *The Darling* (1898), about a woman who can find material for gossiping only in the interests of her several successive husbands and lovers. In the end, deserted by them, she is forced to attach herself to a small schoolboy, and

to talk of nothing but school and how the masters treat the pupils!
Chekhov's light treatment of the subject offended Lev TOLSTOY,
who considered the woman exemplary in that she sacrificed her
own personality for those whom she loved; what Tolstoy failed to
realize was that she hardly possessed any personality to sacrifice!
Still, there is nothing essentially unkind in Chekhov's satire, and
we feel that the "darling" is a universal type, and her need a
universal need which leads all men to desire love.

Chekhov's neurotic, frustrated heroes may suddenly revolt
against their fates, like Uncle Vanya, with a petulance which is
melodramatic but also childish and ineffective. We laugh at
Vanya as he waves his pistol in the air and shoots wildly at his
chief persecutor, but we hardly cease to pity him.

Chekhov's personages sometimes hold out hope for one another,
but it is usually a vague, dream-like hope of the distant future,
after they will all be dead and buried. Thus, Colonel Vershinin,
in *The Three Sisters*, talks continually of how much better life
will become in "two or three hundred years." Chekhov himself
was probably ambivalent in his attitude toward human progress.
He believed in life's amelioration by means of enlightenment and
science, but he also sensed keenly the hopelessness of the reality
around him, and realized that no transformation could be quick
enough to save the generation of the fin de siècle which were his
contemporaries.

Several of Chekhov's later stories deserve special comment.
Ward No. 6 (1892) is an ethical and philosophical tale, in which
an educated and sensitive doctor, bored in his position as director
of an insane asylum, develops a fondness for talking philosophy
with one of his patients. His unscrupulous assistant takes advantage of this eccentricity, has him declared insane and confined
in his own asylum, where he is subsequently beaten to death. We
never know if he is really mad or not, only that he ironically deserves his fate in that he has never made the slightest attempt
to improve conditions in the asylum. *The Black Monk* (1894) is
popular as a horror story, but is not especially successful. *Peasants*
(1897) and *In the Ravine* (1900) are naturalistic portrayals of the
life of peasants and shopkeepers, backward, ignorant and selfish
—as grim and sordid pictures of such life as any the radical
writers of the day could produce.

Chekhov's plays are better known than his stories in the English-speaking world, though hardly to Russian readers. There is no doubt that his plays are unique in world literature as lyrical dramas of inaction, and that they are masterpieces. It must be realized, however, that they adhere to a very narrow pattern, and show much less variety than do Chekhov's stories. Still, they are probably the most remarkable body of modern dramas since Ibsen.

With the exception of the early farces such as *The Proposal* (1888-89) and *The Bear* (1888), all the plays concern the frustrations and hopeless dreams of neurotic intellectuals. As dramas they are essentially static, for Chekhov is not concerned with action or change, but rather the portrayal of frustration. "Life goes on but nothing has changed," one of his characters says, and the sentence is the key to understanding his dramas. The play of mood, melancholy and grey, brings a poetized lyrical treatment which is almost akin to music. The characters, each isolated in his own frustration, deliver monologues of self-pity which merge into each other like contrapuntal themes: each is contrasted and individualized, yet each forms part of a universal refrain of unsuccess, weakness and frustration. Another analogy with music is that of leit-motif construction: the plays are held together not by action, but by the recurrence of moods and of a few motifs, many of them lyrical in character. Sounds, snatches of music and the repeated use of the pause are other musical elements in these "dramas of inaction."

The structure of Chekhov's plays is looser, less rigid, less compact than his stories, and the plays appear more uniform in their character of mood pieces. For the most part they lack a single hero, and their poetry of mood demands a sensitive interpretation by a whole company of actors, in which overplaying or "star" performances must be avoided. This is why Chekhov's plays gained such success in the interpretation of the Moscow Art Theater (see Drama and Theater).

Though Chekhov's plays are melancholy in mood, he insisted that most of them were comedies. No doubt they all contain elements of comedy, and sometimes even farce. But more probably what he intended was that the plays and their heroes, though often pathetic, lack the essential dignity and stature of tragedy.

We view Chekhov's frustrated neurotics with a mixture of pity and ridicule (a sympathetic ridicule) hardly proper to tragedy.

In his early years Chekhov made several attempts at serious drama, but only with *Ivanov* (1887) did he attain success. *Ivanov* is the study of a neurotic who tries to forget his problems in an illicit love affair, but unable, ends by killing himself. *The Sea Gull* (1896) is a study of the mutual jealousy of mother and son, both artists, the failure of the son to find himself, and his self-destruction. *Uncle Vanya* (1897) is the portrayal of an intellectual who realizes that his whole life, which he supposed he had sacrificed nobly for idealistic reasons, has been wasted. *The Three Sisters* (1901) depicts the neurotic apathy of an entire family, who dream of losing their frustrations and ennui by moving from their boring provincial city to Moscow, but never seriously make the attempt. The last play, *The Cherry Orchard* (1904), is lighter than the others, though it still has deep pathos. Its theme is the decay of the landowning gentry and the break-up of its way of life, symbolized by the chopping down of a cherry orchard.

Chekhov is one of the finest of Russian letter writers. His letters show the depth of his tolerance and humanity, as well as an attractive modesty and restraint rare among writers.

Chekhov's influence has been considerable both in Russia and abroad. The great popularity of the short story in Russia in the 1880's and 1890's is due partly to his success. The lyrical monotony and nostalgic atmosphere of stories like *The Steppe* influenced BUNIN and, in Soviet literature, FEDIN. Chekhov's methods of dramatic construction were imitated by Gorki (see Peshkov), though unsuccessfully; in the American theater his techniques have become models for a whole tradition in the drama, and his *Cherry Orchard* has even been rewritten with an American setting. Chekhov's story of mood, which customarily ends without a sharp *pointe*, has also enjoyed wide international popularity and influence, particularly in England and America.

Cherny, Sasha. See Glückberg, A. M.

Chernyshevski, Nikolay Gavrilovich (1828-89), a leading Russian political thinker and critic of the mid-nineteenth century. The son of a priest, he was educated at theological school and at the University of St. Petersburg. In 1855 he joined the staff of the journal, *The Contemporary*, as its literary critic. His critical and esthetic point of view he embodied in his *Studies in the Age of Gogol* (1855-56) and in his master's dissertation, *The Esthetic Relations of Art and Reality* (1855); in the years which followed he devoted himself more to economic and political writing. In 1862 he was arrested as a leader of the radicals, and confined in the Petropavlovsk Fortress. There he wrote his first novel, *What Is to Be Done?* (1863). In 1863 he was exiled to Siberia. Not until 1883 was he permitted to return west as far as Astrakhan, and finally to his native Saratov, where he died in 1889.

As a literary critic, Chernyshevski was a follower of BELIN-SKI, though he was far less interested in esthetic values, and criticism was more of a pretext for him to preach his ideas than anything else. Art, in his view, is a reproduction of reality, to which, as a copy, it is necessarily inferior. Literature can have little justification, therefore, save as it manifests a progressive social tendency. But Chernyshevski also argues that literature cannot change society; it can only reflect it. His novel, *What Is to Be Done?*, provided a model for the kind of writing which he advocated. Its subject is the social and economic emancipation of women. It also portrays a radical hero, Rakhmetov, an ascetic young man who gives up pleasure in order to serve his cause more completely. The book was intended in part as a refutation of TURGENEV's *Fathers and Children*, in which a young radical, Bazarov, ends in failure. Though unimaginatively written, the novel was tremendously popular with the Russian radicals.

In his political theory, Chernyshevski was, along with HER-ZEN, a forerunner of the radical movement of the POPULISTS. A socialist, he held that the complete reorganization of Russian economic institutions was necessary for progress. He was singularly free from the Pan-Russian messianism which characterized many other nineteenth-century Russian radicals.

In his philosophy Chernyshevski was a materialist and a positivist. He believed in the complete sufficiency of science to answer man's questions; life itself could be reduced, he thought, to a simple set of scientific principles. In his ethical views he was a utilitarian.

Chernyshevski's influence helped set the tone of positivism and materialism fashionable among the radicals of the 1860's. The NIHILISTS, led by PISAREV, took over much of his enthusiasm for natural science, as well as his contempt for purely esthetic questions. Along with BELINSKI, Chernyshevski has enjoyed a revival of influence in the Soviet Union today, as a great nineteenth-century critic and revolutionary leader. (See Philosophy.)

Chirikov, Yevgeni Nikolayevich (1864-1932), a novelist of the early twentieth century. A radical, he published with Gorki's press, *Znanie* ("knowledge"), and was a follower of Gorki (see Peshkov) in his realism. Many of his stories are based on his own childhood. After the 1917 Revolution he emigrated from the Soviet Union.

Chorny, Sasha. See Glückberg, A. M.

Christianization of Russia. The date of Russia's official Christianization is 988 or 989, but it is clear that some Russians had been baptized earlier. Christianity was formally accepted from Byzantium and enforced on the pagan populace by the Russian Prince Vladimir (978-1015), subsequently canonized. In return Vladimir obtained the hand of the Greek princess Anna. He seems to have been motivated by a desire to establish a closer relationship with Constantinople; perhaps also by a wish to use the new Russian Church as a tool of the state in setting up a Russian Empire in imitation of Byzantium. If so, he was probably disappointed, for the young Russian Church was dominated by Greek clergy.

Our chief source of information on Russian Christianization is the *Primary Chronicle* (see Chronicles). It relates several colorful legends, including the visits paid to Vladimir by representatives of the Mohammedan, Jewish and Roman faiths. Vladimir rejects Mohammedanism when he learns that drink is forbidden Moslems; Judaism when he learns from the Jews that they wander in exile from their native land. The Greek faith is accepted when Russian envoys sent to Constantinople return and describe the splendor of the Greek churches, saying, "We did not know whether we were in heaven or on earth." Also legendary is the tale of an earlier Christianization by St. Andrew the Apostle, as well as the tale of Vladimir's miraculous recovery from blindness just before his conversion, clearly influenced by the legend about the Emperor Constantine and his baptism.

The Chronicles give us reason to believe that there was strong popular resistance to Christianity among the people. Great distances in Russia also made conversion of the masses difficult, and the majority probably remained pagan for several centuries. So-called "dual belief" in both Christianity and certain elements of paganism, such as witchcraft and agricultural magic, has survived among the populace into modern times.

Chronicles, Old Russian. The Russian chronicles were annals, compilations of historical facts entered in chronological order by years. Hence their Russian name of *letopis* ("writing by years"). Besides descriptions of historical events, they contain much legendary material, oral tradition and personal reflections of the chroniclers, especially of a moral and religious nature. Generally compiled by monks in the larger monasteries, they often expressed the "official" ideology of the state as well as the Church.

Modern scholarship has shown these chronicles to be complex compilations of diverse materials, oral and written. Entire literary productions, such as legends, lives of saints and princes, and battle narratives, some of high literary value, were included in chronicles, along with more factual and prosaic entries. Hence different parts of the chronicles vary greatly in their accuracy, style, literary value, and even interpretation of historical events. As time went on, older chronicles were often revised or recompiled in accordance with new political or ideological needs.

The beginnings of Russian chronicle writing can hardly be traced. A. A. Shakhmatov supposed that the oldest chronicle compilation was produced around 1039, during the reign of Yaroslav the Wise, at the time of the beginnings of intense literary activity in Russia (see Literature). The first compilation which has been preserved as a unit is the so-called *Primary Chronicle,* which treats events up to 1110. It has not survived as a separate work, however, but is found in similar form in a number of later compilations. The best texts are those of the *Laurentian Chronicle* of 1377 and the *Hypatian Chronicle* of the 1420's. The *Primary Chronicle* was formerly known as "Nestor's Chronicle," and was attributed to the monk NESTOR of the Kiev Crypt Monastery, but this attribution is uncertain. This chronicle has also been attributed to a certain Silvester, prior of another Kiev monastery, but he may have been little more than a copyist or reviser.

The *Primary Chronicle* is our principal source of information on Russian history up to the beginning of the twelfth century, a period which includes the formation of the Kievan Russian State and the CHRISTIANIZATION of Russia. It begins with the Biblical flood and the settlement of the Russian land by descendants of Japheth, son of Noah. Much of its contents are legendary and unreliable, especially for the older periods. Such parts are valuable, however, for their preservation of elements of folklore and old traditions: pagan and early Christian legends, superstitions, proverbs, customs, etc. In ideology, the *Primary Chronicle* shows a strong nationalist tendency. The Russian people are depicted as favored by God; their misfortunes, on the other hand, are interpreted as God's punishment for their sins.

Chronicles were kept in many medieval Russian cities. The earliest chronicle of Novgorod is almost as old as the *Primary* (Kiev) *Chronicle*. Suzdal, Rostov, Ryazan, Nizhni Novgorod, Tver, Pskov, Moscow and other cities began to keep chronicles as they became regional centers. Many of these works have been lost, but they can in part be reconstructed from later compilations. As Russia came under the domination of Moscow between the thirteenth and sixteenth centuries, local chronicles were incorporated in the chronicles of Moscow, and for the most part ceased to exist separately. Russian chronicle writing continued to be practiced at least until the end of the seventeenth century.

Chulkov, Mikhail Dmitrievich (ca. 1743-92), an early Russian writer of realistic and fantastic novels and tales. His most important work is his picaresque novel, *The Fair Cook, or the Adventures of a Debauched Woman* (1770), slightly reminiscent of *Moll Flanders*. His *Scoffer* (1766-68) is a collection of tales, some realistic and satirical, others fantastic, influenced in part by the *Arabian Nights*. Chulkov's interest in folklore resulted in his large *Collection of Various Songs* (1770-74), and in a *Dictionary of Russian Superstitions* (1782).

Church Slavonic. See Old Church Slavonic language.

Civic critics, a name given to those Russian critics, particularly of the nineteenth century, who evaluated literature primarily on the basis of its social and political content and its expression of progressive ideas. They opposed the unideological estheticism of the PARNASSIAN POETS, as well as the writings of those more conservative in their ideology, such as TURGENEV. BELINSKI, CHERNYSHEVSKI and DOBROLYUBOV were the leading critics of the civic tendency. (See Criticism.)

Civic poetry, the name applied to the long tradition in Russian nineteenth-century literature of poetry expressing a definite social and political consciousness, usually of a liberal or radical nature. Beginning with RYLEYEV in the 1820's, the tradition of civic poetry extends to the end of the century, and includes such poets as OGARYOV, NEKRASOV, PLESHCHEYEV, Ivan NIKITIN, Ivan AKSAKOV, NADSON and Minski (see Vilenkin). The civic tradition ended with the rise of SYMBOLISM, which was largely non-political in its interests.

Civil War. See Revolution of 1917; Literature, Soviet.

Classicism. Russia did not undergo the Western European Renaissance, at least directly, and her roots in the culture of classical antiquity were weaker than those of Western Europe. It is something of a paradox, therefore, that classical influence has been so strong on Modern Russian literature, and particularly on poetry. Classical Greek, as distinct from Byzantine, literature had little influence in Russia until the eighteenth century. Certain passages from classical writers were quoted in the didactic anthology called *The Bee,* brought, presumably, to Russia from the South Slavic lands sometime before the end of the twelfth century. KLIMENT SMOLYATICH, Metropolitan of Russia in the middle of the twelfth century, refers to his knowledge of the writings of Homer, Plato and Aristotle. But such cases are isolated ones, and in general Old Russia assimilated only the Greek Christian tradition, while the pre-Christian classical tradition remained an alien one.

In the mid-seventeenth century, classical influences began to enter Russia by way of the Ukraine, where writers already possessed some familiarity with Greek classical culture. SIMEON POLOTSKI's long poem, *The Russian Eagle,* is full of classical allusions.

The classical period par excellence in Russian literature is the eighteenth century. This period is customarily referred to as Pseudo-Classicism or Neo-Classicism, in order to denote its artificial character, as well as the fact that it was based on a misunderstood or exaggerated adherence to classical standards. Pseudo-Classicism entered Russia as part of the general wave of enlightenment from the West and the new taste for things European characteristic of Russia in the eighteenth century. At that time the predominant literary movement in Western Europe was Neo-Classicism; the writers of the newborn Russian literature merely followed suit. Borrowing from the neo-classical tradition of the West, particularly from France, as well as directly from Greek and Roman sources, Russian writers deliberately imitated the classical genres and rules for poetry. The chief poetic forms cultivated were the ode, tragedy, comedy, fable, eclogue and satire; forms not considered classical, and in particular prose fiction, were held in contempt. Writers such as Horace, Pindar, Anacreon, Homer, Boileau, La Fontaine, Racine and Molière served as models. Classical and neo-classical rules were applied to Russian literature, particularly in PROSODY; the doctrine of the three dramatic unities was introduced, as well as the doctrine of three levels of style (see Lomonosov). References to classical mythology were used frequently as symbols or conceits; thus the writer of a love poem would probably mention Cupid or Venus. The literature which resulted had a largely imitative character, and was of interest only to a small group of readers of the upper classes who had been educated under the Western Enlightenment. There was, to be sure, a less elegant literature of the middle classes which was scarcely affected by classical influences, but serious writers paid little attention to it. Efforts to Russianize the new pseudo-classical literature were largely unsuccessful; even when Russian subjects were treated, the character types, style and technique often remained arbitrary and derivative. A major exception to this is comedy, in which greater freedom was permitted and a more natural style could be attained. Attempts were also made, as in BOGDANOVICH's narrative poem, *Dushenka,* to replace classical mythological allusions by references to Russian legend and folklore, but these were rendered abortive by lack of real knowledge in these fields.

Though it is difficult to point to an exact beginning for the Russian pseudo-classical movement, KANTEMIR is generally considered the first writer to follow the new style systematically. His nine satires were written during the decade, 1729-39. After him TREDIAKOVSKI, LOMONOSOV and SUMAROKOV were the major fountainheads of Russian Classicism. The last great classical poet was DERZHAVIN, though his work showed relaxation of the strict classical styles and genre divisions. Toward the end of the eighteenth century, the introduction of new sentimentalist and romantic trends from the West (see Sentimentalism, Pre-Romanticism) sounded the death knell of Classicism as a systematic literary movement. Classical subjects and forms persisted well into the nineteenth century, however, in the work of such poets as BATYUSHKOV, PUSHKIN, DELVIG and others. A revival of classical themes also characterized the work of several poets of the 1860's, including SHCHERBINA and APOLLON MAYKOV.

A more important classical revival occurred again at the end of the nineteenth century under the Symbolist Movement (see Symbolism). Here the impulse was primarily esthetic and esoteric. MEREZHKOVSKI in fiction and literary criticism, and ANNENSKI, VOLOSHIN and VYACHESLAV IVANOV in poetry were its leading representatives. In the Soviet period, interest in classicism has remained at a minimum, in accordance with prescriptions to writers to deal with national, socialistic and contemporary themes. (See Criticism.)

Clement Smolyatich. See Kliment Smolyatich.

Communism and Literature. See Literature, Soviet; Criticism, Soviet; Socialist Realism.

Conflict in Soviet Literature. See Criticism, Soviet; Virta.

Constitutional Democrats. See Revolution of 1905.

Constructivists, a group of young poets organized in 1924, who included SELVINSKI, INBER and others. K. L. Zelinski was their chief theoretician. From the Futurists (see Futurism) these poets took their interest in technology and other contemporary themes, but they were not so anti-traditional as their predecessors. In their view a poem should be a "construction," in which, by analogy with engineering, the maximum effect should be achieved from the potential. This could be accomplished, in their view, by so-called "localization," i.e., by directing all the images and devices of a poem toward the poem's subject, as, for example, in the use of a marching rhythm in a poem about war. The Constructivist poets soon surmounted this rather narrow esthetic. As a movement they broke up in 1930. Politically they supported the Bolshevik regime, and were on the side of the proletarian writers in the literary disputes of the 1920's (see October).

Cosmists. See Smithy Poets.

Cossacks (Russian *kazaki),* frontiersmen of a number of regions in southern Russia and southwestern Siberia. Descended in part from runaway Russian and Ukrainian serfs, they conquered large areas of the southern steppe from the nomads who had held it. They played a major role in conquering and opening up Siberia. The Cossacks are celebrated for their bravery, independence, fierceness in battle, and, in modern times, for their conservative loyalty to the tsars, whose crack cavalry units they manned. Under tsarism they received special privileges, including a degree of local autonomy and the traditional right to elect their own leaders, or *atamans.* Most famous were the Ukrainian Zaporozhian Cossacks of the Dnieper, who were organized in the fifteenth century. The Cossacks were a heroic and colorful people, frequently depicted in Russian literature, particularly in works by GOGOL, L. N. TOLSTOY, SHOLOKHOV and others.

Criticism. The second quarter of the eighteenth century saw the beginnings of systematic literary theory, in which principles were modelled, for the most part, on contemporary French literature and the tradition of classical antiquity (see Classicism). The modern Russian system of accentual versification was formulated by TREDIAKOVSKI and LOMONOSOV (see Prosody), while a hierarchical system of three literary styles was laid down by LOMONOSOV. The latter proved too rigid and archaic, however, and at the end of the century the three styles were reduced by KARAMZIN to a single one, more elegant and flexible, as well as more receptive to foreign lexical and stylistic influences.

PUSHKIN was perhaps the first Russian literary critic of genius. His criticism was unsystematic, however, and to a large extent concerned with Western European rather than Russian literature. Still, his critical writing was penetrating, witty, and far more sensitive to esthetic values than most nineteenth-century Russian criticism.

During the 1820's, book reviews and critical articles became a regular feature of Russian journals; the first systematic critics were writers such as POLEVOY and NADEZHDIN, who attacked the aristocratic and cosmopolitan literature of the "Golden Age" and called for a literature of greater ideological and national consciousness. This trend, associated with the rise of a middle-class reading public and the transition to a literature of prose, was destined to have tremendous consequences in Russian criticism.

The great critic BELINSKI, who dominated literary criticism during the 1840's, demanded that literature embody both naturalism (fidelity to life) and national character; at the same time it should be imbued with progressive and liberal ideas. Belinski is the father of the so-called "civic" tendency in Russian criticism, according to which literature should be evaluated primarily in terms of its social and political ideas, rather than its esthetic merits. This civic trend was brought to its height under Belinski's successors of the 1860's, CHERNYSHEVSKI, DOBROLYUBOV and PISAREV. They tended to ignore esthetic factors almost entirely, and their reviews and critical articles were actually more essays on social, economic and political questions than literary criticism as such. In spite of official literary CENSORSHIP and other controls, these radical critics were extremely influential, since they helped to form the opinions of a large share of the reading public, and even relatively conservative writers tried to placate them. The civic critics were to a large extent responsible for convincing Russian readers (and even writers) that literature is primarily a vehicle for expressing ideas, and that questions of artistic form and style are secondary, even unessential. Indeed, such an attitude was scarcely unnatural in view of the currents of the times. Tsarist CENSORSHIP rendered direct expression of liberal or radical social and political ideas next to impossible, and the writers were forced to express such ideas obliquely, either in the form of imaginative literature, or in essays which discussed literary works rather than the proscribed reality. This emphasis on ideas rather than esthetic values has become almost a fixed characteristic of Russian criticism—even, in large part, of Russian literature itself—and was displaced only temporarily under the SYMBOLISTS at the end of the century.

Opposed to the civic critics at the middle of the nineteenth century were a small number of "esthetic" critics, including ANNENKOV, DRUZHININ and V. N. MAYKOV. They tended towards a conception of art for art's sake. Though their work was both able and original, it had little influence. More significant than they as a critic was Apollon GRIGORIEV, who combined estheticism with an emphasis on the depiction of the Russian national "character" in literature, which Grigoriev found embodied in the people's humility, passionate feeling and traditional, un-Europeanized culture. Another, slightly earlier nationalistic group were the SLAVOPHILES, such as I. S. AKSAKOV. Like the later civic critics, however, they were actually more concerned with publicist activity than literary criticism as such.

During the latter part of the century the civic tendency was continued in the work of N. K. MIKHAYLOVSKI. The political reaction and widespread disillusionment of the end of the century helped to weaken the civic trend, however, and a new type of philosophical criticism appeared, cultivated by such thinkers as LEONTIEV, ROZANOV, MEREZHKOVSKI, SHESTOV and BERDYAYEV. This new trend persisted in Russia until the 1917 Revolution, and, among the emigration, until the present. TOLSTOY and DOSTOYEVSKI were the favorite subjects of these critics, who were primarily concerned with the manifestation of ethical and metaphysical ideals. Tolstoy himself advocated the primacy of ethical considerations for literature in his *What Is Art?* At the same time a new estheticism appeared in the writings of the Symbolist critics, such as FLEXER, BRYUSOV and others (see Symbolism).

Psychological criticism, never strong in Russia, appeared as a separate school at the end of the nineteenth century in the work of D. N. Ovsyaniko-Kulikovski (1853-1920) and his followers. Freudian trends appeared briefly in the 1920's, but soon vanished under the hostile attitude of the Communist Party. Sociological criticism was most strongly represented by the Marxist critics of the late nineteenth and twentieth centuries, such as PLEKHANOV, BOGDANOV and LUNACHARSKI. They viewed literature primarily as an ideological reflection of the class struggle; the latter two were actively concerned with the problem of creating a radically new "proletarian" literature which would replace the older "bourgeois" literature (see *Soviet Criticism,* below).

The foundation in 1916 of OPOYAZ, the Society for the Study of Poetic Language, brought the beginnings of a significant new movement in Russian criticism, Formalism. The Russian Formalists sought methodologically to divorce the work of literature from the biography of its author, and to concentrate on purely esthetic and literary criteria in analyzing a work of literature, rather than on its psychological, sociological or historical content. Literature they viewed primarily as language; the language of artistic literature (indeed, of each writer) can be studied as a language system opposed to the language of everyday speech, of journalism, or of technical prose. Hence much of the Formalists' work was centered on the study of poetic language. They also devoted attention to the analysis of motifs in narrative fiction. Leaders of the Russian Formalists included the writers Viktor SHKLOVSKI and Yuri TYNYANOV, as well as the scholars Roman Jakobson, Boris Eichenbaum, Boris Tomashevski, and the more moderate Viktor Zhirmunski. Formalism continued to exist until about 1927, when the Formalists began to modify their approach under the attacks of hostile Marxist critics, though certain problems and methods of the school persisted throughout the 1930's. The Formalists had close relations with the Futurist poets, on one hand (see Futurism), who were likewise interested in the poetic functions of language; on the other their theory of literature as device (see Shklovski) influenced a number of prose writers of the 1920's, especially Kaverin (see Zilberg) and OLESHA.

Criticism, Soviet. Literary criticism is literary theory in action, or, as a recent writer has phrased it, "applied aesthetics." This is particularly true of Soviet criticism, which is always careful to relate critical judgments consciously to a literary theory which has its basis in Marxist philosophy. This philosophy, known in the Soviet Union as "dialectic and historical materialism," holds that the social structure of a given society depends on the manner in which that society satisfies its economic needs. Upon the basis of production and the relationship of social groups to one another in the process of production there is erected, according to this theory, the complex structure of ideas and institutions, religion, art, and literature which make up the culture of a given society. If the society is divided into classes the cultural "superstructure" will reflect the needs, aspirations, and view of life of the dominant class. Only after the proletariat has succeeded in establishing a classless society will it be possible for literature, for instance, to express the thought and feeling of humanity as a whole.

There has never been complete agreement among Soviet critics as to the proper application of "dialectic materialism" in literature.

The conformity which has been observed during the Stalin period is not natural and has been artificially induced: the normal state of affairs among Marxist literary critics is one of acrimonious debate. Within the framework of Marxist doctrine disputes have arisen, and there is every reason to expect that they will continue.

It is possible to distinguish three schools of thought in the Soviet criticism of literature since 1917. The oldest of these derives from the work of G. V. PLEKHANOV (1857-1918), a publicist and philosopher whose literary criticism was based on the Marxist analysis of social and economic determinants in the cultural sphere, and also on the ideas of the Russian philosopher V. G. BELINSKI (1811-1848), whose aesthetics in turn derived from Hegel. Many Soviet critics of the twenties were conscious followers of Plekhanov and Belinski. Perhaps the most important of them was Alexander VORONSKI (1884-?), who, while he subscribed to the doctrine that literary works are part of the cultural superstructure and therefore bear the impress of a particular economic and social environment, insisted nonetheless that sociological analysis provides only a partial understanding of literature. For literature, and indeed all art, has the same function in human life as science has: to provide knowledge of the world. The difference between art and science is that the scientist expresses this knowledge of the world in logical concepts while the artist embodies it in immediate, sensible images of reality. The artist "thinks in images," according to this school of thought, and the critic must not, therefore, limit the activity to discovering the class content of a work of art but must also assess its objective value as a concrete "cognition of life." This theory of literature, in which the Hegelian ingredients are still visible though filtered through Belinski, Plekhanov, and Voronski, was a liberalizing force in the Soviet Union during the early twenties. The critic operating with such concepts was able to find objective value not only in the art of past and dead societies but also in the work of contemporary "bourgeois" writers, whose work was defended in spite of ideology or class background as a revelation of the world.

Strict and exclusive application of sociological criteria in literary criticism was characteristic of a second school of thought, the leading representatives of which were A. Bogdanov (see Malinovski; 1873-1928), V. F. Friche (1870-1929), and V. G.

Pereverzev (1882-?). Bogdanov was the founder and leading theoretician of the Proletarian Educational and Cultural Organization, known in abbreviated form as the PROLETKULT, whose purpose was to develop through the training of working class writers a specifically proletarian "class" literature. The dominance of the proletariat in all cultural fields, was, Bogdanov believed, a prerequisite to the establishment of the power of the proletariat over society as a whole. Art is simply a "means of organizing the forces of a given class." This extreme position seems to have met with an eager response among party intellectuals and a part of the urban working class in the first years after the Revolution, though it found no sympathy among higher Soviet officials, who were concerned that the Russian proletariat acquire the barest elements of human culture before attempting to create "its own" literature.

V. F. Friche, another representative of the strict sociological tendency, owed many of his ideas to Plekhanov, but placed the main emphasis on the sociological rather than the cognitive aspect of literature. And Friche tended to reduce sociology to simple economics. Typical of his approach is an essay on the *Sociology of Literary Styles,* in which he accepts the idea (advanced by Spengler and others) of the unity of styles in all fields of culture during a given period, but rejects as idealistic and metaphysical any but the economic interpretation of this unity: "The first task of sociology in this field [literary criticism] is to work out the relationship of a particular poetic style with a particular economic style." Friche was a rationalist of the purest water who believed that in an industrial society and in the socialist world which grows out of it, man becomes an exclusively rational being and that literary style will more and more reflect the modern "rationalization" of all life. Evidences of non-rational factors at work in the contemporary scene he did indeed observe, but contended that these survivals would disappear as socialism developed.

V. G. Pereverzev was another exponent of strict economic determinism in literary criticism. He maintained that in order to understand a given writer the critic should direct his attention not to peripheral matters such as the writer's biography or his conscious view of the world, nor even to the social and political environment of his times, but exclusively to the position occupied by the given writer in the process of production. Thus Dostoyevski's frequent split personalities he explained as so many projections of Dostoyevski himself, a declassed nobleman torn between the values and standards of bourgeois productive relations and his own aristocratic traditions and antecedents. Pereverzev maintained, further, that the process of literary creation is subconscious and that the writer cannot by taking thought himself or by responding to directives from the party alter the class nature of his "system of images." Indeed the writer works within a "vicious circle" of images subconsciously determined by his economic environment. If the writer is a proletarian his images are certain to be of proletarian character, even though he deck them out as bourgeois. The writer of one economic "class" cannot even imagine a character of another "class." The creation of literature is directly determined by productive processes and the author's place in them, and such creation cannot be mediated by educational, political, or governmental bodies. The proletarian state, therefore, can produce nothing in literature by its decrees and manifestoes, though it can and should silence the literary voice of hostile classes. Obviously the theorizing of Pereverzev could have no place in the Soviet Union of the thirties, where the demand was that all writers, both proletarian and non-proletarian, consciously engage in tasks assigned by the Party. This explains the violent attack on Pereverzev which took place in 1930, and also the fact that his ideas are now scornfully characterized as "vulgar sociology."

A third school of thought has been dominant in the Soviet Union since the early thirties. This school is the source of the doctrine of "socialist realism" and a number of ideas and slogans associated with that phrase: "party spirit" or "partisanship" (PARTIYNOST), "revolutionary romanticism," "the positive hero," and some others. The spokesmen of this school of thought appeal ultimately to the authority of Lenin, quoting with particular insistence an article which he wrote in 1905 defending the idea of "partisanship" in literature, by which Lenin meant the frank and open service of the proletariat. It should be obvious that the pre-eminence which this school of thought enjoys was achieved not as a result of debate and persuasion but through the direct application of political power in the literary world, and LENIN's "partisanship" has come to mean simply conscious support of the Party and the Soviet state.

The voluminous literature on "SOCIALIST REALISM" reveals an authoritarian bias in its emphasis on precept and admonition. The theorists of socialist realism are much less interested in investigating what literature has been and is than they are in pointing out what Soviet literature is and must be. Literature is described as a means of education consciously employed and directed by the socialist state. Maxim Gorki (see Peshkov), in his speech at the First Congress of Soviet Writers in 1934, provided a theoretical basis for this viewpoint when he drew a distinction between "critical realism" and socialist realism. Gorki pointed out that in modern times the great realistic writers had been critical of their bourgeois environment and that the main body of nine-teenth-century realism is a protest against social reality. After the establishment of socialism, however, a critical realism of the old type would seem to be an anomaly. ". . . . This form of realism," said Gorki, ". . . cannot serve to educate a socialist personality, for while criticizing everything it never affirmed anything . . ." And he continued: "Life, as asserted by socialist realism, is deeds, creativeness, the aim of which is the uninterrupted development of the priceless individual qualities of man."

Gorki is the source of many of the phrases, attitudes and ideas characteristic of Soviet criticism. His ideas, applied in practice by official critics such as Andrey ZHDANOV (1896-1948), Alexander FADEYEV and V. V. Yermilov, have been reduced to a few quite simple demands. Soviet literature, said Zhdanov, must be quite honestly tendentious. "Soviet literature is tendentious and we are proud of its tendentiousness because our tendency consists in liberating the whole of mankind from the yoke of capitalist slavery." Soviet literature is optimistic regarding the future of mankind, and in today's reality it must see "the promise of tomorrow." Soviet literature must present to the reader images of "positive heroes" embodying the socialist virtues and thus provide him with models of behavior. Soviet literature must eschew decadent "formalism" and barren avant-garde experimentalism in favor of the use of standard language and literary forms intelligible and acceptable to the mass of working people. Soviet literature should be positive, affirmative, and healthful; it is, to quote Zhdanov once again, "saturated with enthusiasm and heroism."

Certain kinds of writing have been firmly rejected as having no part in "socialist realism." Among these should be mentioned "formalism," a term of disapproval which includes all varieties of modernism not only in literature but in the other arts. Pornography is the frequent target of virtuous criticism, and such condemnation might be desirable except that the term is made to include any frank and direct treatment of sexual experience, and has been applied in the recent past to such a writer as Panteleymon ROMANOV. Concern on the part of the writer with his own peculiar experience of the world is certain to attract unfavorable attention. In the case of ZOSHCHENKO's unfinished novel, *Before Sunrise,* a subjective account of the first years of the author's own life, the mildest expression of critical disapproval was that "Zoshchenko ignores . . . the social factors which form the consciousness of man."

In the immediate post-war period Soviet criticism reached so low a level and the abuse of deviant writers was so violent that much of what was written during those days can hardly be treated as literary criticism at all. ZHDANOV's attack on Zoshchenko in 1946 was an example of intellectual regimentation in which no regard was paid to literary or human considerations, and the literary critics both high and low were obliged to take their tone from Zhdanov. During that time curious literary theories appeared the function of which was simply to rationalize a kind of behavior that seemed unavoidable. The "no-conflict theory," now firmly rejected, declared that Soviet drama should not be based on conflict since there can be conflict only between the bad and the good and in "our Soviet reality" the bad is so unusual that it should not even be shown on the stage. If conflict does occur it can only be between "the good and the better." Much was written about the meaning of "the typical" in Soviet literature, a discussion motivated by Engels' definition of realism as the treatment of "typical characters in typical situations." This was essentially a problem of exegesis, the solution of which made possible the inclusion in realism of the quite untypical positive heroes of Soviet literature. The solution was provided by Malenkov, who said at the Nineteenth Party Congress in 1952: "Typicalness corresponds to the essence of the given social-historical phenomenon; it is not simply the most widespread, frequently occurring, and ordinary phenomenon. Conscious exaggeration and accentuation of an image do not exclude typicalness but disclose it more fully . . . The typical is the basic sphere of the manifestation of Party Spirit in realistic art . . ." And then: "The force and importance of realistic art lie in the fact that it can and must disclose . . . the high spiritual qualities and typical positive features in the character of the ordinary man, create his vivid artistic portraits as an example and an object of imitation for the people." Thus Malenkov offers an explanation of "the typical" which includes the outstanding, unusual, and heroic, and a definition of realism which would seem to include many elements of romanticism.

Since the death of Stalin there have been important changes in the standards of Soviet literary criticism, and the movement has seemed to be in the direction of allowing the writer greater individual freedom and more discretion in working out his own style within the somewhat broadened confines of "socialist realism." By 1955 critical writing, while it still depended on the manipulation of phrases and slogans, had acquired a repertory of somewhat more liberal ones. Thus there has also been a marked improvement in the quality of Soviet writing.

Edward J. Brown

Cyril of Turov. See Kirill Turovski.
Cyrillic alphabet. See Alphabet.

D

Dahl, Vladimir Ivanovich (1801-72), an ethnographer, lexicographer, and writer of tales. Dahl is remembered chiefly for his monumental *Dictionary of the Russian Language* (1861-68), still the most complete dictionary of popular spoken Russian, as opposed to the standard language of the intelligentsia. Under the pseudonym of Kazak Luganski, Dahl published a number of stories and anecdotes in the 1830's, 1840's and 1850's, significant for their use of a pure Russian popular style, as well as for the introduction of lower-class characters and their social milieu. But his tales and sketches are weak in their characterizations, and lack unity. He also compiled an outstanding collection of Russian proverbs (1862).

Daniil the Pilgrim, a Russian abbot who made a journey to Palestine between 1106 and 1108, and left an interesting and informative account of his pilgrimage. The work contains many colorful legends of the Holy Land.

Daniil "the Prisoner," an Old Russian author who probably lived at the court of Prince Yaroslav Vsevolodovich of Pereyaslavl in the early thirteenth century. He is known for the petition which he addressed to his prince, begging to be taken into the latter's favor and made a counsellor. The work is noteworthy for its secular character and lively wit, though written at a time when literature was generally monopolized by the Church. Daniil quotes many proverbs, and invents ingenious puns. Attempts to interpret his *Petition* as a social document have failed, and we do not even know to what social class the writer belonged. The tradition that Daniil was a prisoner *(zatochnik)* seems to be of later origin and spurious.

Danilevski, Grigori Petrovich (1829-90), a novelist of the late nineteenth century. His early novels, such as *Fugitives in Novorossiya*

(1862, published under the pen-name of A. Skavronski), are full of ethnographical details; later he wrote light historical novels, such as *Moscow Burned* (1886), which were extremely popular.

Danilevski, Nikolay Yakovlevich (1822-85), a historian and philosopher of the second half of the nineteenth century. He formulated a doctrine of national types, in terms of which nations produce distinct cultures according to their national character. Russia and the Slavs were, for him, a unique type, while one cultural achievement of the Slavic peoples was, in his view, the creation of a form of political absolutism. Russia should remain indifferent to the West, Danilevski taught, for her cultural traditions were distinct from those of the West; rather she should seek to unite the Slavs and form a new empire around Constantinople. His most important work, *Russia and Europe* (1869), had great influence, particularly on the German philosopher Spengler. Danilevski was one of the most violent opponents in Russia of the Darwinian theory of evolution.

Davydov, Denis Vasilyevich (1784-1839), a poet of the early nineteenth century. An officer in the army, Davydov led a partisan unit in the War of 1812 against Napoleon. He cultivated a kind of "hussar style," celebrating military valor, comradeship, wine, women and song. Besides his hussar's songs, he wrote love lyrics, elegiac epistles and political fables. Davydov's colorful personality supposedly served as the prototype for the character of Denisov in TOLSTOY's *War and Peace*.

Decembrist Movement, a revolutionary movement of liberal noblemen, who led an uprising in December, 1825—hence the name, "Decembrist." The Decembrists were influenced by the French and American Revolutions, and were dissatisfied with the growing reaction of the regime of Alexander I and with its feeble foreign policy. Soon after 1815 secret societies of army officers and other young noblemen were formed. Their programs agreed on the need for the abolition of serfdom and for agrarian reform; in other respects they differed. The Northern Society, led by Col. Nikita Muravyov, favored retention of the monarchy, which would be limited by a constitutional, federal system. The Southern Society, led by Col. Pavel Pestel, advocated a democratic republic.

The societies waited for a favorable occasion for an uprising. On November 19, 1825, Alexander I suddenly died, leaving the throne to a younger brother, Nicholas. Nicholas had an elder brother, Constantine, who had renounced the succession to the throne, but his renunciation had never been made public. Taking advantage of the confusion which resulted, the Decembrist officers led their regiments into the Senate Square in St. Petersburg on December 14, 1825, and raised a cry of "Constantine and a constitution!" They counted on immediate popular support for their uprising, but in this they were cruelly deceived. They had no real plan of action, and had failed to propagate their cause among the people. Some of their soldiers supposed that "Constitution" (Russian *konstitutsiya*) was the name of Constantine's wife. Nicholas rallied support and crushed the uprising. Hundreds of arrests were made, and some 120 persons brought to trial, among them members of leading noble families. Five of the prisoners were hanged; the others were imprisoned or exiled to Siberia.

Among the Decembrists were three outstanding poets of the period: RYLEYEV, one of the leaders, who was hanged, KÜCHELBECKER, who spent the rest of his life in prison and exile, and ODOYEVSKI, who was sentenced to exile, then to serve in the army ranks. The last fate also met the talented writer BESTUZHEV. Many other young writers were sympathetic to the movement. Both PUSHKIN and GRIBOYEDOV were arrested for their close associations with the conspirators, but were subsequently released.

The Decembrist Uprising was at once the last of a series of palace revolutions so typical of the eighteenth century, and the first attempt—if an abortive one—at a modern revolution. Its memory persisted among liberal and radical writers, though the censorship prevented any direct reference to the movement. PUSHKIN addressed a famous lyric to the Decembrists in exile, while TOLSTOY originally planned his *War and Peace* as a novel about the Decembrists. It is the Decembrist Movement which is clearly indicated at the end of the novel in its final form, when Pierre announces his intention of joining a secret political society.

Delvig, Baron Anton Antonovich (1798-1831), a poet and journalist, the contemporary and close friend of PUSHKIN. A descendant of a Russianized German family, Delvig pursued a career in the civil service. He also edited several journals. Notorious for his laziness, he published little poetry. His work is mostly classical in feeling, sensuous, but cold and unemotional. His favorite classical forms were the idyl and the epigram. His idyl, *The Bathing Women* (1825), is remembered for its precision of manner and vivid classical feeling. More popular were his stylized imitations of folk songs. Largely forgotten in the late nineteenth century, Delvig has enjoyed a certain revival in modern times.

Derzhavin, Gavriil Romanovich (1743-1816), the greatest Russian poet of the eighteenth century. Born in a family of impoverished nobility, Derzhavin was educated in Kazan high school. In 1762 he entered the army as a private, a thing unusual for a man of noble descent. In 1772 he was promoted to officer rank, and distinguished himself in the suppression of the Pugachov Rebellion of 1773-75. In 1777 he went to Petersburg and entered the civil service. He had already begun to write and publish poetry several years earlier. In 1783 he published his "Felitsa," a semi-humorous ode addressed to CATHERINE THE GREAT, whose identity was transparent under the mask of "Felitsa," a coined name derived from Latin *felicitas*, "happiness." The poem made his success at once, and Catherine rewarded him by making him governor of a province (1784), and in 1791 her secretary. He was independent and difficult in temperament, however, and was several times removed from office. In 1802 Alexander I made him Minister of Justice, but a year later he was retired because he was too conservative for the young emperor.

Derzhavin's poetry is for the most part lyric. As with LOMONOSOV, his odes form his greatest body of work. They are sonorous and majestic in tone, but are very different from Lomonosov's cold, impersonal stanzas. Derzhavin frequently introduces nature descriptions, scenes from real life, glimpses of his personal thoughts, even bathetic digressions. Thus, while preserving much of the grandeur and solemnity of the classical ode (see Classicism), he weakened its restrictions and made it more intensely lyric. Most famous is his ode to "God" (1784), a striking statement of man's contradictory position in the universe as both "tsar" and "slave"; "worm" and "god"; the poem is also a rebuttal of atheism, and man's significance is shown as following from God's care for him. "On the Death of Prince Meshcherski" (1779) is one of his grandest odes; in it he preaches the Epicurean philosophy of *carpe diem*. "The Waterfall" (1798) is an evocation of sublimity in nature. Most of his odes are didactic in tone, and their morals are often magnificently expressed commonplaces. But Derzhavin was a stern advocate of right, and his ode, "To Potentates and Justices," rejected by the censorship in his day, is a ringing denunciation of any rule which is less than divine in its justice.

Derzhavin worked in a great variety of poetic genres, including Anacreontic poetry, dithyrambs, ballads and tragedies. His Anacreontic verse strikes a note of strong sensuality and love of life. His prose writings include criticism and his *Memoirs* (1811-12).

Derzhavin's style is uneven, alternating flights of magnificent language (his so-called "mighty line") with passages which are flat, even bathetic. His diction is also impure, and Pushkin, who admired his poetry, said that he wrote "like a Tartar." Although Derzhavin's influence was great in breaking down the strictures of the classical genres and in introducing elements of a freer expression, the rapid change in genres and styles made his legacy largely unusable for the generations which followed him. His most important successor was the mid-nineteenth century poet TYUTCHEV. Derzhavin's poetic flights show him as an almost solitary giant in Russian eighteenth-century poetry.

De Tournemir. See Salias de Tournemir.

Diaghilev, S. P. See Drama and Theater.

Dimitri Rostovski, St. (1651-1709), a monk of Cossack descent and pupil of the Kiev Academy, later Metropolitan of Rostov. He founded schools for children of all classes, introducing the study of Latin and Greek into the curriculum. He supported the reforms of PETER THE GREAT, and attacked the Old Believers and the low level of education of the Russian clergy. He compiled a popular collection of lives of saints, and wrote several mystery plays, baroque in their humorous treatment of the sacred and supernatural.

Dmitriev, Ivan Ivanovich (1760-1837), a poet of the end of the eighteenth century. A friend and follower of KARAMZIN, Dmitriev applied Karamzin's new and cultivated style to poetry. He is remembered primarily for his fables, but he also wrote songs, odes, elegies and verse tales. His manner is clear, cold and lucid, uncomplicated by profound ideas. He lived to see his polished style become outmoded, and withdrew from literature after 1803.

Dobrolyubov, Alexander Mikhaylovich (1876-?), an early symbolist poet, who published several small pamphlets of verse and then disappeared mysteriously "into the people" to become the leader of a small religious sect. Besides exemplifying the mixture of estheticism and religious mysticism so typical of the Russian symbolists, Dobrolyubov was significant for his early discovery of French Symbolism. In his poems he cultivated poses, such as Satanism, in the style of Huysmans.

Dobrolyubov, Nikolay Alexandrovich (1836-61), a leading radical critic of the mid-nineteenth century. The son of a poor priest, he was educated in a theological seminary and in a pedagogical institute. In 1856 he met CHERNYSHEVSKI and came under his influence; at the same time he began to contribute to *The Contemporary,* and in 1857 he took over Chernyshevski's place as chief critic of that journal, a post which he held until his premature death.

Dobrolyubov shared Chernyshevski's materialistic esthetics and his belief that literature merely reflects reality and cannot essentially change it. As with his teacher, his criticisms were more pretexts for social commentary than actual esthetic analyses. Still, Dobrolyubov was more particularly interested in literature than Chernyshevski, and possessed a keener critical judgment. His greatest contribution to Russian critical theory was his discovery of social types in Russian literature and their importance both for the expression of the author's ideas and for the analysis of Russian society. In the so-called "SUPERFLUOUS MAN," and especially in GONCHAROV'S Oblomov, an idealistic dreamer who gives way to a life of sloth and inaction, he found such a type, a proof that the liberal nobility were impotent as leaders. The plays of OSTROVSKI were significant for him as exposing the backward life of the Russian merchant class, which he characterized by the eloquent name of the "Kingdom of Darkness."

Dolmatovski, Yevgeni Aronovich (1915-   ), a Soviet poet. He served as a reporter during World War II, and published several volumes of war poems. He is best known for his songs, which are among the most popular in the Soviet Union today.

Domostroy, a book of rules and admonitions for the successful regulation of a household, dating from the sixteenth century. Supreme authority over the family is vested in the father, who is likened to the tsar himself in his power. Strict corporal punishments are prescribed for the transgressions of wives, children and servants. Order and respect for authority are presented as the supreme virtues. Thus the work's title (which means "Household Management") has come to be synonymous with the strict, humorless and tyrannical domestic morality which supposedly characterized Muscovite society, and which persisted among some classes, such as the merchants, into modern times.

Doroshevich, Vlasi Mikhaylovich (1864-1922), a leading journalist of the late nineteenth and early twentieth century. His newspaper feuilletons and reviews are witty and pointed and, with their short phrases, have a characteristic staccato tone. Their style was much praised and imitated around the turn of the century.

Dostoyevski, Fyodor Mikhaylovich (1821-81), an outstanding nineteenth-century novelist. Dostoyevski was in fact the creator of the modern psychological novel, and it is perhaps no exaggeration to say that he has been the strongest single influence on the twentieth-century novel.

Dostoyevski was born in Moscow, the son of a doctor. His father was of noble birth, but the family had no property, and its way of life was rather typical of the middle class. Fyodor grew up in not impoverished, but hardly well-to-do circumstances. There were eight children in all, but only Mikhail, Fyodor's elder brother, was close to him in later life.

Dostoyevski's mother died when he was seventeen. A year earlier he and his brother had been sent to boarding school, where Fyodor, shy and lonely, was exposed to the cruelty of the other boys, who mistreated or ignored him, hardships which he described later in *Notes from Underground* and *A Raw Youth.* Mikhail and he then went on to military school, where they studied engineering. Fyodor gave proof of being an able student, but rather impractical; on one occasion he designed a fortress but forgot to provide it with gates.

While Fyodor was in cadet school, his father was murdered. Dr. Dostoyevski had purchased a small property on which he indulged in drunken living and cruel treatment of his serfs. Ultimately they rose up and murdered him. Anxious to avoid any scandal, the family hushed the whole matter up. The news was a tremendous shock to Fyodor, and he states that his epileptic fits, which became very common later, originated at this time. Actually he had had earlier attacks, it seems. Freud argues, with some apparent reason, that Dostoyevski unconsciously desired the death of his father, and that when he found this wish involuntarily realized, he felt guilty of the death, a fact which may indeed have aggravated his tendency to epilepsy. Oedipal guilt is no doubt a major theme in Dostoyevski's novels: thus, Ivan Karamazov asks the question, "Who does not desire his father's death?" After his imprisonment in Siberia Dostoyevski admitted that he was actually guilty and deserved punishment, perhaps because he unconsciously associated his revolt against the tsar and against God with his earlier wish for the death of his father.

In 1843 Dostoyevski was graduated from cadet school, but, instead of taking a commission, he entered the civil service, in which he remained for about a year, though he hated the work. The state service supplies a background for many of his early stories, the heroes of which are petty officials. He and his brother then decided to become writers, and Fyodor published a translation of Balzac's *Eugénie Grandet*. Soon he was working on his first novel, *Poor People* (1846). He submitted it to NEKRASOV, the poet and publisher, who accepted it eagerly, coming to see Dostoyevski late one night to congratulate him on his success. The two men talked all night, and the next day, without going to bed, they took the manuscript to BELINSKI, the leading critic of the day. Belinski also greeted the book enthusiastically. The public, too, welcomed *Poor People,* and Dostoyevski experienced a success rare indeed for a young writer. It must be said that to a considerable extent Belinski and the public misinterpreted Dostoyevski; they overemphasized the element of sympathy for the poor in the novel, to the neglect of its psychological interest. Contrary to their belief, there is little of the proletarian novel in this first work.

Fired with success, Dostoyevski produced a second short novel, *The Double* (1846), a whole series of tales and novelettes, and the beginning of a long novel, *Netochka Nezvanova,* which he never completed. But, though much of this work, and especially

The Double, is on a higher level than *Poor People,* it failed to duplicate the success of his first novel. Belinski and Nekrasov did not find the element of social sympathy which they had exaggerated in *Poor People,* and hence lost much of their enthusiasm for Dostoyevski's work.

Meanwhile, in 1847, Dostoyevski had joined a group of Utopian socialists, the so-called PETRASHEVSKI CIRCLE. They were a circle of intellectuals who met to read and discuss proscribed political and economic literature. They had a printing press but never employed it. In April, 1849, Dostoyevski and the other members of the circle were arrested. The extent of Dostoyevski's personal involvement in the group is difficult to determine. His chief crime, besides attending the circle's meetings, lay in reading the famous letter from BELINSKI to GOGOL in which Belinski accused Gogol of betraying the liberal cause. Probably Dostoyevski's radicalism was a passing phase of his youth, which he would have soon outgrown. Significantly, he was repelled by the atheism of many members of the circle.

After a long trial, the Petrashevtsy were condemned to various terms of imprisonment in Siberia. Dostoyevski was sentenced to four years of confinement in a prison house and an indefinite term of service in the ranks of the army. But Nicholas I planned a cruel torture for the condemned: they were to be led out as if for execution, and only at the last minute reprieved. This sadistic joke resulted in one of the prisoners going mad.

Dostoyevski spent the next four years in prison at Omsk in Siberia, living in conditions which would have taxed the endurance of a much stronger and less sensitive person. His experiences there among common thieves and cut-throats are described in the slightly fictionalized *Memoirs from the Dead House* (1862), one of the finest and most moving studies of prison life in any literature. On leaving prison, he was sent to the town of Semipalatinsk as a soldier. After two years in the ranks he was made an officer, but was still not allowed to leave Siberia or the army. Nor could he publish. He hated the narrow, provincial life of the Siberian town. Meanwhile, in 1857, he married a widow, Marya Dmitrievna Isayeva, to whom he was deeply attached. Ill with tuberculosis and a hypochondriac as well, she tried his patience, but he testified that she was the best woman he had ever known.

Only in 1859 were Dostoyevski and his wife permitted to return to Russia; about the same time he received permission to publish again. Settling in St. Petersburg, Dostoyevski joined his brother Mikhail in editing a journal, *Time* (1861-63). In *Time* they sought to strike a compromise between the views of the SLAVOPHILES and the WESTERNERS, and to be moderately liberal. But in 1863 the publication of an article on the Polish Revolt brought government suppression of the review. A second journal, *The Epoch,* founded in 1864, failed to win the success of *Time*. Meanwhile, Mikhail Dostoyevski had died, and Fyodor nobly but unwisely accepted his brother's debts. Unable to settle with the creditors, he was forced to leave the country, and spent much of the next five years in Germany and Switzerland.

Dostoyevski had already gone abroad in the summer of 1862, after which he had published a series of articles called *Winter Notes on Summer Impressions* (1863). Though he considered himself an admirer of Western cultural traditions, in fact he was anti-Western. An irrationalist, he was especially irritated by what he saw as the cold rationalism of the French. He felt that the West had lost God, while Russians were more devout, and at the same time emotionally more open and honest.

In Germany Dostoyevski gave way to a passion of gambling which for years he could not control. Time and again he wagered and lost everything he had at the roulette tables of the German resorts. Meanwhile he fell victim to another passion, his unhappy love for Polina Suslova, a woman considerably younger than he, and a beauty. She treated him cruelly, but was apparently capable of bursts of sympathy as well; something of this duality of character entered into the portrayals of Dostoyevski's heroines.

With the publication of *Notes from Underground* in 1864, Dostoyevski began what may be called his great period. Up to this time his novels had for the most part been psychological studies of personality. With *Notes from Underground* he adds a serious interest in philosophical and moral problems, and with *Crime and Punishment* (1866), in religious problems. *Crime and Punishment* was followed by a less important novel, *The Gambler* (1866), inspired by Dostoyevski's own passion for gambling. He dictated the novel in less than a month in order to satisfy the demands of an unscrupulous publisher. Later he married his secretary (his first wife had died in 1864), Anna Grigorievna Snit-kina, whom he had hired to take dictation. Younger than he, she was a woman of no great intelligence but of immense sympathy and understanding, and she helped to make the final years of his life happier. Meanwhile, however, she was called on to endure her husband's frequent fits of temper and his ruinous mania for gambling. Doubtless her affectionate sympathy for her husband helped him finally to conquer his weakness.

When, in 1871, Dostoyevski finally settled with his creditors and returned to Russia, life became easier for him. He resumed his career as a journalist, editing in 1873 a review called *The Citizen*, in which he published a regular column under the heading of "The Diary of a Writer." His views were by now quite conservative, but the owner of the journal proved too reactionary for him, and he left the editorial staff after about a year. A frustrated journalist most of his life, Dostoyevski now undertook to continue *A Diary of a Writer* as a separate monthly publication (1876-77; 1880-81). It contained *feuilletons*, editorials and even several stories. It is paradoxical that Dostoyevski's social and political ideas are often as petty as his novels are great, and the reader may well find his extreme chauvinism, anti-progressivism and racial prejudice hard to stomach.

Gradually during his final period Dostoyevski acquired a great reputation and influence. In 1880 he gave a speech on the occasion of the dedication of a monument to Pushkin in Moscow. In the speech he returned to his favorite aim of reconciling the WESTERNERS and the SLAVOPHILES (though in fact his own views stood far closer to the latter); PUSHKIN, he asserted, combined a truly Russian spirit with one which was cosmopolitan and universal. So, too, in his view, did the Russian people, and hence Russia was destined to save Europe from the collapse of her spiritual values.

The following year Dostoyevski died from a hemorrhage, caused, in one account, by a family quarrel; in another, by moving a heavy piece of furniture. His funeral was a great event, and thousands followed the coffin to its grave.

Dostoyevski's character shows a mass of conflicts and contradictions, and he even may be said to resemble one of his own ambivalent, "double" heroes. He was by no means a simple or even very pleasant person; still, it was to a considerable extent this contradiction in personality which makes his work so rewarding. He was well aware of these contradictions and hence was able to portray his characters with a depth almost unparalleled in modern literature. Emotionally open and expansive, he alternated, like so many of his characters, between bursts of warm sympathy and a haughty contempt for his fellows. A similar contradiction is evident in his religious feelings: though he strove to believe in God, his letters as well as his novels suggest that he was torn by doubt and by a proud refusal to accept God as a power whose existence would necessarily limit the self-assertion of his own ego. God Dostoyevski conceived as the principle of love; the road to God lies through humility, for him the supreme virtue. Acceptance of God, personal humility and love of our fellow men are for him all aspects of one attitude, which is the religious spirit. Its negation is found in pride and contempt, and in man's desire to make himself a god, as Kirilov seeks to do in *The Devils*. No stranger himself to egoistic pride, Dostoyevski well realized the strength of this temptation to exalt self and to deny God. It is perhaps true, as has been claimed, that in *The Brothers Karamazov* (1879-80), his final novel, Dostoyevski came to a less troubled acceptance of Christianity, though it is in this book that Ivan Karamazov propounds the most tormenting doubts. In any event, Dostoyevski's significance as a religious "thinker" seems to rest in his ability to feel deeply both belief and unbelief, just as his significance as a philosopher lies in his ability to feel ideas intensely and to make them come alive in literary form. Ultimately, Dostoyevski's greatness is that of a novelist, and critics who exalt him as a profound religious thinker or philosopher inevitably overlook the full implications of the fact that he considered himself a novelist (rather than a philosopher), and that his non-fictional writings are mediocre both in content and manner. As a psychologist, Dostoyevski is perhaps more significant, and it is just conceivable that his views on human personality might be abstracted from his writings and erected as a psychological system. Yet here, too, as in his religious, ethical and philosophical thought, there are inconsistencies, and his brilliant psychological insights are often alloyed with sentimental and quite hackneyed biographical formulas. His heroines, for example, so often come from good families which have become impoverished, a detail which seems intended to create pathos rather than enrich their characterization.

Dostoyevski's first novel, *Poor People* (1846), has been overestimated; it contains many technical faults. Quite implausible is the device of telling the narrative in a series of letters written by two people who actually live almost next door to one another. The novel's hero, Makar Devushkin, is an indigent civil service clerk who fights a constantly losing struggle with poverty. He befriends a poor girl, Varvara, who is trying to support herself with her sewing. But he is weak and too poor to help her, and, in order to spare him the burden, she ends by marrying a dissolute landowner. Too late Devushkin realizes that he loves her with something more than fatherly feeling.

The novel shows the strong influence of GOGOL; at the same time, however, Dostoyevski asserts his independence of the older writer. The figure of Devushkin is obviously modelled on the poor clerk in Gogol's story, *The Overcoat;* at the same time Dostoyevski resents Gogol's "unfeeling" caricature, devoid of sympathy as well as realism. Gogol's clerk seems scarcely to feel or think; Dostoyevski, on the other hand, has made Devushkin pathetic and human. Not that Dostoyevski is never cruel; he pokes fun at Devushkin's simplicity, for example, and his silly taste for cheap erotic tales. But Dostoyevski's cruelty to his weak heroes never precludes his sympathy for them, and his contradictory attitude towards weakness is, in its way, thoroughly human.

Though *Poor People* is weak in construction, the character of the writing is often striking, especially in the style of Devushkin's letters, corrupted by the office jargon which he writes in his capacity as a clerk.

More successful and more original, though it failed to please the taste of the day, was *The Double* (1846), which also shows the influence of GOGOL, this time of his story, *Memoirs of a Madman. The Double* again concerns a civil servant, unloved and despised by his fellows, who finally goes mad and sees his own double. His madness may be interpreted either as a pathological split in personality, or as the paranoid delusion that he is being subjected to the persecutions of a supposed "double" who in fact does not exist.

Besides these two novels, Dostoyevski wrote a large number

of tales and stories before his Siberian exile. Some of these contain interesting anticipations of the later novels, especially in the psychology of their characters, while others show experiments which are quite unrelated to his later work. Thus, *The Landlady* (1847) is a melodramatic horror story, with a use of folk narrative style which Dostoyevski never repeated. *White Nights* (1848) and *A Little Hero,* the latter written in 1849 when Dostoyevski was in prison, show a strong lyricism of landscape, of feelings of love and of adolescent yearning which are more strikingly poetic than anything in his later works, and which bring him close to TURGENEV and the high "poetic" style in Russian prose, which Dostoyevski generally shunned. The story called *An Honest Thief* (1848) is perhaps closer to his later novels. It tells how a drunkard, rescued from the streets, betrays his benefactor by stealing from him, but then dies of remorse for his own guilt. We see here the almost infinite sensitivity of the meek hero, as well as the exaggerated weakness of will so characteristic of this type.

Dostoyevski's first writings after imprisonment (if we except *Memoirs from the Dead House*) show little fruit of his Siberian experiences. The evident influence of Siberian imprisonment on his religious and moral views did not mature at once, it would seem. His first works published after his return from exile continue to be intense psychological studies, the first of which are even partly humorous.

Uncle's Dream (1859) is an involved tale of intrigue, in which a provincial lady tries to marry her proud daughter to a decrepit old prince. In the end her scheming leads to a terrible scandal; her daughter is forced to give up the man she really loves, but in reprisal rebels and herself assumes a tyrannical power over the household. Her nature, proud, resentful and sensitive, is also capable at times of warmth and generosity, and thus she is a first example of the double heroine in Dostoyevski's work. The story's most striking quality, however, lies in the wonderful humor of unexpected incident.

The Village of Stepanchikovo (1859; English translation as "The Friend of the Family") is perhaps the finest of all Dostoyevski's early works. It describes in almost excruciating detail the sufferings endured by a sensitive, meek-spirited landowner at the hands of his tyrannical mother, who considers it her son's duty to support her in every luxury. She is abetted in her tyranny by her companion, the hypocritical and despotic Foma Fomich Opiskin. The latter is a richly conceived character, worthy of ranking with the great hypocrites and parasites of world literature. Opiskin has sustained a lack of recognition from others earlier in life; forced by a tyrannical old general to play the part of a buffoon, he assumes the role to perfection, but on the general's death seeks vindictive revenge and becomes a sadistic tyrant himself. In the end he goes too far, and his insinuations concerning the chastity of a pure young girl bring the landowner to drive him from the house. Finally he is forgiven, but, thoroughly chastened, now becomes a mere shadow of his former tyrannical self.

Dostoyevski published his first long novel, *The Insulted and Injured*, in 1861. It has all the faults of his long novels, with few of their virtues. It is prolix, with a profusion of characters, plots and sub-plots, and with much overly melodramatic atmosphere which often merely confuses the reader. Its subject is a tormented quadrangular relationship among two men and two women. The character of one of the heroines, Natasha, represents that peculiar blend, so typical for Dostoyevski, of sadistic and masochistic impulses. Burdened with this ambivalence of nature, she is fated never to find happiness in love: one of the men she despises; the other she dominates as a mother does a child. Neither satisfies her thirst for suffering, a longing forced on her by a sense of her own guilt. In the end she gives up all chance for married happiness.

Dostoyevski's *Notes from Underground* (1864) shows a new depth of psychological and philosophical penetration. The first part of the work is in the form of a journal, kept by the "man from underground," who is described as such because he has long since given up the struggle for love and success and has retreated to his "hole" underground. A shy, sensitive boy who experienced rebuffs at the hands of his schoolmates, and who at the same time felt himself far superior to them in intrinsic worth and especially intelligence, he early in life loses his capacity to love or to be loved; for love he substitutes a desire for despotic power. But this drive is just as impossible of fulfillment as is his need for love or recognition, and in the end he can only torment himself by turning his sadistic impulses inward. Dostoyevski's underground man

is an early—almost a first—example of the modern neurotic intellectual in literature, and it is typical of him that he attempts to
substitute his own intellectual superiority for his emotional
deficiencies.

The Underground Man keeps a journal which contains his reflections on life, and which constitutes the first half of the work.
Here Dostoyevski launches his first attack on the socialists and
on all rationalistic, utilitarian conceptions of human nature and
social progress. Any society based on rational principles will fail,
Dostoyevski's protagonist argues, for man himself is profoundly
irrational. It is useless, then, to attempt the application of "scientific" principles calculated to assure man's happiness, for man
will ultimately only reject them in the name of his own independence, for the sake of having his own way. Here Dostoyevski
anticipates the dilemma of freedom and happiness to which he
later returns in *The Brothers Karamazov*. War is an illustration of
the fact that society is not governed by rational principles, and
Dostoyevski pokes savage fun at Buckle's thesis that, in proportion as mankind progresses, wars grow less numerous and less
severe.

The second part of *Notes from Underground* shows the protagonist frustrated by his own inability to love. He begins a relationship with a prostitute for the sake of the sense of power
which it gives him. But she has genuine feeling for him and, much
as he wants and needs her love, he is too proud to accept it, and
in the end drives her away.

In spite of its deficiencies from the formal point of view, *Notes
from Underground* has a pivotal importance in Dostoyevski's
work, as the critic ROZANOV first realized. It introduces Dostoyevski's views on the nature of human society and the possibility
of Utopia, themes to which he returned in his final novels. It
gives perhaps the clearest portrayal, at least in terms of childhood
development, of the ambivalent nature of his heroes, who alternate between love for their fellows and haughty contempt, and
it thus prepares the way for the emergence of such personages
as Raskolnikov and Ivan Karamazov. Dostoyevski had even
planned to introduce his characteristic religious ideas in the
book; the Underground Man was to advocate Christianity as an
alternative to atheistic socialism and materialism. But he aban-

doned the plan, perhaps because his hero turned out too unsympathetic.

Crime and Punishment (1866) is the first of Dostoyevski's masterpieces, and one of the great novels of world literature. Its hero, Raskolnikov, is a poor student who commits the bloody murder of an evil old woman pawnbroker for money, and who subsequently is forced to kill her gentle and pious sister as well. Unnerved by his double crime, he steals little or nothing, goes home and falls seriously ill from shock, a fact which first brings him to the attention of the police. Tormented by his crime, he will obviously give himself up sooner or later. But he restrains his impulse to confess, and it is only after he is subjected to a whole series of diverse spiritual influences that he can voluntarily accept his punishment. Chief among these is the friendship of Sonya, the gentle-spirited prostitute who loves him and whose love it is so hard for him to admit; another is that of Svidrigaylov, a dissolute landowner whose long career of evil serves as a warning to Raskolnikov that his path of self-isolation and crime leads only to spiritual self-destruction. But Raskolnikov is a double, who, throughout the book, goes on alternating between a good side and an evil one, between sincere love and proud contempt. It seems inevitable that he should continue this alternation until death (presumably a self-inflicted death brought by the hopelessness of his tormented position); his final conversion in Siberia, which comes almost on the last page of the novel, is too schematic and unconvincing. Raskolnikov is a greater achievement as a creature of doubt and negation than as a repentant criminal who accepts God and his fellow men.

Besides the pattern of Raskolnikov's repeated alternation, the novel is built on a progressive revelation of the motive for his crime. At the very outset it appears that poverty—his poverty and that of his mother and sister—is the motive. But we soon discover deeper and more tangled motives beneath this superficial, rationalistic one. Raskolnikov's sister Dunya is engaged to be married to a rich official whom she hates, in order to save her mother and brother from poverty. She, like her brother, is a double, and he realizes that part of her motive in making such a sacrifice is to place him eternally in her debt. His pride cannot tolerate the idea of her winning such moral superiority over him, and through the murder he seeks to thwart her marriage by stealing enough to make himself and his family financially independent. No doubt his rivalry with his sister goes back to their childhood, but Dostoyevski never depicts this earlier period in their lives.

Lastly, there is a motive, or rather, a complex of motives associated with Raskolnikov's strange theory of his destiny as a superman. He believes that there are certain men capable of great good as well as great evil, who are outside the moral law; they are able to commit crimes without feeling compunction; on the other hand, they are also capable of becoming saints and benefactors of humanity. Raskolnikov regards himself as such a superior being, and feels that he must commit a crime to prove that he is indeed a superman and beyond the law; at the same time he needs money to begin his great career as a benefactor of mankind. His theory fails him, however, for his weakness after the murder proves he is not a superman at all. Nor is his theory valid, for obviously a man need not do great evil to prove his capacity for doing good.

Raskolnikov's theory is in fact only a rationalization. His theory of the superman-benefactor is no more than egotistic longing for despotic power, rooted in his pride, in his contempt for others, and in his exaggerated sense of the value of his intellect. It is his demonic pride, more than anything, which brings him to the murder. And his power theory is only the first stage of the "reformer's" dream of Utopia which Dostoyevski was later to expose so thoroughly in *The Devils* and *The Brothers Karamazov,* in which the idealism of the reformer turns out to be nothing but a mask for his drive for power.

Crime and Punishment is a novel which can be admired on many levels. As a novel of crime and detection it is superb. The terror of the murder, of Raskolnikov's escape from the scene of the crime, and of his dreams is perhaps unsurpassed in any other work of literature. As a Christian story of sin and retribution the work is perhaps less perfect, and Raskolnikov's final redemption may seem unconvincing. Lastly, the novel may be viewed as a drama of man's revolt against God, or of impulses within the human soul which work against man's happiness and his salvation. As such, it is almost perfect.

The Idiot (1868-69), Dostoyevski's next major novel, is far less successful. It has a brilliant opening, but tends to fall to pieces, overweighted with too many plots and characters. In the character of the "Idiot" himself, Prince Myshkin, Dostoyevski strove to create a Christ-like figure, a task impossible of perfect fulfillment. True, as a man Myshkin is not unconvincing. But his weakness—his epilepsy, his implied sexual impotence, as well as his tendency toward "idiocy"—all make him fall short of the Christ ideal. He hardly changes anyone around him; though all are impressed by his perfection, they go on living as before and his attraction for them only seems to hasten the final tragedy. Evidently the artist in Dostoyevski won where the moralist lost, and the book is perhaps most successful if we consider its theme to be the frequent impotence of the good in human life.

Opposed to the "Idiot" is the allegorical figure of Rogozhin, who represents passion. He recognizes Myshkin's purity and respects him, but is too weak to control his own vicious impulses. Too melodramatic, Rogozhin falls short of being real. In Dmitri Karamazov Dostoyevski later created a more convincing figure of this type.

Last, there is the richly inspired figure of Nastasya Filipovna, the most dramatic of all Dostoyevski's double heroines. Violated as a child and brought up to play the part of a kept woman, she conceives an intense, neurotic loathing for herself and a longing to suffer. She cherishes the wrongs done her, and cannot conceive of any redemption for herself which would enable her to give up her sense of injury. At the same time she seeks to avenge herself on others. At once sadistic and masochistic, she cannot be saved by Myshkin, and in the end chooses to be killed by the jealous Rogozhin.

The Eternal Husband (1870) is a kind of interlude in the series of great novels, and is shorter and has fewer characters and themes. It is almost as tortured as the other novels, however, though its style is lighter and more bantering. The story concerns a husband's discovery after his wife's death that she has deceived him, and that the child he thought to be his is illegitimate. Inflamed by jealous hatred, and at the same time fascinated by a strange admiration for the man who possesses the very attraction to women he himself lacks, he seeks out his wife's former lover. The two of them fight a macabre duel, culminating in the death from neglect of the unwanted little girl and in the husband's

unsuccessful attempt to murder the lover. In the lighter epilogue
we see the husband again married to a young and beautiful girl.
He is still an "eternal husband," possessed of the same ambivalent
feeling: a fear of being deceived mixed with a secret desire to be;
he is so unattractive to women that he feels it is only right for
them to cuckold him.

The Devils (1871-72; also known as "The Possessed" in English
translation) is perhaps the most complex and tortured of all Dostoyevski's novels, though it is hardly the most successful. The
main subject of the book is a savage attack on the radical younger
generation of Nihilists (see Nihilism), whose political significance
Dostoyevski overestimated. The basis for the novel was an actual
political murder, the so-called "Nechayev Affair." Though Dostoyevski no doubt did an injustice to the Russian radicals in depicting
them as unfeeling, savage brutes, still he was too keen to fail
entirely to understand the nature and motives of revolution, and
the novel serves as a frightening prophecy of the Bolshevik Revolution. For Dostoyevski power is the motive which makes men
revolutionaries, and their idealistic talk of reform is only rationalization. He saw in revolution a new form of man's eternal attempt to dispense with God and create a materialistic earthly
paradise of his own design. In the novel the revolutionary theorist,
Shigalyov, designs a plan for a totalitarian order, the keystone of
which is absolute equality. Everyone will be happy, he argues,
for all men will be absolutely equal, and hence there will be no
envy among them. Equality will be achieved by levelling down-
ward; the citizens will have to toil, and the level of education,
science and art will be lowered. Geniuses are not wanted, and
will be destroyed in infancy.

For Dostoyevski political revolution was only a part of man's
greater revolt against God. In the enigmatic character of Stavrogin he sought to demonstrate (as he had earlier implied with
Svidrigaylov in *Crime and Punishment*) what would happen to a
man who could reject God and fellow man completely. Such a
man would not become a benefactor of society, as Raskolnikov
had fancied. Nor would he even be a power-mad despot, though
this temptation might attract him for a time. In the end, without
a goal in life, recognizing no law above him, he would give himself over completely to vice and to grotesque sensuality, to crimes

striking in their very pointlessness. One can hardly help but feel that Dostoyevski created this type of character, described by his commentators as the "proud" or "self-willed" type, more for melodramatic reasons than as the result of deeper religious or moral observation. In the end Stavrogin is profoundly bored by evil, and finds himself completely alone, isolated in a universe in which he can accept neither God nor men. He makes desperate attempts to find love, but, incapable of feeling affection, he finally kills himself, not from a sense of guilt, but rather out of boredom and loneliness.

A *Raw Youth* (1875) is sometimes grouped with Dostoyevski's great novels. Its extreme complexity, unnecessarily melodramatic atmosphere, and, above all, the anti-climax of its over-anticipated denouement, make it a failure. It introduces no new themes or character types to Dostoyevski's work, except perhaps that of the "raw youth" himself, some part of whose youthful vigor and naiveté Dostoyevski may have taken from his own youth.

The Brothers Karamazov (1879-80) is without doubt the most complex, profound and artistically the finest of Dostoyevski's novels. Its chief fault is that it is essentially unfinished, and the fates of the major characters are never satisfactorily resolved. Had he lived Dostoyevski might have attempted the sequel, but he died within three months after the end of the novel's publication.

The three brothers Karamazov are allegorical figures, though their allegorical significance does not deprive them of reality. The eldest, Dmitri, like Rogozhin in *The Idiot*, represents feeling and passion. The slave of his sensual desires, Dmitri is too weak to control his passions. Still he realizes that God is above him, and thus, in Dostoyevski's eyes, he is capable of being saved. Ivan represents intellect; pride in his intellectual powers brings him to reject God. Yet Ivan's revolt against God also proceeds from a keen sense of justice and revulsion at the existence of irrational evil in God's universe. Ivan's rejection of God, unlike that of Raskolnikov or Stavrogin, is based partly on altruistic grounds. It seems, perhaps, that even he may be saved, therefore, though Dostoyevski no doubt realized how difficult it could be for an intellectual to accept God. The third son, Alyosha, is less actualized, more potential, than the other two. Presumably he was to have become the main hero of the promised sequel. We may say tentatively that he represents humility and active love, with the restriction that Dostoyevski may have intended (in the sequel) that he first fall into sin and later be redeemed as a saint. It is to such a fate, apparently, that his elder, Zosima, sends him out from the monastery into the world.

The father of these three brothers is old Fyodor Karamazov, one of Dostoyevski's most magnificently portrayed characters. In his sensuality and indecent buffoonery he seems to be something like a creature of absolute evil. Yet he too has a sense for God and his justice, though he treats them blasphemously. His sensuality seems to represent the nature of man, the root of Dmitri's inherited sensuality as well as Ivan's cold pride.

The drama of the book is the murder of the father by the sons; behind this lies the deeper drama of man's revolt against the heavenly father. Both Ivan and Dmitri desire the death of their father, and both are involved in it and guilty of it; though neither actually commits it, both are guilty and are destined to suffer for it. But suffering, in Dostoyevski's view, is capable of teaching man humility, and hence it may be that both will be saved.

The real murderer is the fourth, and illegitimate, brother, the lackey and epileptic Smerdyakov. In him Dostoyevski seems to have sought to create an embodiment of grotesque, petty evil, and Smerdyakov may seem more of a petty demon than a real human being. He apes Ivan's arguments and conceives the idea of the murder from Ivan's doctrine that "If there is no God, then all is lawful"; thus Smerdyakov's discipleship also makes Ivan indirectly guilty of his father's death.

The books ends with the fates of the three brothers unresolved. Dmitri is convicted of the murder on circumstantial evidence and is to be sent to Siberia; he says that he wishes to accept his suffering, but in fact it is uncertain if he actually will go to Siberia or not. As for Ivan, the consciousness of guilt drives him partly mad, and he sees his own double, masquerading as the devil. The latter conducts philosophical conversations with him about God. Alyosha's fate is likewise unresolved, but the novel ends with the warm and joyful picture of his friendship with a group of boys and the reconciliation which he brings them. Closing the novel on this episode, Dostoyevski may be said to have ended on a resolution which surmounted—at least for a time—his customary spiritual doubts.

The Brothers Karamazov contains a philosophical chapter, "The Legend of the Great Inquisitor," in which Dostoyevski returns to the problem of a totalitarian "Utopia." Again, as with the system of Shigalyov in *The Devils*, he envisages an authoritarian state in which complete equality together with loss of moral and political responsibility would insure happiness for the average citizen. Dostoyevski now sees that freedom and happiness are irreconcilable, for freedom means not only the responsibility for making personal and political choices which involve our own welfare, but the far heavier responsibility of making final ethical and religious choices. Ultimately freedom means the responsibility for accepting or rejecting God. Such freedom is at the root of man's unhappiness, in Dostoyevski's view, for man can hardly find permanent and lasting answers to his dilemmas; even more, moral responsibility implies suffering for the evil and injustice of human existence. Yet, though he finds freedom and unhappiness, Dostoyevski remains on the side of freedom, for it is the latter, in his view, which is the divine spark implanted in man by God.

It has become customary for the twentieth-century critics to praise Dostoyevski as a psychologist, and to find in his novels remarkable anticipations of the ideas of the modern psychoanalytic school. There is no doubt that certain passages in his novels contain brilliant insights into human behavior which are far in advance of psychological modes of thinking in his time. It is a mystery how he came to his ideas on the human mind, and it would seem that to a truly remarkable extent he simply intuited them. In his system of thought he is closer to Adler's view of the human personality than to that of Freud. For him the basic human need is love, but love considered as affection or recognition rather than as eros. When this need is frustrated, as in the case of the Underground Man, Raskolnikov, or the Raw Youth, man comes to develop a substitute craving for despotic or even sadistic power over other human beings. The sexual drive in Dostoyevski's work is relatively unimportant; it becomes significant largely as an occasion for the display of perverted power-seeking attitudes (sadism and masochism). Dostoyevski anticipates clearly the modern psychological association of masochism and sadism, in which masochism appears as sadism turned inward on the self. He is aware of the role which the unconscious plays in psychic life; this is well demonstrated in *Crime and Punishment*, where Raskolnikov's dreams and semi-conscious ideas themselves form an organic chain of thought culminating in the murder, or in *The Brothers Karamazov*, where Ivan Karamazov goes away because he unconsciously realizes that by doing so he will help set the stage for his father's murder. Finally, we find the conception of the Oedipus Complex realized in *The Brothers Karamazov*, reflected in the hatred of Dmitri and Ivan for their father and their wish to kill him.

It has also been customary to praise Dostoyevski as a great religious thinker. Here his two most characteristic ideas are his belief in the chastening power of suffering, and his postulation of freedom as man's highest spiritual birthright. Suffering, accepted voluntarily, teaches us humility, which for Dostoyevski is the greatest virtue, to be identified with complete love and the acceptance of God and our fellow men. The opposite of humility is pride, which is the greatest sin, for it involves the rejection of God, and ultimately an erroneous and self-destructive belief in our own divinity. It is pride far more than any intellectual doubts which brings Raskolnikov and Ivan Karamazov to reject God.

In his ideas on freedom Dostoyevski has had great influence, as, for example, on BERDYAYEV, and has even been proclaimed a great "Orthodox" thinker. Yet it would seem that here as elsewhere, his real aim was not so much the elaboration of ideas as their dramatization.

To a large extent critics have ignored the purely artistic achievements of Dostoyevski's work, or have even denied that these exist. Thus, his style is often regarded as "incorrect" or at least inadequate. No doubt it has a certain "middle-class" character so strongly in contrast with the refined style of "aristocratic" writers like Turgenev, and it is not the sort which is usually given to school children to imitate. Suffice to say that it is at least adequate to Dostoyevski's purpose. His characters' speeches (dialogues have a particular importance in his work, since he is in essence a "dramatic" writer) are always faithful and accurate in their style and intonation. At times he is capable of using language with great effect, as in the parody of TURGENEV's prose poems which he gives in *The Devils.*

Much the same is true of the structure and composition of his novels. No doubt the form of his novels, with their intrigue and the great number of plots and characters, is old fashioned and excessive. Still Dostoyevski chose his form deliberately; he wanted the melodrama of intrigue, the freedom of an exposition which could provide suspense. His use of minor characters to recount the narrative may at times seem awkward, but is ultimately justified by the greater vividness which he attains. The rapid flow of events, almost impossible chronologically, likewise makes for suspense. No doubt at times there is too much mystery and melodrama in his novels. Still it is impossible to imagine his work without these qualities, or to suppose that it would have such startling effect or such power.

Dostoyevski's influence on the contemporary novel has been immense. Thomas Mann, Gide, Wassermann, Kafka—these are only a few of the writers whom he has influenced. In Russian literature his influence was at first slight; he was slower in gaining recognition than, for example, was Tolstoy. By the end of the nineteenth century he had only a few lesser followers, such as ALBOV and Prince D. P. GOLITSYN. But with the symbolist movement he came into his own: MEREZHKOVSKI, HIPPIUS, Vyacheslav IVANOV, BLOK, Bely (see Bugayev), REMIZOV —almost every one of the non-realist writers of the time was influenced by him, and, in the early Soviet period, LEONOV and OLESHA. Since then his influence on Soviet literature has declined, along with his official popularity. His morbidity, real or apparent, his political conservatism and religiosity have brought official disapproval of his work, and his novels and tales have seldom been republished in Soviet Russia. At the present writing it seems that there will be some relaxation of this policy, and that he will be re-evaluated as a great, "national" artist, the formula which has been applied by Soviet critics to reclaim so many older conservative writers.

Drama and Theater. *Beginnings of Russian Drama.* Harvest and spring festivals in early Russia may have had a semi-dramatic character, and later there were travelling actors and clowns who appeared at great houses and at fairs. School religious plays were performed in West Russian schools. The usual date assigned, however, as the beginning of the Russian theater, is 1672. In that year Tsar Alexey Mikhaylovich ordered a German pastor and school teacher, Johann Gottfried Gregori, to stage a comedy, using the Book of Esther as a subject. Dwellers in the German suburb of Moscow had for some time been staging amateur productions based on ecclesiastical school plays of the type common in Europe in the late Middle Ages and early Renaissance.

The theater formed by Gregori was short-lived, beset by problems of language, personnel, and finance. The plays were performed in German, and later, when Russian actors had been trained, in Old Church Slavonic. Perspective paintings were used for scenery. Apart from the school plays, the repertoire supplied by Gregori was apparently derived from that of the English Comedians, a group of English actors who had gone from England to Holland in the early seventeenth century. An anthology of their plays had appeared in 1620, and it was prototypes of these plays which went into the Russian repertoire. One of these was a piece called *Bayazette and Tamerlane,* presumably a version of Marlowe's *Tamburlaine.* The Russian repertoire was supplemented by verse morality plays written by Simeon POLOTSKI (1629-80), a graduate of the Kiev Academy and tutor to the tsar's children. With the tsar's death in 1676, the theater was disbanded.

Eighteenth-century Theater and Drama. PETER THE GREAT helped to renew interest in the theater. He hired a company from Danzig; led by Johann Kunst, they arrived in Moscow in 1702. The problem of finding Russian-speaking actors was again acute, however, and the Moscow theater was closed in 1706. Various temporary theaters, many in unoccupied private houses, gave performances in Moscow during and after Peter's death.

The tsar's example stimulated interest in private theatricals among the nobility and wealthy merchants, with the result that private theaters, in which servants, professional actors, and members of the noble households took part, began to appear at this time. Some of these theaters came to give public performances as well as purely private theatricals. Peter's example also inspired his youngest sister, who staged and even wrote plays with propaganda overtones. The repertoire of the theater during Peter's time also included plays from the German Johann Felten's repertoire —and this group included versions of Molière; the Russian translations of these, however, may have been made directly from the French. Realistic interludes of coarse, gross humor, played by buffoons, were a standard part of a theatrical evening at this time, and mark the beginning of the Russian realistic drama.

The reign of Anna Ivanovna (1730-40) brought new interest in the court theater. One room in the newly built Winter Palace in Petersburg was equipped as a theater. *Commedia dell'arte,* interludes, and, in 1735, Italian opera and ballet, appeared. A Russian ballet troupe began training in 1738; it quickly came under French influence. German, French and Italian dramatic companies came to Russia for brief visits in the 1740's, and in the next century for more frequent and extended stays.

Yelizaveta Petrovna, Peter's daughter and the next empress (1741-62), was a patroness of the theater, and was responsible for bringing to Petersburg the real founder of the Russian professional theater, Fyodor Volkov (1729-63). He had founded a company in Yaroslavl; the group, coming to Petersburg, began public performances there in 1752. A. P. SUMAROKOV (1718-77), the first well-known Russian dramatist, was appointed director. Sumarokov had played with an amateur group in the Corps of Cadets, where some of the Yaroslavl group were sent for a more general education. Volkov, second in command and the chief actor, had a professional attitude toward the stage; he imported properties, and systematically studied acting techniques.

CATHERINE THE GREAT (1762-96) encouraged the theater to the extent that she herself adapted scenes from Shakespeare and wrote original satirical and didactic plays. In 1779 a dramatic school was founded in Petersburg, for which the educated actor I. A. Dmitrevski was named supervisor. He had travelled in Europe to study Western acting, and subsequently proved the greatest Russian actor in the grand French declamatory style.

Catherine took an interest in the personal and professional lives of actors. The social position of theater people gradually improved over the course of the century, but, as in other countries, actors and actresses were long held inferior. At first women's parts were taken by men, and when women did appear on the stage, the character and behavior of the first actresses did little to raise their social level. At the beginning, salaries were as irregular as the performances, but as the theater itself became established, actors were paid better and more regularly. In addition to their stipends, they were often provided with housing by the State. Benefit performances were occasionally granted for special players or in time of special need.

Until Catherine's time Russian plays had been almost entirely adaptations of Latin, German, Italian, French and English plays. The eighteenth-century repertoire continued to lean heavily on translations and adaptations, but real attempts to write Russian plays on European models now resulted in some creditable work. SUMAROKOV wrote tragedies based on Russian history (*Mstislav* and *The False Dmitry*) in the style of French classical drama. His version of *Hamlet* in Alexandrines, observing the unities, made a new play of Shakespeare's work but demonstrated Sumarokov's subservience to Boileau. The conflict of love and duty was his major theme, as it was Racine's. Sumarokov's comedies were also influenced by the ideals of post-Renaissance classicism, and the didactic style he used proved helpful to another writer of comedy, Denis FONVIZIN (1745-92). Fonvizin's two satirical plays, *The Minor* (1782) and *The Brigadier-General* (1786), show signs of the influence of the Dane Holberg and of English eighteenth-century comedy; the plays are of such merit that, unlike all other Russian eighteenth-century plays, they remain in the repertoire today.

After Fonvizin, other successful writers of comedy were Yakov KNYAZHNIN (1742-91), with *An Accident with a Carriage* (1779), and Vasili KAPNIST (1757-1823), whose satire of the legal profession, *Chicane* (1798), probably influenced later Russian comedy. Comic opera was represented in the later eighteenth century with Alexander ABLESIMOV's *The Miller as Wizard, Quack and Matchmaker* (1779).

A taste for theater spread to all parts of Russia by the end of the century, and the great nobles founded their own theaters, in which serfs were often trained as actors, musicians and dancers. Some of these private serf theaters were exquisitely constructed and equipped.

Nineteenth-century Theater. In 1805 came the decree instituting the Imperial theaters in Moscow in addition to those in Petersburg. The act established the crown monopoly in both cities, a state which continued until late in the nineteenth century. In 1809 the Moscow state dramatic school was established. The Maly Theater in Moscow officially became a state theater in 1824; in Petersburg the opera and ballet were combined into one theater (the Bolshoy), and the drama went to the Alexandrinski Theater in 1836. A decree of 1839 defined the civil-service rank of state-employed actors.

During the nineteenth century the style of Russian acting shows a steady progression towards realism. In the first part of the century there was intense rivalry between the actors V. A. Karatygin (1802-53) at the Alexandrinski in Petersburg and Pavel Mochalov (1800-48) in Moscow. Karatygin represented the carefully calculated approach to acting; he studied all connected historical and psychological data to familiarize himself with his roles, and was thus able to play a wide variety of different characters. Mochalov represented the instinctive approach; he achieved inspired performances, but his work was uneven, not only from role to role, but from night to night. His Hamlet was his most famous creation and indicates the pre-eminence of Shakespeare in the repertoire of the 1830's and 1840's.

Mikhail Shchepkin (1788-1863), born a serf, became an actor in the provincial theaters and from there made his way to the Imperial Theater in Moscow. It was he who practised so-called "natural acting" and made it the dominant style in the Russian theater. He also stressed the importance of ensemble work. His influence was felt on actors of his own day, and afterward down to K. S. Stanislavski (see below), who gave credit to Shchepkin for the latter's influence.

The next generation brought Prov Sadovski (1818-72) to the stage of the Moscow Maly Theater. His talent was especially compatible with the realistic plays of Alexander OSTROVSKI, whose first play was produced in 1852. The middle years of the century found Moscow far ahead of St. Petersburg in the level of acting.

In 1882 the ban on private theaters in the capitals was lifted. New public theaters, some financed by wealthy merchants, began to appear, and enthusiasm for the theater was widespread. Many amateur groups sprang up and home productions were common.

From one of these amateur groups, the Society of Art and Literature, there came the famous Stanislavski (pseudonym of Konstantin Sergeyevich Alexeyev, 1863-1938). Together with the playwright Vladimir NEMIROVICH-DANCHENKO, he founded the
Moscow Art Theater, which opened in 1898. Stanislavski and
Nemirovich-Danchenko were theatrical reformers, who aimed at
elimination of the star system and at the principle of co-ordina-
tion of the entire production by the director. The Art Theater also
stood for a consistent—at times too extreme—realism in stage production.

Nineteenth-century Drama. The nineteenth century produced
most of the enduring drama which Russia has created. The early
years of the century were dominated by vaudeville, "tearful
comedy," romantic tragedy and sentimental historical plays. V. A.
OZEROV (1769-1816) had resounding success with a historical
patriotic play, *Dmitri Donskoy* (1807), a neo-classic drama with
a strong sentimental effect, which played on the emotions of
Russians before and during the Napoleonic invasion.

Vaudeville, which almost monopolized the stage in France, also
became the main theatrical fare in Russia. At first, as usual, the
plays were more or less accurate translations or adaptations of
French models. By the 1820's there were Russian experts in the
genre, dependent though they were on French sources. N. I.
KHMELNITSKI (1789-1846) and A. I. PISAREV (1803-28) accounted for many of the earlier plays; D. T. Lenski's (1805-60)
Lev Gurych Sinichkin is a typical popular vaudeville of the 1840's.

The first truly great play of the nineteenth century is the
comedy, *Woe from Wit,* by A. S. GRIBOYEDOV (1795-1829). It
has been considered a masterpiece almost from the time it began
to circulate in manuscript about 1825. This satire of stultification
in Russian society, as seen through the eyes of a young man who
has just returned from Europe with liberal ideas, is written in
rhymed verse; phrases and characterizations in the play were so
meaningful for Russian audiences that much of the play has gone
into the language as proverbial speech.

Woe from Wit is still in the tradition of the eighteenth-century
satirical play, but Alexander PUSHKIN's (1799-1837) *Boris
Godunov* introduces Romanticism and the influence of Shakespeare. The plot was based on the romantic Russian history of

KARAMZIN; the structure was that of the Shakespearean history play. *Boris Godunov* is in blank verse; after the model of Shakespeare the play contains crowd scenes and low-life characters, both innovations on the Russian stage. The play was never performed during the poet's lifetime, and his apparent plan to provide a more serious model for Russian drama bore little direct fruit.

Pushkin also wrote the so-called "Little Tragedies," more properly dramatic studies than actual plays. They are taut examples of dramatic conflict, written in concise, brilliant verse. *The Stone Guest* is an unexpectedly fresh treatment of the much-used Don Juan theme, while *Mozart and Salieri* is a study of the envy of a skilled artist for a genius. *The Avaricious Knight* contains a miser's monologue worthy of ranking with that in Jonson's *Volpone*. Pushkin also wrote a few articles on the theory of the drama, and he was an acute critic.

The dark side of Romanticism was represented by the work of M. Yu. LERMONTOV (1814-41). The major influences on his plays were those of Schiller, Shakespeare and Lessing; Byron contributed to his characterization. Although Lermontov wrote several plays, only his verse play, *The Masquerade,* is well known. The romanticist approach is apparent in this play with its brooding hero, dark intrigue in a corrupt world, and passionate emotion. The play was not produced in its complete version until 1862.

Of all Russian plays the one perhaps best known abroad is Nikolay GOGOL's (1809-52) *The Inspector-General,* first performed in Russian in 1836. The play is in the tradition of Russian satire, with a new talent for grotesque caricature which is distinctively and inimitably Gogolian. The influence of Molière on Gogol's characterization and situation is in traditional Russian style.

Gogol's peculiar blend of realistic detail with grotesque exaggeration was unique, but his plays influenced later construction and characterization. His earlier play, *The Marriage,* contains characters from the merchant milieu. His *The Gamblers* is a short piece of characteristic Gogolian grotesque satire on a vice as popular in nineteenth-century Russia as it was in Restoration England.

In the 1850's there appeared a Russian dramatist as concerned for the ideals of realism for the stage as were the great novelists who were his contemporaries in fiction. A. N. OSTROVSKI (1823-86), the first great professional Russian playwright, devoted almost his entire literary production to works for the stage, and created a body of drama which has since remained the backbone of the Russian repertoire. He also made efforts to improve the lot of the playwright and actor in Russia and sought to reform the Imperial theaters, of which he was appointed director only a year before his death.

Ostrovski created realistic characters from the merchant and provincial social milieu. His diction is a more accurate transcription of real speech than any in Russian drama before him. His plots and, to a certan extent, his theses come from European melodrama and bourgeois *drame*. His aim was to write thoroughly Russian plays, but he learned from playwrights who had gone before him, both Russian and European. It is not surprising to find Latin drama, Molière, Shakespeare, Holberg and Goldoni as influences—they influenced many Russian dramatists. Ostrovski kept abreast of contemporary European dramas as well, and translated some for Russian production.

Ivan Sergeyevich TURGENEV (1818-83), better known for his novels, was a contemporary of Ostrovski's. There is a strong French influence in all his theater pieces, culminating in his best-known play, *A Month in the Country*. It has as a central situation the rivalry of an older woman and her niece for the attentions of the same young man, the theme of Scribe's *Bataille des dames*. This *pièce bien faite* of the French stage takes on an added dimension with Turgenev, however, and moves forward toward the Chekhovian drama. The action of the play is not outward and obvious, but inward and complex; the flow of conflicting emotions constitutes the "action" of the play.

The generation of the 1860's brought more self-conscious social criticism into the drama. Thus, A. F. PISEMSKI's (1820-81) *A Bitter Lot* is a powerful exposé of the relations between landlords and their serfs. It is a strong play in situation, characterization and diction. A. V. Sukhovo-Kobylin (1817-1903), in his trilogy (*Krechinski's Wedding, The Affair*, and *The Death of Tarelkin*), combined Scribean methods with a satire of legal justice in Russia.

A. K. TOLSTOY (1817-75) contributed a trilogy to the older

line of Russian historical drama: *The Death of Ivan the Terrible,* *Tsar Fyodor Ioannovich,* and *Tsar Boris.* Tolstoy was as much influenced by Schiller as by past Russian historical drama. *Tsar Fyodor Ioannovich* was the play chosen for the first production of the famed Moscow Art Theater at its inception in 1898.

Lev TOLSTOY (1828-1910) was long interested in writing drama, but discouragement by friends such as the poet FET, as well as difficulties with the censorship, kept his production small. None of the plays from the early part of his career was played, while his middle years were occupied with writing novels and stories. It was not until the late 1880's that he began to produce the plays for which he is known. His interest in theater was renewed at this time by the growth of popular theater, and he originally designed *The Power of Darkness* as a play for the people. The play was first produced by Antoine's *Théâtre Libre* in Paris (1888). This realistic tragedy of peasant life is based on an actual court case, but it is informed with Tolstoy's moral ideas.

The first draft of the *The Fruits of Enlightenment* was written at the request of Tolstoy's family for a play to be performed at home. It is a comedy satirizing the superstition of the decadent nobility and contrasting the practical realism of the peasants. *The Living Corpse* and *Light Shines in Darkness,* two unfinished and posthumous plays, are interesting. *The Living Corpse,* also based on a real case, concerns a man who pretends to kill himself so that his wife can marry the man whom she loves. It has been performed more often than the other plays. *Light Shines in Darkness* seems autobiographical in part, concerned as it is with a pacifist-moralist at odds with his conventional family. Tolstoy also wrote several short plays, such as *The First Distiller,* for production before peasant audiences. These are almost morality plays in the medieval sense.

The continuity of Russian drama is demonstrated in the plays of Vladimir NEMIROVICH-DANCHENKO (co-founder with Stanislavski of the Moscow Art Theater), who wrote plays about merchant life, like Ostrovski, and in the plays of Anton CHEKHOV (1860-1904). The latter is the most important Russian playwright of the late nineteenth century. *Ivanov,* his first full-length play, was staged in 1887, and had some success. *The Wood Demon* was next (1888-89), but the performance was unsuccessful, and it was rejected so resoundingly by his friends that Chekhov abandoned serious drama for almost a decade. Meanwhile he wrote several one-act plays, including the vaudeville farces which continued the tradition of this popular Russian genre of the nineteenth century. Chekhov's vaudevilles have been widely played in professional and amateur groups in many countries. In 1896 he wrote *The Sea-gull*, which was first produced at the Alexandrinski Theater in Petersburg. The production was so badly received that Chekhov was again ready to give up the theater. He was persuaded by the newly formed Moscow Art Theater to give the play to them for their second production, and with their performance of the play (1898) the theater found its writer and the writer found his theater. A reworking of *The Wood Demon* as *Uncle Vanya* was next staged (1899), and then *The Three Sisters* (1901), to be followed by his last play, *The Cherry Orchard* (1904).

Chekhov's immediate forerunners in Russian drama are OSTROVSKI and TURGENEV. Thus, Madame Ranevskaya in *The Cherry Orchard* has a psychological resemblance to the heroine of Turgenev's *A Month in the Country*. Chekhov's first plays contain spectacular and melodramatic events, such as suicide and even a half-hearted attempt at murder. Even *The Three Sisters* has a fatal duel; *The Cherry Orchard*, however, chronicles unspectacular grief, mixing irony, tragic loss and humor in life-like quantities. Events represented in his plays usually form the climax of a long development previous to the opening of the play. The exposition of the complex pre-plot is accomplished in the course of the play with a minimum of artificiality. The effect is that of getting to know the characters and their problems gradually, as one does in life.

With *The Cherry Orchard*, Chekhov's drama verged on the symbolic, and in the years preceding the 1917 Revolution, several Russian Symbolist plays were written and presented. Leonid ANDREYEV (1871-1919) wrote both realistic and symbolic plays —both with the same theme: the hollowness of life and the preeminence of death. In Alexander BLOK's (1880-1921) "lyrical drama," *The Stranger*, a poet longs for the return of a mysterious lady, symbolizing divine wisdom, whom he once has known. Zinaida HIPPIUS (1867-1945), the wife of MEREZHKOVSKI and a leading poet, contributed *The Green Ring* (1914) to the body of symbolist drama. A. M. REMIZOV (1877-   ) turned the folk play *Tsar Maximilian* into a symbolic mystery play.

Maxim Gorki (see Peshkov; 1868-1936) began writing plays in 1901 with *The Petty Bourgeois,* and went on to the play taken to be the masterpiece of Russian naturalism, *The Lower Depths* (1902). *The Lower Depths* has been played in every country of Europe and in the United States. It is one of the most widely-known Russian plays, a fact to be accounted for partly by the brilliant original production of the Moscow Art Theater. The sordid environment of a flop-house which it depicts and the varied characters who find shelter there made it a popular addition to the naturalistic repertoire. Gorki's later plays include *Yegor Bulychov* (1932), a powerful picture of a merchant on the eve of the Revolution; we see him alienated from the "bourgeois" existence which he himself leads.

The period before the Revolution saw a reform in the ballet, led by the famous impresario Sergey Pavlovich Dyagilev (Diaghilev, 1872-1929). This reform, which eventually influenced Russian theatrical *mise en scène,* centered around the strict subordination of all elements of the ballet to a unity of impression. Dyagilev sought to find serious modern music and decor for his productions. He employed such outstanding composers as Stravinski and Ravel, and such designers as Alexander Benois and L. N. Bakst to produce new ballets of unparalleled brilliance. Dyagilev sought to give ballet a new importance; his estheticism links him closely to the symbolist poets and to other artists of the period (see Symbolism).

Post-Revolutionary Theater and Drama. With the Revolution, Moscow again became the capital, and the Moscow theater acquired pre-eminence in the Soviet Union. The value of the theater as a political instrument was quickly turned to account by the government after October, 1917. A special section of the People's Commissariat of Education was established as early as January, 1918, to manage theatrical affairs. And in 1919 all theaters, former Imperial and private ones, became state property. Members of the staffs became members of an all-Russian trade union.

During the period of the New Economic Policy (1921-28) many theaters reverted briefly to private ownership, only to return to state control in 1929, under the Committee on Art Affairs. This committee was responsible to the Council of People's Commissars (known since 1946 as the Council of Ministers). The Communist Party Central Committee and the local Party committees exercised direct and indirect supervision over the art committees and theaters. One means of control was through the Main Repertory Committee and its local branches, under the Commissariat of Education; another was through the granting of subsidies. Government grants kept the theaters going in difficult years and made possible the flowering of theatrical art in the twenties and early thirties.

Stanislavski, realizing long before the Revolution the necessity for further experimentation, began training new directors and encouraging them to assume their own independence. The mere existence of so vital a body as the Art Theater gave genius a place to develop. The years just before and the chaotic years just after the Revolution brought the brilliant directors Yevgeni Vakhtangov, Vsevolod Meyerhold and Alexander Tairov, as well as the lesser but still fascinating experimenters Bykov and Burdzhalov. Vakhtangov stood for what he called "synthetic theater," a blend of realism and theatricalism, while Meyerhold's rejection of Stanislavski's realism took the form of expressionistic theatricalism. Tairov, director of the Kamerny Theater, brought the arts of drama, music, decor and gesture to a new rhythmic unity as a single and complete theatrical art.

The First Five-Year Plan brought a tightening of government control over theaters. A 1932 declaration stated for the first time the doctrine of SOCIALIST REALISM, which became the prescribed style for Soviet theater. The middle thirties are marked by the suppression of Meyerhold's theater and others, and the exile or death of many actors and actresses. In 1946 a further effort was made to encourage an art "socialist in content, realistic in method" by the excoriation of "cosmopolitan critics," that is, of those critics interested primarily in esthetics rather than the message of the plays they reviewed. Changes as recent as 1955 have re-instated some of these men. What the future holds for the Soviet theater can only be guessed.

If the Soviet theater has been relatively productive, in spite of the reported decline in luster after the early thirties, Soviet drama has had continuous difficulties. It was almost ten years before a Soviet play of stature appeared, a fact understandable considering the severe social upheaval. One common form in the early post-revolutionary years was the "living newspaper." Workers in blue blouses acted out sketches based on the news of the day. Historical pageants and plays celebrating the theme of the triumphant workers were popular.

Several attempts at plays depicting the Civil War were made before Konstantin TRENYOV'S *Lyubov Yarovaya* was successfully produced at the Maly Theater in Moscow in 1926. The following year the Moscow Art Theater staged a sensational play showing some sympathy for the White forces which had been defeated in the Civil War. The play was M. A. BULGAKOV's *Days of the Turbins;* it was soon banned from every stage except that of the Art Theater, however, in spite of (or perhaps because of) its success.

The First Five-year Plan and the extension of government supervision over the theater resulted in many plays about the difficulties of transforming the Soviet Union into an industrial nation. Nikolay Pogodin (see Stukalov) was one of the more successful writers of this sort of play; his *Chimes of the Kremlin* and *Tempo* are examples. The new plays of the forties generally reflect important government policies; anti-German plays replaced pro-German plays after the German invasion of Russia; anti-American plays replaced the anti-German ones in the era of the cold war. Soviet émigrés abroad and Party critics at home have pointed out the theater's inability to keep contemporary plays in the repertoire. Apparently the plays have no lasting value, so closely are they related to contemporary events, so shifting is Soviet policy, and so restricted in expression are the dramatists. The recent controversy concerning the "conflictless" drama (see Virta) illustrates how little freedom writers are allowed.

In spite of all these difficulties, however, the Soviet theater today continues to be a great theater, and splendid ballet and fine acting, especially in classic Russian and foreign plays, distinguish it. However restricting the current Soviet doctrine may be, the tradition of realism developed from so many strands of influence in the nineteenth century is being carried forward.

Martha Bradshaw Manheim

Drozhzhin, Spiridon Dmitrievich (1848-1930), a poet of the late nineteenth century. Self-educated, he was the first of a series of "peasant poets" important in Russian literature at the end of the nineteenth and beginning of the twentieth centuries. His poetry, which describes the hardships of peasant life, is largely imitative of such poets as PUSHKIN, KOLTSOV and NEKRASOV.

Druzhinin, Alexander Vasilyevich (1824-64), a novelist and critic of the mid-nineteenth century. His most famous novel, *Polinka Sachs* (1847), influenced by George Sand, was one of the most popular of its period. It tells the story of a young married woman whose progressive husband gives her a divorce so that she may continue her liaison with a romantic lover. She dies realizing that it was the husband whom she really loved, and not the lover.

As a critic, Druzhinin was one of the first Russians to deny that literature should be subordinated to the needs of society; art, in his view, is not utilitarian, and should not serve the needs of the times. PUSHKIN, and not GOGOL, was for him the great master of Russian literature, a preference unusual for the period in which Druzhinin wrote. Thus his views represent a reaction against the critical theories of BELINSKI.

Dunin-Martsinkevich, Vikenti (1807-84), a leading Belo-Russian writer (see Preface).

Dyagilev, S. P. See Drama and Theater.

Dzhugashvili, I. V. See Stalin.

Dzyubin, Eduard Georgievich (1895-1934), a Soviet poet who wrote under the pseudonym of Eduard Bagritski. He came from the family of a poor shopkeeper of Odessa. As a young poet he joined the new movement of the CONSTRUCTIVISTS, but he was never spiritually a member of their group. Though he had already been writing poetry for over a decade, he published his first collection only in 1928. His poetry, like that of GUMILYOV and TIKHONOV, is essentially optimistic in its search for the heroic and for elemental life forces, which he finds in the past, in the events of the Revolution and the Civil War, as well as in a romantic passion for nature. His chief poem which deals with this period, *The Lay of Opanas* (1926), is the story of a Ukrainian peasant who is pressed into service by Makhno, leader of a famous Ukrainian anarchist band. There he is forced by his superiors to shoot a Red leader, though he admires the latter's heroism; in the end he is himself executed by the Reds, and accepts his fate with the same stoicism. Bagritski's later poetry, published in *The Victors* (1932) and *The Last Night* (1932), continues to be romantic, though he encounters greater difficulties in treating the contemporary realities of Soviet life. Bagritski also translated from English poetry, including Burns and Scott.

E

E- (names beginning in). For those not listed here, see under Ye-.

Ehrenburg, Ilya Grigorievich (1891-), a Soviet novelist and
journalist. Of middle-class origin, he left Russia in 1909 and went
to Paris, where he entered the Bohemian literary world. His first
poetry appeared in 1911. During the First World War he remained in France as a Russian war correspondent. The October
Revolution of 1917 found him on the White side; he returned to
Russia but lived in the South under the Whites. In 1921, after the
Red victory, he was arrested, but soon released after he had
"accepted" the Revolution. He returned to Paris, and spent most
of his time before 1941 in the West as a journalist and writer.
In 1936-37 he was a Soviet war correspondent in Spain during
the Spanish Civil War. During World War II he was one of the
most active of Russian writers in war journalism and propaganda.
His innumerable articles were extremely popular and are considered to have played a large part in inspiring Russian resistance
to the German invasion. Since the war Ehrenburg has visited the
United States, and has published many anti-American articles in
the Soviet press.

Ehrenburg is almost unique as a Soviet writer who possesses a
good knowledge of Western life and culture. Hence he is one of
the few Soviet writers who can write about the West, however
critically, with some degree of comprehension for its way of life.
His novels are related to his journalism, and many of them are
not far above newspaper articles in their quality. He writes
easily and at times with considerable force, but his work lacks
polish as well as depth, and the characters are wooden. Ehrenburg is a writer who can conceive of intriguing themes, but who
usually fails to carry them off.

Ehrenburg's first successful novel was his *Extraordinary Ad-*

ventures of Julio Jurenito and His Disciples (1922; the actual title is much longer), a series of satirical portraits of representatives of various nations; their leader, Julio Jurenito, is a man of anarchic inclinations who seeks to expose the hypocrisy and evil of modern society. Apparently a satire on the West, the book is actually more a reflection of the author's own cynical attitude toward life.

Ehrenburg produced a large number of novels in the 1920's and 1930's, few of which are of serious literary merit. *Trust D. E.* (1923) describes the conquest of Europe by capitalist America. *The Second Day* (1933; English translation as "Out of Chaos") depicts the construction of a Siberian steel plant.

The Fall of Paris (1941) is Ehrenburg's most ambitious novel, and portrays the degeneration of French society between 1935 and 1940. The novel contrasts the "decadent" French bourgeoisie with the "resourceful" Communists. Ehrenburg continued to live in France after the Nazi invasion, and the novel reflects an immediate knowledge of events as well as a strong feeling for France and her people.

The Storm (1948) is a novel about World War II, depicting the war in France and in Russia, and the development of strained relations between the Soviet Union and her Western allies after the war. The work is a leading example of the post-war anti-American trend in Russian fiction.

Ehrenburg's recent novelette, *The Thaw* (1954), has caused much discussion abroad, and apparently indicates that the literary atmosphere in the Soviet Union has become somewhat more liberal since the death of Stalin. Indeed, the very title seems symbolic, referring to the recent easing of tensions within the Soviet Union. The story violates several taboos of Soviet literature; for example, it mentions the purges of the 1930's, and portrays the tragedy in the life of a boy whose father has been sent into exile. The contrast between two painters—one, a successful artist who paints only officially approved subjects, and the other, who goes his own way and remains unrecognized—implies that "official" Soviet art is actually philistine. These and other indications are slight ones, but they suggest that Ehrenburg's story may have served as a kind of trial balloon, sent up to explore the new atmosphere in Soviet letters and to challenge the hegemony of the Party critics. They reprimanded him severely, but still it can be said that the political line in literature has relaxed slightly, if not substantially. In particular, the treatment of a less stereotyped and less rigidly optimistic psychology now seems possible in Soviet fiction. Ehrenburg, who up to now has been so adroit in following changes in Soviet policy, may himself have grown secure enough in his position to lead such a change.

Emigration. The October Revolution found very few established writers on the Bolshevik side. The most prominent of these were Gorki (see Peshkov), MAYAKOVSKI and BRYUSOV. Others, such as BLOK and Bely (see Bugayev) were enthused by the Revolution for reasons of their own, but lived to regret their enthusiasm. The initial "wait and see" attitude of some writers soon gave way to wholesale disillusionment and emigration. Among those who emigrated were BUNIN, REMIZOV, ANDREYEV, KUPRIN, MEREZHKOVSKI, HIPPIUS, BALMONT, Vyacheslav IVANOV, TSVETAYEVA, SHMELYOV, ZAYTSEV, Shestov (see Schwarzman), BERDYAYEV and Sergey BULGAKOV. Kuprin and Tsvetayeva returned to the Soviet Union not long before their deaths. Others who emigrated and later returned include A. N. TOLSTOY and EHRENBURG. There were also writers who remained in the Soviet Union but participated in an "internal emigration," as the Communists called it, either writing little or nothing, or attempting to write in a markedly individualist and non-conformist manner. Among the first group were KORO-LENKO, ROZANOV and Sologub (see Teternikov); Akhmatova (see Gorenko) maintained a long silence after 1922, broken only in 1940. The second group, those who attempted to ignore Party demands in literature, included YESENIN, KLYUYEV, ZAMYA-TIN, MANDELSTAM, and, to an extent, PASTERNAK. Vere-sayev's novel, *In a Blind Alley* (see Smidovich), is non-conformist in its objective view of the Civil War, but Veresayev was later reconciled to the party line. This list does not include the large number of younger non-conformist writers of the 1920's who developed after 1917. (See Literature, Soviet.)

Emin, Fyodor Alexandrovich (1735?-1770), an eighteenth-century writer of tales of romance and adventure, the first Russian writer of prose fiction who is not anonymous. His chief work is the *Letters of Ernest and Doravra* (1766), an imitation of Rousseau's sentimental novel, *La Nouvelle Héloïse*. Emin's work was attacked by the classicists, but found an eager audience among the less cultured reading public.

Erenburg, Ilya. See Ehrenburg.

Ertel, Alexander Ivanovich (1855-1908), a writer of the late nineteenth century. Politically he was an adherent of the POPULISTS. Ertel's major work, a two-volume novel, *The Gardenins, Their Retainers, Their Adherents and Their Foes* (1889), is remarkable for its panoramic view of country life, with a great gallery of characters drawn from the peasantry, middle class and gentry. Ertel's views on the agrarian problem were close to those of the POPULISTS, but founded on a better knowledge of peasant life. The novel was republished in 1908 with a preface by Lev TOLSTOY, who praised Ertel's language for its variety, force and beauty.

F

Fadeyev, Alexander Alexandrovich (1901-56), a Soviet novelist. Of peasant origin, he grew up in the Siberian Far East. He joined the Communist Party in 1918 and served on the Red Side during the Civil War. Fadeyev has been active as a Party leader. In 1939 he was made secretary of the UNION OF SOVIET WRITERS, a post to which he was re-appointed in 1946. In 1953, after the death of STALIN, he was made chairman of the Union, a move which may actually have been a demotion; in any event, the office was abolished the following year.

Fadeyev's first important work was his short novel, *The Rout* (1927; English translation as "The Nineteen"). It depicts Red guerillas fighting against the Whites and the Japanese in the Far East. The author employs some of the techniques of TOLSTOY's *War and Peace*, particularly in his methods of psychological and moral analysis and his battle descriptions. The novel depicts a number of types which were later much imitated in Soviet literature: Levinson, the heroic and resourceful commander whose one error of judgment brings the almost complete destruction of his detachment; the disorderly but courageous proletarian Morozka; the naive shepherd, Metelitsa, who is taken prisoner by the Whites and suffers martyrdom at their hands. Apart from them is the young student Mechik, an intellectual who has no real faith in the Red cause, and who deserts at the crucial moment and betrays the detachment to its fate. The figure of Mechik perhaps reflects Fadeyev's distrust of the intellectual, and in fact offended many members of the Soviet intelligentsia.

Fadeyev's lengthy *Last of the Udegs* (1928-36) is only part of an unfinished epic novel on the Civil War in the Far East; the author had intended to portray the changes made by the Revolution in the life of an almost extinct Far Eastern tribe. Fadeyev has admitted his difficulty in bringing the work to a successful conclusion. Meanwhile he published *The Young Guard* (1945), one of the most popular novels on the Second World War. It deals with the partisan resistance of young people living under the German occupation, and is based in part on actual events. In spite of the somewhat conventional conception of patriotism which the book embodies, the characterizations are striking. The novel was soon attacked by the critics, who accused Fadeyev of giving insufficient attention to the role of the Party in leading guerrilla resistance. Fadeyev yielded and subsequently revised the book.

Fainzilberg, Ilya Arnoldovich (1897-1937), a Soviet humorist who wrote under the pen-name of Ilya Ilf. Born in Odessa, he moved to Moscow, where he met Yevgeni Petrov (pseudonym of Yevgeni KATAYEV); in 1927 the two writers formed a literary partnership. At times they wrote under humorous pen-names such as that of "Fyodor Tolstoyevski." Their principal works were the novel, *Twelve Chairs* (1928; English translation as "Diamonds to Sit On"), and its sequel, *The Little Golden Calf* (1931). These are picaresque novels, dominated by the character of the swindler and knave, Ostap Bender, the "great manipulator." In the first novel Bender seeks some diamonds which have been hidden in one of a set of a dozen chairs; in the end the diamonds are found by others and used to build a club for workers. Bender is killed, but is "revived" by the authors in the sequel, in which he pursues a disguised millionaire and tries to extort his millions. Both novels present a certain satire on Soviet life, which is shown as unreal and grotesquely comical.

Ilf and Petrov visited America in the 1930's and published a book about their journey, *One-storied America* (1936; English translation as "Little Golden America"). The work is mildly amusing, and, though the writers find much to criticize in America during the economic depression, they are far less critical than Soviet writers were to be after World War II.

In 1937 Ilf died from tuberculosis, and the collaboration came to an end.

Fairy tales. See Folk tales.

Fedin, Konstantin Alexandrovich (1892-   ), a Soviet writer. He came from a family of mixed aristocratic and peasant descent.

During the First World War he was interned in Germany. In 1918 he returned to the Soviet Union and served in the Red Army during the Civil War. He joined the literary organization of the SERAPION BROTHERS and published his first significant story, *The Orchard,* in 1920. He was subjected to repeated attacks by Soviet critics, and only recently can he be said to have been generally accepted as a leading Soviet writer whose orthodoxy is reasonably above suspicion.

Fedin's early stories have a delicate lyricism of description and mood which recalls CHEKHOV and BUNIN. Several of these stories express nostalgic regret for the passing of the pre-revolutionary way of life. His first novel, *Cities and Years* (1924), was one of the earliest attempts to depict the impact of the Revolution on a Soviet intellectual and the difficulties in the way of his acceptance of the revolutionary cause. Fedin's hero is an intellectual who is swept up for a short time by enthusiasm for the Soviet regime, but soon loses it. In the end he is killed as a traitor by a former friend, a German who has become a staunch Bolshevik. The novel presents a broad panorama of events, with scenes in both Germany and the Soviet Union. Original is the treatment of the chronology, continually interrupted by jumps backward and forward in time, in which the denouement is placed at the start of the novel. The critics accused the author of sympathizing with his weak-willed hero, and, indeed, it is possible that the hero's doubts are Fedin's own.

Fedin's early story, *Transvaal* (1928), depicts the career of a powerful *kulak* (well-to-do peasant) of Boer origin. Becoming wealthy, he rules the whole neighborhood, over which he holds an economic stranglehold, as a despot. Though the story is relatively objective, and later turned out to be based on an actual case, Soviet critics accused Fedin of idealizing the *kulaks*.

Fedin's second novel, *The Brothers* (1928), was more conservative in its technique than his first one. Its theme is the mission of the artist, whose right to individualism is opposed to the obligations of Soviet life. Again the author seems sympathetic to the intellectual who cannot conform to the new way of life.

In the early 1930's Fedin seems to have surmounted his objections to the Soviet regime. His next novel, *The Rape of Europa* (1934-35), is concerned with trade relations between Western

Europe and the Soviet Union, a theme which serves to contrast the "decadent" West with the "progressive" Soviet Union. But the novel is poorly integrated, and the second, "progressive" part never really comes off.

Fedin's most recent cycle of two novels, *First Joys* (1945-46) and *An Unusual Summer* (1948), constitute perhaps his finest work and, indeed, probably the finest in Soviet literature since the Second World War. In keeping with the principles of SOCIALIST REALISM, they are conservatively realistic and lack the experimental tendencies of Fedin's earlier writing. They excel in their depth of psychological portrayal, and are free from the usual simplified, sentimental psychology of recent Soviet novels. The two novels depict a small town on the Volga, the first on the eve of World War I, and the second in 1919, after the Revolution has had its effect.

Fedin's career has been a long one; he has matured by developing from a romantic lyricist to a psychological realist. His work, though hardly great, has a freshness, vividness and an intellectual honesty which make him one of the most truthful of Soviet writers.

Fedorov. See Fyodorov.

Fellow Traveller. See Trotski; Literature, Soviet.

Feofan Prokopovich (1681-1736). A monk and pupil of the Kiev Academy, Feofan completed his education in Poland and Rome, and was perhaps the best-educated Russian of his generation. In 1720 he was named Archbishop of Novgorod. He lent his full support to the reforms of PETER THE GREAT, and his sermons are in fact secular political tracts propagandizing Western learning and the idea of enlightened absolutism. Feofan assisted Peter in carrying out his reform of the Russian Church. His most famous sermon was pronounced at the funeral of Peter the Great (1725), and is one of the greatest examples of Russian oratory. His poetry also praises the Petrine reforms. His play *St. Vladimir* (1705) treats the introduction of Christianity into Russia.

Fet, Afanasi Afanasievich (1820-92), a leading Russian poet of the mid-nineteenth century. His parents were a Russian squire, Shenshin, and a German woman named Fet (Foeth). Since they were wed according to the Lutheran rite, their marriage was not recognized under Russian law, and the poet, as illegitimate, was forced to use his mother's name until 1873, when he was legitimized. He studied at the University of Moscow, where he first began to publish in 1840. From 1845 to 1858 he served in the army in order to obtain by promotion the rank denied him by birth. Meanwhile he published two volumes of verse, in 1850 and 1856. As a poet he belonged to the group of esthetic or PARNASSIAN POETS, and this, combined with the extreme conservatism of his views, won him the hostility of the radical CIVIC CRITICS of the 1860's. They succeeded in reducing him to silence, and after 1863 he published nothing for twenty years, though he continued to write. In 1883 he came back, publishing a series of volumes of poetry under the collective title of *Evening Lights*.

In personality Fet was vain, callous and selfish, almost the direct contradiction of his sensitive, musical, ethereal verse. In spite of these personal deficiencies he became the close friend of both TURGENEV and LEV TOLSTOY. He saw no conflict between his personal standards and his poetic vision; poetry itself for him was a withdrawal from practical life, from which, in his view, it was completely divorced.

Fet's early poetry specializes in the sensual pictures of nature and themes from classical antiquity characteristic of the Imagist or PARNASSIAN POETS. His nature poems have less of a purely imagistic quality, however, than those of his contemporaries; they are at the same time more musical as poetry and more emotional and spiritual in their expression. He is an impressionist of associations, nuances and fleeting images. Behind his images there lies a strong pantheistic conception of the unity of all nature.

Fet's later poetry, published in the 1880's, is more metaphysical in content. Beauty becomes more and more an abstract idea for him, rather than a sensual quality, leading him to a Platonic conception of reality as unified and one. The identification of the self with nature, the cult of love as the worship of beauty and the eternal feminine—these are favorite themes of the later poetry. Reality appears more and more as a dream, not dreamed by man himself, but by the universe, a dream of life which veils the world of eternal ideas. Fet's metaphysical poetry brought him close to the poetic movement of SYMBOLISM of the 1890's, and he is one of the chief precursors of the Symbolist poets, particularly Sologub (see Teternikov) and BLOK.

Fet was also a translator, and rendered examples of Latin

poetry, as well as the writings of the philosopher Schopenhauer, into Russian.

Five-year Plan Literature. See Literature, Soviet; RAPP.

Flexer, Akim Lvovich (1863-1926), a critic of the late nineteenth and twentieth century, who wrote under the pseudonym of A. Volynski. He was one of the leading defenders of the new movement of SYMBOLISM at the turn of the century. He attacked the materialistic positivism of contemporary radical writers, and advocated a rather vague and mystical idealism.

Florenski, Pavel Alexandrovich (1882-?), a religious philosopher of the twentieth century. He taught history of philosophy at the Moscow Theological Academy. In 1911 he was ordained a priest. The range of his intellectual activity was extremely broad: he was an electrical engineer, physicist, painter, musician, and a symbolist poet. Under the Soviet regime he was arrested and imprisoned several times; finally he disappeared completely, and must be presumed dead.

Florenski's thought is archaic in its tendency, with a pronounced antipathy for those areas of modern learning which, in his opinion, still challenge Orthodox faith. Thus, he is an astronomer who still defends the geocentric theory.

The key to Florenski's thought is his notion that all created personalities are consubstantial with one another. Love for him is a manifestation of this consubstantiality, the end of which is that "two may become one," as his favorite motto expresses it. A follower of Vladimir SOLOVYOV, Florenski identifies Sophia, Divine Wisdom, with the "original substance of creatures, and the creative Love of God in them." Sin proceeds from absorption in self; in his opinion, such self-absorption may lead to neurotic and psychotic states of personality.

Foeth, A. A. See Fet.

Fofanov, Konstantin Mikhaylovich (1862-1911), a poet of the late nineteenth and early twentieth century. Unlike most of his contemporaries of the 1880's and 1890's, who were "civic" poets, he wrote a pure lyric poetry of nature and emotions, uninfluenced by radical social ideas. His verse is musical, but uneven in its technique. Many of his poems have been set to music.

Folk literature. The various types of Russian folk literature, including songs, tales, proverbs and other forms, are richly preserved.

Russia, and especially far-northern Russia, isolated economically and culturally since the beginning of the eighteenth century, has preserved a variety of archaic types of folklore no longer found in the West. Such are the heroic epic songs, or *byliny* (see *Bylina*), the religious epic songs and epic funeral laments (see Folk songs), as well as vestiges of songs and plays which once served as elements of seasonal fertility rites. Magical incantations contain other vestiges of pagan folk beliefs dating from pre-Christian times. Many works attest the confusion of Christian and pagan points of view among the folk, resulting in a kind of dual belief, known as *dvoyeverie* ("double faith"). Of the folklores of the Slavic peoples, only that of the Serbs is more archaic. One reason which has been advanced for the relatively archaic character of Russian folk literature is Russia's adherence to the Orthodox Church, less rigorous in practice, if not in principle, than the Roman Catholic Church in its opposition to folk literature and customs. Other explanations are the long period of Tartar domination from the thirteenth to the fifteenth centuries, Russia's predominantly agricultural economy, and the widespread illiteracy and general cultural backwardness of the great mass of Russian people. Still it must be said that, like all folklores, the Russian is constantly changing and developing, and contains many modern elements as well as archaic ones.

Folklore is primarily the property of the peasants, though certain professions, such as soldiers, carters, bargemen and even factory workers have had their specialized forms. To an extent, indeed, oral literature is the property of all classes and professions, as is the case with many proverbs.

Aside from FOLK SONGS and FOLK TALES (treated separately), the genres of Russian folk literature include folk plays, magical incantations, proverbs, riddles and jokes. The folk drama is but slightly developed in Russia, probably because of Church opposition and, more important, the failure of the Church to provide dramatic models analogous to the mystery and morality plays of the West. The few folk plays which are found are fanciful, often grotesque blends of tragedy, comedy and broad farce. The texts depend to a considerable extent on written literature, and there is some parody of the upper classes, their manners and institutions. The most popular play, *Tsar Maximian*, was probably an adaptation of the Czech baroque drama about the martyrdom of St. Dorothy. It apparently became popular in Russia during the reign of Peter the Great, and represented a protest against Peter's marriage to a Protestant wife and his execution of his son, themes reflected in the play in Maximian's marriage to a pagan woman and his persecution of Christians. There is also a Russian puppet theater, which is humorous and farcical, with the clown Petrushka as the leading character.

Incantations are preserved in great quantity in the Russian tradition. Though they contain pagan elements, their resemblance to Christian prayers shows that they have been influenced by the Church, and may even have been cultivated in some cases by churchmen. A largely professionalized genre, they were pronounced for the most part by sorcerers and witches to whom the people had recourse. Persecution for witchcraft was probably less thorough than in the West, and the Russian people had a somewhat more sympathetic attitude towards its practice.

Proverbs and bywords are extensively used by the Russian folk. They are usually bipartite in structure, and tend towards a regular rhythm and even rhyme. A kind of rhymed speech is also characteristic of the folk, and improvised verses are pronounced at wedding ceremonies. Riddles are close to proverbs in their form. Both proverbs and riddles are frequently incorporated in FOLK TALES and FOLK SONGS.

Folk songs. Russia is famous for the beauty and variety of her folk songs. These have a reputation for melancholy, but there are many light and humorous songs, as well. At present popular songs, some of literary origin, have largely crowded out the more archaic type of folk songs, but the latter have been preserved in numerous song books, beginning with the eighteenth century, and in scholarly collections, such as those of Sobolevski and Sheyn, made in the nineteenth and twentieth centuries. Many songs of the older type are still sung in remote areas.

Folk songs are classified as epic and lyric. Epic songs are in turn divided into *byliny*, or heroic songs (see *Bylina),* historical songs and religious epics. The difference between the heroic, sometimes vaguely historical *byliny* and historical songs proper is not great, but the latter tend to be shorter and less fantastic or exaggerated. The subjects of historical songs concern events of

Russian history from the sixteenth through the nineteenth centuries; most famous are the songs from the reign of Ivan the Terrible in the sixteenth century, such as those describing the conquest of Siberia, the taking of Kazan, and others. Later songs, such as those about the seventeenth-century revolutionary leader Stenka Razin, or about Peter the Great, are relatively short and more lyric. Religious epics, once sung by wandering pilgrims, are a distinct group. These retell in popular form lives of saints, miraculous legends and Biblical narratives, with much admixture of fantasy. All the epic songs have a rigid style featuring elaborate repetitions and parallel constructions, use of fixed epithets (e.g., "*fiery* head," "*fair* maiden," "*white* hands," etc.), and frequent comparisons of persons and events to objects in nature.

A transitional form between epic and lyric songs are the ballads, which to some extent resemble the English and Scottish ballads. They deal mostly with anonymous persons, and concern such themes as love, adultery, murder and brigandage. Formerly neglected by scholars, they are actually a rich and intriguing genre.

Another transitional group are the chanted laments for the dead. These are found for the most part in northern Russia, where women improvise them for the occasion. Professional mourners are sometimes employed. Unique in Russia were recruiting laments, sung for men going into service. Since service in the tsarist army before 1874 lasted for many years, the parting was almost equivalent to death, and these laments are very like funeral laments.

The great body of Russian songs are lyric. These have little or no plot, and are more intimate in manner than the epic songs. Like them, however, their form is highly stylized and patterned. Nature comparisons, fixed epithets and parallel constructions are also characteristic of lyric songs. Especially beautiful are elaborate nature metaphors built on symbols, usually birds or plants. Thus, the swan symbolizes a bride, the falcon a bridegroom or hero, the cuckoo a sorrowing woman, etc.

Ritual lyrics include wedding songs and calendar songs. Of especial beauty in the first group are the elaborate laments sung by the bride in parting from her family. Calendar songs contain elements of agricultural magic, and are sung during the traditional seasons of pagan festivals: before Christmas, Shrovetide,

Midsummer, and harvest time. They are sometimes accompanied by survivals of magical practices designed to encourage fertility, though belief in their efficacy is generally dead.

Love songs form a large group of lyric songs. They are chiefly the property of the young, especially girls. They treat love, even outside of marriage, unmorally, as an enviable state. Many of them reflect sadness, however, at betrayal or parting.

Family songs are chiefly the property of married women. They complain of the wife's hard lot.

Two important groups are dancing songs and songs sung as accompaniments to games. These overlap to a great extent with other categories; thus, a love song may serve as accompaniment for dancing. Lullabies and children's songs are also important groups.

Many professions have special songs: such are the songs of soldiers, carters, bargemen, etc. There is a large group of Cossack and brigand songs, extolling a life of roving and plundering. Themes of violence and death are also common.

A relatively new development is the *chastushka* (pl. *chastushki*), a short song, easily improvised, usually of four lines. They are often humorous and epigrammatic in character. *Chastushki* arose around the middle of the nineteenth century, and have had an ever increasing popularity, at the expense of the more archaic lyric. They may concern almost any subject proper to the lyric, but the largest group are love songs, and they are for the most part the property of young people. *Chastushki* on political events, such as the World War, Revolution, agricultural collectivization, etc., are also known. Undoubtedly many express anti-Soviet attitudes, but unfortunately these have not been collected.

Songs may be sung as solos, or chorally. Traditional instruments used in accompaniment are the balalaika and guitar; more recently the accordion has been predominant.

The older lyrics have a free rhythm, based on a regular number of accented syllables, with a varying number of unstressed syllables. Cadences are usually feminine or dactylic, and these are regular, while a metrical tendency, usually trochaic, may characterize the whole song. Rhyme is sporadic. The *chastushki* and modern popular songs are rhythmically more regular, and are rhymed.

Folk tales. Russia is rich in folk tales, both of the fantastic type and in more realistic, satirical and humorous tales and anecdotes. Like FOLK LITERATURE in general, folk tales are today chiefly the property of the peasants. The oldest recorded tales were written down for the Englishman Charles Collins, physician to Tsar Alexey Mikhaylovich, in the seventeenth century, but oral narratives have doubtless been told through all of Russian history. Historical narratives recorded in the Old Russian CHRONICLES may have originated either from prose legends or poetic historical songs, probably from both. Many Russian folk tales have plots strikingly similar to those of Western Europe and other lands, attesting to the migration of tale plots from one people to another. In the nineteenth and twentieth centuries important scholarly collections of tales were made by Afanasyev, Azadovski, the Brothers Sokolov, and others.

Folk tales may be classified as: (1) fantastic, or fairy tales; (2) realistic tales and anecdotes; (3) animal tales; (4) myths; and (5) legends. A comparison with Western Europe shows that the Russian stock of tales is considerably poorer in animal tales, and slightly poorer in fantastic tales (despite the international reputation of this class of Russian tales). Much richer, on the other hand, is the group of Russian realistic and satirical tales and anecdotes. True myths—tales symbolizing religious and philosophical truths about the universe—are quite rare, though undoubtedly the Russians had them before their Christianization. Survivals of mythic elements are found, however, such as the figures of Grandfather Frost and of wood demons and water sprites. Legends—tales narrating some pseudo-historical or fantastic event—are well known; a large number are religious in content.

As elsewhere, many Russian fantastic tales relate the hero's triumph over all obstacles and his passage from anonymity to fame, fortune and the possession of a beautiful bride. The usual apparatus of fairy tales is present: witches, enchanters, giants, golden apples, magic carpets, self-setting tables, caps of invisibility, and so on. Fairies of the sort known in Western European tales are rare, however; the hero is helped to his success by men of hyperbolic or magical powers, animals, old women or even witches. A favorite hero is Ivan the Tsarevich, described as so handsome "that one cannot take his eyes from him." At the beginning of the tale he may be known as Ivan the Fool, held in contempt by all for his fancied stupidity. The heroines, who are saved from misfortune by the heroes, are embodiments of virtue and beauty; some are simple, modest and tender; others are heroic warrior maidens. The most common villain is the witch, Baba-Yaga. She is described as "having a long foot, riding in a mortar, chasing people with her broom." Another evil figure is the enchanter Koshchey the Immortal, who sometimes appears as a dragon. His immortality depends on the clever concealment of his soul, which the hero must find and destroy. A unique creation is the wondrous fire-bird, whom the hero must catch, and who may then offer him help, or herself turn into a lovely maiden.

Quite different are the realistic tales and anecdotes. These are often broadly didactic or satirical. They deal with such subjects as stupidity, laziness, infidelity, fate and fortune, wealth and poverty, etc. Often they contain improbabilities and even fantastic elements, but they lack the magical apparatus and supernatural beings of the fantastic tales. They may end with the success of the hero or the punishment of the villain, or both. Often the hero and the villain are a sharply contrasted pair, as in tales about two brothers, one rich, the other poor. The character of Ivan the Fool also appears in these tales, but here he is usually a real fool. Social as well as moral satire is frequently found; there are older tales which poke fun at the clergy and the landowning aristocracy from the peasant viewpoint, but Soviet scholars have probably exaggerated their importance.

Russian tales tend towards a poetic style of narrative, and certain passages, even entire tales, may actually be in verse. Cliché expressions are often rhymed, and the characters sometimes speak in a kind of rhymed proverbial speech typical of the Russian peasantry. The tales are rich in puns, proverbs and sayings. As with FOLK SONGS, tales are sometimes the property of social groups other than the peasantry, such as soldiers and bargemen. The tellers are generally specialized amateurs who perform for the public; in some localities mothers also tell stories to their children. Professionalized tellers, often serfs, have been known, as at the courts of the tsars and on the manors until the nineteenth century, or even more recently in the pre-Soviet Siberian work cooperatives.

Folk tales have served as material for many Russian writers, such as PUSHKIN, OSTROVSKI, L. N. TOLSTOY and REMIZOV. Even greater has been their influence on the Russian opera, ballet and symphonic music, as in works by Rimski-Korsakov, Lyadov and Stravinski.

Fonvizin, Denis Ivanovich (1745-92), the leading Russian playwright of the eighteenth century. The descendant of a Russianized German family, Fonvizin received a good education at the University of Moscow, and entered the civil service as a translator for the Ministry of Foreign Affairs. In 1769 he became secretary to Count Panin, an influential liberal nobleman, whose views concerning limitation of absolutism and of serf ownership Fonvizin shared. He also dreamed of a return to the spirit of the reforms of PETER THE GREAT, when the nobility had been compelled to serve the state, a requirement abrogated by CATHERINE THE GREAT's charter to the nobility. As a result of his liberalism, he fell into disfavor with Catherine, and in 1783 the empress forced him to retire from literature.

Fonvizin's fame rests chiefly on his two great satiric comedies, *The Brigadier-General* (written about 1768, published 1786) and *The Minor* (1782), which hold the stage even today. *The Brigadier-General* satirizes the Russian eighteenth-century mania for things French, with its superficiality and lack of real understanding of French culture. *The Minor,* though less perfect in construction, is more popular and more significant. It attacks the vulgarity, ignorance and cruelty of the Russian provincial gentry, almost untouched by Western enlightenment. The hero, Mitrofan (the "minor"), a lout and ignoramus, is being educated by ignorant tutors for a post in the civil service. His mother, Mme. Prostakova ("Simpleton"), a bully and tyrant almost without human feeling save for her son, feels that such an education is really superfluous, and that the requirement that civil servants be educated is unjust. In her view nobility is a privilege, and not an obligation; members of the gentry should not be expected to work, when serfs and flunkeys can work for them. Her love for her son, a purely animal emotion, leads her to kidnap a wealthy and beautiful young heiress as his bride. In the end her plot is foiled by the virtuous characters of the play, and Prostakova is deprived of her tyrannical power over her serfs in a completely artificial denouement reminiscent of the plays of Molière. Her beloved Mitrofan proves completely ungrateful for all his mother's efforts in his behalf.

The villainous personages of the play are brilliantly drawn, but the good characters are artificial and boring both in their virtue and their manner of speech. Oddly enough, Fonvizin believed them to be the better part of the play. They are quite without reality, however, while the members of the Prostakov family, with their barbarism and swinishness, are among the most real of Russian satiric characters. In addition to Prostakova the author has created a whole gallery of brutish figures: her spineless husband; her brother, Skotinin ("Beastly"), who loves pigs more than humans; the incompetent and rascally tutors, and others.

Fonvizin also wrote non-dramatic satires. His *Universal Courtiers' Grammar* (written around 1783) contains prescriptions for a courtier's success through flattery, and is a sharp attack on the favoritism and hypocrisy of Catherine's court. His letters from abroad (he made two trips to Western Europe in 1777 and 1784) are models of elegant prose style for the period, and reflect his impatience at Russia's cultural subservience to the West.

Forsh, Olga Dmitrievna (1875-   ), a Soviet historical novelist. Of aristocratic birth, she published stories before the Revolution under the pseudonym of A. Terek. Her *Clad in Stone* (1927) is a historical novel about the Russian revolutionaries in the late nineteenth century. *The Contemporaries* (1927) treats fictionally the career of the Russian painter Alexander Ivanov. The writer GOGOL, a friend of Ivanov in Rome, also appears. Forsh's later historical trilogy, *Radishchev* (1934-39), treats the life of the eighteenth-century liberal writer and his era. Her historical fiction shows the influence of MEREZHKOVSKI.

Frank, Simon Lyudvigovich (1877-1950), a twentieth-century philosopher. He taught philosophy at the University of Saratov and later at Moscow. In 1922, along with other anti-Soviet philosophers, he was expelled from the Soviet Union. He lived in several Western countries, and finally in England.

Frank's thought, following that of Vladimir SOLOVYOV, is

constructed on a metaphysics of total-unity; for him nothing exists without being related to something else. Even the Absolute Deity is inconceivable, he argues, without that which he has created. Much of Frank's thought is devoted to the elaboration of logical, epistemological and metaphysical constructions designed to support his philosophy, and he is one of the leading systematists among Russian philosophers. The problem of evil presents considerable difficulty in his monistic system; striking is his refusal to attempt any explanation of evil on the ground that to explain evil would be to justify it.

Franko, Ivan (1856-1916), a Ukrainian writer (see Preface).

Freemasonry. Masonry came to Russia in the 1730's, and spread rapidly during the second half of the eighteenth century. It offered the aristocracy and intelligentsia an opportunity for philanthropic activity combined with a mystical spirituality which replaced the conservative creed of the official Church, discredited by the sceptical spirit of the Enlightenment. The Russian Masons engaged extensively in publishing activity and in molding progressive public opinion; in this respect the writer NOVIKOV was most energetic. The secrecy of the Masonic lodges attracted the suspicion of CATHERINE THE GREAT, and she wrote a number of satirical works against them. In 1792, frightened by the French Revolution, Catherine arrested the leading Masons, including Novikov, and their activity ceased. The Masons reorganized during the reigns of Paul and Alexander I, and in their lodges the secret societies of the DECEMBRIST MOVEMENT were formed. In 1822 the government suppressed the organization.

Friche, V. F. See Criticism, Soviet.

Furmanov, Dmitri Andreyevich (1891-1926), a writer of the early 1920's. During the Civil War he served as Bolshevik commissar to the guerilla forces of General Chapayev. His novel, *Chapayev* (1923), is more a record of his experiences than a work of fiction, and its technique is direct and unsophisticated. The work draws a sharp contrast between the strong but emotionally undisciplined revolutionary feeling of Chapayev, and the collected, calculating rationalism of the Bolshevik commissar. The book was much praised by Soviet critics as one of the best novels on the Civil

War, and is still cited by them as a major classic of Soviet literature.

Futurism, a modernist poetic movement founded in 1910. Its leader was Viktor (Velemir) KHLEBNIKOV, a talented poet whose primary interest was in coining new words and creating a "trans-sense language" *(zaumny yazyk),* a language which would be "beyond sense." Futurism was to a large extent a revolt against SYMBOLISM, especially against its mysticism and its estheticist cult of pure beauty; the Futurists were interested in the realities of modern life. But they went much further than opposing the Symbolists; their aim was *épater le bourgeois,* to shock at any cost. Their manifesto, published in 1912 and signed by KHLEBNIKOV, KRUCHONYKH, MAYAKOVSKI and BURLYUK, was entitled "A Slap in the Face of Public Taste." It called for scrapping the whole cultural tradition of the past, which it described as "stifling"; Pushkin, Dostoyevski and Tolstoy were to be thrown "overboard from the steamer of modernity." The reader is told to wash his hands, "filthy with the slime of books scribbled by countless Leonid Andreyevs." Further on the manifesto calls for "uncompromising hatred for the language used hitherto," and for "enriching the vocabulary with arbitrary and derivative words."

Russian Futurism was an offshoot of Italian Futurism, founded by Marinetti. But the differences were greater than the similarities. The Russian Futurists, particularly the Cubo-Futurists who signed the 1912 manifesto, were interested in depicting life of the twentieth century, but placed somewhat less emphasis on the cult of technology and the machine, and were opposed to war, which Marinetti, who later became a Fascist, advocated as the "hygiene" of modern civilization.

After the 1917 Revolution, the Futurists, many of whom were radicals, suddenly found themselves in key official positions for the control of literature. But this was only temporary, and Futurism proved too "high-brow" and avant-garde for permanent official acceptance. In 1923 the Futurists founded an organization and a journal called LEF ("Left Front"), in which they asserted their claim to dominate the art of the future, and opposed the tendency, already manifest, toward a return to a conservative realism. But the Party turned a deaf ear to such claims, and early in 1925 *LEF* ceased publication. A *New LEF* appeared in 1927, but it, too, died very soon.

Fyodorov, Innokenti Vasilievich (1836-83), a radical novelist and poet of the second half of the nineteenth century. He published under the pseudonym of Omulevski. His novel, *Step by Step* (or *Svetlov*, 1870), was popular for its fictional presentation of certain social questions, such as the emancipation of women, the education of the masses, etc.

G

Gan, Y. A. See Hahn.

Garin, N. See Mikhaylovski, N. G.

Garshin, Vsevolod Mikhaylovich (1855-88), a writer of the late 1870's and 1880's. He came from the landowning aristocracy, and was a painter of social subjects as well as a story writer. In 1877 he enlisted in the army as a volunteer in the war with Turkey. Though a pacifist, he believed that it was his duty to take part in war since others were suffering and dying. He was wounded and sent back to Kharkov, where he wrote his first story, *Four Days* (1877). It describes vividly the sensations and sufferings of a wounded soldier who lies four days on the battlefield before he is found. The story had a tremendous success, and Garshin turned to writing as a career. Sensitive and morbid, he was subject to fits of insane melancholia; during one of these he attempted suicide by jumping down a stairwell, and died five days later in terrible agony.

Garshin's total production is very small, less than two dozen stories. For the most part concentrated and quite short, they helped to begin the new vogue for the short story, which became the leading literary genre of the 1880's and 1890's. Most of his tales are concerned with the problem of evil, frequently symbolized by him in allegorical terms. Thus, in *The Red Flower* (1883), a madman evades the watch of his guards to pluck and crush a red poppy which grows in the asylum yard; in its flowers, he believes, all the evil of the world is contained. He succeeds in the attempt, but the supreme effort exhausts his strength and he dies. *Attalea Princeps* (1880) is another allegory, about a palm which breaks the glass of the conservatory in which it is confined; instead of freedom it finds only the cold and death of the Russian winter. *A Very Short Novel* (1878) is about a crippled war veteran whose disability causes the girl he loves to throw him over. *The Signal* (1887) is strongly influenced by TOLSTOY's later didactic manner in its simplicity and the elemental quality of its moral point. It tells how a radical gives himself up to save an old signalman who has risked his life to prevent the very wreck which the radical had plotted.

Garshin is hardly a great writer, though he was extremely popular in his own day. His importance lies chiefly in his new use of the story form, which, in his treatment, becomes more single in impression than the older, loosely constructed tale. The particular merit of his stories is their atmosphere, usually of gloom, melancholy or horror.

Gartny, T. See Hartny.

Gastev, Alexey. See Smithy Poets.

Gerasimov, Mikhail. See Smithy Poets.

German, Yuri. See Herman.

Gershenzon, Mikhail Osipovich (1869-1925), a philosopher, essayist and literary historian of the early twentieth century. His literary reputation rests chiefly on his remarkable exchange of letters with Vyacheslav IVANOV, *Correspondence between Two Corners* (1921), written while the two men were living in the same rest home for writers in Moscow. In these letters Gershenzon expresses the idea that the Revolution would prove beneficial to Russia and free her from what he considers the dead weight of culture and tradition.

Gertsen, A. I. See Herzen.

Gippius. See Hippius.

Gladkov, Fyodor Vasilievich (1883-   ), a Soviet novelist. A school teacher of radical sympathies, he began to publish as early as 1899. In 1912 he published *The Outcasts*, a novel of the life of political prisoners. His greatest success was *Cement* (1925), the first Soviet novel to place much emphasis on industrialization, and a best-seller both in the Soviet Union and abroad. The work describes the reconditioning of a cement factory which has fallen into decay during the Civil War. The hero who leads the work succeeds in re-opening the factory, but fails to find personal happiness; his wife insists on her freedom to devote herself to social work and to indulge in extra-marital relations. Their daughter, placed in a nursing home, dies from lack of love and proper care. Gladkov seems unable to solve the problems of the family and home which he himself raises. The novel is written in a crude and blatant style, influenced by such writers as AN-DREYEV.

Gladkov's novel, *Energy* (1932-38), written during the First Five-year Plan, describes the construction of the Dneprostroy dam. But its story bogs down in the author's attempt to give masses of engineering detail.

Gladkov's *Story of My Childhood* (1949), a collection of childhood reminiscences, shows the influence of Gorki's autobiographical works (see Peshkov). The book is stronger than his fiction, and creates real feeling and nostalgia for the events of childhood.

Glikberg. See Glückberg.

Glinka, Fyodor Nikolayevich (1786-1880), a Russian poet, cousin of the famous composer, Mikhail Glinka. He is primarily a writer of mystical religious poetry of high quality, though somewhat monotonous in its tone. He wrote several songs in the folk style, such as his *Troika* (ca. 1830), which have actually survived among the people as folk songs.

Glückberg, Alexander Mikhaylovich (1880-1933), a satirical poet of the early nineteenth century who wrote under the pseudonym of Sasha Chorny. His poems are parodies of the Symbolist poets (see Symbolism), and make fun of their mysticism, eroticism and general pretentiousness. In 1920 he left the Soviet Union. He attacked the Bolshevik regime sharply in his subsequent poetry.

Gnedich, Nikolay Ivanovich (1784-1833), a Russian poet of the early nineteenth century. His original productions, including a few lyrics and a long idyl, *The Fishermen* (1822), are slim in quantity. He is best remembered as a translator; his rendering of Homer's *Iliad* in Russian hexameters (1829) is one of the finest translations in Russian. The language, archaic and rich in Slavonicisms, is sonorous and majestic, and the translation is noted for its fidelity to the original.

Gofman, Viktor. See Hoffman.

Gogol, Nikolay Vasilyevich (1809-52), one of Russia's greatest writers. Born in the town of Sorochintsy in the Ukraine, he was the son of a family of Cossack petty gentry. From 1821 to 1828 he studied at the lycée at Nezhin, and there he made his first attempts to write. In 1828 he went to St. Petersburg to make his career. His hopes of becoming an actor failed; he then published at his own expense, under the pseudonym of V. Alov, a long narrative poem called *Hanz* (sic) *Küchelgarten* (1829), about a German student of Byronic character. It met with ridicule, and Gogol bought up all the copies and destroyed them. Disillusioned, he set out on a trip to the west, but returned after getting as far as Lübeck. He then entered the civil service, but was disappointed at his humble position as a junior clerk. At the same time he began to write stories, the first of which he published in 1830. He was introduced to the literary world, and met ZHUKOVSKI and PUSHKIN, who encouraged him. He secured a position as teacher of history in a ladies' institute; meanwhile he brought out his first successful work, a collection of tales called *Evenings on a Farm near Dikanka* (1831-32). In 1834 he was made professor of history at the University of St. Petersburg; his lectures were occasionally brilliant, but more often empty and boring. In spite of his limitations as a historian, he projected such undertakings as a history of the Ukraine and a world history, but these remained mere dreams. The following year he resigned his chair, and soon determined to dedicate himself entirely to literature.

The volumes of tales which followed *Evenings on a Farm near Dikanka* established Gogol as a leading figure in the literary world. The successful production of his comedy, *The Inspector-General* (1836), made him the hero of the liberals, though the conservatives attacked the play fiercely, and only the personal intervention of Nicholas I allowed it to be performed. Confused by the mixed reception of his play, Gogol left Russia for Italy the same year. He spent the next twelve years, with brief interruptions, abroad, for the most part in Rome, a city which appealed both to his baroque sense of fantasy and to his obsession with religious problems. There he worked on the great novel—or epic, as he called it—which was to be his masterpiece, *Dead Souls*, the first part of which was published in 1842.

Gogol was now regarded as the leading Russian writer by the liberal and radical intelligentsia, who interpreted his mature works as an indictment of serfdom and the autocratic political order. These readers were dumbfounded when, in 1847, Gogol published his *Selected Passages from a Correspondence with Friends*, a collection of moralizing sermons (few of which were taken from actual correspondence) preaching a return to the conservative virtues and defending established Russian institutions, including autocracy and serfdom. Even the SLAVO-PHILES, who had been close to Gogol, were disgusted by the work, while the radical critic, BELINSKI, one of Gogol's warmest admirers, now castigated him in the bitterest terms. Belinski's famous letter of reproach to Gogol from abroad (1847), though banned in Russia, became a profession of political faith for the radicals.

More and more preoccupied—even haunted—by moral and religious problems which his earlier works had echoed, Gogol undertook a pilgrimage to Palestine in 1848. But he found little spiritual satisfaction. Returning to Russia, he attempted to follow an ascetic regimen which undermined his health. His reason gave way, and, apparently dissatisfied with his failure in the second part of *Dead Souls* to embody the positive spiritual values which he himself was seeking, he destroyed the manuscript. A few days later, in 1852, he died, almost literally of self-starvation and exhaustion.

Gogol's character was in many ways complex and contradictory. Though his writings, as well as his private conversations, were humorous—both on the surface and in a deeper sense—he himself was unhappy and warped in personality. Closely attached in youth to his unbalanced mother, he seems literally to have had no other relations with women. Tormented by a fear of spiritual retribution and a never-ending quest for ethical values, he failed to embody positive spiritual qualities in his works; in their stead he could only caricature the weakness, ugliness and petty foibles of mankind. The greatest Russian humorist, he is also, paradoxically, the greatest Russian master of the horror story. Both his humor and his horror seem to flow from the same source, a terror of life, which he perceived as a kind of spiritual void; thus he laughed at other men's lack of spirituality, but had perforce to realize that it was also his own.

The common denominator of almost all Gogol's fictional writing is its exuberant prodigality of invention, which transfuses both his language and his vision of life. His language has two main styles: a dignified, rhythmically flowing rhetoric; and a grotesque, sometimes earthy humor. Both are always brilliantly orchestrated and alive. The humorous style embraces many verbal devices: the use of comic or suggestive names, plays on words, invented words, incorrect use of connectives, long sentences with sudden, ironic twists of thought, or rhetorical heights followed by the sudden bathos of inelegant words or ideas. But in its essence his style is unanalyzable and inimitable; nor is it susceptible to translation.

Gogol's creative genius is also manifested in his prodigious gift for imagery. No other Russian prose writer has conjured up such a rich and exotic world of images, which become almost visible to the reader. The main focus of this gift is in caricature, the seizing on grotesque human features which are exaggerated and distorted until they threaten to envelop the whole person. This gift of visualization—not of the real world, but of a world in which everything has a kind of spiritual or metaphysical significance—extends to objects as well; in *Dead Souls* Chichikov's coach and his mysterious trunk seem living parts of his personality. Clothing, food, even scenes of nature, depicted as completely transformed and fantastic, an exotic world alien to man—all these become grotesquely alive in Gogol's work. His imagery and his tendency to caricature resemble Dickens', but with the important difference that Dickens' caricature and satire are placed at the service of his positive social consciousness; with Gogol they rather serve the function of peopling a world which, without them, would be nothing but a spiritual void.

Gogol's first successful stories, the tales of the collection, *Evenings on a Farm near Dikanka* (1831-32), though strikingly different from his more mature works, are masterpieces in their genre. Set in Gogol's homeland, the Ukraine, they are light, partly fantastic stories stylized in the tradition of folk tales and the Ukrainian puppet theater. Comic witches and devils appear in several of them, and the apparatus of the supernatural is used with humorous effect. The very opposite of realism, they are nonetheless vivid in their pictorial color and joyous vitality. They depict a heroic, romantic and light-hearted people, whose exoticism at once made the tales popular with Russian readers. One story, *The Terrible Vengeance*, influenced, like much of Gogol's subsequent work, by the German romanticist story-teller of the supernatural, E.T.A. Hoffmann, stands apart as a tale of horror.

Haunting and oppressive, it suggests that Gogol was perhaps not so gay and carefree as the other stories might imply.

The *Evenings* were followed in 1835 by two volumes of stories entitled *Mirgorod,* the name of a Ukrainian town. Romance, horror, humor and satirical caricature are the diverse elements represented in this collection, which has no unity except the Ukrainian setting. *Vi,* the name of Ukrainian folk demon, is a horror story on a theme taken from popular superstition; unlike *The Terrible Vengeance,* it also strikes a humorous note. *Taras Bulba,* a historical novel which forms part of the collection, is set against the background of the Cossack-Polish wars of the seventeenth century. The hero, Taras, is a heroic Cossack in the grand manner, whose braggadocio and earthly vitality are living and colorful; the other characters are romantic types, however, and seem artificial. The novel is an apotheosis of the heroic past of the Ukraine and the Zaporozhian COSSACKS; it suffers somewhat from romantic idealization, and the love story is wooden and conventional. Still *Taras Bulba,* with all its defects, is one of the most vivid and popular of Russian historical novels.

The story called *Old World Landowners* portrays two old people, husband and wife, who live a self-satisfied, purely vegetable life on their tiny estate. Their only interest is in food, and the story reads almost like a menu. Neither hilarious nor terrifying, the tale is mildly satirical. The theme of vegetative, self-satisfied existence recurs in Gogol's later work frequently, as in *The Inspector-General* or *Dead Souls.*

The *Tale of How Ivan Ivanovich Quarreled with Ivan Nikiforovich,* also contained in *Mirgorod,* is one of the funniest in all literature. It describes two Ukrainian squires, comic, slothful and self-satisfied, who fall out over a fancied slight. They become involved in endless lawsuits and counter-suits with each other. Hilarious almost to the very end, the story closes on a note of sudden gloom when the author describes the ruin of both, and ends with the famous line, "It is dreary to live in this world, gentlemen."

The same year *Mirgorod* appeared Gogol published a new collection, *Arabesques* (1835), containing, besides some essays, three tales. Gogol now deserts the Ukraine and turns to St. Petersburg. But his vision of life in the Russian capital is as fantastic and grotesquely distorted as was his view of life in the Ukraine. *Nevski Prospect* (the name of the principal thoroughfare in Petersburg) describes the fate of two young men who follow girls. One, an artist, falls hopelessly in love with a prostitute whom he follows home, but she rejects him scornfully. He takes refuge in his dreams of her, invoked with the aid of drugs; in the end he kills himself. Though romantic, the story is a vivid picture of developing schizophrenia. The second hero, a young officer of less serious bent, follows the prosaic but beautiful wife of a German shopkeeper; at the outcome he gets only a drubbing from her husband for his pains.

Memoirs of a Madman, though still influenced by Hoffmann, is even closer than *Nevski Prospect* to a clinical study of the development of mental disease, in this case paranoia. A petty clerk, rejected by the daughter of his superior, consoles himself with the fantasy that she is really in love with him, and that their two dogs are carrying on a correspondence. Reading in the paper that the throne of Spain is vacant, he imagines himself to be the vanished heir; his trip to the asylum he interprets as his arrival at the royal palace. The story is in the tradition of PUSHKIN's *Bronze Horseman,* in which a petty clerk is driven mad; along with Gogol's later tale, *The Overcoat,* it was of great influence on DOSTOYEVSKI.

The Portrait, the first version of which is contained in *Arabesques,* is another tale of the supernatural in the style of Hoffmann, but here the moral element is more prominent than in any of Gogol's earlier tales. A poor artist is attracted by the portrait of a demonic old man. He buys it, and in the frame discovers a large sum in gold. Rejecting the impulse to go to Italy and study, he sets himself up as a fashionable portrait painter. The eventual realization that he has sacrificed his talent for wealth and success destroys him, and he dies in an insane delirium. In an epilogue we learn how the portrait came to be created. An evil and strong-willed old merchant, about to die, has his portrait painted and conceals the gold in the frame in order to insure that his evil influence will live after him. The artist who paints the picture is so tormented by the experience that he passes the remainder of his life in asceticism. Here in Gogol's work we see for the first time the clear expression of a higher, symbolic plane of meaning. Besides its obvious message of the importance of artistic integrity, the story suggests a great cosmic drama of evil and its infectiousness, of guilt and expiation.

Meanwhile Gogol had written his great comedy, *The Inspector-General* (1836). The subject involves the artificial device of mistaken identity, and need hardly have been suggested to Gogol by Pushkin, as legend has it. Its unique quality lies in the skill of its character portrayal and in the complete absence of sympathetic personages. The hero, Khlestakov, a minor clerk mistaken by a crew of thieving officials for a government inspector, is himself almost as great a rogue as they, and as silly in the complete lack of restraint with which he tries to play the role of a great gentleman. The officials, like most of Gogol's characters, are caricature portraits of vulgarity and petty vice. The mayor, their leader, is more terrifying in his cupidity and tyrannical absolutism, and he is almost unique in Gogol's work as a portrayal of evil on a grand scale. Intended as a moral satire on evil and vulgarity, the play was interpreted rather as a satire on political corruption and despotism. Even Nicholas I, outraged at the custom of bribe-taking, apparently understood it on this level when he permitted the play to be performed. But Gogol's own interpretation, that the final arrival of the real inspector is actually a summons to the Last Judgment, may not be so fantastic as it seemed, for it accords with the trend of his ideas on evil and moral guilt.

Besides *The Inspector-General*, Gogol wrote several other plays, none of the same stature. The best is *The Marriage* (1842), a hilarious comedy of match-making and marriage among the merchant class.

Meanwhile Gogol had continued the cycle of his Petersburg tales in *The Nose* (1835) and *The Overcoat* (1842). The first is an essay in sheer fantastic humor. The story concerns a government clerk whose nose, apparently shaved off by a drunken barber, assumes a separate existence of its own, until it is apprehended by the police and restored to its rightful place on its owner's face. The tale may well have as its basis the castration fear of modern psychoanalysis.

The Overcoat is Gogol's greatest story. It describes the life and death of a petty civil service clerk, a grotesque personality who takes no pleasure in anything but his copying work. In desperate need of a new overcoat, he focuses his whole life's energy on the task of procuring it, even denying himself his former pleasure of copying in order to economize on candles. But on the first day that he wears the new overcoat, it is stolen. He catches a severe chill and dies; in the end his ghost returns to steal a coat from a high official who had refused his plea to intervene and find his stolen garment. The story contains a profound symbolism on several levels. Psychologically, the overcoat suggests a kind of cloak or mask which the clerk (or man in general) needs to conceal his spiritual poverty. On the metaphysical plane, the ironic loss of the coat and the clerk's vain protests to higher authority suggest man's spiritual isolation in a universe which is hostile or indifferent to his plight. The public of Gogol's day interpreted the tale as an example of social realism; of realism there is hardly a shred, however, and the profound "social sympathy" which made the story so celebrated is only one sketchily developed motif among many. If anything, Gogol makes fun of the clerk as much as he sympathizes with him. The poverty with which Gogol is concerned is a spiritual, rather than a material, poverty.

The novel, *Dead Souls* (first part, 1842), is Gogol's masterpiece, despite its incompleted state. Though Gogol destroyed the manuscript of the second part, some excerpts from it have survived in various drafts, and we know a little of the plan of the whole, which was to have contained three parts in all. It was to have been a great drama of sin and redemption, the three parts of which would parallel the three sections of Dante's *Divine Comedy*. The hero, a swindling civil servant, was to come to grief in the second part and repent of his crimes. The third part would then show his final salvation. But the fragments of the second part which have survived continue the gallery of caricatures of petty evil which animate the first part; the positive characters and themes are few in number, and are treated palely and without real conviction. Apparently the consciousness that his essential gift was for caricature, and that he could not create positive characters, led Gogol to destroy the second part of the novel.

The first part is a finished whole, however, and can be considered by itself. In form it is a picaresque novel, influenced by such writers as Le Sage, Sterne and NAREZHNY. The hero, Chichikov, is an embodiment of the petty egoistic vices; self-complacency, shrewd and dishonest dealing, and a hankering for personal comfort. Like the personages of *The Inspector-General*, his chief sins are pettiness and vulgarity. He conceives a plan for a gigantic swindle: he will buy up dead serfs whose names are still carried on the tax registers, and who are therefore legally still alive. The title of the work—*Dead Souls*—refers to this scheme, since in Russia serfs were numbered as so and so many "souls." It has also, of course, a deeper significance; the personages in the book are spiritually dead. The purchase of these "dead souls" could be accomplished for a nominal sum, since the landowners would be anxious to erase them from the list of their tax obligations. Chichikov would then buy cheap land (serfs were more valuable in Russia than unsettled land), "settle" his serfs on it, mortgage the estate, and disappear abroad with the proceeds.

Though intriguing, the plot subject is no more than a frame, a pretext for Chichikov's travels about Russia. On his way he meets different types of landowners. These are all caricatures, hyperbolized personifications of individual vices. Sobakevich, brutal, beast-like and silent; Nozdryov, the engaging liar, cheat and hypocrite; Manilov, the sentimental milksop; Plyushkin, the miser; Korobochka, the stupid widow who fears that Chichikov may cheat her by paying less than the market value for "dead souls" —all these are classic types in Russian literature, as memorable and as forceful as those of Dickens or Shakespeare are for us.

In the end Chichikov comes to grief. Korobochka's anxious inquiries as to whether he may have cheated her expose his scheme, and he is forced to leave town in great haste. The final passage of the work is one of the most powerful in all Russian literature. Chichikov's troika is gradually transformed into a symbol of Russia herself; its glorious, intoxicating speed, without real goal or purpose, is a moving characterization of Russia—a silent, powerful giant who rushes somewhere, she knows not where.

The meaning of Gogol's work and the question of his influence have remained controversial to the present day. Following the lead of the critic BELINSKI, the reading public of his day accepted Gogol as a realist who described the social and political faults of Russian life. *Dead Souls* was interpreted as a denunciation of the institution of serfdom and of the corruption of the

Russian social structure. Considered thus, Gogol became the founder and inspirer of the Russian realist movement. Unfortunately, this view is oversimplified. It overlooks the fact that the great majority of the Russian realists, with the exception of the young DOSTOYEVSKI, and to some extent PISEMSKI and OSTROVSKI, were quite unlike Gogol and were hardly influenced by his work. Such realists as TURGENEV, GONCHAROV and TOLSTOY do not caricature, they are not interested in grotesques, and are not humorists. The style of most of the realists, unlike Gogol's brilliant and colorful rhetoric, tends to be colorless and placid. If anything, Russian literature after Gogol moved away from his work, rather than following in its path, as the critic ROZANOV pointed out. Dostoyevski's famous declaration that "We all came out of Gogol's *Overcoat*" (supposedly said of himself and the writers who were his contemporaries) is at best apocryphal, and one scarcely knows to what writers it could be applied other than Dostoyevski himself. Writing in a period when Gogol's *Overcoat* was accepted without question as an expression of social sympathy, Dostoyevski was nonetheless alive to Gogol's real lack of sympathy for his hero, and he criticized *The Overcoat* in his early novel, *Poor People*.

Such a view of Gogol's work also divides it into a number of parts, disjointed and contradictory. His early tales are unquestionably romantic, and contain few if any motifs of political satire or social sympathy. They are followed by the three great works of the mature period, *The Inspector-General*, *The Overcoat* and *Dead Souls*, supposedly "realistic" and inspired by liberal sentiments. But these, in turn, are followed by a sudden about-face: the turn to reaction represented by the *Selected Passages from a Correspondence with Friends*, for which BELINSKI bitterly denounced the author. Such a view splits Gogol's work into irreconcilable segments.

Closer inspection reveals other discrepancies. How can we reconcile the ghost episode which ends *The Overcoat* with any sort of realism, or the author's obvious amusement at the expense of his hero with genuine social sympathy? Gogol's so-called "realism" consists largely, perhaps entirely, in his ignoring the taboo on the depiction of vulgar characters and crude human actions.

Only if we abandon this view do we obtain a picture of Gogol's work which is unified and consistent, which accords with the facts of his life and even, to a great extent, with what he said about his own writings. From the first he is a writer preoccupied with spiritual and moral problems, for whom man is ultimately alone and helpless in a universe which is unsympathetic. Penance and self-abnegation become significant for him as means of buying the good will of this hostile universe. But he also sees man as incapable of either heroism or self-renunciation in his spiritual isolation, which man hardly even senses. Futile and sunk in a kind of vice which Gogol almost always depicts as petty because man himself is petty, he appears ridiculous in Gogol's eyes, and he caricatures him. Certainly Gogol is a satirist; we may even admit that at times he is a political and social satirist, if it also be remembered that his ultimate personal aim was to create *moral* satire. But as well as a satirist, he is a master of the grotesque, of irony, and of metaphysical terror. Far from being an objective realist, he is a writer who projects his own subjective fears and anxieties into the world around him.

Gogol's influence on subsequent Russian literature was not great. To the realistic movement which followed him he gave little more than a precedent for the depiction of lower-class personages, along with one or two stereotyped figures, such as the petty clerk, who passed into the heritage of Russian literature. His humorous method, unique in its combination of verbal creativity and grotesque imagery, was perhaps too distinct to be imitated. The most successful Russian writer to make use of Gogol's legacy of humor is the Soviet humorist and satirist ZOSHCHENKO, though the latter's own originality is quite considerable. The satirical methods of Gogol's play, *The Inspector-General*, were rather more widely and successfully imitated, particularly in the writing of plays which lacked sympathetic characters, such as those by OSTROVSKI and SUKHOVO-KOBYLIN.

With the emergence of the school of SYMBOLISM at the end of the nineteenth century, the existing interpretation of Gogol was partly overthrown, and Russian writers became more sensitive to the moral and metaphysical strain in his work. This reinterpretation enabled the post-symbolist writer ANDREY BELY to become perhaps the only Russian writer who absorbed more than a single facet of Gogol's method and used it creatively in his own novels. Yet Gogol's lack of influence does not dim his significance. He is a superlative artist, one who both created his own private world of art and exhausted it.

Golenishchev-Kutuzov, Count Arseni Arkadievich (1848-1913), a poet of the late nineteenth century. The chief subject of his lyrics is nostalgia for the vanishing aristocratic way of life. Many of his poems were set to music by Rachmaninov, Mussorgski and other composers.

Golitsyn, Prince Dmitri Petrovich (1860-1919), a minor writer of the late nineteenth century, who published tales, novels, poems and travel sketches under the pseudonym of Muravlin. His favorite subject is the decadence of the landowning class. Influenced by DOSTOYEVSKI, he gives much attention to the depiction of pathological types.

Gomberg, Vladimir Germanovich (1894-   ), a Soviet writer who publishes under the pseudonym of Vladimir Lidin. His earlier lyric stories, first published in 1916, show the influence of CHEKHOV and BUNIN. He has written many short stories of Soviet life, as well as several novels. *The Renegade* (1928) depicts the spiritual transformation of a student who has taken part in a murder conspiracy and who later confesses his guilt. *Great or Pacific?* (1932) is a regional novel about the Far East and the development of socialism there. Lidin's later work has met sharp criticism because of his preference for individualistic themes.

Goncharov, Ivan Alexandrovich (1812-91), a leading Russian novelist of the mid-nineteenth century. Born in Simbirsk, on the Volga, the son of a wealthy merchant family which had acquired estates, he was brought up in the atmosphere of the life of the provincial gentry. In 1834 he was graduated from Moscow University, and entered the civil service, at first as an employee in the Ministry of Finance. He began to write around 1832, publishing translations and poems, but these had no success. His first novel, *A Common Story*, published in 1847 and enthusiastically greeted by the critic BELINSKI, brought him immediate recognition. In 1852-55 he was sent as secretary on a mission to Japan; the voyage around the world which he made he described in his volume of travel reminiscences, *The Frigate Pallas* (1856). Otherwise his life was largely unmarked by unusual events. In 1856 he was transferred in the civil service to the censorship, where he remained until 1867. He was inclined to be indolent and self-satisfied, fond of comfort and ease, like his most famous character, Oblomov. His personality, apparently staid, was unstable, and at one time he made fantastic accusations against the writer TURGENEV for plagiarizing parts of his novel, *The Precipice.*

Goncharov's three novels all have the same theme, the spiritual inertia and impractical character of the Russian nobility, particularly of its younger and more liberal members. They are to a considerable degree autobiographical, and the heroes resemble Goncharov himself in their circumstances of life, upbringing, and vegetative character. Though based on introspection, the autobiographical element in Goncharov's creation never leads him into subjectivity, and his characters achieve a degree of universality which is rare even in the Russian novel. They, and in particular, Oblomov, are the final stage (in the sense of being the best defined and best conceived in sociological terms) of the long tradition of Russian SUPERFLUOUS MEN, those sensitive, intelligent heroes of the Russian novel who are too impractical and inactive to become leaders or creators.

Goncharov's first novel, *A Common Story* (1847), describes the fate of a young provincial, Aduyev, who comes to St. Petersburg full of hopes and ambitions for a career, love and friendship. But he avoids hard work, wasting his time in idle daydreams. His uncle, a successful bureaucrat and industrialist, destroys his lofty ideals, instilling in their place a gospel of practical common sense and hard work. Instead of writing poetry, he advises his nephew to translate practical articles on agriculture. In the end Aduyev is converted, sheds his ideals, makes a successful career and a profitable marriage, and becomes a solid if prosaic citizen. The novel was popular as part of a reaction against the exaggerated romantic idealism of the period, and for its formulation of a more practical, materialistic conception of progress. Goncharov seems to accept the philosophy of the uncle, but one suspects that his deeper, unconscious sympathies lie with the disillusioned nephew. It is significant that the uncle himself undergoes a breakdown at the end of the novel, the result of his own unresolved conflict between idealism and a practical business mentality.

In his second novel, unquestionably his greatest, *Oblomov*

(1859), Goncharov sees the split between idealistic dreaming and practical industry as irreconcilable. Oblomov, like Aduyev, is a young dreamer who comes to Petersburg with the same high hopes. But he finds his career in the civil service not to his liking, and his new-found friends prosaic and vulgar. He withdraws from the world, gives way to inaction, and literally spends all his time in bed. He is roused from his lethargy by a practical, hard-headed friend, Stolz, and by his love for a beautiful girl, Olga. New dreams of marrying Olga and settling down to become a progressive estate manager and contented father of a family now replace his former ones. But at last Oblomov realizes that he is too weak to achieve his dreams, and gives up Olga, who then marries Stolz. Oblomov ends by marrying his own landlady, a woman who is far beneath him culturally and socially, but who is well able to insure his indolent comfort. He dies in total listlessness, smothered in the mire of a vulgarity and sloth which he accepts as substitutes for the peace and contentment he had so longed for.

In the beautiful lyric interlude called "The Dream of Oblomov," Goncharov gives a vivid picture of Oblomov's upbringing, and propounds an explanation for the failure of the Russian nobility to grow to active leadership. As a child Oblomov is petted by his relatives, surrounded by servants who do his slightest bidding, and protected against every conceivable harm. This almost Oriental upbringing destroys his moral fibre, leaving only a nostalgic dream of peace and contentment which he cannot find again in the adult world. Whether Oblomov's history was typical of the Russian nobility or not, he was accepted as a convincing example of the liberal nobility's failure to act. The critic DOBROLYUBOV used the name "Oblomovism" for this disease of inaction and its social roots in the manorial and provincial existence of the Russian nobility.

In sharp contrast to Oblomov is Stolz, who is the positive, didactically inspired hero of the work. Of German descent (as if Goncharov could not imagine a practical Russian!), his upbringing is the exact opposite of Oblomov's. But the figure of Stolz is pale and artificial, and the reader's sympathies lie with Oblomov.

Goncharov's final novel, *The Precipice* (1869), is inferior to

Oblomov. It presents a kind of compromise between the path of practical common sense and that of idealistic daydreaming. The hero, Rayski, tries to discover a middle way in art. But he is a dilettante, and finds himself in a society which cannot yet afford professional artists. He gives over to a series of love affairs, finally falling in love with his proud, passionate cousin, Vera, only to discover that she loves Volokhov, a nihilist and scoundrel. Infatuated with Volokhov, she gives herself to him, only to realize that she was wrong in betraying her social background and traditions. In the end Rayski goes abroad, while Vera acquires a new interest in Tushin, a practical, honest business man reminiscent of Stolz. The character of Volokhov is notable as an addition—far less sympathetic than TURGENEV's Bazarov—to the series of portraits of NIHILISTS in Russian literature.

Though only one of Goncharov's novels, *Oblomov,* is of first importance, his position in Russian literature is secure. Russians would rank him alongside of TURGENEV, though his popularity abroad has never been so great. No doubt Goncharov has many weaknesses, such as his failure to portray convincing positive heroes. The pedestrian character of the virtues of hard work, thrift and honesty which he holds up for emulation is hardly likely to enthuse readers with the didactic side of his novels. Though much praised, largely on the basis of "The Dream of Oblomov," for its lyrical qualities, Goncharov's style is actually (and deliberately) flat and prosaic. The most that can be said for it is that it is entirely adequate to his purpose. His unique talent consists in his ability to embody subjective elements of his introspection as a generalized, compelling social symbol almost without equal in Russian literature.

Gorbatov, Boris Leontievich (1908-54), Soviet novelist. His most popular work, *The Unvanquished* (1943), also known as *The Taras Family,* is set against the German occupation in South Russia, with the life of an average family and its participation in the underground resistance movement depicted. The relation of the father and his two sons reminds the reader of GOGOL's novel *Taras Bulba.* Gorbatov's final novel, *The Donets Basin* (1951), was the first part of a longer work which remained unfinished. It deals with the introduction of new machines and of workers' competitions in a Soviet colliery.

Gorbunov, Ivan Fyodorovich (1831-95), a writer and actor of the second half of the nineteenth century. He specialized in humorous monologues and dialogues, as well as sketches of peasant and middle-class life. His most famous character, General Dityatin, is a retired general who served under the reactionary Nicholas I. He delivers humorous tirades against reform and calls for a return to the good old days of reaction.

Gorenko, Anna Andreyevna (1888-   ), a poet of the twentieth century who published under the pseudonym of Anna Akhmatova. In 1910 she married the poet GUMILYOV, and joined him in the new movement of ACMEISM which he founded in 1912. She divorced him in 1918 and married Vladimir Shileyko, an Assyriologist and a minor poet. Akhmatova had published a number of volumes of poetry between 1912 and 1922, but after 1922 she was silent for almost two decades. She did publish several important studies on PUSHKIN in the interim, however, including a demonstration of the dependence of Pushkin's *Tale of the Golden Cockerel* on Washington Irving's *Tale of the Arabian Astrologer*. In 1940 she took advantage of the greater official leniency which prevailed during the war years and published *A Selection from Six Books*, which included her earlier poetry as well as a few new poems. Although her poetry is melancholy and is to a large extent concerned with personal sorrow in love, a "bourgeois" theme in the eyes of Soviet critics, still it seems that she won great popularity among young Communist intellectuals. To stop this defection by youth, the Party found it necessary to purge her, and the attack on her by A. A. ZHDANOV in 1946 led to her prompt expulsion from the Union of Soviet Writers, which meant the loss of her right to publish. But in 1950 she printed a number of official patriotic verses as excerpts from a cycle entitled *In Praise of Peace*. The quality of these poems is painfully low; subjected to official pressure to conform, it is obvious that she finally gave in.

Akhmatova's poetry is intimate and personal; her favorite subject is love and the melancholy and disillusionment which it brings; rejection or betrayal seems for her the usual lot of a woman in love. Some of her poems are simple love lyrics; others are ironical comments on love; others are nature poems in which landscape serves as a release from sensuality. Her poetry is musical, with a clarity of description and a concreteness of manner typical of the Acmeists. Her leading collections are *Evening* (1912), *The Rosary* (1914) and *The White Flock* (1917). *Anno Domini MCMXXI* (1921) is a volume of lyric verse on the time of the Civil War.

Gorki, Maxim. See Peshkov, A. M.

Gorodetski, Sergey Mitrofanovich (1884-   ), a poet of the early twentieth century. His first collection, *Yar* ("Vital Sap," 1907), was distinguished by its varied rhythms and its use of an exotic and largely invented Russian mythology. In 1912 he participated with GUMILYOV in publishing the manifesto of the new poetic school of ACMEISM. In 1915 he left the Acmeists and identified himself with the young group of peasant poets, including KLYU-YEV and YESENIN. After the 1917 Revolution Gorodetski became a Communist, and when, in 1921, Gumilyov was shot by the Soviet government, he issued a public vilification of his former friend and a denial of his own connection with Acmeism.

Granovski, Timofey Nikolayevich (1813-55), a Russian historian and political philosopher of the mid-nineteenth century. Professor of history at Moscow University, he belonged to the Russian party of WESTERNERS. More moderate than BELINSKI or HERZEN, he neither believed in nor advocated a revolution for Russia, but felt that the historical process would itself bring reform, and lead to a constitutional monarchy.

Grech, Nikolay Ivanovich (1787-1867), a journalist, literary historian, philologist and writer of the mid-nineteenth century. A conservative, Grech allied himself with BULGARIN and the reactionary party in journalism and literature.

Green, A. See Grinevski, A. S.

Grek, Maxim. See Maxim Grek.

Griboyedov, Alexander Sergeyevich (1795-1829), a leading playwright of the early nineteenth century. The son of an officer, he studied science and law at the University of Moscow. He served in the army during the Napoleonic Invasion of 1812, later entering the civil service in the Ministry of Foreign Affairs. He joined the camp of the literary conservatives, led by SHISHKOV, and in 1815 produced his first play, an adaptation from the French. In 1818 he was sent to Persia as secretary to the Russian Mission. In 1826 he was arrested because of his associations with the

Decembrists (see Decembrist Movement), but succeeded in clearing himself. He was returned to his diplomatic post in the Caucasus, where Russia was now fighting a war with Persia. Griboyedov negotiated the peace treaty in 1828, and was appointed Russian Minister to Persia. In the Russian legation at Teheran he was attacked by a mob. Infuriated by the Russian demands made in accordance with the peace treaty, which included a provision for the return of Christian women held prisoner in Persian harems, the rioters hacked him to pieces.

Griboyedov is the author of a few lyric poems and a number of comedies in prose and in verse. One of them, *The Student* (1817), is a satire directed against the young generation of romanticist poets. But for practical purposes he is the author of but one work, the comedy, *Woe from Wit*. Written in 1822-24, the play was not passed by the censor, but in 1825 fragments of it were published, and it was widely circulated by the author in manuscript.

Woe from Wit is written in rhymed verse, in iambic lines of varying lengths, a meter already used by KRYLOV in his fables. Influenced by Molière, and in particular by his comedy, *Le Misanthrope,* the work is nonetheless completely Russian in situation, characters and style. The hero, Chatski, a sensitive and idealistic young nobleman, returns to Moscow from travelling abroad, to find that the Russian society for which he has been nostalgic is reactionary, stupid and petty. His love for a childhood sweetheart, Sophia, the daughter of a high official, is blighted when he discovers that Sophia loves not him, but a worthless fop, Molchalin. To silence Chatski's barbed thrusts, father and daughter spread a rumor that he is insane. Alienated from society, Chatski sets out again on his travels.

Though the figure of Chatski is not quite perfect—PUSHKIN first observed that an intelligent man would not have wasted his time in conversation with the stupid people who surround him— it nonetheless had great influence on subsequent Russian literature. Together with PUSHKIN's Onegin, Chatski is the prototype of the so-called SUPERFLUOUS MAN, who feels the need for social and political change, but does nothing to bring it about. Even his talkativeness became a symptom of the character type, and reappears in TURGENEV's hero, Rudin. But Chatski's wit is unique, and the play is a solitary example of a great Russian comedy of wit.

The other characters of the play constitute a great gallery of satirical portraits. Famusov, the father, whose ideal is to be wealthy and respectable; Sophia, his heartless if witty daughter; Molchalin, the fawning hypocrite; Repetilov, the drunkard and fashionable "liberal"—all are perfect types, representatives of a society which is vain and foolish.

The play owes much of its appeal to its language and rhymed verse. Griboyedov was amazingly successful in using an easy, colloquial speech and subjecting it to the restrictions of verse form; the effect is one of spontaneous naturalness and lightness. Many of the lines are memorable, and have become popular proverbial expressions.

Grigoriev, Apollon Alexandrovich (1822-64), a leading Russian critic and poet of the mid-nineteenth century. Born into a middle-class family, he studied law at Moscow University. In 1850 he became editor of POGODIN's journal, *The Muscovite*. Its failure in 1856 left him unemployed, and in great economic distress. He led a dissolute Bohemian life, and was always in financial difficulties. A large part of his last years he spent in debtor's prison. In 1861 he joined the staff of DOSTOYEVSKI's journal, *Time*, and became a close friend of that writer.

As a critic, Grigoriev rejected the civic view of literature held by BELINSKI, predominant in his day. He believed that art should be organic and intuitive, that it should obey its own laws, rather than serve the needs of society. He made a cult of all that was distinctly Russian; literature should be a "product of the soil"; it should mirror those elements and areas in Russian life which were traditional and conservative, which had not yet been displaced by the Europeanized culture of the upper classes. Thus, Grigoriev was close to the SLAVOPHILES, though he did not share their specific political views. For him the greatest Russian writer was his contemporary, the playwright OSTROVSKI. But the passionate romanticism of his temperament also attracted him to writers who were more revolutionary and less traditional, such as LERMONTOV, Byron and Schiller. Grigoriev was a keen intuitive observer, and his recollections, called *My Literary and*

Cultural Wanderings (1864), are a brilliant record of the intellectual and cultural life of his times.

As a poet Grigoriev is less significant, and his verse shows the technical imperfections characteristic of the period. He wrote poems about love, carousing and gypsy music, some of them adaptations of popular gypsy songs. Certain of these, such as his *Two Guitars,* are still sung as cabaret songs, though Grigoriev has almost been forgotten as their author. He enjoyed a certain revival under Russian SYMBOLISM, and the poet BLOK published his collected poems in 1916.

Grigorovich, Dmitri Vasilyevich (1822-99), a Russian prose writer of the mid-nineteenth century. His two tales, *The Village* (1846) and *Anton Goremyka* (1847), gained fame for their sympathetic description of the miseries of peasant life, though they were soon eclipsed by TURGENEV'S *Sportsman's Sketches.* Grigorovich continued to publish novels and stories about peasant life throughout the 1850's. He stopped writing after 1864, but returned to literature in the 1880's and 1890's with several stories and his literary reminiscences.

Grin, A. See Grinevski, A. S.

Grinevski, Alexander Stepanovich (1880-1932), a Soviet writer of fantastic tales and novels who published under the pen-name of A. Grin. He was influenced by E. T. A. Hoffmann, Poe, Stevenson and other writers of stories of fantasy and adventure. In spite of the many attacks on his work by Soviet critics, he succeeded in keeping his work free of political and social elements and in writing stories of pure adventure and fantasy, many of which are set in the purely imaginative country of "Grinland." His work is not on a very high level, but it provided Soviet readers with an escape from the tedium of a literature concerned only with reality, and has consequently been very popular.

Grossman, Vasili Semyonovich (1905-   ), Soviet novelist. His major novel, *Stepan Kolchugin* (1937-40), in three volumes, depicts the Bolshevik underground before the Revolution. Grossman served at the front in World War II, and his novel, *The People Is Immortal* (1942), attempts to portray different kinds of officers and men and to analyze the character of the successful fighter. A second war novel, *For the Just Cause* (1952), dealt with the defense of Stalingrad. It was condemned for its "idealist" philosophy and for the insufficient attention it gave to the role of the Party in winning the war (see *Partiynost*).

Gumilyov, Nikolay Stepanovich (1886-1921), a poet of the early twentieth century, the principal founder of the movement known as ACMEISM. He studied under the poet ANNENSKI at the Tsar's Lycée in Tsarskoye Selo; besides Annenski, he was most strongly influenced by the symbolist BRYUSOV. His first book of verse, *The Path of the Conquistadores*, was published in 1905. In 1910 he married the poetess Anna Akhmatova (see Gorenko). They separated during the war, and she divorced him in 1918. Interested in the ethnography of exotic lands, Gumilyov went to Abyssinia in 1911, where he collected folk songs. In 1912, together with GORODETSKI, he founded the Guild of Poets, a group of young poets who soon acquired the nickname of "Acmeists" (see Acmeism). In 1913 Gumilyov went to Somaliland on an expedition for the Museum of Anthropology and Ethnology. In 1914 he volunteered for the army as an officer, and was twice decorated for bravery. After the Revolution of 1917 he was openly anti-Bolshevik. In 1921 he was arrested for supposed complicity in an anti-Soviet conspiracy, the Tagantsev Affair, and was shot by a firing squad, though his guilt has never been proven.

Gumilyov's poetry is almost unique in Russian literature for its descriptions of the exotic lands in which the poet travelled and for its cult of adventure and heroism. The heroes of his poems are explorers, conquerors, sea captains and virile adventurers. He was repelled by the mysticism, softness and vagueness of the symbolist poets (see Symbolism), and his reaction led to the founding of the new movement of ACMEISM, with its stress on clarity, precision, concreteness and vividness of imagery. Some of his more important collections are *Pearls* (1910), *The Pyre* (1918) and *Pillar of Fire* (1921). His translations include a successful version of Coleridge's *Rime of the Ancient Mariner*.

Gusev, Sergey Ivanovich (1867-   ), a novelist of the late nineteenth and early twentieth century. He was born in Orenburg, and took the pen-name of Gusev-Orenburgski. He served as a priest until 1898, and his main subject is the life of village priests, depicted realistically. After the 1917 Revolution he came to the United States, where he worked as an editor.

Gusev-Orenburgski. See Gusev, S. I.

H

Hagiography. See Literature, Old Russian.

Hahn, Yelena Andreyevna (1814-42), a Russian writer of tales, who wrote during the 1830's and 1840's under the pseudonym of Zeneida R—va. The wife of an artillery officer, she followed her husband from one military post to another, and her tales describe the vulgarity and ennui of provincial and garrison life. Concerned with the position of women in society, her work was influenced by the French writer George Sand, and she was even described as the "Russian George Sand." Her tales, with their conventional plots, naive heroines and deceitful, knavish heroes, are of little artistic significance.

Hartny, Tsishka, pseudonym of D. Zhilunovich (1887-?), a leading Belo-Russian writer (see Preface).

Herman, Yuri Pavlovich (1910-), a Soviet novelist and story writer. His early novel, *Our Friends* (1936), dealt with the life of average people and the regeneration of a young woman who drifts without purpose through life, failing to find its meaning. In the end she is redeemed by her marriage to an OGPU (secret police) official.

Herman's later novel, *A Lieutenant Colonel of the Medical Corps,* was never completed, though the opening installments were published in *Zvezda* in 1949. The hero, an army doctor, was apparently too introspective and eccentric to satisfy official demands for a literature of optimism.

Herzen, Alexander Ivanovich (1812-70), a leading Russian revolutionary thinker and philosopher of the mid-nineteenth century. Born the natural son of a wealthy nobleman, Herzen was brought up by his father, who treated him generously. The boy attended Moscow University, which he completed in 1833. In 1834 he was arrested for belonging to a socialist political circle, and was exiled to the provinces, though as a civil servant. In 1840 Herzen was permitted to return to Moscow, where he met the young literary critic and philosopher BELINSKI, whom he influenced strongly. He published a series of articles on questions of philosophy, science and history under the pseudonym of Iskander, as well as several stories and a novel, *Who Is at Fault?* (1841-46). In 1847 he inherited a large fortune from his father and, after many difficulties, secured permission to go abroad. He arrived in Paris in time to witness the Revolution of 1848, which he hailed enthusiastically, thus making it impossible for him to return to Russia. His enthusiasm was short-lived, however; the unfavorable course which the revolution took destroyed much of his optimistic faith in progress and his former idealization of the West. He went from country to country, finally settling, in 1852, in England. He established a Russian press there and, with the help of his childhood friend, the poet OGARYOV, who had followed him into exile, published a free Russian weekly newspaper, *The Bell*, which first appeared in 1857. Smuggled into Russia, it had an enormous influence, and was read regularly even by the Emperor Alexander II. The government's promulgation of REFORMS in the 1860's somewhat weakened Herzen's influence in Russia; in 1864 he transferred the paper to Geneva, and it appeared only sporadically. He died in 1870 in Paris.

Herzen was well acquainted with many of the leading European revolutionists of the nineteenth century, such as Garibaldi, Proudhon, Mazzini and BAKUNIN. His own early radical thought grew out of the French enlightenment and French Utopian Socialism. He was also strongly influenced by German idealist philosophy and its more liberal Russian followers, such as STANKEVICH. A leader among the Russian WESTERNERS, his Westernism was characterized by a devotion to the most radical political thought of the West. The disillusionment which attended the failure of the revolution of 1848 and his life in the West cooled his ardor, however, and his socialism subsequently acquired a strong agrarian and Russian nationalist tinge. Like the later POPULISTS, he came to regard Russia as a primarily agrarian country, in which socialism would develop out of existing peasant communal institutions. Thus, though far more radical, his thought tended to approach that of the Russian SLAVOPHILES.

Herzen's philosophy had its roots in Schelling and Hegel. But he was too sceptical and positivistically inclined to persist in the German idealist tradition for long. Embittered by the personal tragedies of his life, he developed a philosophy of history in which an important role was played by chance. History became for him a kind of "improvisation" of events. But he did not lose heart for the future, though he no longer saw it as the necessary product of a rational historical process. In the will and creative freedom of the individual he, like BELINSKI, saw the possibility for human progress.

Herzen's writings are significant not only as historical records of the European revolutionary movement, but as works enlightened by a keen understanding and an objective point of view on people and history. He had great literary gifts, and even his philosophical and publicist works are eloquent and animated. His early novel, *Who Is at Fault?* (1841-46), is of lesser importance, though it was one of the most popular books of the 1840's. It is Herzen's contribution to the series of novels about SUPERFLUOUS MEN, and presents a liberal hero who returns from his studies abroad to find Russian provincial society petty and vulgar. He fails to make a successful career, and in the end goes abroad again, more disillusioned than ever.

Herzen's literary reputation rests chiefly on a volume of political articles, *From the Other Shore* (1847-50), and his memoirs, *My Past and Thoughts* (1855). The first is a critique of the revolutionary movement of 1848, which Herzen saw as a failure because of the over-optimism of the revolutionaries and their lack of realistic thinking. In it he expressed his new-found disillusionment with the West. *My Past and Thoughts* is an autobiography, but it is also much more; it is a brilliant picture of Russian intellectual life in the 1840's, as well as of the European revolutionary movement, with a broad and sweeping manner and a wealth of characters.

Herzen's influence on Russian political thought was great. The Russian POPULISTS were to a large extent his followers, and after them the Socialist Revolutionary Party of the early twentieth century. He is perhaps the most honored and respected (by Russians of all political persuasions) of all nineteenth-century political thinkers.

Hilarion. See Ilarion.

Hippius, Zinaida Nikolayevna (1867-1945), a symbolist poet. She married D. S. MEREZHKOVSKI in 1890, and was associated with him in his activity in the Religious and Philosophical Society, though she did not always share his mysticism. Like him she became a revolutionist in 1905, and after 1917 an intransigent anti-Bolshevik. She even succeeded in publishing a volume of anti-Bolshevik verse in Russia soon after the October Revolution. In 1919 she and her husband emigrated.

Hippius' poetry shows a morbid preoccupation with her ego, and is full of feelings such as guilt and self-disgust. Her best-known poem, *Psyche*, expresses her loathing for her own complicated and ambivalent personality. Like Sologub (see Teternikov), she strikes a decadent pose of Satanism and worship of evil. Her use of complex psychological analysis, tendency toward morbid introspection and feelings of duality all suggest their relation to the novels of DOSTOYEVSKI. Her poetry shows great wit and intellectual brilliance, and is technically on a high level, though it tends to be too cold and rational. An important part of her poetic production consists of witty and biting political verses, whether pro-radical or anti-Bolshevik. Her prose includes a number of stories and several plays and novels. These are influenced by DOSTOYEVSKI, with attempts to give deep psychological analysis and to portray abstract ideas. Her play, *The Green Ring* (1914), deals with the problems of a young generation which feels spiritually lost.

Hippius also published brilliant and unconventional essays in literary criticism under the pseudonym of Anton Krayni ("extreme"). Between 1905 and 1917 she conducted a salon in Petersburg which became a meeting place for the younger symbolists. She has left reminiscences of BRYUSOV, Sologub (see Teternikov) and BLOK in her collection called *Living Faces* (1925).

Hoffman, Viktor Viktorovich (1884-1911), a minor poet of the early twentieth century. Melancholy and neurotic, he committed suicide in 1911. His poetry, which was very popular in his day, expresses the nostalgia of a decadent of the city for return to nature and the country.

I

Ia- (names beginning in). See under **Ya-**.

Ideynost, or "ideological expression," along with *PARTIYNOST* and *NARODNOST,* one of the requirements demanded from literature under SOCIALIST REALISM. According to Soviet critics, literature must embody ideas, and, in particular, political and social ideas of a progressive character. They deny value to literature which lacks ideological content, which is pure narrative or which seeks only to entertain. (See Criticism, Soviet.)

Igor Tale, or **Tale of Igor's Campaign,** the greatest work of Old Russian literature. It describes a campaign undertaken by Prince Igor Svyatoslavich of Novgorod-Seversk against the nomad Polovcians in 1185. According to the tale, Igor's pride leads him to undertake the campaign without sufficient preparation. His forces are almost annihilated, and he is taken prisoner. Later he escapes and returns to Russia.

The *Igor Tale* was composed within two years after the events which it describes, judging by internal evidence. The author is anonymous. He may have been a noble or a member of a princely retinue, but there is little reason to suppose that he necessarily took part in the campaign, as is sometimes claimed. His point of view is secular, and he uses pagan references as part of an elaborate system of symbols. It is unlikely, however, that he believed in the pagan gods whom he mentions. His extensive use of pagan references is unparalleled in Old Russian literature, generally dominated by a strict Church point of view.

The *Igor Tale* is a summons to the Russian princes to settle their differences and unite in resistance to the Polovcians before it would be too late. As such, the work served as a gloomy prophecy of coming doom; in 1223, four decades later, the Russians were first defeated by the Tartars, another nomad people from the east.

The *Igor Tale* has often been compared to the epics of Western Europe, such as the *Nibelungenlied* and *Beowulf*. Though artistically on a level with these, the tale is not purely epic, but contains many lyrical and oratorical passages, even stylistic elements which suggest that it is a kind of political pamphlet. The author refers to his work as an address *(slovo)*, a tale *(povest)*, and a song *(pesn)*, showing that it is a mixture of these genres, and as such highly original. It is also shorter than the Western European epics, and has relatively meagre action, but much lyrical treatment of moods and emotions which events produce in the author and his characters. A constant device is the depiction of nature as alive and emotionally involved in the tale; the forces of nature sympathize either with the Russians or the Polovcians. Nature is also prophetic; an eclipse of 1185 (May 1) foreshadows the Russian defeat.

Scholars have disputed whether the *Igor Tale* is written in prose or in verse. Attempts to discover a regular verse pattern have been unsuccessful, and the form is more probably poetic prose. Both in form and in the style of certain passages, the tale is clearly related, however, to Russian lyric and epic FOLK SONGS. Other sources of influence are the Old Russian CHRONI-CLES, translated historical narratives such as Flavius Josephus' *Jewish War,* and sermons, with their rhetorical and occasionally lyric character (see Literature). Direct influences of works of Byzantine literature, such as the *Chronicle of Manasses*, have also been traced.

The tale opens with a discussion of the style to be followed. The author announces his preference for a more factual style, rather than a highly ornate one. The second part treats the campaign, with the omen of the eclipse, the initial success of a minor action, and the Russians' heroic defense and final defeat on the River Kayala (probably a small river flowing into the Sea of Azov). The third section relates how Prince Svyatoslav of Kiev, Igor's cousin and his senior, hears of his defeat; Svyatoslav expresses the author's conviction that Igor should have united with the other princes before undertaking such a campaign. The fourth section contains a series of apostrophes to other Russian princes of the times. It ends with a curious digression treating the career of the dead Prince Vseslav of Polotsk, a sorcerer whose magic brings him victory at the expense of the unity and peace of the land. The final section opens with the beautiful lament of Yaroslavna, Igor's wife, for her husband. Her speech contains many elements borrowed from folk literature, especially laments and incantations. After her appeal to the forces of nature to bring back her husband, Igor escapes from captivity and returns to Russia.

The *Igor Tale* survived in a single manuscript of the sixteenth century, discovered in 1795. The manuscript perished in the Moscow fire of 1812, after an edition had been published in 1800, and a second copy prepared. Both the published edition and the copy are faulty, however, and the lack of the older manuscript makes the production of a perfect text difficult, if not impossible. A number of obscure passages are found in the work as we have it. These circumstances, along with the fact that the tale is a relatively unique work in Old Russian literature, have led some to question its authenticity. Today there is almost universal agreement, however, that the tale is authentic. On this question, see the *Zadonshchina,* an early fifteenth-century work influenced by the *Igor Tale.* The *Igor Tale* provided the subject for Borodin's opera, *Prince Igor.* Paraphrases of the *Igor Tale* have been made in modern Russian by the poets ZHUKOVSKI, A. N. MAYKOV and others.

Ilarion, the first Russian to be made Metropolitan of the Russian Church, in 1051. By 1055 he had been replaced; whether he had died or had been ousted is not certain. Ilarion is famous for his *Sermon on the Law and the Grace,* composed between 1037 and 1050, a masterpiece of Old Russian rhetorical art. The author argues that, even though Christianity has come to Russia later than to other lands, the grace of God makes the Russian Church the equal of others. St. Vladimir, the prince who Christianized Russia, is called the "equal of the apostles." Thus Ilarion is apparently calling for the Russian Church's independence from Constantinople. The sermon is also noteworthy for its remarkable use of the Byzantine type of allegorical interpretation of the Scriptures. (See Christianization.)

Ilf, Ilya. See Fainzilberg.

Ilyin, Mikhail Andreyevich (1878-1942), an émigré writer who wrote under the pseudonym of Mikhail Osorgin. He left Russia after the Revolution of 1905. His best-known work is the novel *Sivtsev Vrazhek* (1928; English translation as "Quiet Street"), a picture of peaceful life upset by the terror of the Revolution of 1917. His other novels, such as *An Eye-Witness to History* (1932), and *The Book of Ends* (1935), also concern the Revolution of 1917. His writing is sincere, warm and humanitarian in tone.

Imaginism, a poetic movement organized in 1919. The Imaginists stressed the use of imagery, particularly of the metaphor, as the true basis of poetry. They included YESENIN, Marienhof, Ivnyov, SHERSHENEVICH and Kusikov; the only major poet of the group was Yesenin. They favored free verse forms, and sometimes wrote poems which were little more than catalogs of images, often deliberately designed to shock in that crude and vulgar images were presented in close proximity to exalted ones. As a group the Imaginists, who lived in Moscow, were given to tavern and café life, drunkenness and a rowdiness which they celebrated as "hooliganism." Their Bohemian way of life expressed their disillusion with the Revolution and defiance of the Bolshevik regime, as well as their discontent with the stern conditions of life during the Civil War years. After 1924 the Imaginists fell apart as a group.

Imagists. See Parnassian Poets; Imaginism.

Inber, Vera Mikhaylovna (1890-   ), a Soviet poet. She began to publish in 1911 as a follower of GUMILYOV and Akhmatova (see Gorenko); in the 1920's she joined the group of young poets known as CONSTRUCTIVISTS. Her earlier lyrics, with their strongly feminist mood, gave way during the 1920's to optimistic, frequently humorous poems about the Revolution and Soviet life. The Second World War brought her the inspiration which her earlier work had lacked, and her long narrative poem, *The Pulkovo Meridian* (1942), is one of the finest war poems. It depicts the siege of Leningrad, as does her prose work called *Nearly Three Years, a Leningrad Diary* (1945).

Istomin, Karion (died 1717). A pupil of SIMEON POLOTSKI, he advocated the introduction of a Byzantine-Greek type of enlightenment, rather than a Western one. A successful court poet under both Princess Sophia and PETER THE GREAT, Istomin's leading works were two primers written for Peter's son Alexey, containing many verses, including an acrostic poem on the tsarevich's name.

Iu- (names beginning in). See under Yu-.

Ivan the Terrible (Ivan IV, 1530-84; reigned 1533-84). Famous in history for his repressions of the boyar nobility, as well as for his fits of insane cruelty (which often alternated with terrible remorse), Ivan is also known as a writer of letters. The most famous of these are his two surviving letters to Prince ANDREY KURBSKI, in which he answers Kurbski's charges that he had become a tyrant; Ivan declares that he is the legitimate sovereign and the chosen of God, who does not need to justify his actions, for his subjects are only his slaves. The style of Ivan's letters, especially the first, is egregious for its length and diffuseness, and for its use of the long, rhetorical and repetitious manner popular in Muscovite writing. Ivan's barbed thrusts show a keen sense of irony, however, as when he observes that if Kurbski were really sure of the justice of his cause, he might better have refrained from running away, and have chosen instead a righteous martyrdom at the tsar's hand. Ivan's personality and career are the subjects of literary works by LERMONTOV, A. K. TOLSTOY, A. N. TOLSTOY, and others.

Ivanov, Vsevolod Vyacheslavovich (1895-   ), a Soviet writer. In his youth he wandered about, working at various jobs, including that of circus fakir. He published his first story in 1915. Later he attracted the attention of Gorki, who helped and advised him. He fought in the Civil War in Siberia, at first on the White side (he may have been conscripted by the Whites), and later with the Reds. His war experiences, which included being captured and nearly shot several times, are as fantastic as anything in his tales. In 1920 he came to Petersburg, where he joined the SERAPION BROTHERS.

Ivanov is one of the most typical practitioners of the stylistic tendency popular in the 1920's, known as ORNAMENTALISM. His writing is rich in dialect forms and a frequently ornate, colorful and exotic lyricism. Like Pilnyak (see Vogau) and BABEL, he is fascinated by the passion and violence of the Civil War. In his early stories, such as *Partisans* (1921) and *Armored Train No. 14-69* (1922; later dramatized, 1927), and in the novels

Colored Winds (1922) and *Azure Sands* (1922-23), he describes guerilla fighting in Central Asia and Siberia. He sees the Civil War, with all its carnage and horror, as a cruel and meaningless struggle, in which there is little to choose between the Whites and Reds. Man, as Ivanov depicts him, is the creature of impulse and the plaything of evil forces of nature. His later *Mystery of Mysteries* (1927), a collection of tales of village life, shows much the same primitive conception of human behavior, and highlights the unrestrained sexual freedom of his heroes.

Ivanov was attacked by Soviet critics for his pessimism and failure to accept the Revolution. He attempted to conform, and is today an established Soviet writer. But his later work lacks much of the power and originality of his first collections. *Adventures of a Fakir* (1934-35) is a semi-autobiographical novel based on his colorful experiences in the circus. *The Taking of Berlin* (1945) is a large-scale novel on the Second World War.

Ivanov, Vyacheslav Ivanovich (1866-1949), a symbolist poet. He studied classics and ancient history at the Universities of Moscow and Berlin, where he studied under Theodore Mommsen. Ivanov published his first volume of poems, *Pilot Stars,* in 1903, and was at once recognized as a leading symbolist poet (see Symbolism). His apartment, which was called the "Tower," became the meeting place of the Petersburg symbolists. In 1913 he moved to Moscow, however, and his influence came to an end. In 1921 he was appointed Professor of Greek at the University of Baku. In 1924 he left the Soviet Union on an official mission to Italy. He remained in Italy, where he taught classical studies at several universities, and became a convert to Roman Catholicism.

Ivanov's poetry is dignified, ornate, full of erudite classical references, quotations and scholarly allusions. Linguistically it combines archaisms from Old Church Slavonic with Greek idioms and neologisms borrowed from the modern European languages. It is a poetry of declamation, majestic and solemn, in the tradition of the eighteenth-century odes of DERZHAVIN. Ivanov's chief subject is art, which, in his conception, becomes a form of mystical, collective religious activity. The function of art for him lies in the creation of religious myths. His best collections are *Eros* (1907) and *Cor Ardens* (1911). The later *Winter Sonnets* (1920) are simpler and more human than most of his poetry;

they describe the poet's struggle for existence during the cold and famine of the Civil War.

Ivanov's philosophy originates in Nietzsche's dichotomy of Apollonian and Dionysian temperaments. Dionysus, the god who is slain and resurrected, is identified by Ivanov with Christ. Hence Christianity can be identified, in his view, with Dionysian art, which is frenzied, ecstatic or tragic, and opposed to the Apollonian art of reason and contemplation.

Ivanov's prose writings share the majestic style of his poetry. His critical study, *Dostoyevski* (1932), is unusual in that it stresses the mythic side of that writer's creation.

Ivanov exchanged a curious correspondence with the literary historian GERSHENZON when the two were living in the same rest home for writers in Moscow: *Correspondence between Two Corners* (1921). In these essays Ivanov defends the value of culture and tradition, which Gershenzon hopes Russia has cast off with the Revolution.

Ivanov also translated from Aeschylus, Dante, Novalis, Byron, Nietzsche and many others.

Ivanov-Razumnik. See Scythians.

Ivnyov, Ryurik. See Imaginism.

Izmaylov, Alexander Yefimovich (1779-1831), an early writer of Russian fables characterized by a crude but vigorous style. He is also one of the first modern Russian writers of prose fiction, and produced didactic tales of adventure, noted for their realistic manner.

J

Journals, Literary. *Eighteenth Century.* The first Russian literary and cultural magazine was the *Monthly Compositions, to Serve for Profit and Amusement (Yezhemesyachnye sochineniya, k polze i uveseleniyu sluzhashchie;* 1755-97), edited by the academician Gerhardt Friedrich Müller, and published by the Academy of Sciences. Its models were the Western European journals of the early part of the century, such as *The Tatler* and *The Spectator* of Addison and Steele. SUMAROKOV and other contemporary poets published in this magazine. A wave of private journals, published by poets of the period, followed: Sumarokov's *Industrious Bee* (1759), KHERASKOV's *Profitable Amusement* (1760-62), BOGDANOVICH's *Innocent Exercise* (1763) and others. Sumarokov and his followers did much to develop the standards of Russian taste and lay the foundations for systematic literary criticism.

CATHERINE THE GREAT initiated the short-lived vogue of the satirical journal in 1769, with her *Omnium-Gatherum (Vsyakaya vsyachina).* Her intention was to focus Russian satire on such social vices as provincialism and resistance to enlightenment. But independent satirical journals, and in particular NOVIKOV's *The Drone (Truten;* 1769-70) and *The Painter (Zhivopisets;* 1772-74), sought to create a significant satire which would attack the evils of absolutism and SERFDOM. In 1774, as a result, Catherine suppressed all the satirical journals. Novikov later attempted to revive social satire with a series of journals published after 1781, but in 1792 he was arrested, while KRYLOV's satirical periodical, *The Spectator (Zritel),* founded the same year, was suppressed.

KARAMZIN's short-lived *Moscow Journal* (1791-92) marked the beginnings of the new literary period of SENTIMENTALISM and PRE-ROMANTICISM. Besides Karamzin himself, who published his *Letters of a Russian Traveller* and *Poor Liza* here, the poets DERZHAVIN and DMITRIEV wrote for this magazine.

Early Nineteenth Century (1800-1860). KARAMZIN later founded *The Messenger of Europe (Vestnik Yevropy;* 1802-30), which published the poets ZHUKOVSKI, DERZHAVIN, BATYUSHKOV and VYAZEMSKI; PUSHKIN printed his first poem in this magazine in 1814. It represented the views of the conservative aristocracy, and was the first journal of the nineteenth century to combine literature with discussion of political, economic and social questions; thus it helped to set the pattern for Russian literary journals throughout the century. A leading conservative and nationalist journal was *The Son of the Fatherland (Syn otechestva;* 1812-44; 1847-52), edited by the reactionary N. I. Grech. He was joined in the editorship after 1825 by the notorious Faddey BULGARIN, a careerist who combined journalism and literature with espionage. Liberal journals of the period were shorter lived. *The Polar Star* (1823-25) of BESTUZHEV and RYLEYEV ended with the disastrous failure of the DECEMBRIST MOVEMENT.

The 1820's saw the introduction of Western Romanticist influences in Russia. POLEVOY's *Moscow Telegraph* (1825-34) did much to popularize French literary Romanticism. PUSHKIN, ODOYEVSKI and other poets published in its pages. It was immensely popular, especially among the middle classes. POGODIN's *Moscow Messenger* (1827-30) performed a similar function for German Romanticism.

During the reign of the reactionary Nicholas I (1825-55), CENSORSHIP and official repression made publishing extraordinarily difficult. Open expression of political opinion was well-nigh impossible, and the government insisted that even the right to praise its actions was a presumption on the part of private citizens. Polevoy's journal was suppressed in 1834 for printing a criticism of a chauvinistic historical play by KUKOLNIK which had won court favor. PUSHKIN's repeated requests to found a literary journal were refused until 1836, the year before his death. He then founded *The Contemporary (Sovremennik;* 1836-66), destined to be the most famous journal of the nineteenth century. Under Pushkin's successor, PLETNYOV, the magazine stood for a Romanticist estheticism. A sharp critic of Romanticism, on the other hand, was NADEZHDIN, who called for a literature of greater ideological significance. His journal, *The Telescope* (1831-36), was suppressed for publishing the famous *Philosophical Letter* of CHAADAYEV. On the reactionary side the most popular journal was SENKOVSKI's *Library for Reading* (1834-64), the most widely circulated magazine of the 1840's.

This same decade witnessed the split of the Russian intelligentsia into the two opposed camps of SLAVOPHILES and WESTERNERS. The former published in POGODIN's *The Muscovite* (1841-56), together with such younger writers as OSTROVSKI, GRIGORIEV and PISEMSKI. Pogodin's earlier journal, *The Muscovite Observer* (1835-39), had proved unsuccessful, although such important writers as GOGOL, BARATYNSKI and YAZYKOV had written for it. The leading journal of the WESTERNERS in the 1840's was *The Fatherland Notes (Otechestvennye zapiski;* 1839-84), in which writings by TURGENEV, NEKRASOV and HERZEN appeared. BELINSKI, who had earlier been an editor of NADEZHDIN's *Telescope,* now became the new journal's literary critic. He stood for "naturalism" of depiction and for the expression of social consciousness in literature; thus he established the "civic" trend later so powerful in Russian CRITICISM. In 1846 he went over to *The Contemporary,* which NEKRASOV acquired and which now became the chief organ of the Westerners. Such distinguished writers as DOSTOYEVSKI, GONCHAROV, OSTROVSKI, GRIGOROVICH and A. K. TOLSTOY wrote for *The Contemporary;* both TURGENEV and Lev TOLSTOY published their first works in its pages. But between 1858 and 1861 a split took place between the liberal and radical writers of the journal, and both Tolstoys, Turgenev, Goncharov, Ostrovski and Grigorovich left *The Contemporary* (Dostoyevski had meanwhile been sent to Siberia). Most of these writers now went over to KATKOV's *Russian Messenger (Russki Vestnik;* 1856-1906). At first this journal represented the views of the liberal landowners; during the 1860's, however, Katkov became a sharp reactionary. In spite of the fact that he sometimes dictated reactionary changes to his writers, Katkov's *Russian Messenger* was the most brilliant of all Russian literary journals: it carried TURGENEV's *Fathers and Children,* the first part of TOLSTOY's *War and Peace* and the whole of *Anna Karenina,* and DOSTOYEVSKI's *Crime and Punishment, The Idiot, The Devils* and *The Brothers Karamazov.* LESKOV, PISEMSKI and OSTROVSKI also published in its pages.

With the defection of the liberals, NEKRASOV's *Contemporary* became the journal of the young radical generation, and as such perhaps the most widely read magazine of the 1860's. It published the literary criticism of CHERNYSHEVSKI and DOBROLYUBOV, followers of BELINSKI; another of its editors was the great satirist, SALTYKOV.

1860-1917. The 1860's saw a considerable increase in the Russian reading public, and the emergence of large-scale journalism in the modern sense. The attempt on the life of Alexander II in 1866 brought the suppression of several radical magazines, *The Contemporary* and PISAREV's "nihilist" *Russian Word* (1859-66). But the revision of CENSORSHIP regulations in 1865, though it did not protect editors against government repressions, largely did away with preliminary censorship and thus made the practice of journalism easier. Political and social satire, which had almost vanished after the eighteenth century, returned around the middle of the nineteenth century and became a permanent feature of Russian journalism.

In 1861 DOSTOYEVSKI founded his journal, *Time (Vremya),* with his brother Mikhail. It was the organ of the so-called *pochvenniki,* including GRIGORIEV, STRAKHOV and Dostoyevski himself. They stood for the development of an original and independent Russian culture according to indigenous traditions. *Time* was suppressed in 1863 because of official misinterpretation of an article it carried on the Polish Uprising. Dostoyevski's second journal, *The Epoch* (1864-65), failed to win the same success.

After the closing of *The Contemporary,* NEKRASOV and SALTYKOV took over *The Fatherland Notes* in 1868. In the 1870's this journal became the chief organ of the POPULISTS; besides MIKHAYLOVSKI, one of its editors, such writers as Gleb USPENSKI, ZLATOVRATSKI, GARSHIN, NADSON and BOBORYKIN published in it. Another Populist journal was *Russian Wealth (Russkoye bogatstvo;* 1876-1918), in which MIKHAYLOVSKI and KOROLENKO played leading roles after 1895. Gorki's early story, *Chelkash,* was published here (see Peshkov). In the twentieth century it took a moderate (National Socialist), anti-

Marxist point of view until it was closed in 1918. In 1884 the government suppressed the Populist *Fatherland Notes* because of its evident connection with the radical terrorists. The Populists then went over to *Russian Thought (Russkaya mysl;* 1880-1918), one of the most popular journals of the period. Beginning with 1905 it was edited by STRUVE, who by then had deserted his earlier Marxist position, as the journal of the liberal Constitutional Democratic Party. After 1918 Struve continued to publish it in Prague. It printed works by LESKOV, GARSHIN, CHEKHOV, KOROLENKO, MAMIN and ERTEL.

The leading journal of the middle-of-the-road liberals was the new *Messenger of Europe (Vestnik Yevropy;* 1866-1918). It tolerated a wide latitude of ideological expression, and published the radical satire of SALTYKOV as well as the mystical religious philosophy of Vladimir SOLOVYOV. TURGENEV, GONCHAROV and BOBORYKIN also published in this journal.

The last decades of the century saw the development of large popular magazines, often illustrated. The most successful of these was *The Field (Niva;* 1870-1918), which published works by LESKOV, FET and Lev TOLSTOY.

The appearance of "modernist" literary trends at the end of the century, particularly SYMBOLISM, brought new literary magazines to the fore. In the 1890's *The Northern Messenger (Severny vestnik;* 1885-97) published the critical articles of Volynski (see Flexer) in defense of the new literature, as well as such Symbolists as BALMONT, MEREZHKOVSKI and Sologub (see Teternikov). *The World of Art (Mir iskusstva;* 1898-1904), founded by the wealthy dilettante Sergey Dyagilev (Diaghilev), published Balmont, Merezhkovski, Sologub, BRYUSOV and HIPPIUS. The Merezhkovskis also founded their own journal, *The New Way (Novy put;* 1903-04), primarily religious in interest. The most significant of the Symbolist journals was *The Scales (Vesy;* 1904-09), supported by BRYUSOV. It published almost all the Symbolist writers.

The revolutionary years 1905-06 saw the birth of a great number of little magazines. Most of these specialized in political satire, and between 1905 and 1908 over four hundred humorous magazines existed in Russia. Almost all of them were closed down at once by the government. The most famous of these magazines, *The Satyricon* (1908-17), produced a small school of humorous writers: AVERCHENKO, Sasha Chorny (see Glikberg) and Teffi (see Buchinskaya). The poet MAYAKOVSKI published here for a brief period.

The first Social Democratic (Marxist) journal was *The New Word,* founded in 1894 by liberals and Populists. It passed into the hands of the Social Democrats in 1897, but was suppressed by the end of that year. LENIN, PLEKHANOV and STRUVE wrote for this journal, as did Gorki. There followed a series of short-lived magazines, the most important of which was the "idealist-Marxist" journal, *God's World (Mir bozhi;* 1892-1906), which took a more moderate position. In its publication STRUVE and BERDYAYEV played important roles; writers for the journal included ANDREYEV, BUNIN, KUPRIN, ARTSYBASHEV and MAMIN. Gorki's *Annals (Letopis;* 1915-17) was important for its pacifist stand during the war. The young MAYAKOVSKI and BABEL published here.

Soviet Literary Journals. In 1918 and 1919 most independent "bourgeois" journals were liquidated, though several small ones continued to exist until the mid-1920's. During the 1920's a few new independent journals were also founded, including those of such non-conformist literary groupings as the IMAGINISTS. But more and more during the 1920's, the publication of journals became a monopoly of the Communist Party, or of officially sponsored organizations and agencies.

The first official journals (of which there was a large number), such as those of the PROLETKULT, or LUNACHARSKI's *Creation (Tvorchestvo;* 1918-20), encountered organizational or ideological difficulties, and soon ceased publication. *Red Virgin Soil (Krasnaya nov;* 1921-42), founded at Gorki's incentive by the critic VORONSKI, fared better. It published such leading Soviet writers as Gorki, MAYAKOVSKI, LEONOV, GLADKOV, A. N. TOLSTOY, FEDIN, FADEYEV and V. KATAYEV. In the mid-1920's it was controlled by Voronski and the PEREVAL group, whose views on literature were more liberal than those of other Marxist journals. In 1934 it became an organ of the UNION OF SOVIET WRITERS.

The so-called "proletarian" writers, who agitated for official recognition from the Party (see October, RAPP), founded their monthly, *October*, in 1924. Since 1932 this journal has been published by the Union of Soviet Writers, and today it is the leading literary magazine in the Soviet Union. FADEYEV, SHOLOKHOV and GLADKOV have published in its pages, among many others. *On Guard (Na postu;* 1923-25) and *On Literary Guard (Na literaturnom postu;* 1926-32) were proletarian journals which called vehemently for the suppression of independent opinion in literature. But the Party, anxious to reconcile dissident intellectuals, rejected such demands for a time as too leftist, and only with the triumph of RAPP in 1929 did the proletarian writers gain the upper hand. Another "deviationist" Marxist journal of the 1920's was Polonski's *Press and Revolution (Pechat i revolutsiya;* 1921-30). Polonski followed TROTSKI's view of the impossibility of creating a proletarian literature; he also opposed the officially accepted doctrine of "social command" as the only proper source for the writer's literary inspiration. *Lef* ("Left Front"; 1923-25) was the journal of Soviet Futurists; it also sought official recognition for its views (see Futurism). Unable to gain this, it ceased publication in 1925. *The New Lef* (1927-28) likewise failed to win Party acceptance. MAYAKOVSKI, and later ASEYEV and TRETIAKOV were editors of these journals.

Though founded by the Association of Proletarian Writers of Leningrad, *The Star (Zvezda;* 1924-   ) had a somewhat broader character, and Formalists (see Criticism) and other non-proletarian writers took part during the 1920's. LIBEDINSKI, FEDIN, TYNYANOV, FADEYEV and A. N. TOLSTOY have published in this journal.

The official literary journal of the Communist Party was *The New World* (1925-   ). Gorki, A. N. TOLSTOY, LEONOV, SHOLOKHOV, FEDIN and others have published in its pages. Since 1947 it has been published by the Union of Soviet Writers.

The victory of RAPP and the proletarian writers at the outset of the First Five-year Plan in 1929 brought the reorganization of contending literary groups and their magazines (see Literature, Soviet). But the rule of RAPP was itself short-lived. The decree of the Central Committee of the Communist Party of April 23, 1932, liquidated all existing literary organizations, including RAPP, and created a single UNION OF SOVIET WRITERS.

This put an end to the last vestiges of independence in Soviet literary organizations and their periodicals.

Besides *Red Virgin Soil* and *October*, described above, which now became the major organs of the Union, several new literary journals were founded. *The Banner (Znamya;* 1931-) specializes in the publication of stories and articles on national defense and the war; EHRENBURG, SIMONOV, PANOVA and others have printed works here. *The Literary Gazette* (1929-) is the professional newspaper of the Union, but actually much of its contents is devoted to political news and propaganda.

In 1946 literature was the first field to be attacked in the postwar wave of official restriction led by ZHDANOV in the arts and sciences. In his famous report, passed on August 14 by the Party Central Committee, Zhdanov attacked the two Leningrad journals, *The Star (Zvezda)* and *Leningrad*. Their principal "sin" was the publication of works by ZOSHCHENKO and Akhmatova (see Gorenko), whose expulsion from the Union of Soviet Writers Zhdanov now demanded. Zhdanov insisted on the reorganization of the editorial board of *The Star* and the complete suppression of *Leningrad*. These measures were immediately carried out.

K

K.R. See Romanov, K. K.

Kamenev, Gavriil Petrovich (1772-1803), a minor poet of the end of the eighteenth century, member of the school of KARAMZIN. Influenced by German and English poetry, including Ossian (Macpherson) and Edward Young, his *Gromval* (1804), a chivalric narrative in verse, has been called the first work of Russian ROMANTICISM.

Kamenski, Anatoli Pavlovich (1877-   ), a writer of the early twentieth century. His three volumes of stories, published between 1907 and 1910, deal with the subject of free love, and are closer to pornography than literature.

Kampov, Boris Nikolayevich (1908-   ), a Soviet novelist and journalist who writes under the pseudonym of Boris Polevoy. His best-known novel, *The Tale of a Real Man* (1946), concerns the war exploits of A. P. Marasiev, a daring Soviet pilot of World War II. The book has been one of the war novels most praised by Soviet critics.

Kantemir, Prince Antioch Dmitrievich (1708-44), often regarded as the founder of modern Russian literature. His father, Prince of Moldavia, fled to Russia after his failure to free that land from Turkish rule. The son received a brilliant education, and in 1732 was sent to London as the Russian ambassador, and in 1738 to Paris, where he remained until his death. Here he met French writers and underwent French literary influence.

Kantemir was an enthusiastic supporter of the reforms of PETER THE GREAT, and championed them in his writings. His chief works are nine satires, written 1729-39, first published in French translation in 1749, after his death. The Russian text was published only in 1762, though the satires had been widely circulated in manuscript. They are composed in syllabic verse (see Prosody) and according to the classical models of Horace, Boileau and others. Their principal targets are the foes of Russian enlightenment and those reactionaries who sought to undo Peter's work after his death: barbarous landowners, ignorant clergy, and foppish nobles who adopted a mere surface veneer of European culture. Kantemir contrasted Peter's conception of a nobility based on service to the older boyar concept of nobility by lineage. His language is vigorous and colloquial, and he avoids the use of archaic Slavonicisms (see Old Church Slavonic), but he failed to create a satisfactory new style, and his choice of language is often crude. His characters, though somewhat distorted in the mold of classical tradition, are alive and even distinctly Russian.

Kantemir is usually considered the first writer of the Russian pseudo-classical tradition, which was to dominate the literature of the entire eighteenth century (see Classicism). He translated works by Fontenelle, Montesquieu, Horace and Anacreon. He also began an uncompleted epic poem on PETER THE GREAT. At the end of his life he opposed the introduction of tonic verse by TREDIAKOVSKI and LOMONOSOV (see Prosody).

Kapnist, Vasili Vasilyevich (1757-1823), a poet of the eighteenth century, friend and brother-in-law of DERZHAVIN. He wrote lighter odes in the Horatian manner, as well as several satires, including one on serfdom, which he was not permitted to publish. His most famous work is a satirical comedy in verse, *Chicane* (1798), a savage attack on the dishonesty of judges and court officials.

Karamzin, Nikolay Mikhaylovich (1766-1826), a leading writer and historian of the late eighteenth and early nineteenth century. Born in a family of provincial gentry. Karamzin was educated in Moscow, where he came under the influence of NOVIKOV and contributed to the latter's publications. In 1789-90 he travelled in Western Europe. He returned to Russia and founded a new monthly review, *The Moscow Journal* (1791-92), in which he published his impressions of his trip abroad as *Letters of a Russian Traveller*. In 1802 he founded a new journal, *The Messenger of Europe*. He soon gave up literary work, however, for research in Russian history, and in 1816-18 published his eight-volume *History of the Russian State*. He was the intimate friend of the Emperor Alexander I; like Alexander, he was a liberal in his youth, but became increasingly conservative and absolutist in old age.

In literature Karamazin is noted for his reform of the Russian literary language and for his introduction of the new Western literary current of SENTIMENTALISM. He sought to bring the literary LANGUAGE closer to spoken Russian, particularly to the speech of the aristocracy. He excluded archaic Slavonicisms (see Old Church Slavonic); at the same time he introduced many new words, particularly abstractions, from Western European languages, and especially from French. Many of these were calques—new compounds formed by substituting several Russian or Slavonic roots for their Western European equivalents. Most of the neologisms which he introduced persisted, in spite of the opposition of Admiral SHISHKOV and the "Slavonic" party, who were opposed to Western influence on the Russian language. Though Karamzin's language was more tasteful and elegant than that used by eighteenth-century writers, and was more unified and consistent, his reform was by no means an unmixed blessing. Since court speech was taken as a model, the new style tended to be too soft and refined. It also limited possibilities for expression, since, by excluding both archaisms and vulgarisms, Karamzin in effect reduced LOMONOSOV's system of three styles to a single one: a middle style. His reform also increased the gap between the language of the upper and lower classes. Karamzin's innovations were most exaggerated in his youth; in his later writings, and especially in his *History*, he rejected many of his more extravagant borrowings, and even reinstated the archaic Slavonic element to a limited extent. Karamzin's language served as the basis for the poetic language of most of the poets who followed him, some of whom joined in a society, ARZAMAS, to support his reforms and oppose the views of SHISHKOV. These poets, especially PUSHKIN, preserved the elegance and flexibility of Karamzin's language, but gave it a vigor and colloquial ease which it had lacked. In this modified form Karamzin's language became the basis for the standard literary language of the nineteenth century, as well as for the spoken language of the intelligentsia.

Karamzin's cultivated style accorded with his general view of literature as a medium for the expression of elegant and noble feelings. Influenced by such Western writers as Rousseau, Sterne, Goldsmith, Macpherson, Kleist and others, Karamzin introduced the literary cult of sensibility into Russia. Interest in landscape, exaltation of personal feelings (as opposed to the classical cult of reason), tenderness in personal relations and sympathy for misfortune were important traits of the new school. Known as SENTIMENTALISM, the new writing was in fact often guilty of excessive sentimentality. Still, as a transitional step toward ROMANTICISM, it served as a healthy corrective to the cold, impersonal CLASSICISM previously dominant in Russia, which had outlived its day.

Karamzin provided models for Russian sentimentalist writing in his *Letters of a Russian Traveller* (1792) and in his tales. The first are elegant and polished reflections of his travels in Western Europe; they do not so much describe as mirror the author's emotions and feelings. Of the tales the most important is *Poor Liza* (1792), the story of a peasant girl who, deserted by the lover who had seduced her, commits suicide. The success of the story was such that the pond in which Liza had supposedly drowned herself became a favorite place of pilgrimage for the citizens of Moscow. Karamzin also wrote several historical tales. His poetry is important for its use of new meters and for its somewhat greater freedom of lyric expression.

Karamzin's *History of the Russian State* is his greatest work. Though pro-autocratic in ideology, and concerned largely with the actions of Russian sovereigns rather than with the people, it was strikingly dramatic, and written in an eloquent, dignified style. The first history of Russia to be read widely, it played a great role in the rising wave of Russian national feeling which developed after the Napoleonic Wars.

Kareyev, Nikolay Ivanovich (1850-1931), a historian and philosopher of the late nineteenth century. He was a critic of Hegel's philosophy of history, arguing that the notion of chance must be introduced into history; history for him is "a chaotic concatenation of chances." The significance of historical events lies not in their adherence to an absolute pattern, in his view, but in their relativistic significance for man. The individual for him is significant and fundamental in the historical process. Kareyev was the first Russian philosopher to take Lev TOLSTOY's philosophy of history seriously and to give a systematic criticism of Tolstoy's views. (See Philosophy.)

Katayev, Valentin Petrovich (1897-), a Soviet writer. The son of a high-school teacher of Odessa, he began to write poetry very early as a follower of Ivan BUNIN, whom he knew personally. He served as a soldier in the First World War. During the Civil War he was arrested and imprisoned by both sides at different times. In 1922 he began to devote himself to fiction. An optimistic writer with a flair for humor, Katayev has been one of the most popular of Soviet authors. His first novels and stories were tales of adventure, or lyrical character portraits such as *The Father* (1925), the study of a loving and conscientious father whose son finally deserts him.

The *Embezzlers* (1926) is a picaresque novel about two bank officials who embezzle funds and squander them in a merry pleasure trip over Russia, on which they meet strange people and have all sorts of adventures. In the end they give themselves up to justice. Though light-hearted, the subject is a reflection of the decline in socialist "morality" typical of the time of the New Economic Policy.

Katayev's *Time, Forward!* (1932) is one of the best Five-year Plan novels. It deals with the construction of the Magnitogorsk chemical combine. The book celebrates the increase in work tempos, exemplified by a brigade's successful attempt to break the world's record for pouring concrete. The hero of the novel is the entire brigade. Katayev has succeeded in giving the novel a feeling of climactic excitement and a vivid, cinematographic quality. The work's ideological significance seems to lie in its discovery of a natural enthusiasm for machines and technology among the Russian people; Americans, on the other hand, once world leaders in technology, are portrayed as already tired of their superiority.

Lonely White Sail (1936; also translated as "Peace Is Where the Tempests Blow") is a lyrical picture of the childhood of two boys in Odessa, set against the background of the REVOLUTION of 1905. The same boys, grown to manhood, appear in Katayev's most recent novel, *For the Power of the Soviets* (1949), about the partisan movement in Odessa during World War II. The book brought strong denunciation of the author for "neglecting" the role of the Communist Party in underground resistance.

Katayev has been a successful playwright. His *Squaring the Circle* (1928) has been one of the most popular Soviet comedies. It deals humorously with a situation produced by the relaxation of the Soviet divorce laws in the 1920's: two couples who share the same room find themselves mismated and solve their difficulties by exchanging partners. The play is a light, farcical comedy, rather than a serious satire. *The Road of Flowers* (1930) has a similar theme.

Katayev, Yevgeni Petrovich (1903-42), the younger brother of Valentin KATAYEV, who wrote under the pseudonym of Yevgeni Petrov. All his significant work as a humorist and satirist was written in collaboration with Ilya Ilf (see Fainzilberg). In 1937 the collaboration ended with the death of Ilf, while Petrov was killed in 1942 in the siege of Sevastopol.

Katenin, Pavel Alexandrovich (1792-1853), a pre-romanticist Russian poet of the early nineteenth century, especially noted for his ballads. He belonged to the literary camp of the archaists led by SHISHKOV, and attempted to make his ballads Russian by using realistic details of questionable taste. Thus he opposed the (in his view) too cloying ballads of ZHUKOVSKI, which were translated or adapted from foreign sources. Though PUSHKIN valued his work highly, he has almost been forgotten.

Katkov, Mikhail Nikiforovich (1818-87), a publisher and journalist of the second half of the nineteenth century. Though he had been a moderate liberal in his youth, by the 1860's Katkov had become more reactionary in many of his views than the government itself. He opposed certain of the REFORMS of Alexander II, including the establishment of the Zemstvos, and the introduction of trial by jury. Together with his journal, *The Russian Herald,* Katkov's name became a synonym for reaction in Russian literary and political history.

Katyryov-Rostovski, Prince I. M., supposed author of a history of the "Time of the Troubles," a disturbed period early in the seventeenth century. The work was written in 1626, and is interesting for its inclusion of passages composed in the so-called pre-syllabic verse (see Prosody).

Kavelin, Konstantin Dmitrievich (1818-85), a philosopher of the second half of the nineteenth century. The pupil of BELINSKI, he was a member of the conservative wing of Russian WESTERNERS. He advocated a moderate positivism: mind for him is relatively independent of material reality, though he fails to develop any precise relation between the two. He is confident of the power of science and of psychology to provide a basis for the solution of the problems of being and for the construction of a system of scientific ethics.

Kaverin, Veniamin. See Zilberg, V. A.

Kazin, Vasili Vasilievich (1898-), a leading member of the Moscow SMITHY POETS. A follower of YESENIN, he differed from most of the other Smithy Poets in his dislike for the city and the new industrialization. His chief subject, aside from the village, is the joy of physical labor freed from exploitation and enslavement.

Khemnitser, Ivan Ivanovich (1745-84), the first Russian fabulist of note. His *Fables* (1779) are less crude and more original than the earlier ones of SUMAROKOV, and are notable for their use of colloquial style.

Kheraskov, Mikhail Matveyevich (1733-1807). An eighteenth-century writer and follower of SUMAROKOV, Kheraskov was the son of a Wallachian noble who had settled in Russia. Educated in cadet school, he became an official of the newly founded Moscow University in 1755, and in 1763 its director. He was a prolific writer, who cultivated all the recognized literary genres of the day (see Classicism). He is remembered chiefly for his two epic poems, the first Russian works in this form. Modelled on Voltaire's *Henriade,* they are the *Rossiada* ("Russian Epic"; 1779), which depicts the taking of Kazan in 1552, and *Vladimir Reborn* (1785), concerned with the introduction of Christianity in Russia. Both are attempts to create a national epos, while *Vladimir* reflects Kheraskov's mystical and pietist sentiments as a Freemason (see Freemasonry). Though called the Russian "Homer" in his own time, Kheraskov is almost completely forgotten today.

Khlebnikov, Viktor (Velemir) Vladimirovich (1885-1922), the chief founder of Russian FUTURISM. He replaced his given name with the Old Slavic surname Velemir. Khlebnikov sought to reform the lexicon of poetry by creating his own original poetic vocabulary. His first "etymological" poem, published in 1910, consisted of nothing but a set of newly invented derivatives of the root *smekh*, "laughter." Under his leadership, the Futurists sought to create a "trans-sense language" *(zaumny yazyk)*, to free words from their meanings, a startling revolution which ultimately threatened to make the pure sound values of language the basis of poetry. Khlebnikov was a gifted etymologist, however, and his linguistic derivations have interest which gives his "trans-sense" poems a certain suggestive quality, whatever their value as poetry.

A mystic with Slavophile leanings, Khlebnikov dreamed of a pan-Russian culture which would combine the cultures of the various minority nationalities of Russia and be free of Western elements.

Khmelnitski, Nikolay Ivanovich (1789-1846), an early nineteenth-century writer of comedies and vaudevilles, most of them translations or adaptations from the French.

Khodasevich, Vladislav Felitsyanovich (1886-1939), a Russian poet of the twentieth century, of Polish origin. He first published in 1908 as a symbolist poet, but his more characteristic work was done after the Revolution of 1917, when he emigrated. His poetry is witty, ironic; it deals with the soul's imprisonment in the world of material reality. His poems, with their sometimes morbid imagery and witty, epigrammatic endings, have been popular with Russian émigrés.

Khomyakov, Alexey Stepanovich (1804-60), a leading Russian poet, philosopher and theologian of the mid-nineteenth century. The descendant of a great noble family, he was educated at the University of Moscow. He served for a time as an officer in the Guards, fighting in the war against Turkey in 1828-29. He retired from the army in 1829, occupying himself with study, writing, polemic disputes, and with the management of his estates.

Khomyakov was one of the leaders of the Russian party of SLAVOPHILES, and much of his poetry is devoted to his conception of Russia's high historical and spiritual mission. His poems inspired by political events, such as the Crimean War, are dignified and eloquent, and among the finest examples of Russian political verse.

Khomyakov is equally noted as a theologian and philosopher of history. He saw man's freedom as attainable only through membership in a greater whole, the Church, without which man lives in impotence and discord, and seeks to subject himself to blind necessity. The opposition of these two poles of freedom and necessity animate all human history. In common with the other SLAVOPHILES, Khomyakov finds true unity and freedom manifest in Russia's history; Russia, though unworthy, has the historical task of redeeming the West from the chains of individualism and materialistic necessity. Khomyakov's theological writings were banned by the Russian Church in his own day, but he has since been accepted as one of its greatest lay theologians, and his work has influenced the great Russian religious thinkers who followed, such as VLADIMIR SOLOVYOV and BERDYAYEV. (See Philosophy.)

Khvorostinin, Prince Ivan Andreyevich (died 1625), author of a *Prologue*, a polemic work against heresy, written shortly before his death. Khvorostinin was exiled to the Kirillo-Belozerski Monastery in 1622 for his sympathies with Roman Catholicism; there he retracted his former non-conformism and was pardoned. His *Prologue*, which contains more than 500 rhymed couplets, is notable for its use of pre-syllabic verse (see Prosody).

Khvylyovy, Mykola (1893-1933), a leading Ukrainian writer (see Preface).

Kievan Literature. See Literature, Old Russian.

Kireyevski, Ivan Vasilyevich (1806-56), a philosopher, critic and journalist of the mid-nineteenth century, one of the leaders of the Russian SLAVOPHILES. He viewed the West as decadent, and criticized it for its overemphasis on reason. Russia's strength he found rather in the faith and feeling characteristic, as he believed, of the Orthodox Church. Hence he saw Russia as destined to become the dominant nation, culturally and spiritually, in the arena of history. (See Philosophy).

Kirill Turovski, Bishop of Turov in Southwest Russia in the second half of the twelfth century, and the author of a number of sermons, prayers and other religious writings. He excelled in the art of panegyric sermons, usually in praise of some Biblical person or event. Kirill indulged in the allegorical interpretation of Scriptures so popular in Old Russia. His description of the resurrection of nature in spring (from his sermon for the First Sunday after Easter) is famous for its poetic imagery; it now appears, however, that it is derived from Byzantine models.

Kirillov, Vladimir Timofeyevich (1889-   ), a leading member of the Moscow SMITHY POETS. His poetry shows the characteristic themes and ideological and stylistic excesses of that group. His poem, *The Iron Messiah* (1921), greets the machine as a new savior of man, while *We* (1921) calls for the destruction of monuments of art and museums, antiquated, in the poet's opinion, by the Revolution.

Kirshon, Vladimir Mikhaylovich (1902-37?), a Soviet playwright. He wrote about contemporary Soviet life. His best-known play, *Bread* (1930), deals with the government's struggle with the *kulaks* (well-to-do peasants) to stop the hoarding of grain. The play also dramatizes the pointed conflict between a disciplined, cold Party member who follows the correct line, and his over-emotional, unbalanced rival whose feelings lead him into error. As a former leader of RAPP, Kirshon was arrested in 1937; his fate is unknown.

Kliment Smolyatich, Metropolitan of Russia from 1147; he was subsequently deposed several times when the Greek clergy in Russia refused to recognize his election. Kliment was celebrated as a philosopher, and his letter to the Presbyter Foma shows that he was familiar with the works of Homer, Plato and Aristotle. This is an evidence that the Greek classic writers were known, at least to an extent, in Old Russia. (See Classicism.)

Klychkov, Sergey. See Leshenkov, S. A.

Klyuyev, Nikolay Alexeyevich (1885-1937), a poet of the early twentieth century. A peasant from the Onega country northeast of Petersburg, Klyuyev was the first representative of the so-called "peasant poets." He astonished the public with the remarkably finished quality of his verse, which he began to publish in 1912. The mystical faith of the Russian peasantry is his principal theme, and his poems are full of the exotic imagery and estheticism of religious ritual. Folklore and popular tradition are other sources of his subjects and images. The conflict between city and village is another of his themes. Klyuyev at first accepted the REVOLUTION of 1917 as a mystical religious achievement of the people which, he believed, would bring a peasant paradise on earth. In his long poem, *Lenin* (1924), he compared the Bolshevik leader to AVVAKUM and the sectarian Old Believers of the seventeenth century. But Klyuyev soon lost his faith in the Soviet regime and its agrarian program, and expressed his disillusionment in such poems as *The Village* (1927) and *Lament for Yesenin* (1927). Finally, it seems, he was arrested and sent to a concentration camp, and apparently died there in 1937. His poetry, popular immediately after the Revolution, was soon condemned by Soviet critics for its *kulak* (well-to-do peasant) ideology. Klyuyev's influence was strong on the more famous peasant poet, YESENIN.

Knyazhnin, Yakov Borisovich (1742-91), an eighteenth-century playwright, the son-in-law and follower of SUMAROKOV. A civil servant, Knyazhnin was degraded to the army ranks for embezzling government funds. He was pardoned in 1777 and reinstated in his former rank, but was compelled to go into retirement.

Knyazhnin wrote comedies, comic operas and tragedies. His comedies, based on French models, are perhaps his best work. He was a revolutionary liberal, extremely critical of Russian absolutism, and his comic opera, *An Accident with a Carriage* (1779), is a witty satire on the institution of serfdom. Most famous is his tragedy, *Vadim of Novgorod*, written after the French Revolution. It idealizes the ancient democratic institutions of the Russian city of Novgorod; its hero, Vadim, kills himself rather than submit to tyrannical rule. Published posthumously in 1793, copies of the play were destroyed by the government, and for a long time it was prohibited on the stage.

Kochkurov, Nikolay Ivanovich (1899-), a Soviet novelist who wrote under the pen-name of Artyom Vesyoly. His novels and stories of the Civil War reflect the influence of Pilnyak (see Vogau), and, like Pilnyak, he is impressed by the violent and destructive sides of the war. His novels, such as *Russia Washed with Blood* (1927-28), have almost no plot, but show the colorful use of SKAZ narration and of ornamentalist techniques (see Ornamentalism). His later *Gulyay-Volga* ("The Sporting Volga," 1934) is a historical novel about the conquest of Siberia by Yermak.

Kokhanovskaya. See Sokhanskaya, N. S.

Kolas, Yakub, pseudonym of K. Mitskevich (1882-), a leading Belo-Russian writer (see Preface).

Koltsov, Alexey Vasilyevich (1809-42), a Russian poet of the 1830's. The son of a cattle dealer, he received little formal education.

His poetry attracted the attention of STANKEVICH, who first published his poems in 1835, and of the critic BELINSKI, whose close friend he became. Koltsov's father was unsympathetic to his poetic career, and forced him into his own business; ultimately he had to give up poetry.

Koltsov's early poems are imitations of PUSHKIN and other established poets of the day, and show little originality. His later "Meditations" on philosophical questions are relatively naive, and also unsuccessful. He is remembered almost entirely for his imitations of Russian folk songs, which in fact represent a kind of synthesis of the folk-song manner and the stylized tradition of "folk-like" songs of DELVIG and others. Still, they strike a truly popular note, and many have survived among the folk itself. They treat such themes as peasant labor, the beauties of farmland and steppe, the joys and sorrows of love, and the hard lot of the peasant woman. Rich in dialect expressions, many are in short, unrhymed lines suggestive of the true folk song, though in the more regular meters of the written poetry of Koltsov's day. Fresh and unsophisticated in their appeal, they have often been compared to the lyrics of Burns. Though such a comparison overlooks vast differences in national psychology, it is just in describing Koltsov's close tie with the people and with the folk song, as well as the simplicity, immediacy and frank emotion of his songs.

Konevskoy, I. See Oreus, I. I.

Korniychuk, Alexander (1905-   ), a Ukrainian Soviet writer (see Preface).

Korolenko, Vladimir Galaktionovich (1853-1921), a writer of the late nineteenth and early twentieth century. Born of mixed Polish and Ukrainian descent, he was at first brought up as a Pole; only after the Polish Uprising of 1863 did his family declare itself Russian. He studied technology and agriculture in Moscow, but was expelled from school for belonging to an organization of the POPU-LISTS. In 1879 he was arrested and exiled, eventually to the Yakut country in northeastern Siberia; only in 1885 was he permitted to return to European Russia and settle at Nizhni Novgorod. He returned to literature (he had already begun to publish shortly before his arrest), and made his first great success with a story called *Makar's Dream* (1885). In 1895 he was permitted to move to Petersburg. At this time he virtually deserted literature, devoting himself to progressive journalism and to exposing the injustices of the police and the courts, as well as defending the rights of persecuted minorities. After the Revolution of 1905 he was energetic in attacking martial law and capital punishment, weapons of government terror in the despotic reaction to the Revolution. He remained in the Soviet Union after the Revolution of 1917, but was bitterly and openly opposed to Bolshevik rule.

Korolenko's best literary work was in the genre of the lyrical tale, with much poetic nature description. Exquisitely lovely are his pictures of the vast Siberian wildernesses, in which he catches the frosty grandeur and dazzling brilliance of the far north. *Makar's Dream* (1885), which has this Siberian setting, is his best and most popular tale. It tells of a poor Yakut who dreams as he dies of cold that he is on his way across the snowy wastes to Yakut "heaven." There he is condemned to be put out for his sins, but he replies eloquently that, poor and crushed by toil, he has never had the time or energy to do good deeds, and this answer tips the scales of justice in his favor. The warm humanitarianism which inspires this story is typical of Korolenko's writing. Many of his tales are about the lower classes: peasants, Siberian exiles, tramps, etc. For the most part they are optimistic, cheerful, often sentimental and full of warm humor. For Korolenko man is essentially good; it is tyranny and exploitation which debase him.

Korolenko's last literary work is the autobiographical account of his early years, called, curiously, *The History of My Contemporary* (1906-22). It depicts important events which he witnessed, such as the Emancipation of the serfs in 1861 and the Polish Uprising of 1863.

Kosmisty. See Smithy Poets.

Kostylyov, Valentin Ivanovich (1884-1950), Soviet novelist. He began to publish as early as 1903, but only in the Soviet period did he achieve popularity. His trilogy, *Ivan the Terrible* (1942-47), was an early attempt in fiction to popularize Ivan and to depict him as a progressive ruler of the Russian people.

Kotlyarevsky, Ivan (1769-1838), a leading Ukrainian writer, the founder of Modern Ukrainian literature (see Preface).

Kot-Murlyka. See Wagner, N. P.

Kotsyubinsky, Mykhaylo (1864-1913), a leading Ukrainian writer (see Preface).

Kozakov, Mikhail Emanuilovich (1897-), a writer of the 1920's. His stories and novels show the influence of DOSTOYEVSKI, and his short novel, *Adameyko the Philistine* (1927), resembles *Crime and Punishment* in that it concerns the murder of a "useless" old woman usurer.

Kozlov, Ivan Ivanovich (1779-1840), a minor poet and contemporary of PUSHKIN. He specialized in the Byronic narrative poem; his principal work was *The Monk* (1825), a tremendously popular tale of evil and redemption which influenced LERMONTOV. Today he is remembered almost entirely for his translations, which include renderings of Thomas Moore's *Evening Bells* and Charles Wolfe's *Burial of Sir John Moore at Corunna.*

Kravchinski, Sergey Mikhaylovich (1851-95), a Russian émigré writer of the late nineteenth century, who published under the pseudonym of S. Stepnyak. A revolutionary terrorist and member of the POPULISTS, he was involved in the murder of General Mezentsov, chief of the political police. He emigrated in 1882, eventually settling in England. *Underground Russia* (1882), originally written in Italian and translated into Russian by the author, is a sensational picture of the Russian revolutionary movement. Kravchinski also wrote a revolutionary novel, *The Career of a Nihilist* (1889), in English. His work gave Western readers a thrilling if not always accurate picture of the Russian revolutionary movement.

Krayni, Anton. See Hippius, Z. N.

Krestovski, Vsevolod Vladimirovich (1840-95), a reactionary writer of the second half of the nineteenth century. His most popular work, *The Dens of St. Petersburg* (1864-67), is a melodramatic novel in the style of Eugene Sue. Terroristic NIHILISTS constitute the villains of his sensational fiction.

Kropotkin, Prince Pyotr Alexeyevich (1842-1921), a Russian philosopher of the late nineteenth and early twentieth century, a leader of the political movement of anarchism. In his youth he served as an army officer, and took part in several important geographical survey expeditions to the Far East. In 1872 he visited Switzerland, where he joined the Russian anarchist party led by BAKUNIN. Returning to Russia, he was arrested in 1876 and imprisoned, but escaped to Western Europe two years later. He was again imprisoned in France in 1883, for three years. After 1886 he settled near London. He returned to Russia after the February Revolution of 1917, supporting the Kerenski Government, but took no part in political events.

Kropotkin attempted to develop a scientific foundation for anarchist theory. Law for him is the consequence of man's tendency to oppress his fellows; it is nourished by violence and superstition. Society was first governed only by custom and spontaneous agreement, in his opinion. Kropotkin brings evidence from the animal world to show that those species which practice mutual aid multiply more rapidly than others. Capitalism, in his view, cannot achieve full productivity, for it aims at maximum profits, not at production for human needs. Manual labor should be the obligation of all persons, even intellectuals, who should contribute it voluntarily. Economic goods should be distributed according to individual needs, of which each man should have the right to judge for himself.

Kruchonykh, Alexey Yeliseyevich (1886-   ), a poet and member of the Cubo-Futurists (see Futurism). Along with KHLEBNIKOV, Kruchonykh developed so-called "trans-sense language" (*zaumny yazyk*), in which the lexicon of poetry, even of each poem, became a new and original creation of invented words. Kruchonykh had a weaker sense of etymology than Khlebnikov, and his word coinages are of interest for the most part only as curiosities.

Krylov, Ivan Andreyevich (ca. 1769-1844), the leading Russian writer of fables. The son of a poor army officer, Krylov entered the civil service when still a boy. Transferred to St. Petersburg in 1783, he began a literary career, writing comedies and comic operas and editing several magazines, the second of which was soon closed down by the government for its satirical attacks. From 1793 to 1805 Krylov virtually disappeared from literature. During this period he worked as a secretary, tutor, and "parasite" for several families, even as a professional card player. He subsequently returned to the drama, writing several popular comedies which satirized the prevalent Gallomania. But he had already discovered his real talent in his fables, the first edition of which appeared in 1809, and which proved tremendously popular. In 1816 he was given the comfortable post of librarian in the St. Petersburg Public Library, where he remained until his retirement in 1841. Indolent and self-satisfied, his subsequent literary production was extremely small, and he sometimes produced no more than two or three fables a year.

Krylov's fables are the Russian classics in this genre, and have replaced those of the eighteenth-century fabulists in popularity. Of his several hundred fables, some are translations or adaptations from La Fontaine, Aesop and others, but the great majority are original, and completely Russian in their style and characterizations. They represent a common-sense, practical, hard-headed philosophy of life; the vices satirized are corruption, stupidity, ineptitude and even ambition. Some are veiled social or political satire, but from a strongly conservative point of view. They are humorous, picturesque, racy and popular rather than elegant. Krylov used a poetic line of varying lengths, and this freedom, slightly reminiscent of the Russian folk song, was well suited to the popular manner of his verse. An outstanding innovation is his use of language. Though somewhat archaic, it was popular and colloquial in style, far closer to average Russian speech than either the dignified manner of eighteenth-century poetry or the elegant new language of KARAMZIN. A gift for natural, easy statement makes his lines eminently quotable, and many of them have become popular proverbs.

Krymov, Yuri. See Beklemishev, Yu. S.

Küchelbecker, Wilhelm Karlovich (1797-1846), a poet of the 1820's. Of Russianized German parentage, Küchelbecker was sent to the lycée established for children of the nobility at Tsarskoye Selo. There he met PUSHKIN, whose close friend he became, though he never came under Pushkin's influence. He took part in the Decembrist Uprising of 1825 (see Decembrist Movement), for which he spent ten years in prison and the last ten years of his life in Siberian exile.

An early romanticist and follower of ZHUKOVSKI in the task of introducing the German romanticist poets in Russia, Küchelbecker turned more and more to Classicism, and joined the party of the literary conservatives, led by SHISHKOV. He took the poet DERZHAVIN for his model, and called for a revival of the classical ode. He described himself as a "romantic in classicism." This inconsistency made his poetry strange and even ridiculous for his contemporaries, and it is rarely successful. He was more significant as a literary critic and theoretician, if one whose influence was largely abortive, than as a poet.

Kukolnik, Nestor Vasilyevich (1809-68), a Russian playwright of the mid-nineteenth century. The author of romantic plays in blank verse in the style of Schiller, Kukolnik was tremendously popular in his day, especially among the less-discriminating theater-going public. His plays, such as *Torquato Tasso* (1833), were unrestrained in their emotionalism and highly rhetorical. Some of them, such as *The Hand of the Almighty Saved the Fatherland* (1834), about the founding of the Romanov dynasty, followed an obsequious patriotic and nationalistic line.

Kulish, Mykola (1892-?), a leading Ukrainian writer (see Preface).

Kulish, Panko (1819-97), a leading Ukrainian writer and critic (see Preface).

Kupala, Yanka, pseudonym of I. Lutsevich (1882-1942), a leading Belo-Russian writer (see Preface).

Kuprin, Alexander Ivanovich (1870-1938), a leading novelist and story writer of the early twentieth century. He was educated in cadet school, and served for several years as an army officer. After retiring from the army, he wandered about from one job to another. The many colorful professions in which he worked gave him material for his stories. His first great success came with the publication of a novel on army life, *The Duel* (1905).

After the 1917 Revolution Kuprin emigrated from the Soviet Union, settling in Paris. Emigration apparently destroyed his talent, and his writings abroad are negligible. His health broke, and in 1937 he accepted the Soviet government's invitation to return to Russia, where he died a year later of cancer.

Kuprin's characteristic genius was for the story of action, adventure and sensation. He was influenced by the American writer Jack London, to whom he has often been compared. He is at his best in depicting the various exotic and Bohemian *milieux* in which he worked: as an actor, a singer, a newspaperman, etc., as well as such colorful settings as the circus and the race track. Kuprin did not always realize where his real talent lay, however, and his writings on social themes and his more pretentious experiments in new literary forms are weaker than his stories of action. Of the latter type one of the best is *Captain Rybnikov* (1906), about a Japanese spy in Petersburg during the Russo-

Japanese War who succeeds in passing himself off as a retired Russian officer, and is detected only when he cries "banzai!" in his sleep in a house of prostitution. *The Bracelet of Garnets* (1911) is an extravagantly romantic but touching tale of the love of a poor clerk for a society lady.

The most successful of Kuprin's writings on social themes is his first novel, *The Duel* (1905), an exposé of the brutality and purposelessness of army life and the sadistic behavior of officers to their men. The hero, a sensitive officer, seeks to escape army life, but just after he receives his retirement papers he is killed in a senseless duel which the army code of honor forces him to fight. The novel was extremely popular with the liberal intelligentsia. More sensational and more famous (or notorious) was Kuprin's *Yama* ("The Pit," 1909-15), a journalistic study of life in a house of prostitution in Odessa. It suffers from its too conscious attempt to shock the public, an attempt at variance with its conservative morality of chastity.

Similarly unsuccessful were Kuprin's experiments with the exotic. The story *Izumrud* (1908) is an attempt to analyze the psychology of a race horse. *Sulamith* (1908) is a long and ornate prose poem on a love affair of King Solomon, suggested by the Song of Songs; Kuprin's style is inadequate for such exoticism.

Kurbski, Prince Andrey (1528-83). A pupil of MAXIM GREK, Kurbski belonged to the progressive party in Russia during the reign of IVAN THE TERRIBLE. In 1564, fearing Ivan's displeasure at his defeat by the Lithuanians, Kurbski went over to the enemy. In Lithuania he became acquainted with Western humanist culture. His four letters to Ivan reflect his study of classical literature and rhetoric, and contrast sharply with Ivan's rantings in their restrained, logical style. In these letters and in his history of Ivan's reign (1576-78), Kurbski accused Ivan of cruelty and injustice, and of undermining the rights of the boyar nobility, to which Kurbski belonged. In Lithuania he also wrote polemic works in defence of the Orthodox faith against the Catholic Poles.

Kurochkin, Vasili Stepanovich (1831-75), a minor radical poet and publicist of the mid-nineteenth century. His poetry contains verses on revolutionary themes, as well as sharp attacks on the liberals, such as TURGENEV, and parodies of their writings.

Kushchevski, Ivan Afanasievich (1847-76), a writer of the 1870's. His principal work is a novel, *Nikolay Negorev* (1871), which depicts the growth of an average boy into a highly successful, selfish and self-satisfied official. The book contains a wealth of picturesque and interestingly depicted characters, as well as much liveliness and humor.

Kusikov, Alexander. See Imaginism.

Kuzmin, Mikhail Alexeyevich (1875-1936), a symbolist poet and writer. Unlike the Petersburg symbolists, of whom he was a member, Kuzmin lacked mystical and philosophical interests, and was primarily an esthete. At one time, however, he made pilgrimages with the sect of Old Believers. His *Songs of Alexandria* (1906) are love songs with occasional homosexual overtones; they are inspired by Pierre Louys' *Chansons de Bilitis*. Kuzmin's pastoral, *Seasons of Love* (1907), for which he also wrote the music, is stylized in the manner of the eighteenth century. He also wrote erotic novels, such as *Wings* (1907), with its defense of homosexual love, or *Travellers by Land and Sea* (1915), an account of the adulteries of the Petersburg Bohemian world.

Kuznitsa. See Smithy Poets.

L

Landau, Mark Alexandrovich (1886-   ), a contemporary Russian
émigré writer who publishes under the pseudonym of Mark
Aldanov. He studied chemistry and law at the University of Kiev.
In 1919 he emigrated from the Soviet Union and settled in Paris,
and in 1941, on the fall of France, he came to the United States.

Aldanov has been most successful as a historical novelist. Best
known is his cycle of novels, *The Thinker*, which deals with the
French Revolution and the reign of Napoleon, subjects which are
allusively linked to the Russian Revolution and the fate of the
Russian emigration. The cycle includes the novels: *The Ninth
Thermidor* (1923), *The Devil's Bridge* (1925), *The Conspiracy*
(1927), and *St. Helena, Little Island* (1923).

One of Aldanov's finest novels, his *Tenth Symphony* (1931),
concerns the life of Beethoven, and deals with the unhappiness
and lack of fulfillment of the composer's life. *The Beginning of
the End* (1939; English translation as "The Fifth Seal") is on a
contemporary theme, the Spanish Civil War and the atmosphere
of fatalism which preceded the Second World War.

Aldanov's historical novels are urbane and cultured, with much
philosophical commentary on the nature of history. He is concerned with analyzing the role of chance in history, which for him
is fundamental, and has published several volumes on philosophy
of history.

Language. The Russian language (properly called Great Russian to
distinguish it from Ukrainian, or Little Russian, and Belo-Russian,
or White Russian) is the largest member of the eastern group of
the Slavic languages, and belongs, with the other Slavic languages, to the Indo-European language family. It is spoken today
as the native tongue of more than 100,000,000 persons in the
Soviet Union. Though dialects exist, the language is remarkably

uniform in the face of the tremendous area of the world which it covers.

Like the Slavic languages generally, Russian is characterized by a high degree of inflection of verbs, nouns, pronouns and adjectives, and by a corresponding freedom in sentence order. Its basic lexical stock is to a large extent inherited from Indo-European. Germanic loan words were an important influence in the period preceding Russia's emergence in history, while Greek influences, especially in religious and abstract terminology, were strong following her CHRISTIANIZATION in the tenth century. The period of the Tartar Yoke (thirteenth and fourteenth centuries) introduced many Tartar words, particularly in the fields of government and communication. In modern times many terms of culture and civilization have entered from the Western European languages, particularly French and German.

Russian has a heavy stress, which, like English and unlike French, is mobile, or not fixed to any particular syllable for all words. The language is egregious for its multiple combinations of consonants, but these hardly impede its fluency. Another marked characteristic is its large number of pallatalized consonants (cf. the *t* in British English *tune*, pronounced "*tyoon*"), which give it a certain mellifluence. The language is capable of both great vigor and softness. Its use of inflections permits multisyllabic rhymes.

Old Russian literature (tenth to seventeenth centuries) is for the most part written not in Russian, but in OLD CHURCH SLAVONIC, a Slavic language which became the Church language of the Orthodox Slavs. Similar to Russian, it could readily be understood by educated Russians. The Russian language was used, however, in some writing, chiefly in works of a non-artistic character, or, in the seventeenth century, in some works of a secular nature. In the eighteenth century Russian finally became the literary language, though with a heavy admixture of Slavonic terms, and the Slavonic stratum has been preserved in the language up to the present. Throughout the eighteenth century Russian writers had great difficulty, because of changing literary taste and the rapid influx of new terms, in achieving a pure literary language. This problem was largely solved early in the nineteenth century, when the standards for the modern literary language were fixed (see Karamzin; Shishkov; Pushkin).

The modern standard language is opposed to sub-standard and folk speech; slang is largely a twentieth-century phenomenon. The Soviet period has seen rapid development in the introduction of new terms, particularly in technology and bureaucracy, and the habit has arisen of coining new words from multiple abbreviations (cf. our NATO, UNRRA, etc.). To what extent this may change the character of the language remains to be seen.

Lavrenyov, Boris Andreyevich (1891-), a Soviet writer. He entered literature around 1913 as a futurist poet (see Futurism). After World War I he began to publish stories, many of them about the Civil War, in which he had taken part. He depicts war romantically, with much idealization of heroism, strong passion and feeling. In these traits, as well as in occasional experimentalism of manner, he shows the influence of Pilnyak (see Vogau). Many of his later stories are fantastic, and suggest a tendency to escape from the tedious realities of Soviet life. His tale, *The Wood-Engraving* (1928), deals with the problem of art in Soviet society. In it Lavrenyov rejects such extremes as radical new proletarian art or futurist crudity and eccentricity as unworthy of the new Soviet order.

Lavrenyov is also a playwright. His recent play, *The Voice of America* (1949), is an attempt to expose the ideological dangers of listening to American radio propaganda.

Lavrov, Pyotr Lavrovich (1823-1900), a political thinker and critic of the second half of the nineteenth century. Arrested in 1866 by the tsarist police, he was exiled to the province of Vologda in northern Russia. In 1870 he escaped from Russia and went to Paris, where he founded a Russian journal in exile, *Forward*. He took part in the First International.

Lavrov's most influential work was his *Historical Letters* (1870), written while he was in Vologda Province, and published under the pseudonym of Mirtov. A positivist and follower of CHERNYSHEVSKI, he emphasized the primary importance of man's ethical nature. History for him is the work of creative and reflective individuals; such persons, in his view, owe a debt to the toiling masses, whose labors have made possible the leisure necessary for their activity. Hence such leaders are morally obligated to work for the emancipation and enlightenment of the people. Though himself isolated from the political activities of the radicals of the 1860's, Lavrov's teachings had great influence on them, and especially on the POPULISTS. He was one of the first Russian socialists to undergo the influence of Marx. (See Philosophy.)

Lazhechnikov, Ivan Ivanovich (1792-1869), a historical novelist of the mid-nineteenth century. A follower of Scott, his novels were more alive and more faithful to history than those of his contemporary, ZAGOSKIN. The best, *The House of Ice* (1835), deals with court intrigue during the reign of the eighteenth-century empress Anna Ivanovna. He also wrote novels of the times of Ivan the Terrible and of Peter the Great.

LEF. See Futurism.

Lelevich, G. See October.

Lenin, Vladimir Ilyich (1870-1924; pseudonym of Vladimir Ilyich Ulyanov), a revolutionary leader and Marxist thinker. The son of a school inspector, he was educated at the Universities of Kazan and St. Petersburg, and was admitted to the bar, but never practiced. From 1893 he worked as a professional revolutionary, and until 1917 spent most of his life in Siberian exile or abroad. From the beginning he opposed the Russian revolutionary POPULISTS and accepted the doctrines of Marxist socialism, which he followed literally, although he did make a few innovations in Marxist political theory and practice. He supposed, for example (contrary to Marx), that revolution might take place in Russia after an imperialistic war, even though Russia's economy had not fully attained the capitalist stage. To a large extent Lenin's political activity was practical rather than theoretical. He insisted on the necessity for strict party discipline, and refused any kind of compromise; in 1903 this insistence cost him the break between the Bolshevik wing of the Party, which he controlled, and the more moderate Mensheviks. He realized the necessity for forming party cells to train experienced revolutionary leaders for the proletariat. He opposed co-operation with liberals; once tsarism would be overthrown, the proletariat, with the help of the peasantry, could make its own revolution, he believed. Returning to Russia in 1917, he realized the wisdom of overthrowing the Kerenski Government before it could become entrenched, and grasped the strategy of using the unpopularity of the war as a weapon against the government. On October 27, 1917, he was selected as head of the revolutionary Council of People's Commissars, and thus in fact head of the new Soviet state, a position which he occupied until his death. An internationalist in his outlook, he mistakenly regarded socialism as imminent in the West, which he supposed would soon follow the example of revolution in Russia.

Lenin's philosophical elaboration of Marxism contains few motifs that are original. According to Marx, socialism would inevitably result from the historical process; Lenin asserted that the inevitability of the historical process in no way lessens the role of the individual in history. This revision of Marxist "fatalism" is typical of the practical character of Lenin's thought; another example is his conception of the revolutionary "leap," the possibility of sudden social transition to the dictatorship of the proletariat. For Lenin such breaks in historical continuity are characteristic of dialectical development in general, which thus progresses to new historical stages not steadily, but in leaps. This doctrine served him as a justification for revolutionary action.

Unlike his contemporary, PLEKHANOV, Lenin devoted little attention to literary theory, though his meagre writings on the subject have been the object of the intensest scrutiny by Soviet students of literature. Lenin is credited with originating the conception of *PARTIYNOST*, the doctrine that literature must manifest "party spirit." But Lenin's pronouncement on party literature, made in 1905, and commonly quoted in support of this view, is actually a denunciation of literary careerism and a summons to writers to join the Party, not a theoretical pronouncement on the esthetic function of "party spirit" as such.

With TROTSKI, Lenin played an active role in the 1920's in restraining those leftist Marxists who sought to throw out the legacy of older "bourgeois" art in order to create a new proletarian art. Lenin advocated the use of bourgeois culture as a basis for the creation of Soviet culture. This position resulted in a considerable degree of freedom for Soviet writers of the 1920's. (See Literature, Soviet; Criticism, Soviet.)

Leonov, Leonid Maximovich (1899-   ), a leading Soviet novelist and playwright. His father was a peasant and a self-taught poet. Leonov attended the University of Moscow, but never completed his studies. He served for three years in the Red Army during the Civil War, and began to write poetry at the beginning of the 1920's, but soon switched to prose.

Leonov entered literature as a "fellow traveller," one who, like so many Russian intellectuals, had serious doubts concerning the Soviet regime and the New Economic Policy of 1921-28, with its partial retreat from socialism. Unlike many fellow travellers, however, Leonov subsequently reconciled himself to the regime and now enjoys the position of one of the most favored, as well as talented, Soviet writers.

Leonov's earliest manner, which he employed in the 1920's, is an intense psychologism, strongly influenced by DOSTOYEVSKI. From this he developed more and more in the direction of the conventional realism demanded in present-day literature. Though he never abandoned psychologism entirely, he became less concerned with the psychology of the pathological and abnormal. His style is complex and many-levelled, often overweighted, with a preference for the ornamental manner popular in the early 1920's (see Ornamentalism); this to some extent he has retained even to the present day.

Leonov's first important work was a long tale, *The End of a Petty Man* (1924), in which the influence of DOSTOYEVSKI becomes apparent. It depicts the fate of a scholar who tries to ignore the Revolution, but in the end, dying with hunger during the famine which accompanied the Civil War, is forced to submit to fate and allow himself to be destroyed.

Leonov's first novel, *The Badgers* (1924), is more realistic, and deals with the theme of the conflict of city and country, an important one in the early 1920's, when the peasants tried to frustrate the grain collections carried on by the government. Two brothers, Semyon and Pashka, side with village and city respectively; in the end Pashka is sent to put down a peasant uprising led by Semyon. The two brothers meet at the end of the novel and are apparently reconciled, but the actual ending is unclear. The author's sympathies seem to be with Semyon, the rebel, rather than the cold and sullen Pashka.

The Thief (1927) is Leonov's greatest novel, though it suffers from extreme complexity and an air of melodramatic mystery, qualities which Leonov inherited in part from DOSTOYEVSKI. The hero of the novel, Mitka, suffers from a spiritual conflict which begins during his service in the Civil War: he cannot decide whether his taking of an enemy's life is justified and, hence, whether the Revolution itself is justified. Disillusioned and disaffected, he becomes a gangster, but in the end gives himself up to the police to be reformed in a Soviet labor camp. The novel contains a great gallery of portraits of profiteers and gangsters who thrive under the New Economic Policy; Leonov uses them as spiritual symbols of what he, like many other Soviet writers, felt to be a betrayal of socialism. In a curious episode a petty official named Chikalyov proposes a system of thought control by the government, according to which every man's thoughts will be read every day by a government official. Chikalyov's ideas are obviously a supplement to those of his near-namesake, Shigalyov, in DOSTOYEVSKI's *The Devils,* and suggest that Leonov, like many other fellow travellers, had serious doubts about the future development of the Soviet system. It is of interest that *The Thief* was omitted from the recent Soviet edition of Leonov's "complete" works.

Leonov produced two Five-year Plan novels. The first, *Sot* (1930, or "Soviet River," as it was also known in English translation), describes the construction of a huge paper mill, the success of which is threatened, as it inevitably is in Five-year Plan novels, by sabotage. A White officer in hiding in the area preaches the coming of a new Attila who will destroy modern industrial civilization and give man a spiritual rebirth. His ideas recall those of the SCYTHIANS. *Skutarevski* (1932) is a largely conventional novel of sabotage in the electrical industry.

Leonov's next novel, *Road to the Ocean* (1935), is a complex work in which different narrative planes intertwine and in which lengthy use is even made of footnotes. The hero is a high Communist official who is about to die, and who realizes how personally unrewarding his life has been. At the same time the author draws a picture of the world of the future, the mysterious city of Ocean, as he and his hero imagine it. He foresees war between the Soviet Union and the non-Soviet world before the final realization of this utopian dream. The novel was not especially successful, and involved Leonov in fresh difficulties with his critics.

Leonov has written a long tale, *The Taking of Velikoshumsk* (1944; English translation as "Chariot of Wrath"), and several plays about the Second World War. The first depicts the life of a Soviet tank and its crew, and their final fate when, isolated from their unit, they sacrifice themselves in a heroic attack on a German column. The characterizations of the crew members give Leonov much opportunity for impressionistic psychological commentary.

Leonov is a leading Soviet dramatist. His play, *The Orchards of Polovchansk* (1936), treats the theme of Soviet family life; melodrama is added in the unmasking of an enemy agent at a family reunion. Of Leonov's two war plays, *Invasion* (1942) and *Lyonushka* (1943), the first is perhaps the finest of the many plays about the Second World War. It deals with the fate of a criminal and social outcast who redeems himself by giving his life in the struggle with the Germans. The second play concerns the activities of a partisan group behind the German lines.

Leonov's latest novel is his *Russian Forest* (1953), which has as its subject Russian love for nature. Besides a wealth of nature description, the novel has a complex range of good and evil characters and a complex intrigue typical of Leonov.

Leontiev, Ivan Leontievich (1856-1911), a dramatist and story writer of the late nineteenth century, who wrote under the penname of Shcheglov. A popular humorist in his own day, he is remembered today chiefly for his friendship with CHEKHOV.

Leontiev, Konstantin Nikolayevich (1831-91), a leading Russian philosopher, critic and writer of the second half of the nineteenth century. He studied medicine at the University of Moscow, and served in the army as a surgeon during the Crimean War. After the war he turned to writing novels, but these had no success. In 1863 he entered the consular service, and served for the next eight years in Greece. In 1871 he fell seriously ill and vowed to spend a year at Mount Athos under monastic rule if he recovered. From then on he was a dogmatic Orthodox Christian of the most rigid cast. He left the consular service in 1873 and returned to Russia, where he attempted to gain a living by work in the censorship and by writing. His chief works, including the collection of political essays, *Russia, the East, and the Slavs* (1885-86), were published in this period. But his writings attracted little attention during his lifetime. After divorcing his mentally deranged wife,

Leontiev spent much time in monasteries. In 1891, a few months before his death, he secretly took monastic vows.

Though estheticism is an important element in Leontiev's thought, it is unfair to describe him as an esthetic amoralist, as his critics have sometimes done. Esthetic amoralism was an early stage in his thought, replaced after his religious crisis by a conservatism and moral rigorism which emphasized the fear of God as the origin of true morality. Utilitarianism and the humanistic delusion of love for mankind without God he rejects as artificial and without comprehension of the "irremediable tragedy of life." Man's purpose is not to be happy, but to fulfill God's will in history. Suffering for him, as for DOSTOYEVSKI, is inevitable and often beneficial.

Leontiev is famous as an anti-democrat and reactionary, and his passionate fear and hatred of the common herd won him the title of the "Russian Nietzsche." He rejects the ideal of human equality as foreign to nature, which does not create men equal. But, though his work appealed to the reactionary circles of the 1880's, he actually did not belong to them, for he insisted on greater autonomy for the Church, and condemned the very nationalism which was the basis of tsarist conservatism.

Leontiev's philosophy of history is rooted in a triune process of development which governs all matter, inorganic as well as organic. This formula of initial simplicity, growing complexity, and final disintegration and death he finds applicable to human historical development. Following DANILEVSKI, he rejects Western Europe as a model for Russia; the West for him is too atheistic, democratic and nationalistic—signs for him of its final disintegration. Like the SLAVOPHILES, he prefers Russia's indigenous institutions, but differs from them in idealizing the Byzantine heritage in the Russian tradition rather than the Slavic.

Leontiev was a capable if strongly prejudiced critic of literature. Though his essays on TOLSTOY and DOSTOYEVSKI condemn these writers for what Leontiev calls their "rose-colored Christianity," he was still able to distinguish manner from content and demonstrate the literary success of these writers on purely esthetic grounds.

Haughty, unyielding and isolated, Leontiev has hardly been popular as a thinker. But his thought is an important link in the development of Russian ideas, and he has influenced both Vladimir SOLOVYOV and BERDYAYEV.

Lermontov, Mikhail Yurievich (1814-41), a leading Russian romantic poet and novelist. His father was a poor army officer, the descendant of a Scottish mercenary who had come to Russia early in the seventeenth century. Apparently he was a distant descendant of the Scottish medieval poet, Thomas the Rhymer. His mother was the daughter of a wealthy family, who died when the boy was only three. His maternal grandmother drove the father away and took over the child's upbringing. She spoiled him badly. A precocious child, he read widely, especially the romantic poets, and among them Byron. As a boy he was three times taken to the Caucasus, and that land of spectacular scenery made a strong impression on him. The Caucasus captured his fancy as a noble setting which symbolized peace and escape from the unhappiness of life.

By the age of thirteen Lermontov was already writing poetry. More and more he felt alienated by society, shy, and ashamed of his own appearance, which he fancied awkward and ugly. He cultivated a cynical wit and a mood of irony which partly protected him from the blows of society. But he never felt at peace with the world about him.

In 1830 Lermontov entered Moscow University, originally to study in the Department of Ethics and Politics, later in that of Literature. An argument with a teacher caused him to leave the University without taking his degree. He then entered military school in St. Petersburg as a cadet. He adapted himself to the atmosphere of the school by assuming a callous exterior, writing coarse erotic verses and engaging in numerous love affairs. In 1834 he received his commission as an officer in the Hussars.

As a poet Lermontov first attracted public attention in 1837 with his poem, *The Death of a Poet*, which circulated in manuscript. The poem denounced the regime of Nicholas I for its culpability in the death of PUSHKIN. The poem came to the attention of the police. Lermontov was arrested, court-martialed, and sentenced to serve in the Caucasus. After a year, however, he was pardoned and returned to the capital, where he found his reputation as a poet established. But he continued to get into trouble; a duel with the son of the French ambassador brought his second arrest. He was sent back to fighting in the Caucasus. There, in July, 1841, he became involved in the duel which cost his life. At Pyatigorsk, a Caucasian watering place, he quarreled with a Major Martynov, a former schoolmate. He and Martynov were paying court to the same young lady, and Lermontov's witticisms at the dandy Martynov's expense brought the latter's challenge. Lermontov was killed at the first shot. Ironically, the duel had an outcome quite unlike the one foreseen by Lermontov in his novel, *A Hero of Our Times,* in which Pechorin, the Lermontov-like hero, kills the dandy Grushnitski.

Lermontov's early death no doubt prevented him from reaching full maturity as a writer, and much of what he wrote is incomplete and unpolished, and was never published in his lifetime. Most of his life Lermontov was under the strong influence of Byron, and he did not have sufficient time to outgrow this influence and come to full originality. Still, it must be said that his Byronism was probably more sincere and more deeply felt than was that of Byron himself. For Lermontov Byronic romanticism was no mere pose, but the withdrawal of a sensitive soul from a life which he considered corrupt and fundamentally unjust.

Lermontov's poetry is extremely musical, rich in images and in mellifluous sound effects. Indeed, it is sometimes too rich, perhaps, and the poetic orchestration at times only highlights the banality and exaggerated quality of the torrent of rhetoric which often accompanies it.

Except for the lyric poem called *The Angel,* little of the poetry which Lermontov wrote before 1836 is of much value. *The Angel,* written in 1832, when he was only eighteen, is a remarkable vision of a paradise which is real but beyond man's attainment; the poem gives an almost mystical vision of perfection and peace. This vision is in sharp contrast to the usual demoniac quality of Lermontov's view of life, but is properly seen as its necessary complement; the major spiritual idea in Lermontov's poetry is the paradox between the memory of a lost paradise and man's actual estate as a rebellious fallen creature.

Sashka, a long uncompleted poem written during Lermontov's cadet years, is an early attempt at a narrative poem in the style of Byron's *Don Juan.* Much of it is erotic or obscene. *Hadji Abrek,* another verse narrative, appeared without Lermontov's permission in a magazine in 1835, and was thus his first published poem. Set in the Caucasus, it is a dramatic tale of revenge.

Lermontov's reputation as a poet is based largely on his two long narrative poems, *The Demon*, completed in 1839 but left unpublished because of the censorship, and *Mtsyri*, which appeared in print in 1840. Both poems, and especially *The Demon*, are exaggerated and unrestrained. Poetically *The Demon* is inferior to Lermontov's best lyrics; thematically and psychologically it is far below his novel, *A Hero of Our Times*.

Mtsyri (the title is a Georgian word which means "novice") tells the story of a young man who, in search of love and freedom, leaves the monastery where he is about to take his vows. But, brought up in seclusion from the world, he learns that he is not strong enough for life, and must die. The poem expresses an idealization of primitive life and a contempt for civilization; Lermontov's strongly anti-religious sentiment is reflected in his choice of the monastery as a symbol of this corrupting power of human society.

The Demon treats a subject which it is difficult today to take seriously: the love of a demon for a mortal maiden. The demon, a fallen angel who is noble but profoundly bored, hopes to rescue himself from the tedium of his existence through love. But his fervent kiss destroys the girl whom he loves, and her soul, taken to heaven by an angel, is lost to him.

Lermontov's lyrics express a passionate condemnation of the injustices of life, of the emptiness of society and the bitterness of his own fate. *The Sail*, probably his best-known lyric, written in 1832, expresses the mood of rebellion and spiritual isolation. *Meditation*, written in 1838, shows Lermontov's low opinion of his contemporaries and his own generation, while *Gratitude*, written in 1840, is the poet's cynical thanks to the God who has destined his life to be so bitter. Only rarely is there a more positive note of hope, as in *The Angel* or *Prayer*, written in 1839, in whch the beauty of poetry itself appears as a salvation.

Lermontov's later poetry tends towards greater restraint and frequent use of understatement. *The Song of the Merchant Kalashnikov*, written in 1837, is perhaps the most magnificent heroic poem in the language. It is modelled on the Russian folk epos (see *Byliny*). *Borodino,* from the same year, is an account of the battle of that name with the French in 1812, as realistically told by an old war veteran.

Lermontov's prose is surprisingly independent of his verse; its manner is more restrained, and there is more psychological analysis. The unfinished novels *Vadim* and *Princess Ligovskaya* are little more than preliminary sketches for his prose masterpiece, *A Hero of Our Times,* published in 1840. It is a novel made up of five tales, united by the common figure of the hero, Pechorin, whose enigmatic character is progressively revealed throughout the novel. Pechorin is a nobleman and officer who partly recalls Lermontov himself. Disenchanted by life, he holds himself aloof, acting only occasionally to relieve the tedium of life or to revenge himself on society for its injustice and neglect. In the tradition of PUSHKIN's Eugene Onegin, Pechorin is a later example of the SUPERFLUOUS MAN, developed in part from the episode in Pushkin's poem in which Eugene kills his friend Lenski out of boredom and suppressed jealousy. Similarly bored, and frustrated in a useless career as an officer, Pechorin is capable of striking back and revenging himself on society. Contrasted to him is the character of Maxim Maximych, a veteran officer who is striking in his openness and devotion to duty. He is totally unable, in his simplicity, to fathom Pechorin's bitter and cynical hatred for life, and his presence in the novel gives it a certain irony.

Lermontov's dramas are youthful works, highly melodramatic in content. The first three are in prose, but *Masquerade,* written in 1835-36, is in the regular, rhymed verse of GRIBOYEDOV's *Woe from Wit.* Highly subjective, their interest rests in the expression of the hero's violent passions.

Lermontov's immediate influence on Russian literature was not great. The transition from verse to prose and from ROMANTICISM to REALISM caused his work to age very rapidly in its day. His chief follower, probably, was the talented poet and critic of the 1850's and early 1860's, Apollon GRIGORIEV. Though Lermontov's poetry, and in particular his narratives, were exceedingly popular in the second half of the nineteenth century, this was due more to their sentimentality and tawdry effects than to their more enduring qualities. Only, perhaps, with the Symbolist Movement of the end of the century, was Lermontov deeply understood. The symbolist poet BLOK, like Lermontov, was preoccupied with the theme of his own fall from the angelic heights of a serene mystical faith.

Leshenkov, Sergey Altonovich (1889-?), a writer of the twentieth century who wrote under the pseudonym of Sergey Klychkov. A follower of KLYUYEV, he belonged to the group of peasant poets, and first published in 1909. His poems, as well as the novels and tales which he published after 1924, are rich in elements, often fantastic, derived from folk tales and fairy tales. Attacked by Soviet critics as a *kulak* (well-to-do peasant) writer, Klychkov disappeared from literature, and may have been arrested during the 1930's.

Leskov, Nikolay Semyonovich (1831-95), a leading writer of the second half of the nineteenth century. He was born in a family of mixed origin; his father was a minor official, while his mother belonged to the landowning gentry. He grew up on the estate, receiving little formal education; the death of his parents forced him to enter the civil service at the age of sixteen. Later he also worked as an estate manager and travelling businessman. His lack of formal education no doubt helped to prevent him from becoming a cosmopolitan, and he is perhaps the most typically and characteristically Russian of all nineteenth-century writers. His work brought him close to the various strata of Russian society, and provided him with sources for the exoticism, the bright, bold color and vigorous humor of his writings. He was interested in folklore and popular literature, and especially in the literature and customs of the sect of Old Believers (see Schism).

In 1860 Leskov entered journalism, and in 1863 published his first short story, *The Musk-ox*. This was followed in 1864 by a novel, *No Way Out*, an attack on the radical NIHILISTS. Another novel, *At Daggers Drawn* (1870-71), was even more critical, and the radicals replied with vicious attacks and attempts to boycott his writings. Leskov acquired the reputation of an ultra-reactionary, an impression which has served to keep him under a cloud almost until the present day. He has always been more popular with the reading public than with the critics. Actually he was not anti-progressive, but, like many Russian writers, was more concerned for moral reform than political progress. Though he remained Orthodox, he was always keenly interested in religious sectarianism and in pietism. Towards the end of his life he came under the influence of TOLSTOY's ethical ideas and advocated a type of Christianity which would be non-denominational and would emphasize ethical values such as charity and humility. This tendency towards quietism is in strange contrast to the exotic color and fierce, passionate quality of much of his work.

Leskov's early anti-nihilist novels are of minor importance. His real talent was for story-telling. He is almost alone in nineteenth-century Russian literature as a writer who tells a story for its own sake. His stories are full of breathtaking adventures, strange atmosphere and strong sensual passions. Whole areas of Russian life appear in his works which are largely foreign to the rest of nineteenth-century Russian literature, or are treated purely tendentiously by other writers: the life of the merchants, the middle classes, and especially the sectarian Old Believers, an interest which Leskov inherited in part from the writer MELNIKOV. Important in Leskov's work is his flair for anecdotal humor, which sometimes becomes almost Rabelaisian.

But Leskov's characteristic attribute is his style, particularly of the works he wrote after 1870. It is of a unique sort, a personal product of that type of narration which in Russian is called *SKAZ*. The term *skaz* denotes a story told by a narrator who has witnessed the events he recounts; in *skaz* narration an effort is made by the writer to fit the style of the narrative to the personality of the fictitious narrator. In Leskov's treatment, the personality of the narrator, sometimes a monk or an Old Believer, is vividly reflected in the language which is put in his mouth. The style even attains a kind of autonomy, in which strange words, often invented by the author, corrupt forms of words, slang and dialect expressions are introduced for their linguistic interest. Leskov studied the language of different social classes, of monks, priests, and Old Believers, and from these sources developed an exaggerated and highly colorful style. His language is far from an accurate reproduction of any kind of popular speech; rather it is an abstraction of certain elements and a distortion in the direction of the grotesque and the humorous. Leskov takes special delight in the use of words corrupted through folk etymology, such as foreign cultural and technical terms misused and mispronounced by uneducated Russians. With his mastery of this elaborate and fantastic style of monologue, Leskov is one of the great stylists in Russian fiction, and the master of the *skaz* type of narration. In the last respect his work was of great influence on early twentieth-century writers, such as REMIZOV, BABEL and many others.

Leskov's early story, *A Lady Macbeth of the Mtsensk District* (1865), though it lacks the *skaz* technique, is his most celebrated narrative, and later served as the basis for the modernistic opera by Shostakovich (1934) which caused that composer's first fall from official favor. It is a tense, horrifying story of lust, adultery and murder. The violent passion of the adulteress, which culminates in murder, seems to exist for its narrative interest rather than any deeper purpose, but the whole constitutes a powerful portrayal of evil. *The Amazon* (1866) is in a lighter but almost equally disturbing vein; it tells of a procuress who is hurt by the ingratitude of one of the unfortunate women she has forced into prostitution.

Leskov's first successful and most important novel, *Cathedral Folk* (1872), is a panoramic novel of a cathedral town. The central figure is a priest, originally conceived on the model of the seventeenth-century leader of the Old Believers, AVVAKUM. The priest's novel attempts to inspire faith among the people call down the disapproval of his superiors. The work has much humor, warm color and Leskov's usual flair for the eccentric and the grotesque.

Leskov's most important genre was the long, rather episodic tale, narrated as *skaz*. The greatest example is *The Enchanted Wanderer* (1873), an absorbing picaresque tale of the life of a man involuntarily driven from one adventure to another until he becomes a monk. The action moves rapidly, and the sequence of adventures allows the author to depict a great number of colorful *milieux*. Another tale, *The Sealed Angel* (1873), tells of the loss of a precious icon belonging to the Old Believers, which is confiscated by the police and sealed over with wax. It is restored to the sect only by a miracle.

Leskov's anecdotal humor finds a good example in the hilarious story called *A Slight Error* (1883), in which a mother begs a crazy old miracle worker to pray for the fertility of her elder daughter, who is childless. The "holy" man confuses the names, however, and it is the younger, unmarried daughter who gives birth instead. A fine quality of whimsy distinguishes another famous story, *The Tale of the Left-handed Smith from Tula and the Steel Flea* (1881), in which English smiths present the Russian emperor with a miniature steel flea; Russian smiths, at a loss to improve on the mechanical wonder, finally provide the flea with tiny gold shoes.

In the last few years of his life Leskov found a new manner, in which he forsook the raciness and passionate quality of his early writing. He adapted stories of early Christian life and lives of the saints, taking them from the eastern patericons and other ancient sources. They often have a rich sensuality and voluptuousness which was new in Russian literature. In general they may be compared to Flaubert's tales in the same genre.

Hare Park is another late tale, published posthumously in 1917. It is a hilarious satire about a brainless reactionary police chief who succeeds in life through brutality and sheer stupidity. He seeks to distinguish himself by catching a radical, but arrests several honest citizens instead, including a police spy also on the lookout for radicals. In the end the radical whom he pursues slips through his fingers, disguised as his own coachman. The police chief, morally and politically confused, goes insane.

An exception and something of an enigma in the current of Russian literature, Leskov has attracted little attention abroad. Fundamentally he is a good story-teller whose work is uncomplicated by religious or philosophical issues, or by political and social causes (in spite of his personal concern for such matters), or by profound psychological analysis. Thus he hardly fits the conventional pattern of Russian nineteenth-century literature. Even his passion, his racy humor and vitality have not succeeded in finding many enthusiasts for his work outside Russia. Undoubtedly he deserves to be better known.

Levitov, Alexander Ivanovich (1837-77), a radical novelist of the second-half of the nineteenth century. Himself a wanderer, he wrote stories about the life of tramps and pilgrims, as well as descriptions of the poverty and vice of city life. His tales combine gloomy pathos with a bitter and savage irony, without hope for the victims of social exploitation.

Levshin, Vasili Alexeyevich (1746-1826), the author of a popular collection of *Russian Tales* (1780-83), partly satirical stories, partly fairy tales and fantastic romances. Because of their similarity to CHULKOV's *Scoffer,* the *Tales* were often erroneously attributed to Chulkov.

Leykin, Nikolay Alexandrovich (1841-1906), a humorist of the 1880's. His principal theme is the humorous depiction of merchant life, as in *Our People Abroad* (1890), about an uncultured young merchant couple who travel over Europe. Leykin's innumerable stories and scenes are crude and often tasteless, and his chief claim to fame is the influence which his style had on the young CHEKHOV.

Libedinski, Yuri Nikolayevich (1898-   ), a Soviet writer. A member of the Communist Party, Libedinski was concerned with the literary portrayal of Party leaders and the description of the workings of the Party. His first novel, *The Week* (1922), describes the suppression of a White uprising by Party leaders. In the later novel, *The Birth of a Hero* (1930), he attempted to describe the private life of a Party official, into which he introduces an unsuccessful love affair; the novel brought much criticism of this "self-indulgent" side of the hero's life. As a former leader of RAPP, Libedinski was expelled from the UNION OF SOVIET WRITERS in 1936. He was re-instated in 1938, but has since been out of favor, and was considered too unimportant to be listed in the *Great Soviet Encyclopedia* in 1954. His novel, *The Guards* (1942), depicts fighting at the front at the beginning of World War II.

Lidin, Vladimir. See Gomberg, V. G.

Lishni chelovek. See Superfluous man.

Literature, Eighteenth-century. See Classicism.

Literature, Nineteenth-century. See Sentimentalism; Pre-Romanticism; Romanticism; Realism; Symbolism.

Literature, Old Russian. Russian literature presumably originates with the CHRISTIANIZATION of Russia under Prince Vladimir in 988 or 989; before this time it is unlikely that the Russians possessed any system of writing. With Christianity, which came from Byzantium and not from Rome, the Russians acquired the liturgical and literary language of the South Slavs, OLD CHURCH SLAVONIC, a language related to Russian and readily comprehensible in Russia. Old Church Slavonic became the Old Russian literary language, though it tended to be Russianized at certain periods; by contrast, the Russian vernacular language was sometimes used in documents of a practical character.

Old Russian literature is largely religious and didactic in content. It must be remembered that churchmen had a virtual monopoly over the copying of manuscripts, and hence over the distribution of literature; to a large extent churchmen were also the readers of early Russian literature. In the Kievan period (eleventh through thirteenth centuries; so called because the leading cultural and political center was Kiev) the religious and moral preoccupation was strong, but more primitive and less formalistic in nature, and elements of interest in secular life and of a literature of entertainment frequently appear. During the Early Muscovite period (fourteenth through sixteenth centuries) the Church achieved its most rigid control over Russian culture and literature. In both Kievan and Early Muscovite literature there is a strong political interest, and a dominant, if sometimes tacitly implied, subject is the drive to unite the Russian land into a single state, or at least into a close-knit federation of states. The lament for disunity is frequently repeated, and finds its supreme embodiment in the *IGOR TALE.*

To a large extent Old Russian literature lacks fiction as such. For the Old Russian reader works of literature were justified by their didactic significance, their truth or wisdom, or their record of historical events. The door was left open, however, for the play of imagination, and lives of saints, such as that of Merkurii of Smolensk, or of historical personages such as Alexander the Great, were often full of fanciful elements. But such stories passed for truth, and even certain legendary heroes of Greek literature, such as Akir the Wise or Devgenii (the Byzantine Digenis Akrites), were apparently accepted as real and historically significant personages. Only in the seventeenth century do we see clear examples of fictional heroes as such.

Most of the literature of the Kievan period was translated from Greek. This does not mean that the translations were always made by Russians. Existing Old Church Slavonic translations already made by South Slavs could be used by Russians with a minimum of difficulty, since the Russian redaction of Old Church Slavonic differed but little from the South Slavic one. In certain cases we are not sure whether the translation was actually made by South Slavs or by Russians.

Among the first works to be translated were the Scriptures and the liturgy, along with many hymns, prayers and other liturgical texts. But the whole of the Scriptures were not brought to Russia at once, and Russia had to wait until the late fifteenth century for the complete Bible. The Bible exercised an immense influence, direct as well as indirect, on Old Russian literature. Of the two artistic styles which dominated in the writing of the Old Russian period, the rhetorical and the lyrical, both have their clear models in the Scriptures: the rhetorical style in much of the Bible and especially the Epistles of St. Paul; the lyrical in the Psalms. Not that the Bible and Church texts were the only stylistic models for Old Russian literature; Russian oral literature (legends, folk tales, epic and lyric songs, proverbs, etc.) and the Russian spoken language itself provided sources.

Another important genre of translated literature were lives of saints. These were replete with miraculous, if frequently stereotyped details. Popular were the lives of Sts. Alexius (known to Russians as Alexey "The Man of God"), Anthony the Great, John Chrysostom, and others. Lives of saints were found in longer versions either separately or in the *Cheti Minei* (Church calendar readings), and in very short versions in the so-called *Prolog*, a misnomer which had resulted from an erroneous translation from Greek.

Certain of the so-called patristic writings on questions of dogma, faith and morals were known in Old Russia, and were sometimes collected, along with sermons, in anthologies. One such collection, the *Pchela* ("Bee"), contains short maxims and quotations taken not only from the Bible and the Church fathers, but also from classical writers such as Plutarch and Aristotle. But later the Muscovite period took no interest in the Greek and Latin classics. Indeed, the availability of the Scriptures to the Russians in Old Church Slavonic, which at first constituted an advantage, in the long run perhaps proved a disadvantage, since it gave Russians no encouragement to learn Greek or Latin, and hence left them without a means of approach to classical learning. For this reason, perhaps, Russia was fated to undergo no Renaissance during her history.

The patericons were collections of anecdotes from the lives of monks, often of a miraculous or fabulous character. Their content, unlike the sermons or patristic writings, was more spectacular and fantastic than edifying. Also colorful were the many apocryphal writings and tales which circulated in Old Russia. Though some heretical apocryphal works spread to Kievan Russia, it seems more likely that heresy as such did not flourish in Old Russia; probably the Church during the Kievan period may be described as "pre-heretical," and had not yet attained that degree of formal exactitude under which precise distinctions of heretical and non-heretical were possible. Of the more colorful apocrypha which circulated in Old Russia one concerns Adam; in it both God and the Devil participate in his creation (this was probably a relic of the Bulgarian Bogomil heresy). Another is a fantastic tale concerning Solomon and the sagacious monster Kitovras, a legend derived ultimately from the Hebrew Talmud. A third is the moving description of the Virgin's journey through Hell. Touched at the sight of the sufferings of the damned, she begs God to grant a partial respite to their torments.

Greek chronicles were also translated into Old Church Slavonic, though unfortunately the Russians read the popular and superstitious Byzantine chronicles of world history rather than the more scholarly treatises which the Greeks produced on specific historical periods and events. Among those translated were the Chronicles of Ioannes Malalas and of Georgios Hamartolus. Also translated was Flavius Josephus' *History of the Jewish War,* which became a principal source for stereotyped descriptions of battle scenes in Old Russian tales.

A number of Byzantine tales were popular in Kievan times. Though in fact works of fiction, they were understood as historical or biographical narratives. The fantastic life of Alexander the Great, deriving from the legendary narrative of the Pseudo-Callisthenes, first came to Russia in the eleventh or twelfth century. It emphasized Alexander's fabulous origin and told of the many strange and monstrous beings he reputedly saw on his march to the East. *The Tale of Akir the Wise* contains a great number of maxims and proverbs. Proverbial wisdom was exceedingly popular in Old Russia; the *Petition* of DANIIL is another work (original rather than translated) which appealed largely for its witty aphorisms. *The Tale of Devgenii* was an epic narrative of a legendary Greek hero who fought against the infidels of the East; we have no exact Greek parallel to its two surviving Old Russian versions.

Against this background of translated literature Russian original literature was created. Original works are relatively few in the Kievan period. Either more did not exist, or they have not survived; it may be that the relatively secular character of much of Kievan literature did not appeal to the copyists of the Muscovite period. Thus, the strongly secular IGOR TALE survived in but a single copy.

The richest original Old Russian genre was that of the CHRONICLES. Chronicle writing perhaps began as early as the reign of Yaroslav the Wise (1019-54), and continued throughout the whole Old Russian period. Each provincial capital compiled and kept its own chronicle accounts, as did many monasteries. The chronicles attempted to list events under the year when they occurred, though this made for many errors. By no means always mere dry factual records of events, the Russian chronicles often contained oral or written narratives of strikingly artistic character. To a large extent they must be considered the original Old Russian genre *par excellence*. (See Chronicles.)

The greatest work of Old Russian literature is the *IGOR TALE*, which recounts in a highly poetic prose the fate of the disastrous expedition of Prince Igor Svyatoslavich of Novgorod-Seversk against the Polovtsy in 1185. In a sense the work is a synthesis of the diverse stylistic trends of both written and oral literature. It is rich in its use of symbols and allusive references. Its conciseness and highly allusive character make it a difficult text to interpret, though it is quite certainly not a late forgery, as has occasionally been supposed. (See *Igor Tale*.)

Of Old Russian lives of saints, the greatest is probably the anonymous *Narrative, Passion and Eulogy of the Sainted Martyrs Boris and Gleb* of the eleventh century. It describes the pitiful end of the two young princes, treacherously murdered by their elder brother Svyatopolk. Its most striking quality is its rich lyrical and pathetic quality. The later *Life of Sts. Boris and Gleb* by

NESTOR is more officious in style, and shows an attempt to follow the stereotyped features of the Byzantine hagiographic genre.

Very significant as a genre are the sermons of the Kievan period. *The Sermon on the Law and the Grace,* written around the middle of the eleventh century by the Metropolitan ILARION, is a bold and original attempt to assert independence for the Russian Church from Byzantium. The sermon is a striking example of the Byzantine rhetorical style, with a rich use of symbolic references and formal antitheses. The symbolic manner was brought to its fulfillment in the second half of the twelfth century in the sermons of KIRILL Turovski.

The coming of the Tartars to Russia in 1223 and again in 1237 began the long period of the Tartar Yoke of the thirteenth, fourteenth and fifteenth centuries. The Tartar invasion and rule had a strong influence on the content of Russian literature, but a lesser one on its form, which was already fixed in Kievan times. From the mid-twelfth century onwards Russia was more and more isolated from Constantinople; the original cultural legacy which she had received from Byzantium tended to remain static rather than develop. The sermons of SERAPION Vladimirski lament the ruin of the land under the Tartar invaders, a ruin which is regarded as God's punishment of the Russian people for their sins. *The Tale of the Ruin of the Russian Land* recalls the *Igor Tale* in its character of a poetic commentary on historical events; it describes the vanished greatness of Russia. The theme of ruin promised by the title is scarcely treated, and what we have is apparently only a fragment of a larger original. *The Life of Alexander Nevski* combines heroic and hagiographic motifs in its characterization of an ideal prince, one who keeps peace with the Tartars while resisting the encroachments of the Swedes and Teutonic Knights to the West. Already at the end of the Kievan period a tendency had appeared to characterize the Russian princes as saints, and this trait grows even stronger in the Muscovite period. Another example is *The Life of Dmitri Donskoy,* the first Russian prince to win a significant victory over the Tartars, the Battle of Kulikovo Pole in 1380. The victory was a great one, and did much to strengthen the prestige of the rapidly expanding Moscow principality. The battle itself was celebrated in three separate accounts. Greatest of these is the *ZADON-*

SHCHINA, or "Battle beyond the Don," of the early fifteenth century, a prose poem in which the style, phraseology and narrative plan of the *Igor Tale* are imitated.

The end of the fourteenth and beginning of the fifteenth century brought the so-called Second South Slavic Influence in Russian literature. Leading South Slavic writers, such as the Serb PAKHOMII Logofet, driven from their lands by the Turkish invasion of the Balkans, continued their literary activity in Russia. They restored a stricter standard for the use of OLD CHURCH SLAVONIC; at the same time they brought a new literary style to Russia, one in which stylistic elements tended to acquire an absolute importance independent of content. The name of "word-weaving" was given to this new style, in which endless rhetorical repetitions, used for decorative effect, played a leading role. The chief Russian practitioner of this style, applied especially to hagiographic works, was the Rostov monk YEPIFANII Premudry. This rhetorical tendency became rooted in Muscovite literature and persisted into the seventeenth century. As Moscow herself grew in power, prestige, and a parochial conviction that only she had the truth, her writing degenerated more and more into a mere show of pomp, lacking any meaning.

Meanwhile Moscow had her religious heresies, crushed through the close co-operation of Church and State. MAXIM Grek ("The Greek," 1480-1556), invited to Russia in 1518 to correct the corrupt Russian Church books, finished by becoming a martyr to Russian intolerance; his work in Russia was largely abortive, but he did leave a few disciples such as Prince Andrey KURBSKI (1528-83) to succeed him. The growing tsarist absolutism found its leading apologist in Ivan PERESVETOV, who advocated a state with a strong sovereign and a subservient aristocracy. The idea of absolutism also found support in its chief exponent, IVAN THE TERRIBLE (1533-84). In his polemic correspondence with Kurbski he asserted his divine right to rule as a complete justification of all his actions.

During the reign of Ivan, Muscovite literature attained its greatest degree of external pomp and splendor, though much of this was merely superficial. The period is relatively poor in original creation, but rich in compilations designed to impress by their sheer weight and grandiose manner. The *Cheti Minei* of the

Metropolitan Makarii was an encyclopedic collection of all Russian religious literature; its most complete copy ran to some 27,000 pages. Another such compilation was the *Illustrated Chronicle* of the 1560's and 1570's, an unfinished history of the world, for which some 16,000 miniature illustrations were prepared. The *Stoglav,* a record of the decisions of the Russian Synod of 1551, attempted to rule on matters of religious dogma and morals, while the *DOMOSTROY* advised concerning the management and government of the household, which it likened to the State itself. For its author the chief virtue is order; the head of the household should keep order just as the tsar does in the State. Like the tsar, his authority over the other members of the family is unlimited, and he can and indeed ought to administer the strictest punishments.

The reign of Ivan the Terrible was followed by the confused Time of Troubles (1584-1613). Political disorder brought to an end the narrow-minded self-assurance of the Muscovite period, and the facade of empty show in literature began to crack. With the seventeenth century we may speak of a new period, the Late Muscovite, transitional between Old and Modern Russian literature. This century brings the secularization of Russian literature, the wholesale introduction of Western influences, and the appearance of new literary genres.

One of the earliest of the new revitalizing influences to appear was that of FOLK LITERATURE. In the sixteenth century the folk influence begins to be felt, as in *The Tale of Pyotr and Favronia,* with its fairy-tale motifs of magic and enchantment; it, together with the seventeenth-century *Tale of the Tver Otroch Monastery,* is a beautiful love story, a rare subject in Old Russian literature. In the sixteenth century folk poems, which had earlier existed in oral form alone, first appear in manuscript versions, and in the seventeenth century folk tales begin to be recorded. In certain cases it is difficult to tell whether we are dealing with a work of folk literature or one only composed in the folk style; such is the case, for example, with the beautiful early seventeenth-century laments of the Tsarevna Xenia Godunova, shut up in a convent after the death of her father, Boris Godunov. Other instances are the epic *Tale of the Kiev Bogatyrs, The Judgment of Shemyaka,* a moral tale satirizing corrupt judges, and *The Tale of*

the Old Man and the Young Maiden. The last is a blunt account
of the fate of an old man who marries a young girl for her
beauty but lacks sufficient virility to remain in possession of his
bride for long.

Perhaps the greatest example of a work in the folk style is the
seventeenth-century *Tale of Misery and Ill Fortune,* a narrative
of the fate of a young man who, for his weakness, is pursued all
his life by the demon of Misery and Ill Fortune, until at last he
takes refuge in a monastery. The work contains many motifs
typical of folk ballads, and is told in the epic verse style of the
BYLINY, or epic folk songs.

Besides the folk type of verse, a literary verse form appears in
writings of the turn of the century, especially in the historical
narratives of the Time of Troubles (1584-1613). The first verse
form is completely free, except for its use of couplet rhymes. This
rather crude verse was replaced in the 1660's by syllabic verse,
brought to Muscovite Russia from Kiev by Simeon POLOTSKI.
Syllabic verse remained the dominant type until the 1740's, and
achieved a relatively high development before it was replaced by
the modern type of syllabo-tonic verse (see Prosody). Besides
Simeon Polotski, the leading practitioners of syllabic verse in
Muscovite Russia were Silvester MEDVEDEV, Karion ISTOMIN
and, in the eighteenth century, FEOFAN Prokopovich and
KANTEMIR. It was used in poetry which was relatively stereotyped in subject: didactic themes and classical poetic genres, such
as the ode, panegyric and the epitaph, were preferred.

Many new kinds of prose fiction entered Russia by way of the
Ukraine and Belo-Russia, where they had come in turn from
Poland and, ultimately, from the West. The long route they had
traversed and the cultural isolation of Muscovite Russia made
their appearance a belated one, and thus we find genres appear-
ing in Russia in the seventeenth century which had been cultivated in the West since the late Middle Ages or the Renaissance.
The medieval moral tale is represented in several collections, including the well-known *Gesta Romanorum.* Collections of Polish
humorous anecdotes with didactic endings were also known.
Fables, and in particular those of Aesop, became very popular.
All this literature presented a superficially didactic aspect which
made it acceptable in Muscovite Russia, but in fact its appeal

was chiefly that of fiction and entertainment. Frankly entertaining was the tale of chivalry and adventure, a number of examples of which appeared in Russia during the sixteenth and seventeenth centuries, beginning with the chivalric adventures of Bevis of Hampton, known to Russian readers as Prince Bova.

The school drama was another didactic form brought from Kiev by Simeon POLOTSKI, though Russian examples are few until the eighteenth century. In 1672 a theater was created at the court of Alexey Mikhaylovich by the German pastor Johann Gregori, but it lasted for several years only, coming to an end with the death of the tsar in 1676 (see Drama and Theater).

Among original Russian works of literature, the highest level was reached by the tale. We have already mentioned an early example in verse, *The Tale of Misery and Ill Fortune;* others are in prose and appear after the middle of the seventeenth century. *The Tale of Savva Grudcyn* reminds us of the Faust legend. Its hero sells his soul to the devil, but apparently the story is independent of the Central European legend. It is remarkable in the richness of its narrative interest and its harmonious use of details. *The Tale of Karp Sutulov* concerns the clever stratagems with which his wife keeps her amorous pursuers at bay during her husband's absence. *The Tale of Frol Skobeyev* is an amusing story of a rogue's success in marrying into a wealthy family by the most brazen and cunning tricks.

Satirical literature also flourished in the second half of the seventeenth century. An unofficial literature, it ridiculed the institutions of Church and State. Parody of the procedure of the law courts is found in *The Tale of Yorsh Yeshovich,* while such stories as *The Tale of the Cock and the Fox* or *The Tale of the Peasant's Son* constitute parodies of the mass itself.

The existence of such burlesques is one consequence of the breakdown of Church authority consequent, in part, on the SCHISM of the mid-seventeenth century. The leader of the schismatics, or Old Believers, the Archpriest AVVAKUM (ca. 1621-82) was himself the greatest writer of the seventeenth century in Russia. His remarkable autobiography embodied a new freedom in its use of the vernacular language. Along with elements of everyday speech, there appear specific details of daily life, rare before this time in Russian literature. The self-portrait of a heroic if bigoted religious leader, Avvakum's *Life* is the first large-scale autobiographical work in Russian literature.

In the reign of PETER THE GREAT (1682-1725) the tale loses in artistic quality but gains a new subject, connected with Peter's reforms: that of travel in the West. Such fantastic tales of adventure as *The History of Alexander, a Russian Nobleman,* illustrate how success may be won by bold adventurers not afraid to venture beyond the borders of their native land. Peter's political reforms are supported by the eloquent Ukrainian preacher and writer, FEOFAN Prokopovich (1681-1736). Peter's reign also saw the beginnings of the sentimental love lyric, which had a considerable vogue among the nobles of the new court at St. Petersburg. Peter himself made efforts to create a court theater (see Drama and Theater), but did not succeed in establishing one which would be permanent.

Literature, Soviet. The term Soviet literature customarily includes all works of the literary imagination written and published within the boundaries of the U.S.S.R. from 1917 to the present. It is essentially an extension of the Russian literary tradition, but it also includes the post-revolutionary output of the Ukrainian, Baltic, Central Asian, Caucasian and other non-Russian minorities. And, conversely, the work of a small group of prominent Russian writers in exile—BUNIN, Aldanov (see Landau) and REMIZOV among them—is excluded for political reasons (see Emigration). But the language of a vast majority of the works published in the Soviet Union is Russian, and the main inherited influences are traceable to the Russian past. Among these influences may be distinguished two kinds of realism, the "classical" and the "socialist."

The classics of Russia's Golden Age have been republished in the U.S.S.R. on an enormous scale and they have loomed larger than any other body of literature as a source of primary reference for writers, critics and scholars. However, they have not established themselves as models for Soviet writers to imitate, nor, in recent years, have they been used as the basis for literary doctrine. SOCIALIST REALISM, the name given to the "new" literary attitudes which were devised to supersede the tenets of classical REALISM, likewise has a native Russian pedigree. All the fundamental ideas of the new theory were first spelled out in the "utilitarian" esthetic developed by the radical political critics, BELINSKI, CHERNYSHEVSKI and DOBROLYUBOV, in the mid-nineteenth century. In fact, the two ways of thinking about literature have existed in a state of tension since the time of their formulation. And it is possible to read the whole of Soviet literary history as a continuation of the mortal contest between them.

The argument between the two factions, briefly summarized, pitted the advocates of an autonomous, freely-investigating, contemplative literature, best represented by the great classical writers themselves, against the advocates of a controlled, didactic, manipulative literature, represented by all those who, since Ivan the Terrible, have sought to make literature speak for a prescribed set of moral or political values. The first is concerned with a kind of total human truth, with man in all his relations to life; the second with a kind of ideological truth in the name of which men illustrate desirable political attitudes. In the first kind of writing the locus of judgment is in the sovereign moral intelligence of the writer; in the second the locus of judgment is elsewhere—in the design of history, in an ethical code, or in a political program, to which the writer must subordinate himself. In the Soviet era this contest has been continuous, bitter, sometimes open, sometimes concealed, and, although victory has apparently gone to the utilitarians, it cannot be said with certainty that it is a final one.

Chronologically Soviet literature divides itself readily into well-defined periods, marked off by important historical events or by basic shifts in government policy. In every case the onset of a new phase of public policy has been accompanied by a change in the attitude of Party and government toward writers and toward literature. There are certain thematic and formal similarities which characterize the works produced in each of these periods. But it is not possible to account for the entire Soviet literary experience merely by classifying writers or their works under one or another of these headings. There are a number of subjects which have a permanent hold on the Soviet imagination —the Civil War, for example, or the problems of industrializing a backward economy, or the continuous and costly conflict between the old way of life and the new. Also there are the permanent problems posed by the properties and "resistances" of the formal media: the possibilities and limits of the novel form, for example, or the general problem of finding suitable ways to dramatize material in an atmosphere of moral absolutes, or the problem of establishing an appropriate poetic idiom in a climate of dogmatic "simplicism." Deeper than any of these questions, because it is where all other questions will be decided, is the continuing tension between a free and a controlled art. Here the Communist Party, which declares itself to be the infallible interpreter of history and the author of all systems of values, will presumably exercise the decisive influence.

1921-1928. When the terrible rigors of the Civil War had lessened, and it became possible again to think of culture, an air of creative excitement and experiment began. There were artists who raised this period of ferment and discovery at times into the realm of brilliance. It was the time of the poet, Vladimir MAYA-KOVSKI, of the great experimental theaters, of Eisenstein in the cinema and of the Formalists in literary criticism, of the new Soviet composers, and of a confident search for new forms in the graphic arts. The promise of the Revolution, where it was still untarnished, translated itself into a widespread feeling of certainty that new forms were about to appear in all the arts.

Among writers and critics it was widely held that the creation of these new forms appropriate to the new era was their first responsibility. It was not agreed among them whether it was to be done through the selective repossession of the classical heritage, both Russian and Western, or through the establishment of a new proletarian culture to replace the old, "bourgeois" culture, or through the Futurist-directed revolution in the literary language itself (see Futurism).

A number of conditions outside literature contributed to the atmosphere of tolerance that made experiment possible. With the end of the Civil War, the Party slowed down the pace of revolutionary change to give the exhausted nation a rest, and to clean up the wreckage of the years of war. The restoration of private retail trade was the key measure in a series of policy changes, which, taken together, are called the New Economic Policy (NEP). They had the effect of relaxing tension and stimulating initiative in many spheres of activity including the arts, sciences and scholarship. The Party made its policy toward literature explicit in a decree by its Central Committee in 1925, in which it announced that it would not attempt to control the literary output, and would not endorse any of the competing literary schools, then engaged in a fierce debate among themselves. Violent attack and denunciation featured this argument in which several of the competing groups aspired to "hegemony" over Soviet literature and would have silenced their opponents if they had achieved it. The Party rejected all such claims, however, and the result was a tense, bitter, but nonetheless stable equilibrium in which a wide range of opinions, attitudes and theories flourished. On the extreme leftward end of this spectrum of attitudes there was a sequence of groups—PROLETKULT, On Guard (see October), On Literary Guard—which advocated a literature based on positive support of the Bolshevik regime, and aimed at the establishment of a new and exclusive proletarian culture, expressing the aspiration and ideology of the working class. Equally extreme, yet no friends of the Proletkult, were the Mayakovski FUTURISTS, who claimed exclusive dominion for their own version of the literary revolution. At the other end of the spectrum two groups deserve mention: the cultivated, brilliant group of scholars and critics, usually grouped together under the label *Formalists* (see Criticism), who denied that political considerations had anything to do with the analysis and judgment of literature, and the writers to whom TROTSKI gave the name "Fellow Travellers," who were loosely organized in the SERAPION BROTHERHOOD and agreed only that literature was an autonomous activity, best kept free of all regulation.

Although the Russian past manifested itself in many ways in the early Soviet years, few of the established, pre-revolutionary writers survived into the Soviet era—intact and still writing as they had before. Those who did not go into exile, died or grew silent in the strange new Bolshevik world. Only Gorki (see Peshkov) lived to become a major figure in Soviet literature, and his position depended more on his activity as a man of letters and literary patriarch following his return from abroad in 1929 than it did on any creative work based on the new order. But the past, protected by LENIN's injunction to repossess the classical inheritance, was felt in the innumerable references to the great classical writers, and by the enormous pressure of their reputations. Even the extremists' loud demands to jettison the classical tradition, ironically echo another powerful tradition, that of CIVIC CRITICISM, which had proclaimed from the middle of the nineteenth century its suspicion of the literary imagination and its willingness to declare expendable any literary work that failed to meet a prescribed standard of social utility.

The literature of the period exhibited a refreshing combination of innovation and traditionalism in its formal solutions. There was much greater uniformity, however, in the choice of subject matter. The Civil War established itself then as the greatest experience in the history of the Soviet imagination: nothing that has happened since has replaced it. The violence itself, and the elemental emotions it gave rise to, have stood as a permanent challenge to the interpreter of Soviet life, offering the most promising clues to the destiny of Soviet man. Some of the early stories, novels and plays have the quality of a raw transcript of experience, often lacking in the most rudimentary kind of formal organization. One of the most celebrated of these, Dmitri FURMANOV's *Chapayev* (1923), the description, in diary form, of the career of a primitive guerrilla military commander, illustrates a kind of hybrid genre typical of the period and of much Soviet writing to follow. It has only the barest pretensions to fiction. It is rather a documentary account of extraordinary events which rises directly to a level of mythic hyperbole bypassing all intermediate stages where it might be subject to imaginative reshaping. If such works are vivid and compelling because of their evident authenticity, the simplicity of the situations and the naiveté of treatment, as well as the formal incoherence, remove them from the realm of literary criticism.

At an opposite pole, Isaac BABEL, the enormously gifted Jewish writer, addressed himself to the same kind of material and produced in his collection of stories and sketches, *Red Cavalry* (1926), a work of great artistic distinction. His literary sophistication, his technical virtuosity, his complex use of irony and his concern with profound moral questions over and above political allegiances give his work a richness and intensity of enduring interest. He is deeply concerned with the far-reaching consequences of violence, and with the complicated tensions between the cultures of Jew and Cossack. His fascination with violence interferes at times with the precision of his definitions, but his failures are the result of overinvolvement in his material, not technical inadequacy.

In a selection of representative fiction, a novel like A. FADE-YEV's *The Rout* (1927) stands at a midpoint between *Chapayev* and *Red Cavalry*. It is an unpretentious yet complete novel, written within the canon of loyalty to the Revolution, but without explicit professions of faith or fabricated evidence of the Party's infallibility. The portrait of its hero, the deformed Jewish commander of an isolated guerrilla unit, makes this a chronicle of plausible human types stretched beyond endurance, yet somehow enduring. Fadeyev's willingness to focus on the human cost, to yield to the pain and terror of the experience, permits a kind of literary truth which is distinct from the mythical-documentary truth of *Chapayev*.

There is an assumption about men's situation in history in *The Rout* which is present in a good deal of the early writing about the Civil War: that each individual enacts the drama of his own expectations within the historical cataclysm, and that there is in the individual examples of bewilderment or defeat a kind of pathos which does not have to be read as a comment on the validity of the Revolution itself. This is sharply different from the assumption in later writing that men take on meaning and worth from their political allegiances alone, and that their fate is interesting only when it is emblematic of Bolshevik victory. A number of the writers were ambivalent toward the question of political commitment, and explored many kinds of men under the stresses of Civil War. Konstantin FEDIN's *Cities and Years* (1924) represents a prominent trend in the fiction of the period: the theme of the intellectual's tragi-pathetic failure to adjust to the brutal and—to him—incomprehensible conditions of the Civil War and the new Soviet order. In this connection many critics have noted the extension into the Soviet era of the "superfluous" stereotype from the pre-revolutionary era (see Superfluous Man). This kind of character permitted a general fictional design that had certain marked advantages for the serious novelist: he was able to avoid explicit political comment, to explore rewardingly complex human types, and to cast the revolutionary regime, in imitation of classical tragedy, as the impersonal, rectifying force, re-establishing the just and necessary order of things.

Leonid LEONOV, one of the most gifted Soviet writers, was particularly successful in keeping political allegiances at a distance while he dealt with the raw material of social upheaval. His novel about warring brothers, *The Badgers* (1924), is an impressive effort to find a measure of human truth in the midst of chaos and violence.

The works of Leonov, Fedin and Babel and others of the "Fellow Travellers" should not be considered as distinguished exceptions, but rather as the best of a large and varied output. The future, however, is better forecast by lesser works (of which there were many) like Serafimovich's *The Iron Flood* (1924; see Popov), a primitive, though vivid, record of mass Bolshevik heroism against superhuman odds.

It is possible to talk of a NEP literature in the same decade, although the distinction between it and the Civil War literature is not a very clear one. These novels and stories are usually set against the squalor and vulgarity of the revival of private trade, the world of the profiteering "Nepmen," and the mood is often one of despair and disillusion. The Civil War is often present in these works, as an object of nostalgic longing, or as a point of contrast with the triviality and stagnation of the NEP, or, occasionally, as the locus of violent events, the consequences of which are worked out in the radically different perspectives of peace time. Such is the design of Leonov's second novel, *The Thief* (1927). Its protagonist, a former Red commissar, has killed a man in cold blood during the Civil War, and undertakes a long journey of expiation through the criminal underworld of Moscow, through the lives of a gallery of eccentrics and outcasts, to the threshold of redemption, when he finally returns to his native village, purged of his guilt. Leonov's resemblance to Dostoyevski has often been noted. Whether or not the comparison is helpful in detail, it points again to the continuity of the Russian humanist tradition, which conceived of the novel as an instrument for defining man's particular condition in a given time and place, against the permanent questions of human existence. None of the writing in the Soviet twenties approaches the universality of the great classics, but the disposition to try is repeatedly apparent.

In this connection, Yuri OLESHA's *Envy* (1927) is one of the most provocative efforts to adjust the novel form to the conflicts of value in the new society. His imaginative formulation of the tensions between old and new and his effort to balance the gains and losses in the new way of life, ends in ambiguity, without open commitment to either side. The new Soviet Babbittry is set against a version of the past, represented by two raffish idlers, romantic misfits, who present themselves as champions of a world of forgotten values and emotions, and organize what they call a "conspiracy of feelings" to preserve them. The smug, mechanized Soviet world with its cult of mindless energy and physical health has simply omitted from its plan for living any provision for a full range of heroic, gallant, sentimental and morbid emotions that have always been a part of human existence. Let the losses be fully measured against the gains, Olesha seems to say. Certainly he came close to the limits of the allowed in this period of relative tolerance, and in the act of raising troubling questions he is closest to the spirit of the Russian tradition.

One other literary mode—satire—which had a rich history in the nineteenth century, also flourished in the first decade of the Soviet epoch. Valentin KATAYEV's *Embezzlers* (1926), the irreverent account of the journey of two engaging crooks through some of the dark corners of Soviet life, and Mikhail ZOSH-CHENKO's acidly witty sketches of all kinds of human (and Soviet) foolishness, indicated that the spirits of Gogol and Salty-kov-Shchedrin had survived. But satire's bite is dangerous in the mildest of despotisms; the restlessness it engenders is beyond control. Despite occasional exceptions, e.g., Ilf and Petrov's *The Little Golden Calf* (1931; see Fainzilberg), the satirical voice was to grow fainter and fainter. In the pious solemnities of the Five-Year Plans, what was out of step, out of joint, began to be viewed as ill-intentioned, malevolent, even treasonable, and was construed as black, melodramatic villainy—not to be laughed at, but liquidated. For this period, marked as it was by promise and by a measure of solid accomplishment, if not by brilliant achievement, was to yield at the end of 1928 to the first experiment in literary orthodoxy. The onset of the First Five-Year Plan, and the rekindling of the mood of revolutionary urgency, brought with it strictures, loyalty tests, and prescribed values, all of which were by nature hostile to the free exercise of the imagination. In the years to come *Chapayev* became a Soviet classic while Babel fell silent and, later, disappeared with all his works from the Soviet scene.

One novel of the first decade, Fyodor GLADKOV's *Cement* (1925), was an indication of the literature to follow. In certain respects the novel reflects a sense of rich disorder found in so much of the better writing of the early 1920's. But theme, characters, setting are all too clearly expressed in this uncompromising title. It is the first of the "construction" novels, in which the central action is concerned with some phase of industrial production. Blueprints, statistics, machinery are the substance of the novel. In these novels, men are masters of the machines in the sense that new production goals are achieved. But in the sense that all human problems are resolved with respect to the needs of the machine, man has become, in Thoreau's phrase, "the tool of his tools." An unpromising milieu for the novelist, but, since it was the central preoccupation of government and Party, it became perforce a major literary preoccupation. Ironically, although this writing aimed at affirmation, it seems rather to document the nineteenth century's systematic attack, led by Marx himself, against the dehumanizing effects of modern industrial civilization. It was this kind of fiction which was to dominate in the years to come.

First Five-Year Plan (1928-1932). Although it did not publicly revoke its 1925 policy of non-intervention in literature, the Party, in effect, reversed its stand when it made the Russian Association of Proletarian Writers (RAPP) its official agent on the literary sector of the "cultural front." Headed by Leopold AVERBAKH, RAPP was a descendant of the PROLETKULT and other groups advocating a literature of "service" to the proletarian revolution. The extent of its control over the total literary output has been questioned by some students of Soviet culture. The literary "means of production"—presses, paper supplies—as well as the power of final editorial decisions, seem to have remained in Party hands. But RAPP occupied the foreground of the literary scene and its strident exhortations and condemnations represented the public face of this effort to make the literary imagination work as an instrument of government policy. In general it was expected that literature would mirror the construction activity of the five-year plan in order to hasten the gigantic effort to industrialize the country. On the level of slogans and popular agitation enormous pressure was exerted on writers to visit industrial sites and to make the "pathos" of construction feats the central theme of their works. Semi-literate "worker correspondents" were encouraged to report on their experiences; the journalistic "sketch" and the "wall newspaper" were celebrated as the most effective of the new literary forms; writers were organized into "shock brigades" and urged into "socialist competitions" with each other. On this level it was a period of barren experimentation which yielded little of literary value. Elsewhere, however, beneath the hysterical sloganizing, it should be noted that RAPP's theoreticians had preserved a core of the classical esthetic in their basic thinking about literature. Apart from the question of loyalty to the Revolution, which was taken for granted and did not have to be attested at every stage of the novel's development, literature must tell a ruthless kind of truth about life. "Tear off all masks," the sloganeers shouted to the writers, and in the treatment of character give us the human being as you see him, the Communist with all his failings and inner conflicts, "the living man," that is to say, the class enemy with all his virtues. There is an unmistakable echo of Tolstoy, Turgenev and Chekhov in this approach. It should be noted that in the critical fulminations accompanying the overthrow of RAPP in 1932 both attitudes were sharply questioned: the indiscriminate ripping off of masks was felt to be dangerously negative, and the call for accurate focus on the human actor regardless of his class allegiances was denounced as "psychologism" and traced to the harmful influence of Tolstoy, Flaubert and other outmoded "bourgeois" writers. The affirmation of Soviet values, which is a feature of all post-RAPP writing, ended literature's function as a "criticism of life," and replaced the "living man" with the new "positive" Soviet hero.

Despite bizarre, superficial experimentation, the good writers continued to write well, within the strictures imposed on them. Whether they were sustained by the muffled echo of the classical esthetic still left in RAPP's program, or whether genuine talent is flexible enough to adapt to a drastic narrowing of the moral range open to it, is a question still to be answered. In any case,

LEONOV wrote two more able novels, *Sot* (1930) and *Skutarevski* (1932), which preserved his views on the complexity of human character and on the costs of intemperate progress. In the first novel the bare melodrama of constraint is enriched with a broader pattern of tensions between the old versus the new, and of the sexual and family dislocation that attends the frenzy of construction. In his second novel, Leonov picked up a theme from the previous decade—the isolation of the intellectual, in this case a scientist—and resolved it "happily." The scientist finds himself increasingly involved in new technological challenges and estranged from the old way of life by the discovery of counter-revolutionary villainy in his own family. This latter detail is very nearly a constant feature in this kind of writing. Because problems of production, of technology and scientific experiment seldom gives rise to interesting human situations, it was often thought to be necessary to impose a dogmatic moral framework, based on political attitudes. The human material is ordered according to this formula and the result, too often, was a pure melodrama in which overworked heroes and concealed traitors did ludicrous battle over the cement mixers and in the planning conferences. Leonov has managed to surmount this element of his narratives with enough story, characters and setting to diminish its impact, but lesser writers, particularly the playwrights, found their representations of life dominated by a simple "for us or against us" moral conflict.

Valentin KATAYEV continued to bypass this problem by casting the whole of his narrative in *Time, Forward!* (1932) in a lighter vein. The problem of production is handled in swift cinematic episodes which emphasize the grotesquely accelerated tempos and allow little time to dwell on virtue or villainy. His heroes are admirable, if slightly foolish in their concentration, and his villains are no more demonic figures than lazy, drunken *kulaks*.

Novels were also written about the collectivization of agriculture, the great revolution in the countryside that paralleled the five-year plan in industry. One, Mikhail SHOLOKHOV's *Virgin Soil Upturned* (1931), stands out above the rest. He set aside his unfinished and much greater epic, *The Quiet Don*, by direction of the "social command" in order to write it. A concealed White officer is the initiator of the resistance to the Party's efforts to collectivize a Cossack village. But a wealth of persuasive detail and a real sense of the human anguish that accompanied the change surround and neutralize the crude political conflict. The novelist's task is made easier because the "production units" are human beings and the problems of the present and the land are charged with emotion. It is a measure of Sholokhov's integrity as a writer that the Communist hero, Davidov, despite his masterful victory over the villagers' resistance to his decrees, stands out clearly in all his monastic aridity and single-mindedness. There is pathos in the image, because the costs of his dedicated, fanatical life are not concealed.

The difficulties of writing novels under these pressures are best demonstrated, perhaps, in EHRENBURG's *The Second Day* (1933; English translation as "Out of Chaos"). The hero of the novel is a self-educated young man who has acquired an extensive knowledge of the great literary classics and has tried to build his life on the kind of permanent truths they contain. He lives in a state of constant friction with the healthy, mindless technicians with whom he studies and works. From his special vantage he is permitted by Ehrenburg to develop a searching critique of the blank spiritual world he inhabits. But there is no resolution of the conflict; the young man's creed is declared to be a rationalization for his self-centered isolation from the group, and the new Soviet truth of dedicated selflessness is proclaimed superior. It is in the effort to enact this predetermined moral outcome that Ehrenburg falls into absurdity. The young man is found to be guilty of anti-social behavior because a companion, to whom he has read Dostoyevski, runs directly to the building site and sabotages an important piece of machinery.

Needless to say, less sophisticated writers than Ehrenburg fared no better than he did. It might be said in conclusion that good writers on the whole continued to write adequately against heavy and mounting pressure, but the mediocre writer was forced into banality. Neither was able to nourish himself sufficiently on the residue of the classical esthetic that lay under the surface of the RAPP program. In any case, it was the poor quality of the average literary product that caused the Party to intervene and call a halt to its first attempt at a legislated orthodoxy. But the liquidation of RAPP by decree in 1932 was followed not by the end of such attempts, but by the institution of the second, subtle, more elaborate and in the end more successful effort to accomplish the same purpose.

1932-1941. The era of SOCIALIST REALISM began with a number of changes in literary theory and in the new field of literary administration. Two contrary tendencies are discernible: one toward liberalism; the other, below the surface and more decisive in the end, toward restriction and control. Except for the attacks on Averbakh, which increased in severity as time went by until he disappeared, charged with Trotskyism, an atmosphere of tolerance and release had surrounded the liquidation of RAPP. A general amnesty was proclaimed for all writers who had been hounded into silence, the practice of securing "loyalty oaths" from writers was denounced, and the harsh regime of slogans was declared at an end. After two years of preparation, the new literary doctrine, SOCIALIST REALISM, and the new administrative apparatus, the UNION OF SOVIET WRITERS, were inaugurated at a great literary conference, the First All-Union Congress of Soviet Writers, in August, 1934. The dual nature of the changeover was made entirely clear in the proceedings of the Congress. On the one hand, invitations were issued, with an air of forgiveness, to all Soviet writers including those who had become most estranged from the regime. On the other hand, a writer who accepted the invitation was to discover that he was being herded into a single literary organization, the new writers' union, with a dominant Party fraction, with an official literary doctrine and with an elaborate set of regulations and by-laws. On the one hand, he was told that in the future he would be deprived of only one right—"the right to write badly"— and he received assurances from Gorki (see Peshkov), Bukharin and others that he stood on the threshold of a new era which called for originality, boldness and experiment. On the other hand, he could not fail to notice in the keynote address by A. A. ZHDANOV, a leader of the Party, that his experiments would not be permitted to transcend a rigidly defined set of doctrinal limits. It was generally asserted that Socialist Realism's only injunction to the writer was that in his investigations of Soviet life, he concentrate on the "emergent kernel of reality," as it collided with and replaced the outmoded and reactionary past. This, in itself, is a very binding commitment: it involves the writer in a particular theory of history and in a set of absolute values derived from it. But Zhdanov spelled out the terms of the writer's obligations far more explicitly than this. He established a standard of literary judgment (derived from the Russian radical past) which was entirely based on extra-literary sources. The standard is the familiar one of utilitarian service, which is to be expressed in a "tendentious" (that is to say, a favorable) treatment of the Soviet status quo. The mood of Soviet literature is to be one of affirmation, and its leading characters are to be the new heroes of "socialist labor," the men and women who carry out government policy in the most exemplary way. It is clear from Zhdanov's speech that the policy changes of 1932 and 1934 had established an effective set of controls on both the doctrinal and administrative levels. They were not immediately applied at their full strength, but they continued to represent a restrictive potential that could be put into effect at any time.

In the 1930's the "Popular Front" strategy on the international scene, and the success of the five-year plans at home made for a policy of tolerance on the part of the literary magistrates, and an attitude of responsiveness to literary influences from the past and from the West, on the part of writers and critics. In the name of the same principles, however, Zhdanov was able, in 1946, to initiate the era of harshest repression in Soviet literary history, not excluding the RAPP period at its worst.

Between 1932 and 1941 the literary product was more varied than might reasonably have been expected. Even in its mild form the new orthodoxy worked a harmful effect on experiment and innovation, but the range in theme, treatment and form is nevertheless impressive. It is best illustrated in four novels which appeared in final and complete form before the Nazi invasion in June, 1941: SHOLOKHOV's *Quiet Don*, LEONOV's *Road to the Ocean*, A. N. TOLSTOY's *Way Through Hell*, and Nikolay OSTROVSKI's *How the Steel Was Tempered.*

SHOLOKHOV's epic of the Cossacks in the throes of revolution is generally accepted as the greatest literary work of the Soviet period. Both Soviet and Western critics refer to Lev TOLSTOY in discussing the origins of this novel, because of the panoramic range of experience contained in it, and because of the depth and solidity of its characterization. Sholokhov may be said to lack the emotional subtlety and the moral awareness of Tolstoy, but these deficiencies may be accounted for by the nature of his human material and by the brutal experiences his characters undergo. The passionate violence of the Cossack ethos in a setting of ruthless Civil War does not encourage Tolstoyan insights, perhaps, but Sholokhov has made superb use of it, nevertheless, in his profound artistic exploration of the roots of Soviet life. Ironically its great success cannot be separated from the fact that it violates both the letter and spirit of SOCIALIST REALISM. The novel's dramatic design is not affirmative, but tragic in a very ancient sense: its hero, the Cossack Melekhov, loses his way in a maze of bewildering choices and finds himself at the end without hope, estranged from life, waiting for the Revolution's impersonal punishment for his fatal errors of judgment. The publication of the final serial episode in 1940 aroused a storm of discussion around the question: "Does Soviet art have a right to tragedy?" Though the novel was an immense popular success, and was welcomed into a realm of Socialist Realism by a number of influential critics, official acceptance has been grudging. Sholokhov's lesser novel, *Virgin Soil Upturned* (1931), has received much greater praise from official sources because of its higher quotient of political uplift.

LEONOV's *Road to the Ocean* (1935) also travels close to the limits of the official canon. Its reception by the critics was unenthusiastic and its complexity (and occasional obscurity) have kept it from achieving popular success. The prevalence of suffering in the novel, the frank emphasis on the blemishes of Soviet life, the fantastic speculations about the future, and the complex time scheme are pointed to by Soviet critics as serious flaws. These are some of the properties of the novel that have brought it to the attention of Western critics.

Leonov has included the obligatory strain of dark melodrama—in this case, the exposure of a villainous wrecker—but the heart of the novel is the spiritual history of a dedicated and sensitive Bolshevik official. With the approach of death from an old injury received in the Civil War, Kurilov, the novel's hero, detaches himself from his oppressive daily routine in order to explore the meanings of his entire life. Against some of the traditional constants of human experience, he strikes the balance of rewards and costs in his bleakly dedicated existence. In the end he concludes that the reward of participating in history's forward movement outweighs the many human deprivations he has suffered. The note of affirmation is heavily muted with sorrow and uncertainty, however, and it is precisely his attitude of skeptical, brooding inquiry that links him with the classical tradition, while it puts him at odds with the magistrates of his society.

Classical concerns are present also in A. N. TOLSTOY's *Way through Hell* (English translation as "Road to Calvary"), which appeared in sections between 1920 and 1941, but they are eclipsed as the novel progresses and replaced by the values of the new mode of writing. The novel has the aspect of a laboratory experiment in converting human truth into political truth. The early episodes contain a large cast of compelling characters, a wealth of careful social observation, and a number of genuine dramatic themes, drawn from the world of the pre-revolutionary intelligentsia of St. Petersburg and developed in the turmoil of Civil War. When Tolstoy abruptly alters his approach after he has made peace with the Soviet regime, the fictional material is drastically rearranged according to standards of political virtue and villainy, and the novel ends on a strident note of political affirmation, the sources of which are entirely lacking in the first half of the novel.

The novel which most directly reflects the esthetic of Socialist Realism and has, therefore, the least relevance to the classical tradition is OSTROVSKI's *How the Steel Was Tempered* (1932-34; English translation as "The Making of a Hero"). It is the story of a Ukrainian Communist from his earliest childhood until the moment when his multiple injuries result in blindness and paralysis and force him to retire from Party work. Still a young man, he engages his "iron" Bolshevik will in the task of becoming a professional writer. This last detail makes it clear to the reader that the book he has just finished is the result of this heroic effort at self-education. It is an autobiographical memoir, then, not a novel, and belongs with *Chapayev* in the category of primitive, journalistic myth-making. Entirely lacking in significant form, the book is held together only by the presence of the hero-narrator in all the major episodes. Immune to doubt, hesitation or fear, he establishes his heroic image by enduring a physical beating over the years that challenges credibility. He is able to do so, he explains, because of his political faith which gives him the strength and wisdom to act effectively in a wide variety of crisis situations. The book is the self-portrait of a Communist paragon, and it is for this reason, undoubtedly, that it has received the highest official praise and has been proclaimed a "Soviet classic." And it may be said that its success forecasts, at the same time, the final defeat of the classical tradition, and indicates a significant deterioration in the situation of the writer and in standards of critical judgment.

The Second World War (1941-1945). War brought important changes to the Soviet literary world. In many ways the war restricted the literary output. Many writers were put on a wartime basis, assigned to front-line units, and made to work as correspondents. A number of these were killed or wounded, and those who survived were forced to endure all the rigors of combat experience. Though it was extremely difficult to write well under such circumstances, new themes and a refreshingly new vision of life began to appear in some of the fragmentary and hastily written material that found its way into print. War brought with it its classical repertory of emotions: terror, solitude and anguish, courage, compassion and comradeship. Soviet writers enforcedly returned to a plane of universal emotion. The only test of political loyalty became a demonstrated willingness to defend the Soviet fatherland, and any one who accepted this elementary challenge might gain entrance to literature without further certification. New human types appeared, more fallible and less doctrinal than the arid, parental figures who dominated the average peacetime novel. It is perhaps ironic that a return to humanist concerns was brought about by the presence of the tangible Nazi enemy on Soviet soil. The emotional atmosphere of Soviet life seemed clarified and deepened in this period of trial by a new awareness of human fundamentals and by the dissipation of the climate of suspicion and bitterness engendered by the intangible menaces of peacetime, the spies, wreckers and distant foreign enemies. This change is most convincingly demonstrated by the reappearance, for the first time in more than a decade, of genuine lyric poetry. It was homely in theme and unpretentious in form, but it reflected more avidly than anything else men's direct, uncomplicated response to a mortal crisis.

Novelists and dramatists, as it turned out, were never to be granted the leisure to dwell at length on the national anguish. During the war few finished examples of the larger forms were produced. There were a number of competent novels—SIMO-NOV's *Days and Nights* (1944), PANOVA's *Travelling Companions* (1946; English translation as "The Train") and LEONOV's *The Taking of Velikoshumsk* (1944; English translation as "Chariot of Wrath") deserve mention—but they are in one sense or another unfinished works. Plays created under the same handicaps produce the same impression of genuine experience, inadequately assimilated.

The Post-War Period. The end of hostilities in 1945 did not bring to Soviet writers, as it did to their Western contemporaries, the tranquillity to recollect the experience just past. By the autumn of 1946 the blight of a new orthodoxy lay on Soviet letters. On September 21 of that year, A. A. ZHDANOV, speaking for the Party, delivered his epoch-making "Report on the Journals *Zvezda* and *Leningrad*," in which he readjusted all the controlling mechanisms of Socialist Realism to exert unparalleled pressure on writers to function as an arm of the propaganda effort. Reconstruction and rehabilitation were prescribed as the only tasks of Soviet literature, henceforth. It is reasonable to suppose that the Soviet people suffered a considerable let down of morale after the war, which might interfere with the program of restoring the national economy. In this atmosphere of apathy and restlessness, any contemplation of the war experience would apparently be rejected as an act of self-indulgent nostalgia. The Soviet people had to be armed against new enemies, and anything that deflected attention from the tasks the Party considered paramount, would not be tolerated. Zhdanov's "Report," therefore, laid heavier emphasis on the restrictive elements in the utilitarian tradition than had any previous interpretation of this approach to literature. Literature was to *serve* in the narrowest sense of the term; it was to act as a kind of animated illustration of whatever policies the Soviet government felt were vital to its security. On questions of taste Zhdanov is perfectly frank: it was entirely wrong, he said, to imagine "that a good, artistic piece of writing" would be published if it contained anything in it "liable to confuse and poison the minds of our young people." Zhdanov's clear exposure of his standards of judgment actually characterizes Soviet post-war writing in terms that are intelligible to Westerners: though it was to deal with adult problems—the rebuilding of factories, the management of collective farms—the level of communication was to be much closer to the kind of writing which, in the West, is called *juvenilia*, complete with contrived situations and uplifting resolutions.

In response to Zhdanov's orders a large number of "problem-solving" novels have appeared in the decade since his "Report," dealing with the most minute aspects of industrial technology and farm administration. According to the basic pattern of this writing, some area of breakdown, disorder or friction in the society, widespread enough, presumably, to be of general interest, is shown in considerable detail, followed by a model solution of the problem through the application of correct techniques and the exercise of exemplary virtues by the Communist hero. In the same spirit, though to a lesser extent, drama and fiction have been brought to bear on the international situation, as well. Plays and novels designed to illustrate American villainy in the cold war were contrived out of the few plausible points of contact between citizens of the two "camps." There were other themes and other kinds of writing during these years—memoirs, historical novels, stories of love and family morality, a few war novels— but the Zhdanov formula predominated in post-war fiction, and nothing of real quality has appeared since his "Report."

The direction of literary policy has not been clear since STALIN's death in 1953. Considerable dissatisfaction with the quality of the literary output under Zhdanov's regime has been expressed, and certain tentative gestures toward liberalization have been made. Evidence of restlessness in the ranks is apparent in EHRENBURG's novel, *The Thaw*, and in a number of controversial articles in the press. But none of the central principles of Socialist Realism had been abandoned by the end of 1955 and no general reversal of policy has been indicated. At a Writers' Congress in 1954 the critical voices were heard but ignored, and Zhdanov's version of Socialist Realism was restored nearly intact.

Until further notice Soviet literature apparently will continue to be written within the confines of the Hegelian-Marxian theory of progress, and will justify its existence by consciously forwarding the progressive trend in history, as defined by history's self-appointed agent, the Party. It will continue, too, to be guided by the utilitarian esthetic which assigns value to art according to the service it performs. Soviet literature is an instrument of social change—a "weapon," as LENIN said—in the hands of political magistrates, and is concerned ultimately with a parochial view of political truth, not with the limitless range of human truth.

Soviet literature, considered as an extension of the Russian tradition, may be said to have betrayed its birthright, though no one can foretell the future. The overall situation of Soviet letters at present is most vividly illustrated by the virtual disappearance of lyric poetry, with the exception of the war years. In the years after the Civil War there were a number of gifted poets, and a lively debate between poetic schools was carried on. Vladimir MAYAKOVSKI, the most gifted representative of this period, displayed enormous vitality in his verse and a striking command of language and image. He put his talent at the service of the Revolution, and seemed to have found in his harshly oratorical declamations (very much in the manner of Walt Whitman) the most viable, perhaps the only possible, relationship between the literary sensibility and the strident energies of the Revolution. His suicide in 1930 cannot be attributed, finally, to political causes, but he left broad hints in his later verse that the cost of surrendering to the "social command" was prohibitively high and that suppression of his lyrical voice was the one price he could not continue to pay. Lyrical statement is most sensitive to alien intrusion: a directed response cannot, in the nature of things, be spontaneously free. If this is the indicated lesson it is most vividly borne out by the silence of Boris PASTERNAK, the poet who is generally acknowledged outside the U.S.S.R. to be the greatest living master of Russian verse. He lives in the Soviet Union at the present time, and has gained considerable public recognition for his translations of Shakespeare. But the lack of an audience for his poetry and the declared hostility of the political magistrates have silenced his private voice, and may have caused him, as

Mayakovski said of himself, to crush "under foot the throat of my very own songs."

Rufus W. Mathewson, Jr.

Logofet, Pakhomii. See Pakhomii Logofet.

Lokhvitskaya, Mirra (or Maria) Alexandrovna (married name: Zhiber; 1869-1905), a poetess of the end of the nineteenth century. Her lyric poems are rich in imagery and passionate emotions. Her poetry is erotic, and idealizes the sensuality of love. Her view of love is essentially feminine: woman's duty in love is to submit to her beloved. Her later poetry is strongly mystical.

Lomonosov, Mikhail Vasilyevich (ca. 1711-65), often called the "father of modern Russian literature." Lomonosov was of humble origin, the son of a fisherman of the White Sea coast. In 1730 he came to Moscow to study, entering the Slavo-Greek-Latin Academy. In 1736 he was sent to Germany to the University of Marburg, where he studied philosophy, physics and chemistry under Christian Wolff. On his return to Russia in 1741, he was made a member of the Academy of Sciences. He was one of the foremost minds of the Enlightenment; besides literature, his activities embraced the fields of physics, chemistry, mathematics, geography, mineralogy, grammar and rhetoric. He was active in the foundation of the University of Moscow in 1755. "Lomonosov was himself a university," Pushkin said. His career was complicated by his disputes with other members of the Academy, almost all of whom were German. Embittered, he took to drink, and his last years were unproductive.

Lomonosov was a legislator for the new Russian pseudo-classical literature (see Classicism). His first major work, the *Ode on the Capture of Khotin* (1739) was written in tonic verse (see Prosody); it was accompanied by a *Letter on the Rules of Russian Versification*, which completed the partial reform of TREDIAKOVSKI; Lomonosov advocated the use of the tonic principle for all Russian poetry. It has been retained to the present time. Following classical theories, he established a system of three literary styles, which for a time resolved the existing stylistic conflict between Russian and OLD CHURCH SLAVONIC (see Language). The high style was to employ words common to both Slavonic and Russian, as well as some Slavonicisms which were still comprehensible to educated Russians; it was to be used in

(237)

odes, epics and dignified orations. The middle style was to be based on spoken Russian, with a slight admixture of Slavonicisms, but with all vulgarisms excluded. It was to serve for satires, eclogues, prose writings and dramas, though the high style was also permitted in tragedy. The low style was entirely Russian; vulgar terms were permitted if used judiciously. This style was to be used for comedies, light epigrams, songs, friendly letters and accounts of everyday matters. This system, though a conservative one, endured in Russian literature throughout much of the balance of the century.

In his *Rhetoric* (1748) and *Grammar* (1757), Lomonosov established rules for the language. He advocated a sentence order influenced by Latin and German; here his reforms were perhaps harmful.

Lomonosov's original literary productions are for the most part odes, in which form he excelled. Their style is solemn and grand, cold and impersonal. Most of them celebrate political or military events; they also praise the reforms of PETER THE GREAT and his daughter, Elizabeth, and call for further progress. Perhaps his greatest odes are his "Morning Meditations" (1751) and "Evening Meditations" (1748), which express a kind of deistic admiration for the grandeur of God and his universe. A curiosity typical of the breadth of Lomonosov's interests is the poem entitled *Epistle on the Use of Glass* (1752). He also wrote didactic poetry.

Though Lomonosov is more important as a legislator for Russian language and literature than as an original writer, it is fair to say that his odes contain some of the most majestic lines in Russian eighteenth-century poetry.

Lossky, Nikolay Onufrievich (1870-   ), a twentieth-century philosopher. He taught philosophy at the University of Petersburg. In 1922 he was expelled from the Soviet Union with other anti-Soviet thinkers. Until 1945 he lived in Czechoslovakia; since 1946 he has resided in the United States.

Lossky calls his thought "intuitivism," and lays stress on intuition as a means of knowledge. Thus his philosophy, though independent, has certain resemblances to that of Bergson. For him everything in the cosmos is immanent in everything else; this immanence makes intuitive knowledge of other beings possible.

For him intuitivism implies no conflict with a rational approach to truth. Lossky is perhaps the most "professional" of Russian philosophers, and has developed his thought into a complete and finished system of ideas.

Lotarev, Igor Vasilievich (1887-1941), a poet of the early twentieth century, member of the so-called "Ego-Futurists," who wrote under the pseudonym of Igor Severyanin. He combined the opulent style of SYMBOLISM with a brilliant command of rhythm and with subjects and new words taken from the world of technology and the modern city. In the latter respect he was a follower of the Italian Futurist Movement (see Futurism). But Severyanin had little to express save a self-centered indulgence, and his poems are cheap and facile dreams of the luxury and sensuality, the erotica of modern urban life. He was extremely popular for several years after the publication of his collection of poems, *The Thunder-Seething Cup* (1913), at first with intellectuals, later with the broad public, who found his sensuous and opulent verse appealing.

Lukin, Vladimir Ignatyevich (1737-94), an eighteenth-century playwright, a predecessor of FONVIZIN in his attempt to create a Russian drama with indigenous problems and characters. In structure his plays are derivative from the French, however; only several, such as his *Prodigal Reformed by Love* (1765), are more original.

Lunacharski, Anatoli Vasilievich (1875-1933), a Marxist philosopher, critic and dramatist of the late nineteenth and twentieth centuries. In 1892 he joined the Social Democratic (Marxist) Party, working as a party agitator. He was arrested a number of times for revolutionary activities. After the October REVOLUTION of 1917 he served for twelve years as Soviet Commissar of Education for the Russian Soviet Federated Socialist Republic.

As a philosopher Lunacharski belonged to a group of Marxists who sought to unite Marxism with the philosophy of Mach and Avenarius. These philosophers were positivists: they denied the opposition of spiritual and material worlds, which they declared to be two aspects of the same experience. This position of "Marxist revisionism" won Lunacharski severe criticism from LENIN. Lunacharski even deviated from the orthodox anti-religious position of Marxism-Leninism to the extent that he characterized socialism as a "religion of feeling." (See Philosophy.)

In his writings on literature and art, Lunacharski advocated the creation of a new proletarian literature for Soviet society. Proletarian literature, in his conception, was neither literature created by the proletariat, nor literature about the proletariat; rather, it was literature which expressed the views of the proletariat in the class struggle. After the October REVOLUTION he became a warm supporter of the PROLETKULT (see Literature, Soviet; Criticism, Soviet).

Between 1906 and 1926 Lunacharski wrote a number of plays, the most interesting of which are attempts to create a proletarian drama. His *Oliver Cromwell* (1920) portrays Cromwell, rather anachronistically, as a modern progressive leader.

Lunts, Lev Natanovich (1901-24), a writer and critic of the early 1920's. A member of the SERAPION BROTHERS, Lunts published an important characterization of that group in 1922. As a critic he argued that Russian literature was too one-sidedly realistic, and that it should learn variety from the West. He published several plays which showed great promise. He emigrated in 1923 and died the following year.

M

Magazines, Literary. See Journals, Literary.

Makarii, Metropolitan. Elevated to the office of Metropolitan of the Russian Church in 1542, Makarii is associated with several literary compilations of a grandiose, encyclopedic nature which were prepared under his direction. The first is the *Cheti-Minei* (Monthly Church Readings; completed in 1552), a collection of almost all the extant Russian Church literature, much of which was reworked. Another is the *Book of Degrees,* a genealogy and history of the Russian princely line, in which many of the princes are depicted as near-saints. This work is an outstanding example of the high-flown, pompous and long-winded rhetorical style of the period.

Malinovski, A. A. See Bogdanov, A.

Malyshkin, Alexander Georgievich (1892-1938), a Soviet writer. His first novel, *The Fall of Dair* (1923), depicted the Civil War in the Crimea; the author drew in part on his own service in the war for his material. The work lacks an individual hero; the people as a whole rather appear in this role. In the late 1920's Malyshkin joined the PEREVAL group. In his later novels, *The Snows of February* (1928) and *Sevastopol* (1929-30), he describes the effect of the Revolution of February, 1917, on the Black Sea Fleet.

Mamin, Dmitri Narkisovich (1852-1912), a novelist of the late nineteenth and early twentieth century. He wrote under the pen-name of Sibiryak ("the Siberian"), and is commonly known as Mamin-Sibiryak. He had political sympathies with the POPULISTS, and specialized in novels about the Ural region, the rapacious growth of capitalism there and the exploitation of the Ural miners. His novels, such as *The Brothers Gordeyev* (1891) and *Bread* (1895), are examples of Russian naturalism; they are wordy and poorly organized, but acquire a certain elemental power from their lengthy accumulation of details. Mamin's attacks on capitalism have helped to bring a revival of his work in the Soviet Union. He has recently become one of the most widely reprinted nine-teenth-century writers, a distinction not entirely commensurate with his true stature.

Mandelstam, Osip Emilievich (1892-1942?), a poet of the twentieth century, one of the poets of the movement known as ACMEISM. His writing is sophisticated and obscure. His distaste for the Soviet regime is obvious; "I have never been anyone's contemporary," he declared, thus asserting the timelessness of his poetry as well as his rejection of life under the Soviet regime. An epigram about Stalin supposedly caused his deportation in the early 1930's. He died some time during World War II.

Mandelstam's poetry is the chief part of his creative work, though he also published several interesting volumes of prose. His collection of essays, *The Egyptian Stamp* (1928), contains recollections of his youth which sometimes give rise to brilliant characterizations of the epoch. His poetry is classical by tendency, with a preference for antique meters; it shows a love of balance, with frequent use of imagery taken from the arts of architecture and sculpture. His style is laconic, but with a curious mixture of archaisms and popular phrases. Mandelstam's content also tends toward classicism, and he even describes a tennis game in terms proper to an antique sport event. His is a poetry of things and images, with a pronounced pessimism, a coldness and a detachment of the poet from the world which he describes. His production has been meagre, and his main collection is a slim volume called *Tristia* (1922).

Manuscripts, Old Russian. Old Russian books were written manuscripts, often ornamented. As in the West, ornament could consist of illumination of beginning letters, or actual illustration. At first written on parchment, later on paper, manuscripts were generally bound, though long scrolls were common in the sixteenth and seventeenth centuries. Bindings were often ornate, employing rich metals, jewels, velvet, etc. The oldest surviving Russian book is the *Ostromir Gospel*, prepared in 1056-57, for Ostromir, Mayor of Novgorod.

Printed letters *(ustav, poluustav)* were customary until the seventeenth century. A kind of broken cursive was introduced, however, as early as the fifteenth century.

Marienhof, Anatoli. See Imaginism.

Markevich, Boleslav Mikhaylovich (1822-84), a writer of the second half of the nineteenth century. He came from a noble family of Polish descent. A reactionary member of the landowning gentry, Markevich attacked not only the radicals of his day, but even criticized the government itself, which seemed too liberal for him in its REFORMS. His novels include the trilogy, *A Quarter Century Ago* (1878), and *The Break* (1880).

Markov, Yevgeni Lvovich (1835-1903), a novelist of the 1870's. His principal novel, *The Black-soiled Steppe* (1877), idealizes the life of the landowning gentry as healthy and natural, and echoes much of the nostalgia of TURGENEV's novels for life on the estate.

Markovich, Mariya Alexandrovna (1834-1907), a writer of fiction who published under the pseudonym of Marko-Vovchok. A Russian by birth, she married a Ukrainian nationalist, A. Markovich. She wrote in both the Russian and Ukrainian languages. Her tales of peasant life, stylized in the folk-tale tradition, are simplified and sentimental pictures of the hardships of peasant life, with the peasants depicted uniformly as good, the landowners as evil. Most significant, perhaps, were her early collections, *Folk Tales* (1858), published in Ukrainian and translated into Russian by TURGENEV in 1859, and *Stories of Russian Folk Life* (1860), in Russian.

Marko-Vovchok. See Markovich, M. A.

Marlinski, A. See Bestuzhev, A. A.

Marxism. See Philosophy; Lenin; Plekhanov; Trotski; Stalin.

Marxism in Literature. See Literature, Soviet; Criticism, Soviet; Plekhanov; Socialist Realism.

Masonry. See Freemasonry.

Matinski, Mikhail, author of a comic opera, *The Petersburg Bazaar* (1779), a satirical treatment of the dishonesty of merchants and government clerks. The author was a freed serf, about whom almost nothing is known.

Maxim Grek ("the Greek"; 1480-1556), a Greek monk who studied in Italy in his youth, where he came under certain Renaissance influences, including, probably, the teachings of Savonarola.

Maxim Grek came to Russia in 1518 to undertake the task of correcting the Russian Church books, long corrupt. His corrections struck his literalist opponents as too extreme, and in 1525 he was condemned to imprisonment for heresy. He remained a prisoner until 1551. Maxim Grek wrote a number of tracts criticizing Russian superstition and unjust government, as well as the cupidity of Russian monasteries. He also wrote didactic treatises and textbooks. He appears in early sixteenth-century Russia as an enlightened teacher far ahead of his times. (See Schism.)

Mayakovski, Vladimir Vladimirovich (1893-1930), a leading futurist poet. Born in Trans-Caucasia, he joined the underground Bolshevik Party at the age of fourteen. He was arrested several times for his political activities, and spent eleven months in prison. After his release, he entered art school, where he joined the newly emerging Futurist Movement in painting and poetry (see Futurism). The poet and painter David BURLYUK provided him with a brief education in poetic technique. Otherwise Mayakovski was self-trained and largely self-educated. In 1912 he signed the manifesto of the Cubo-Futurists. But he did not share the other Futurists' interest in an abstract, invented, "trans-sense language," and the neologisms which he coined by free use of prefixes and suffixes are easily comprehensible.

In 1917 Mayakovski was one of the few established writers who at once accepted the October Revolution. He devoted himself to the Bolshevik cause heart and soul. From 1918 to 1920 he contributed drawings and texts for thousands of propaganda posters calling for Red victory in the Civil War. Most of his poetry during these years was also propaganda. In 1923 he helped to found LEF ("Left Front," see Futurism), a group which sought to continue the principles of Futurism in the Soviet period. But Futurism proved increasingly unacceptable for more orthodox Communist critics, and they subjected Mayakovski to sharp attack. Meanwhile, he had fallen in love with the wife of his close friend and fellow futurist, Osip Brik. In April, 1930, he committed suicide, if not from unrequited love, then from a feeling of increasing estrangement and disillusion with Soviet life.

Mayakovski's poetry is deliberately coarse, loud, and often ugly; it aims to shock, *épater le bourgeois*, and Mayakovski was one of the most vociferous of the Futurists in calling for whole-

sale negation of older culture. The best and most original qualities of his work are his powerful rhythms, grandiose hyperbole,
and original metaphors, often elaborated into long, fantastic conceits. His verse is rhythmically irregular, with a constant number
of stresses to the line but an irregular number of unstressed syllables. The lines are broken down typographically into parts to
facilitate apprehension of the stress pattern. A skilled reader,
Mayakovski intended his verse to be declaimed, and in his own
reading could make it sound like a drum-beat or a powerful
marching rhythm. His rhymes were particularly rich and original,
often extending to four or more syllables and involving several
words.

Mayakovski's first poems were published in 1912. His autobiographical tragedy, *Vladimir Mayakovski* (1914), shocked the public with its use of systematic comparisons to the life of Christ: it
had sections on the poet's nativity, passion, ascension, etc. *The
Cloud in Trousers* (1915) tells of the grief of the poet's unrequited
love; at one point he summons a fire brigade to come and ex-
tinguish his blazing heart. The poem's title is a metaphor for the
poet, whom Mayakovski proposes to bring down from the heavens
and incarnate as a flesh and blood human being.

Mystery Bouffe (1918) is a verse play, a complex allegory with
some resemblance to a medieval mystery play. It prophesies the
eventual victory of the Revolution over capitalism. *150,000,000*
(1920) is a hyperbolic epic in which a giant peasant, Ivan, the
spirit of the Russian people, does battle with Woodrow Wilson,
who represents the capitalist West. At first Wilson seems to be
winning, but the giant breaks up into innumerable little men who
infiltrate everywhere, a motif taken from Russian epic folk songs.

During the early 1920's Mayakovski wrote many short propaganda pieces in support of the Red cause, socialist reform, and
the government manufactured products which competed under
the New Economic Policy with private industry. One of these
poems, *Lost in Conference* (1922), satirizing red tape and bureaucracy, was praised by LENIN for its politics, though Lenin disliked Mayakovski's modernist extravagance and his hatred for
the culture of the past.

On Lenin's death, Mayakovski wrote his *Vladimir Ilyich Lenin*
(1924), a work which shows less crudity and greater restraint than

his earlier writing, and which succeeds in striking a note of true elegiac feeling.

In the mid-1920's Mayakovski travelled to Western Europe, the United States and Latin America, writing a series of poems sharply critical of life under capitalism. He admired American technology, but attacked what he considered the inequality and injustice of capitalism. On his return he wrote a long poem, *Khorosho!* (1927; "All Right!"), a naive eulogy to Soviet progress. But Mayakovski's final attitude was not solely one of uncritical praise; his two satirical plays, *The Bedbug* (1928) and *The Bathhouse* (1929), protested against the growing philistinism and bureaucracy in Soviet life.

Mayakovski's suicide, considered a "bourgeois" act by Soviet critics, almost brought an end to his fame. But the Communists badly needed a poet who had appeared before 1917, and who had lived through the Revolution and accepted it from the beginning. Mayakovski satisfied these requirements as few others could. Today he is celebrated as the uniquely great poet of the Soviet Revolution. But, though the critics recommend his work as a model for young poets, they have little real sympathy for his extremist manner, and the approved poetic style today is far more conservative than Mayakovski's. His influence was strongest during the 1920's, on such poets as ASEYEV and BEZYMENSKI.

Though Mayakovski enthusiastically welcomed the Revolution, it is apparent that he accepted it more because it fitted in with his own rebellion against past tradition and with his radical spirit than because he was a disciplined Communist as such. He liked the nihilism and destructiveness of the Revolution. Its atheism and materialism also appealed to him strongly, with its new cult of technology and machines. His thought is quite superficial: he shares the delusion typical of his day that a little good will and effort, combined with industrialization, would transform Russian life and bring the Soviet people a new happiness. His greatness, in fact, is in his manner and infectious spirit, not in his ideas. He developed his own theory of literature, which he applied to the new Soviet order: the poet should write according to "social command," for the needs of the Soviet proletariat. Poetry itself should take part in revolution, and should become an integral part of Soviet life, which the government ought to treat as seriously as it treats industrial production. Mayakovski even described himself as an "industrial plant manufacturing happiness." This faith in the ability of poetry—and his poetry—to bring happiness seems naive today and a trifle pathetic. Mayakovski's failure to satisfy his own standards—or, indeed, the more traditional ones for poetry—shows clearly that his work is a great, inspired failure, in spite of all its brilliance and originality.

Maykov, Apollon Nikolayevich (1821-97), a poet of the mid-nineteenth century, great-grandson of the eighteenth-century poet, V. I. MAYKOV. He was a painter in his youth, but soon went over to poetry, and published his first volume of verse in 1842. He belonged to the group of Russian Parnassian poets of the mid-nineteenth century, who believed in art for its own sake. An imagist, Maykov's poetry is concerned principally with pictures and images. His work is often sentimental, but contains little real emotion. The world of antiquity furnished him with subjects, such as the struggle between pagan Rome and the early Christians, which he treated in his verse tragedy, *Two Worlds* (1882). Other poems, including the collection, *Sketches of Rome* (1847), show his strongly pagan sympathies. Another favorite subject of Maykov's is nature, and a few of his poems, such as his *Haymaking*, have remained in great favor. His landscapes, noted for their precision, pictorial quality and emotional detachment, are stronger than his more pretentious poems on classical antiquity, in which he attempted to treat philosophic ideas beyond his depth. Increasingly conservative in later life, Maykov's long narrative poem, *The Princess* (1877), ridicules the NIHILISTS.

Though much admired by DOSTOYEVSKI and others in his own day, Maykov has since lost popularity. His failure as a poet is largely to be blamed on the generally low level of poetry in his time.

Maykov, Valerian Nikolayevich (1823-47), a literary critic of the mid-nineteenth century, brother of the poet APOLLON MAYKOV. He sharply attacked BELINSKI for the latter's view that literature ought to be subordinated to the needs of society; art, in Maykov's view, should not serve the particular needs of an era or a nation, but should be universal. His early death by drowning cut short the career of one of the most promising young critics of the period.

Maykov, Vasili Ivanovich (1728-78), a writer of the eighteenth century, who introduced the genre of the mock epic in his poem, *Elisey, or Bacchus Infuriated* (1771). The work describes the adventures of a rogue and drunkard who is under Bacchus' protection. Its details are often crude but realistic.

Medvedev, Silvester (1641-91). A pupil of SIMEON POLOTSKI, Medvedev followed in his teacher's footsteps as an advocate of Western enlightenment and as court poet under the regency of Princess Sophia. Because he had been in favor with Sophia and her party, he was executed by Peter the Great in 1691.

Melnikov, Pavel Ivanovich (1819-83), a novelist of the second half of the nineteenth century, who wrote under the pseudonym of Andrey Pecherski. An archeologist and ethnographer, his most important novels, *In the Forests* (1871-75) and *On the Hills* (1875-81), describe the life of the sect of Old Believers (see Schism) along the upper Volga and in the Urals. Long and perhaps too replete with ethnographical details, they are picturesque in their description of the ascetic and fanatically religious life of this sect.

Merezhkovskaya. See Hippius, Z. N.

Merezhkovski, Dmitri Sergeyevich (1865-1941), a writer and thinker of the generation of SYMBOLISM. He studied at the University of Petersburg, and began to publish poetry as early as 1883. His first poetry was "civic," in the style of NADSON. But his study of Western poetry, particularly that of Poe and Baudelaire, led him to revolt against utilitarian and civic conceptions of the purpose of poetry and to advocate a more esthetic attitude toward literature.

In 1903 Merezhkovski and his wife, the poetess Zinaida HIPPIUS, became central figures in the Religious and Philosophical Society, the chief aim of which was to promote a new and rather mystical spirituality among the intelligentsia, as well as to bring them together with thinking members of the clergy. The circle attracted younger poets, including BLOK and Bely (see Bugayev), whom Merezhkovski early published and encouraged. Previously a liberal, Merezhkovski now inclined to acceptance of the idea of a theocratic autocracy for Russia. But during the REVOLUTION of 1905 he reversed his attitude and launched a violent attack on the tsarist system; his attitude became so critical that he was forced to leave the country and live in France for a time

(1906-12). His influence waned, for most of the Russian intelligentsia moved toward the right, not the left, after 1905, and the radicals distrusted Merezhkovski's mysticism. In 1919 the Merezhkovskis emigrated and went first to Poland, then to France, where they were among the most intransigently bitter of anti-Soviet émigrés. Merezhkovski continued to·write novels as well as anti-Bolshevik propaganda. In the last years of his life he became more and more pro-Fascist in his views, and welcomed Hitler's invasion of Russia.

Merezhkovski preferred to think in terms of sharp antitheses, a tendency which he carried into his historical thought. For him the central antithesis of history is that of the Hellenic principle of the purity of the flesh, and the Judeo-Christian principle of the purity of the spirit. Human history for him represents an oscillation between these two tendencies; when one is on the upswing, the other is on the decline. The goal of history is the synthesis of both tendencies, for each is incomplete, in Merezhkovski's view, without the other. Christian abnegation of the flesh is as wrong for him as Greek neglect of the religious spirit.

Merezhkovski developed this view of history in his trilogy of novels, collectively entitled *Christ and Antichrist: Julian the Apostate, Or the Death of the Gods* (1896), *Leonardo da Vinci, Or the Gods Reborn* (1901), and *Peter and Alexis* (1905). The first describes the death of the Hellenic spirit in the reign of the Emperor Julian the Apostate, the second its rebirth in the Renaissance. The third novel shows the struggle between the principle of secular progress, represented by PETER THE GREAT, and the Old Muscovite theocratic tradition, represented by Peter's son Alexis, whom Peter ultimately put to death as a traitor to his reform cause. In this final novel the author is carried away by other interests, and the subject hardly fits his central thesis. Merezhkovski had considerable erudition, and these novels are successful as popularizations of history, though he often sacrifices history to his fondness for antithetical reasoning.

The same type of antithetical thought characterizes Merezhkovski's principal critical study, *Tolstoy and Dostoyevski* (1901-02). For Merezhkovski, TOLSTOY is the "seer of the flesh," while DOSTOYEVSKI is the "seer of the spirit." He points out that

Tolstoy's ethics proceed from an intense preoccupation with the biological facts of death and sex. The two writers' techniques even correspond to their views of human nature: Tolstoy describes man from outside, as a physical being; Dostoyevski ignores man's external appearance, and gives a naked chronicle of man's spirit. But this last is little more than a half truth. Still, the book was probably the most influential of all the many Russian studies on Tolstoy and Dostoyevski. Merezhkovski also did important critical studies of LERMONTOV, GOGOL, TYUTCHEV and others.

Merezhkovski's stature as an independent thinker and writer is hardly great, but he did have considerable significance as a leader of the Symbolist Movement (see Symbolism).

Merzlyakov, Alexey Fyodorovich (1778-1830), professor at the University of Moscow, poet and member of the school of KARAMZIN. He is noted for his songs stylized in the folk manner, some of which have become actual popular songs.

Metrics. See Prosody.

Mey, Lev Alexandrovich (1822-62), a poet of the mid-nineteenth century, a representative of the so-called PARNASSIAN POETS. His original poems treat subjects from nature and classical antiquity. He imitated the style and subject matter of Russian folk songs. His drama, *The Maid of Pskov* (1860), on a subject from the time of Ivan the Terrible, began the vogue of the historical verse play in the 1860's. Mey is best remembered, however, for his translations, which include renderings of the *IGOR TALE* (1850), Anacreon, Byron and many others.

Meyerhold, Vsevolod. See Drama and Theater.

Mikhaylov, A. See Scheller, A. K.

Mikhaylov, Mikhail Larionovich (1826-65), a minor radical poet of the mid-nineteenth century. In 1861 he was arrested and exiled for circulating proscribed political literature; he died in Siberia. His poems include lyrics on revolutionary themes. He translated Heine into Russian.

Mikhaylovski, Nikolay Georgievich (1852-1906), a writer of the late nineteenth century, who wrote under the pen-name of N. Garin. He is best remembered for his cycle of autobiographical novels: *Tyoma's Childhood* (1892), *Schoolboys* (1893), *University Students*

(1895) and *Engineers* (1908). These novels have great charm and warmth of portrayal, as well as value as a record of education in the latter part of the nineteenth century.

Mikhaylovski, Nikolay Konstantinovich (1842-1904), a Russian political thinker, sociologist and critic of the second half of the nineteenth century. He came of an impoverished noble family, and belonged to those "repentant noblemen"—the phrase is his own —who were motivated by a sense of guilt and an impulse to right the wrongs done by their serf-holding ancestors. Mikhaylovski devoted his life to radical journalism and scholarly writing, but refrained from taking part in political activities lest he be deprived of the right to publish. From 1868 he was a regular contributor to the *Fatherland Notes;* in the early 1890's he became a leading editor of the periodical, *Russian Wealth,* the organ of the revolutionary socialist movement.

A follower of HERZEN and LAVROV, Mikhaylovski was a leading Russian radical theoretician of the second half of the nineteenth century. The philosophical point of departure for his thought is his identification of the concepts of truth and justice (the Russian word, *pravda,* denotes both). For him science and history cannot be studied objectively, independent of ethical considerations or human needs. He conceived of sociology as a subjective science which should be used to serve human progress. He rejected the "struggle for existence" formula of the evolutionists, for, in his view, it ignored the ethical autonomy of the individual. A socialist, and fully aware of the merits of Marx's thought in the field of economics, Mikhaylovski rejected the doctrine of historical materialism, with its one-sided emphasis on economics and its neglect of the moral, psychological and spiritual sides of life. Socialism, in his view, would bring man true happiness and individualism, for it would destroy the contradictions existing between the individual and society, and release the energies of the individual in socially productive labor, thus satisfying the human urge to create.

Though his ideas had great influence on the Russian POPULISTS, Mikhaylovski was critical of their tendency to idealize traditional Russian peasant institutions, such as the village commune, as socialistic. The commune, in his view, might serve as a stepping-stone in a transition to a distinctly Russian form of socialism, but he saw it as no more than a step, not as an end in itself.

Mikhaylovski was a keen critic of literature, though he judged it almost exclusively in terms of its contribution to social progress. His criticism of DOSTOYEVSKI, though hostile to that writer, is penetrating in its revelation of the sadistic cruelty with which Dostoyevski often treated his characters, and which Mikhaylovski found to be a basic element in his view of life. Thus he helped to debunk the notion that Dostoyevski showed a unilateral sympathy and compassion for human suffering. In a study of TOLSTOY's early work, Mikhaylovski correctly predicted the later development of Tolstoy's anarchistic views.

Mikhaylovski's influence was of great importance in Russia, particularly on that segment of the radicals, including the Socialist Revolutionaries, who rejected Marxism. His views are noteworthy for their emphasis on ethical values and on individualism, rather than collectivism, as the basis for a socialist society. (See Philosophy.)

Milovski, Sergey Nikolayevich (1861-1911), a radical writer of the end of the nineteenth and beginning of the twentieth century, who wrote under the pseudonym of S. Yeleonski. His tales portray the provincial clergy as backward and selfish exploiters of the peasantry.

Minayev, Dmitri Dmitrievich (1835-89), a minor poet of the second half of the nineteenth century. He specialized in descriptions of the poverty of the lower urban classes. He translated from Byron, Dante, Molière and others.

Minski, N. See Vilenkin, N. M.

Mirny, Panas, pseudonym of A. Rudchenko (1849-1920), a leading Ukrainian writer (see Preface).

Monomakh, Vladimir. See Vladimir Monomakh.

Mordovtsev, Daniil Lukich (1830-1905), a novelist and historian of the second half of the nineteenth century. His chief novel, *Signs of the Times* (1869), depicted young radicals of the 1860's and the development of the Populist Movement (see Populists).

Muravlin, Dmitri. See Golitsyn, Prince D. P.

Muscovite Literature. See Literature, Old Russian.

Muyzhel, Viktor Vasilievich (1880-1924), a realist writer of the early twentieth century. His early tales depict peasant life with its misery, brutality and poverty. He continued to live and write in the Soviet Union after 1917, but his later works, on themes connected with the Revolution and the Civil War, are very weak.

N

Nabokov, Vladimir Vladimirovich (1899-   ), an émigré writer. His earlier works were published under the pseudonym of Vladimir Sirin. He left Russia after the 1917 Revolution, went to Cambridge University, where he took a degree, and then settled in Berlin. In 1940 he came to the United States; at the same time he stopped writing in Russian and began to publish in English under his own name.

Nabokov's novels and tales tend toward expressionism and surrealism, with much intricacy of style as well as toying with the narrative. These devices are used to distort reality, to make it appear grotesque and fantastic. Nabokov's novel, *The Luzhin Defense* (1930), is the story of a chess champion and his pathological deterioration, which ultimately ends in madness and suicide. Another novel is the macabre *Invitation to an Execution* (1938). The chief theme of Nabokov's stories is that of lyrical and nostalgic reminiscences of the Russia of his childhood, and this subject has been carried over into his recent writing in English. His English novel, *The Real Life of Sebastian Knight* (1941), is an intriguing detective story about the attempt of a young Russian émigré to reconstruct the life of his half-brother, a successful English novelist. Nabokov has also published a critical study on GOGOL in English (1944), in which he emphasizes the surrealistic quality of Gogol's fantasy.

Nadezhdin, Nikolay Ivanovich (1804-56), a Russian journalist and critic of the 1830's, professor of literature at Moscow University. He attacked the early romanticist poets, including PUSHKIN, for their failure to express philosophical ideas. Literature, in Nadezhdin's view, must be "natural, original and national." Nadezhdin is memorable as editor of *The Telescope*, a journal which was shut down by the police in 1836 for its publication of

CHAADAYEV's famous *Philosophical Letter*. As a literary critic and theorist, Nadezhdin is an important predecessor of BELINSKI.

Nadson, Semyon Yakovlevich (1862-87), a poet of the early 1880's. He belonged to the twilight of the long-lived "civic" trend in Russian poetry. His poetry is idealistic and socially conscious (his early poems were influenced by the ideas of the POPULISTS). But his civic idealism grew increasingly frustrated and impotent, and he could not solve the questions of evil and injustice which he posed. Nadson thus reflected the disillusionment of intellectuals of the early 1880's. His sweet, musical verse was tremendously popular in his day, though today it seems too limpid and cloying. Nadson suffered from tuberculosis, and the disease cut short his career only three years after he had begun to publish.

Nagrodskaya, Yevdokia Apollonovna (1866-1939), a novelist of the early twentieth century. Her most famous novel, *The Wrath of Dionysus* (1910), was extraordinarily popular for its erotic manner and its advocacy of sexual freedom for women.

Na postu. See October.

Narezhny, Vasili Trofimovich (1780-1825), a picaresque novelist of the early nineteenth century. Ukrainian by birth, he described Ukrainian and Cossack life, and is thus an important predecessor of GOGOL. His principal work, *A Russian Gil Blas* (1814), was interrupted by the censorship. It is a broad picture of Russian provincial and city life, with an implied attack on the evils of the time, in particular serfdom. His *Two Ivans, or the Passion for Litigation* (1825) suggested both the subject and title of GOGOL's famous tale.

Narodniki. See Populists.

Narodnost, or "national character," along with *PARTIYNOST* and *IDEYNOST*, one of the requirements demanded from literature under SOCIALIST REALISM. Literature, it is maintained, must express typical national thought and character by means of an indigenous national style. Since the term *narodnost* implies "popular" and "folk" character as well as "national" character, much emphasis has been placed on the contribution of folk and popular literature and language to higher literature, and a good deal of confusion has been shown in the whole matter by Soviet critics. STALIN's dictum that proletarian art should be national in form, socialist in content, is a main source of the concept in Soviet criticism. At best the implications of *narodnost* remain vague. The opposite to *narodnost* in art is "rootless cosmopolitanism." (See Criticism, Soviet.)

Naturalism. See Realism; Belinski.

Naumov, Nikolay Ivanovich (1838-1901), a writer of the 1870's and 1880's and adherent of the POPULISTS. His sketches and tales describe the life of the Siberian peasantry.

Nazhivin, Ivan Fyodorovich (1874-1940), a novelist of the early twentieth century. Influenced by the ethical teachings of Lev TOLSTOY, he wrote many popular didactic narratives. He emigrated after the 1917 Revolution. Later he published several historical novels.

Nekrasov, Nikolay Alexeyevich (1821-78), a great Russian poet of the mid-nineteenth century, the leading exponent of the realist and "civic" tendency in Russian poetry. Nekrasov was born in a family of well-to-do gentry. His father, a rude tyrant and profligate, refused to support his son, who almost starved as a student at the University of St. Petersburg. Eventually Nekrasov was forced to give up the university and support himself by working at odd jobs and hack writing. His first collection of poems, *Dreams and Sounds*, appeared in 1840. It was a complete failure, but Nekrasov persisted. He entered the field of publishing, in which he showed indefatigable energy and considerable business ability. By 1845 he controlled his own publishing house, and in 1846 he bought the journal, *The Contemporary*, which he made the foremost literary review in Russia, publishing such distinguished young authors as TURGENEV and LEV TOLSTOY, as well as the radical CIVIC CRITICS, BELINSKI, CHERNYSHEVSKI and DOBROLYUBOV. A radical by conviction, Nekrasov encountered endless difficulties with the censorship. In 1866 *The Contemporary* was suppressed after an attempt on the life of Alexander II, in spite of Nekrasov's belated and fruitless attempt to save his review by composing a sycophantic poem in praise of the reactionary minister Muraviov. Meanwhile, the liberal writers had broken with Nekrasov because of his radical views, and in 1860 TURGENEV and others left *The Contemporary*. In 1868 Nekrasov acquired another established review,

The Fatherland Notes, which he published, with the writer
SALTYKOV, until his death.

Nekrasov was a man of strong contradictions. His work is full
of the deepest and most genuine compassion for suffering, particularly for the hard life of the Russian peasantry. But in business he was calculating and hard. His publishing enterprises
brought him great wealth, which he spent in a life of extravagance
and dissipation. These contradictions in his character brought
him much remorse, an attitude which is strikingly expressed in
his poetry, and which helped, along with the sufferings of in-
curable illness, to intensify his profound sympathy for the Russian
people. Nekrasov's picture of the life of the Russian peasantry
is one of almost unrelieved hardship, poverty and suffering. This
suffering ennobled the Russian people in his eyes, and made it
great. Though he was not blind to the faults of the Russian peasantry, still he idealized it, almost deified it, for that quality of
nobility in suffering which it exemplified for him. This quality
was a proof for him that the people possessed a tremendous elemental force, and would in the future achieve great things.

Nekrasov's early work consists of hack vaudevilles and rhymed
feuilletons. These gave him a dangerous facility in writing verse,
and much of his work is characterized by insufficient attention
to craftsmanship. Most of his great volume of poetry is frankly
bad, whether because it is too sentimental, too imitative, or too
rhetorical and prosaic in language. His standards of taste were
new and radical; he deliberately cultivated a poetry which was
realistic, rhetorical, and which neglected traditional, "esthetic"
canons of taste. Hence it is not entirely fair to judge his work by
traditional standards, as critics have sometimes done. A leading
device of his is a savage irony, which becomes almost cruel when
it is focused on his favorite theme of the sufferings of the people.
This irony helps to redeem the best of his work from sentimentality.

In form Nekrasov's work falls into two broad groups: poems in
traditional meters, and poems in the style and manner of the folk
song. The former, and larger group, is on the whole less successful, for Nekrasov lacked the technical skill and polish for perfection in the traditional forms, and his new expression, rhetorical,
unrestrained and sentimental, was often in conflict with his use

of older verse forms. His more conventional poetry includes verses on social and civic themes, scenes from nature, and love lyrics. His love poems are characterized by a passion, intensity and freedom from sentimentality which make them stand above his more prosaic "civic" poetry.

Nekrasov has a number of narrative poems about peasant life. One of the best of these is *Vlas* (1854), the story of an evil man who repents and becomes a pilgrim, going about to collect money for churches. *Frost the Red-Nosed* (1863) is noteworthy for its poetic incarnation of the majestic beauty of winter, as well as for its eloquent tribute to the Russian peasant woman and her life of toil and suffering. The heroine, a peasant woman who has lost her husband, goes to the frozen forest to find wood for his coffin, and dies from exposure to the cold. Her sufferings are finally transcended and forgotten in death. The poem contains echoes from folklore, particularly in the personification of Frost and the use of the language of funeral laments (see Folk Songs). Another poem which depicts the sufferings of women is *Russian Women* (1871-72), the story of the wives of two Decembrists (see Decembrist Movement) who followed their husbands to exile in Siberia.

Perhaps the strongest and most original of Nekrasov's work is his poetry in the folk manner. For the most part he did not work literally in the forms of the FOLK SONG, but took only certain phrases and devices from folk poetry, using a freer or varied rhythm to suggest the folk verse. Yet he managed to catch the essence of the popular manner, and some of these poems, such as the opening stanzas of his long poem, *The Pedlars* (1861), have since been taken over by the people as true folk songs. In this part of his poetry he transcends his limitations; uniting a vigorous, essentially optimistic and racy style with his themes of tragedy and suffering, he attains a greater objectivity and subtlety of manner.

Besides *Frost the Red-Nosed*, Nekrasov's masterpiece in this style in his long satirical poem, *Who Can Be Happy in Russia?* (1873-76), in unrhymed verse with many phrases and themes from FOLK SONGS and FOLK TALES. The poem tells the story of seven peasants who travel over Russia in search of a happy man. They talk with representatives of all social classes: a landowner, a priest, an artisan, a peasant woman, and others. Nowhere do they find anyone who is happy. In spite of the misery of the individual lives which are depicted, the poem ends on a note of strong optimism for the future greatness of the Russian people. The poem is vigorous in style, ironic, and almost free from Nekrasov's usual sentimentality.

Critical evaluations of Nekrasov's stature as a poet have differed greatly. The radicals of his day adored him for his powerful love for the people, and were ready to forgive the sins of his personal life. His funeral in 1878 was the occasion for a demonstration in his honor, and the funeral orator, DOSTOYEVSKI, was interrupted when he assigned to Nekrasov the third place in Russian poetry, after Pushkin and Lermontov. "Higher than Pushkin!" the crowd insisted. On the other hand, the esthetic critics and poets of his day scorned his poetry as mere doggerel. Only by the end of the century did the controversy abate, and it was possible to recognize in Nekrasov positive and original formal values as well as expressive ones. Today his place among the greatest Russian poets is secure.

Nekrasov, Viktor Platonovich (1911-   ), Soviet novelist. He served as an officer in the Second World War. His novel, *In the Trenches of Stalingrad* (1946), is based in part on his own fighting experience at Stalingrad, and was one of the most popular war novels.

Neledinski-Meletski, Yuri Alexandrovich (1752-1828), a minor poet of the late eighteenth and early nineteenth century. He wrote occasional poems, light salon verse and songs stylized in the folk manner.

Nemirovich-Danchenko, Vasili Ivanovich (1848-1936), a minor writer of the turn of the century, brother of Vladimir NEMIROVICH-DANCHENKO, co-founder of the Moscow Art Theater. He wrote travel sketches and popular novels, of which he turned out more than a hundred volumes.

Nemirovich-Danchenko, Vladimir Ivanovich (1858-1943), a dramatist of the late nineteenth century, brother of the novelist Vasili NEMIROVICH-DANCHENKO. A theatrical reformer, he founded the Moscow Art Theater in 1898 together with Konstantin Stanislavski (see Drama and Theater).

Neo-Classicism. See Classicism.

Nestor, a monk of the Kiev Crypt Monastery at the end of the eleventh and the beginning of the twelfth century. Though

Nestor has been renowned as the chief compiler of the *Primary Russian Chronicle,* often referred to as "Nestor's Chronicle" (see Chronicles), his authorship is open to question. Still, his fame has been so great that for Russians his name has become a synonym for "chronicler" or "historian." Nestor is beyond doubt the author of a life of Sts. Boris and Gleb (see Literature).

Neverov, Alexander. See Skobelev, A. S.

Nihilists, a name given to the radicals of the 1860's, followers of CHERNYSHEVSKI, DOBROLYUBOV and PISAREV. The nihilists were materialistic positivists who made a cult of the methods of the natural sciences, which they considered to be the only valid approach to the problems of life and society. Their attitudes to social and cultural institutions, even to art, were purely utilitarian. Because they criticized most existing institutions, they received the nickname of "Nihilists," i.e., those who believe in nothing. The name was popularized by TURGENEV in his novel, *Fathers and Children* (1862), and though Pisarev had earlier called his party "thinking realists," he eagerly accepted the new name.

Nihilism was more an attitude, even a craze which swept the young radical intelligentsia, than an articulate political movement. Young people affected crudities in manners and dress and advocated free love and equal rights for both sexes. Government persecution provoked them to serious radical activity, and a wave of student strikes and demonstrations culminated in an attempt on the life of Alexander II in 1866, by Karakozov, a Nihilist student. Increased repressive measures by the police followed. To counteract the Nihilists' zeal for natural science, the government increased the proportion of classical subjects taught in the high schools.

With the emergence of more specific political programs in the 1870's, such as that of the POPULISTS, one can speak of the end of Nihilism proper as a phase of the radical movement. But many of its attitudes, such as the cult of materialistic science, and contempt for conventions and existing institutions, remained characteristic for the later radicals.

Though Nihilism itself was a comparatively short-lived phase, it is the subject of a large number of important works of fiction. TURGENEV's portrayal of a Nihilist leader, Bazarov, in *Fathers and Children* (1862) was objective and even sympathetic to the point of antagonizing the conservatives. But, with the exception of Pisarev, the radicals refused to accept Turgenev's characterization. PISEMSKI'S novel, *Troubled Seas* (1863), LESKOV's *No Way Out* (1864), GONCHAROV's *The Precipice* (1869), and, most notably, DOSTOYEVSKI's *The Devils* (or *The Possessed*, 1871-72) sharply criticized the Nihilists, even exaggerated their danger to society and what these writers presumed was the vicious character of their revolutionary intentions. On the other hand, CHERNYSHEVSKI's first novel, *What Is to Be Done?* (1863), provided a sympathetic portrayal which depicted the Nihilists as self-sacrificing heroes and true leaders of the radical cause.

Nikitin, Afanasii (died 1472), a merchant of the city of Tver, who made a trip to India lasting from 1466 to 1472. He left a description of his journey, interesting for its freedom of style and manner, and for its colorful descriptive details.

Nikitin, Ivan Savvich (1824-61), a realist poet of the mid-nineteenth century. The son of a shopkeeper, his education was limited to two years in seminary. Poverty forced him to support himself by keeping a tavern. He died of tuberculosis at the age of thirty-seven.

Nikitin specialized in realistic pictures of the sordid misery of the poor, in particular of the peasants and the lower middle classes, to which he himself belonged. His greatest poem is a long narrative, *The Kulak* (1858), the story of how a peasant is driven by poverty to become the exploiter of his fellow peasants. His lyrics, sometimes sentimental, sometimes poignant and sincere, deal with similar themes. His patriotic and religious poems earned him the enmity of the radical critics, CHERNYSHEVSKI and DOBROLYUBOV, though the latter admired his treatment of social themes. In his technique Nikitin was something of an imitator, especially of PUSHKIN and KOLTSOV.

Nikitin, Nikolay Nikolayevich (1895-   ), a novelist and dramatist of the Soviet period. The influence of Pilnyak (see Vogau) can be seen in his ORNAMENTALISM of manner and attitude toward the 1917 REVOLUTION, which he seems to accept for the intoxication of its passion and violence. His early stories and novels, such as *Fort Vomit* (1922) and *The Flight* (1925), deal with the Civil War, depicted with great detachment.

Nikitin's later novel, *Kirik Rudenko's Crime* (1928), treats sexual freedom and other ethical problems faced by Communist youth in the 1920's. His more recent historical novel, *Aurora Borealis* (1950), concerns British intervention in North Russia in 1919, and shows that he has since come to conform more closely to the conventional manner of SOCIALIST REALISM.

Novikov, Nikolay Ivanovich (1744-1818), a leading satirical journalist of the eighteenth century. An impoverished nobleman who had served as an officer in the army and in the civil service, Novikov founded his first journal, *The Drone*, in 1769. His attacks on serfdom proved too sharp for the supposedly liberal Empress CATHERINE THE GREAT, and the journal was closed the following year. Subsequently Novikov published in succession the journals, *The Tattler*, *The Painter* and *The Purse*, none of which lasted more than a year. In 1774 Catherine shut down all the satirical journals. Novikov then turned to editing and publishing, aiming at public enlightenment and the preservation of historical materials from Russia's past. He also organized philanthropic institutions for the Moscow Freemasons, to whom he belonged (see Freemasonry). Between 1777 and 1785 he again edited a series of journals, but government persecution once more brought his activities to an end. In 1792 he was arrested and imprisoned; he was released only on Catherine's death in 1796. Broken by prison, he retired to the country, to devote the rest of his life to mystical meditation.

Novikov-Priboy, Alexey Silych (1877-1944), a Soviet novelist. He first published in 1917, with a volume of *Sea Stories*. A sailor during the Russo-Japanese War, he was held prisoner by the Japanese for some years. His chief novel, *Tsushima* (1932-35), describes the destruction of the Russian fleet by the Japanese during the battle of that name of May, 1905.

Novodvorski, Andrey Osipovich (1853-82), a writer of the 1870's and 1880's who published under his patronymic as A. Osipovich. An active adherent of the POPULISTS, he described in his ironical tales the failure of the Populist Movement as well as his own personal reservations in committing himself to it. His stories are personal and whimsical, with a keen sense of irony. After 1880 his manner became more sentimental, and his former ironical attitude towards the "SUPERFLUOUS MAN," as he regarded the Russian intellectual, is replaced by sympathy.

O

October, the leading group of proletarian writers of the 1920's. It was formed late in 1922 to replace the PROLETKULT as an organization for proletarian writers. In June, 1923, October began issuing a journal called *Na postu* ("On Guard"), edited by its chief spokesman, G. Lelevich (pseudonym of Labori Kalmanson). The members of October favored the creation of a new proletarian literature which would express the class interests of the workers and peasantry and which would replace older "bourgeois" literature. They also demanded the establishment of a stricter party line in literature and the suppression of all non-conformist writing. In 1925 they organized a union of proletarian writers, known as VAPP (All-Russian Association of Proletarian Writers), and later as RAPP (Russian Association of Proletarian Writers).

The government at first turned a deaf ear to the claims of the proletarian groups, but in 1929 it permitted RAPP to take control of literature and bring it into the scope of the First Five-Year Plan, thus giving proletarian writers essentially what they demanded. (See Criticism, Soviet; Literature, Soviet.)

Odoyevski, Prince Alexander Ivanovich (1802-39), a minor poet of the early nineteenth century, cousin of the playwright GRIBOYE-DOV and of the philosopher, Prince V. F. ODOYEVSKI. He took part in the Decembrist Uprising of 1825 (see Decembrist Movement), for which he was sentenced to exile in Siberia. In 1837 he was transferred to the Caucasus, where he served in the ranks of the army. He died in 1839 of fever.

Odoyevski's poetry, circulated in manuscript and published only long after his death, reflects the sorrows and misfortunes of his life in exile. To him is attributed the poem called *A Reply to Pushkin,* an answer to PUSHKIN's famous lyric, *To Siberia,* which had been sent as a message of hope and encouragement to the exiled Decembrists. His other poetry is mostly patriotic and nationalistic, and glorifies Russian colonial expansion in Georgia and Siberia.

Odoyevski, Prince Vladimir Fyodorovich (1803-69), a mid-nineteenth century philosopher, journalist and writer of tales. He was the cousin of the Decembrist poet, Prince A. I. ODOYEVSKI. In his youth he was president of the society of so-called *lyubomudry* (philosophers), a romanticist group influenced by the German philosopher Schelling. His *Russian Nights* (1844), a cycle of philosophical conversations, present the first systematic Russian criticism of Western European culture and its influence in Russia. Odoyevski attributes the breakdown of Western culture to loss of spiritual faith; a new nation, Russia, must enter the historical scene with a new spiritual force. His unfinished novel, *The Year 4338*, predicts the unification of all peoples of the world under tsarist absolutism. He is important as a predecessor of the SLAVOPHILES. (See Philosophy.)

Ogaryov, Nikolay Platonovich (1813-77), a poet and publicist of the mid-nineteenth century. A close friend of the revolutionary political thinker HERZEN, he followed the latter to England in 1856, where he worked for many years as co-editor of Herzen's newspaper in exile, *The Bell.* Ogaryov's poetry is of lesser significance; it embodies the disillusionment, melancholy and hopelessness typical of the frustrated liberal nobility of the mid-nineteenth century. He also wrote revolutionary and civic poetry.

Ognyov, N. See Rozanov, M. G.

Old Believers. See Schism.

Old Church Slavonic language. Created by the apostles to the Slavs, Sts. Cyril (Constantine) and Methodius, at the time of their mission to the Moravians in 863, this language was based on the spoken Slavic dialect of Macedonia. It also contained many invented words necessary to translate the Bible and other sacred writings. Like medieval Latin in the West, Old Church Slavonic has been preserved as the religious language of the Orthodox Church among the Russians, Ukrainians, Belo-Russians, Bulgarians and Serbs, as well as the Rumanians, a non-Slavic people. It was also used briefly by the Slovenes, Czechs and Poles, and by the Croats down to the present century as an esoteric language for monastic writing. Each people using Old Church Slavonic developed a relatively distinct local variant of the language.

The Old Church Slavonic language and alphabet (see Alphabet) were introduced into Russia following her CHRISTIANIZATION in 988 or 989, as a religious and literary language. Since the Slavic languages were closely related in the tenth century, Old Church Slavonic was readily comprehensible to the Russians, and at the same time possessed the dignity, expressiveness and abstract vocabulary which spoken Russian lacked. Old Church Slavonic, more or less adapted in its pronunciation, spelling, grammar and vocabulary to Russian, remained the language of most Russian literature until the end of the seventeenth century. As time went on, however, it became less and less comprehensible to Russians who lacked special education.

Old Church Slavonic has had an enormous influence on the modern Russian literary language. Slavonic roots are used by preference for coining new abstract, scientific and technical terms. An immense number of Slavonicisms have passed into the Russian literary language and even into the spoken language.

The opposition between "high" Slavonic and "low" Russian has created a dualism in literary style from the oldest period down to the present. In the older period, most literary works were written in Old Church Slavonic, except for business or legal documents. CHRONICLES were sometimes written in a mixture of the two styles, however, as was the *IGOR TALE*, though the latter, as a highly poetic narrative influenced by the oral song tradition, was probably closer in its original form to pure Russian. In the seventeenth century, a middle-class literature in Russian began to appear; it competed with the upper-class Slavonic literature. In the eighteenth century, Slavonicisms continued to be used extensively, especially in serious literature, and LOMONOSOV attempted to legislate concerning the use of the two languages by creating a hierarchy of three stylistic levels. His compromise failed to endure, however, and controversy broke out anew at the beginning of the nineteenth century (see Shishkov; Karamzin). Though the party led by KARAMZIN was victorious, and the most archaic Slavonicisms were eliminated, a vast number of Slavonic words remained firmly embedded in the Russian language. Nineteenth-century poetry and even prose continued to make liberal use of Slavonicisms, including certain archaic ones, especially in formal style. At times Slavonicisms may serve in poetry as rhythmic or stylistic alternants to their Russian parallels, e.g., O.C.S. *grad*, "city" (one syllable); Russian *gorod*, "city" (two syllables). (See Language.)

Old Russian literature. See Literature, Old Russian.

Olesha, Yuri Karlovich (1899-   ), a leading Soviet writer of the late 1920's and early 1930's. He entered literature by writing poetry for a railway workmen's newspaper. In 1927 he published his first novel, *Envy*. It was one of the most promising novels in all Soviet literature, and a brilliant future was predicted for the young writer. But as time went on Soviet critics, who had at first welcomed *Envy* kindly, perceived that it gave a questionable and by no means highly flattering portrait of the new Soviet society. Attacks on Olesha grew more severe. In 1932 he published an open letter and the following year held an interview; in these he "confessed" his "errors" and promised to "re-educate" himself, but insisted on the necessity for following his own path in literature. In 1934 he made a speech at the First Congress of the Union of Soviet Writers in which he pled for the revival of moral problems in Soviet belles lettres. After that year he published only very rarely, in a few articles and reviews. Evidently he is a victim of the rigidity of the official Soviet conception of the function of literature.

Olesha's novel *Envy* (1927) is one of the most original works of Soviet fiction. Its subject is the revolt of the individual against the new collective order. The cause of individualism is represented by Kavalerov, an incarnation of the vice of envy who recalls the hero of DOSTOYEVSKI's *Notes from Underground*, and Ivan Babichev, an incurably romantic eccentric, dreamer and chronic liar. Though these men are unstable and lack character, they are the advocates of a cult of personal feeling which seems to command the author's own sympathies. On the other hand, the representatives of the new order, Andrey Babichev, the "sausage maker," and Volodya, the soccer player, seem vulgar and prosaic, and the Utopia which they envisage a paradise of philistinism. Olesha thus makes it clear that, though he has accepted the new order, he has many doubts and reservations, and in particular seems to feel that a collective society threatens to eliminate personal feelings.

Most remarkable in Olesha's novel is the freshness of the rich and ingenious imagery. Indeed, Olesha so delights in extravagant imagery that it sometimes gets in the way of the novel's structure. Startling new visual effects are often achieved through his use of optical reflections and distortions, as in the blurred images of clouds racing by, seen in a dirty window pane. Olesha seems to follow SHKLOVSKI's theory of literature as "making strange," and seeks to re-form the world as something fresh and new. His imagery is eclectic in style, and may be realistic, romantic or symbolistic. In this blending of styles the author sometimes mixes narrative planes, presenting dreams and lies as reality.

Olesha's stories also oppose an individualism of the emotions to the cold, collective impersonality with which he invests the new order. Thus, in *Love* (1929), Shuvalov, a Marxist, falls in love and sees the world transformed from a realistic one to a romantic one, a change which the author vividly compared to a sudden attack of color-blindness.

Olesha's second novel, *Three Fat Men* (1928), is an adventure story supposedly written for children. It again opposes the world of feelings to that of cold discipline.

Olesha's play, *A List of Blessings* (1931), employs motifs from the films of Chaplin. It depicts an actress' idealization of the decadent capitalist world and her inability to accept the Soviet order; she learns too late to appreciate it when she goes off to Paris, where she is first victimized as an artist, and finally killed by a Russian émigré.

Olesha has also written some film scenarios, and has made dramatic versions of his own novels, *Envy* (as "The Conspiracy of Feelings") and *Three Fat Men*.

Olyosha, Yuri. See Olesha.

Omulevski. See Fyodorov, I. V.

On Guard. See October.

Opoyaz, abbreviated name of the Society for the Study of Poetic Language, founded in 1916 by a group of young philologists and literary theoreticians, including Viktor SHKLOVSKI, Osip Brik and others. Out of it grew the so-called Formalist School in Russian criticism (see Criticism).

Oral literature. See Folk literature.

Oreus, Ivan Ivanovich (1877-1901), an early poet of the Symbolist Movement (see Symbolism), who published under the pseudonym of I. Konevskoy. His promising career was cut short when he was drowned at the age of twenty-four. He attempted to create a new metaphysical poetry in the tradition of TYUTCHEV and FET which would express his mystical ideas of pantheism and the pluralistic nature of the universe.

Orlov, Alexander Anfimovich (1791-1840), a minor writer of the 1830's. He was popular for his didactic and satirical works, which included parodies of the writing of the reactionary journalist BULGARIN.

Ornamentalism, a term used to refer to a highly colored prose style, one in which the manner of narration is usually more significant than its content. An ornamental style is not necessarily beautiful, nor even always ornate, but rather one which calls attention to itself because of some striking effect it makes; it may be mannered or even ugly. The nineteenth-century masters of ornamental prose are GOGOL and LESKOV. As a technical term in Russian literary history, however, ornamentalism applies primarily to the prose of the early twentieth century, and to the school of writers headed by Bely (see Bugayev) and REMIZOV. Their influence actually worked in somewhat different directions; Bely's prose, like his poetry, is rhythmical and musical in character, with much use of interwoven, "contrapuntal" motifs; Remizov's prose tends toward a colloquial style, though one which is highly intricate and mannered.

In the 1920's ornamentalism was the dominant tendency in Russian prose. BABEL, Pilnyak (see Vogau), ZAMYATIN, Vsevolod IVANOV, BULGAKOV and A. N. TOLSTOY are some of the writers who employ an ornamentalist technique.

Osipovich, A. See Novodvorski, A. O.

Osorgin, Mikhail. See Ilyin, M. A.

Ostrovski, Alexander Nikolayevich (1823-86), a leading Russian playwright of the second half of the nineteenth century. The son of a petty government clerk, he was born and grew up in the section of Moscow "beyond the river," the quarter where the Muscovite merchants lived and dealt. Russian merchant life of the period, with its isolation, smugness and double-dealing, became the favorite subject of his dramas. He attended the Law Faculty of Moscow University, but did not take a degree, instead entering the civil service as a clerk in the Court of Commerce. He published his first work, scenes from a comedy, *The Bankrupt*, in 1847. The censorship prevented the play's performance, for by exposing the fraudulent practices of the merchants the work also showed the faults of the system which could tolerate such shady dealings. Ostrovski was forced to resign from the civil service, and was kept under police surveillance for a time. His first play to be performed, *The Poor Bride*, was produced in 1852. His works soon won great popularity on the stage, which they have retained ever since. Ostrovski's plays hardly equal the great dramatic works of GRIBOYEDOV, GOGOL or CHEKHOV in stature, but taken as a whole they form a body of work which has become the backbone of the repertoire of the Russian theater. Whereas the comedies of Griboyedov and Gogol are isolated works, Ostrovski produced some forty plays in prose as well as eight in blank verse.

Besides creating the first great corpus of Russian national drama, Ostrovski devoted his energies in his later years to reform of the theater system. In the Russian capitals the theater was a state monopoly, while the private theaters of the provinces were on a pitifully low level. Ostrovski succeeded in founding several mutual-aid associations, and in establishing a society for the protection of the rights of dramatic authors. Belated recognition was given to his work when, in 1886, he was appointed director of the Moscow Theatrical School, but he died only a few months later.

Ostrovski's prose dramas represent a unique blend of theatricalism and realistic depiction of life. They are hardly "well-made" plays which might compare with those of the Western European theater of the day, in which dramatic construction is usually tight and economical; Ostrovski's plays often contain characters, scenes and motifs which contribute little or nothing to the final conclusion of the play. The climaxes and dénouements themselves are often deliberately dulled in a kind of characteristic understatement. Ostrovski's work contains both tragedies and comedies, but the difference is chiefly in the ending, sometimes almost arbitrary, and his works are more correctly considered as dramas. In spite of their rather loose construction, his plays are perfectly and completely dramatic in effect. This is because his plots, backgrounds and characters are themselves highly dramatic, drawn as they are from the world of greedy and headstrong merchants, of selfish gentry, backward peasantry and corrupt officialdom. Ostrovski deals with vices such as greed, lust, fraud, bribery and tyranny, with crimes and strong passions. Though his plays expose the vice and stagnation of large areas of Russian society, they are not primarily problem plays, but first and foremost theatrical dramas. Thus, Ostrovski may be sympathetic or antipathetic to the patriarchal head of the household, one of his favorite characters, as his dramatic needs dictate. His characters are dramatic in the intensity of their passions, especially in the characteristic Ostrovskian trait of *samodurstvo*, "blind obduracy." The *samodur* is a headstrong, obstinate man who carries his tyrannical power as head of his family and business to the point where it may destroy even his loved ones and himself. Ostrovski's characters have little or no psychological depth; they are closer to manifestations of particular "humors," but they have powerful, elemental dramatic force.

One of Ostrovski's greatest strengths lies in his use of masses of characteristic detail taken from the social milieu which he describes, especially that of the merchants. These details, though they may sometimes seem to get in the way of the dramatic movement of the play, rarely impede it, for they contribute their own peculiar and striking atmosphere, while adding a powerful realism to the author's portrayals. Especially characteristic is his use of language, never poetic, but at the same time never dull or prosaic, full of the racy jargon of merchant life and the business world. This use of the characteristic environmental detail appropriate to various classes and their spoken jargon gives Ostrovski's plays a strong national, Russian flavor which has helped to prevent them from attaining universal appeal. Although he is the most popular Russian dramatic writer on the Soviet stage today, Ostrovski's plays are hardly known outside Russia. They are exotic, but are quite devoid of the ethical and philosophical implications which foreign readers expect from Russian literature, while their very exoticism is so closely bound up with the language, proverbs and customs of particular Russian social classes that they resist any attempt at transplantation.

Ostrovski's first play, *The Bankrupt*, or *It's All in the Family*, the title under which it was first published in 1850, is one of his best. It deals with a colossal fraud engineered by a merchant who plans to transfer his property to his assistant, declare himself bankrupt, settle, at an enormous discount, with his creditors, and then quietly take back his fortune and enjoy his ill-gotten gains. But the assistant whom he trusts proves a greater rogue than he, and refuses to return the fortune once it is made over to him, leaving the merchant to go to prison for debt. The play avoids obvious climaxes, placing the main focus on the fraud itself and on the rascality of the characters.

Poverty is No Crime (1854), the most popular of Ostrovski's comedies, concerns the headstrongness of a merchant father who resolves to marry his daughter to a rich old man, an obvious rake. The girl, though she loves a poor apprentice, is ready to obey her father. But the rich man insults the father, and in a burst of temper the latter resolves to marry his daughter to the first beggar who comes along. This proves to be the apprentice, and a happy ending is thus provided. The play has always been popular, in spite of the extreme looseness of its construction.

The Ward (1859) is, on the other hand, one of Ostrovski's most concentrated and gloomiest plays. It depicts the fate of a poor girl, adopted by a well-intentioned but tyrannical noblewoman, who brings up her protégées in luxury and then marries them off to middle-aged clerks, usually drunkards. The heroine, detected in a love affair with her patroness' son, is sentenced to such a fate. The ending is unresolved: we do not know whether the girl will commit suicide, or what.

Ostrovski's greatest work is his powerful tragedy, *The Thunderstorm* (1859), the only one of his plays to transcend national boundaries and achieve the status of a universal masterpiece. It is also the only one of his prose dramas which is poetic, not because of the language, which is almost as pungent and vigorous as ever, but because the atmosphere of the life represented— narrow, walled-in, inevitably leading to tragedy—is itself poetic. The play tells the story of a young merchant's wife, Katerina, who cannot love her weak husband, and who is driven by her malevolent and tyrannical mother-in-law to destroy herself. She has an affair with a young man, Boris, who is too weak to save her; the affair is both a futile attempt to rescue herself from the family atmosphere which stifles her, and an impulse toward her own destruction. In the end she is driven to suicide by the evil mother-in-law. The latter figure actually dominates the play, and is Ostrovski's greatest creation.

The Thunderstorm was highly praised by the radical critic DOBROLYUBOV for its exposure of the backward and tyrannical atmosphere of merchant life, which he described by the eloquent name of the "Kingdom of Darkness."

Ostrovski's blank-verse plays are on the whole much weaker than his realistic prose dramas. Most of them are chronicle plays of the Shakespearean type, in vogue in Russia at this time. More interesting is his single fairy play in verse, *The Snow Maiden* (1873). Its heroine is a mythological creature, the daughter of Frost and Spring, whose dual nature leads her to long for a love which she is incapable of. In the end her mother, Spring, teaches her to love. But her love destroys her, for it places her in the power of the Sun-God, who has sworn to destroy her as the child of Frost. In spite of the deficiencies of Ostrovski's verse and poetic language, there is a poetry of atmosphere which makes the work a moving and nostalgic play. *The Snow Maiden* has been set as an opera by Rimski-Korsakov.

Ostrovski, Nikolay Alexeyevich (1904-36), Soviet writer. An invalid and cripple, his writing is full of an optimism and courage for life which defied the actual circumstances of his existence. His work is poorly constructed, however, and follows the pattern of the sentimental success story. His novel, *How the Steel Was Tempered* (1932-34; English translation as "The Making of a Hero"), has been one of the leading best-sellers in the Soviet Union, selling more than 5,000,000 copies. It tells the life story of Pavel Korchagin, a poor boy who is employed at various odd jobs. During the Revolution he works for the Red Underground. Though crippled by wounds, he succeeds in his new ambition to become a writer and ideological teacher. The novel is based in part on Ostrovski's own career, but is idealized to a highly implausible degree.

Ozerov, Vladislav Alexandrovich (1769-1816), the leading Russian representative of SENTIMENTALISM in the drama. Using French classical models, Ozerov added elements of feeling, sensibility and national patriotism which made his tragedies overwhelmingly successful in their day. Important are his *Fingal* (1805), on Ossianic motifs, *Dmitri Donskoy* (1807), a romantic treatment of an Old Russian historical subject, and *Polyxena* (1809), on a theme from the *Iliad*.

P

P. Ya. See Yakubovich, P. F.

Pakhomii Logofet, a Serbian monk who, between 1429-36, came to Russia, where he worked as a professional writer. He was one of the first writers to introduce the new style of the Second South Slavic Influence (see Literature), with its dignified panegyric tone. Many works have been attributed to Pakhomii, including lives of saints and a history of the world (1442). The latter work is noteworthy for its analytic treatment of history by topics rather than by years, as was the prevailing Russian manner. It also stresses the biographical element in history, and the significance of the actions of rulers, especially from a moral point of view. In this we see some echo of Renaissance influence. Sometimes attributed to Pakhomii is the *Story of the Princes of Vladimir*, a false genealogy of the Muscovite princes (also princes of the city of Vladimir), in which their line is traced back to a certain Prus, a fictitious "brother" of Augustus Caesar. The work thus served to justify the assumption of autocratic power by the Muscovite grand princes, and the concept of a Russian empire.

Palitsyn, Avraamii, author of a popular history of the turbulent "Time of the Troubles" of the early seventeenth century. This work, which was probably completed in 1620, is remarkable for several passages in verse, among the earliest examples of the so-called pre-syllabic verse (see Prosody).

Panfyorov, Fyodor Ivanovich (1896-), Soviet novelist and playwright. His long novel, *Bruski* (1928-37), depicts the history of a village from the end of the Civil War through the collectivization of the land under the First Five-year Plan. During the 1930's the novel was much attacked for its rough language and lack of artistry. Panfyorov's war novel, *The Struggle for Peace* (1945-47), and its sequel, *In the Land of the Unvanquished* (1948), are crude and sensational novels which describe guerrilla warfare and Russian espionage behind the German lines. His most recent novel, *Mother Volga* (1953), depicts man's struggle against nature in agriculture. Though the author "correctly" recognizes the importance of Party leadership in this struggle, his Communist hero was severely criticized as morally imperfect.

Panova, Vera Fyodorovna (1905-   ), Soviet novelist and playwright. Her short novel, *Travelling Companions* (1946; English translation as "The Train"), was one of the most popular and successful novels about the Second World War. It tells the story of a hospital train, the people who work on it, and how their lives are affected by the war. Panova's later novel, *Kruzhilikha* (1947), describes the work of a factory of that name during the war and the transition to peace. Her most recent novel, *Seasons of the Year* (1953), depicts life in a Soviet industrial town, but, unlike most recent Soviet fiction, is more concerned with human beings than machines. It has been severely criticized for its lack of "Party spirit" (see *Partiynost*).

Parnassian Poets, a term used to describe a number of poets of the mid-nineteenth century, including FET, APOLLON MAYKOV, SHCHERBINA, MEY and POLONSKI, and, to a limited extent, A. K. TOLSTOY. The Parnassians advocated art for its own sake; thus, as estheticists, they opposed the powerful CIVIC CRITICS of the period, with their predilection for political and social ideas. The Parnassians employed precise, vivid, sensual imagery, often to the detriment of emotional expression. Themes taken from the world of classical antiquity are common in their work. Though the movement paralleled French Parnassianism in many respects, it seems to have been indigenous in its origins, going back to PUSHKIN and the poets of the "Golden Age" of early nineteenth-century Russian poetry.

Partiynost, or "party spirit," along with IDEYNOST and NARODNOST one of the chief requirements for literature under SOCIALIST REALISM. The expression of "party spirit," i.e., of identification with the goals and methods of the Communist Party, is a quality demanded from writers by Soviet critics. LENIN is credited with originally stating the necessity for the expression of "party spirit" in literature. The opposite of *partiynost* in art is "bourgeois decadence." (See Criticism, Soviet.)

Party Spirit. See *Partiynost.*

Pasternak, Boris Leonidovich (1890-   ), a leading poet of the Soviet period. His father was a well-known painter, while his mother was a talented pianist. He studied music for some years, then philosophy at the Universities of Moscow and Marburg. He joined the Cubo-Futurists (see Futurism) in 1912, but was only associated with them briefly, and, except for his interest in obscure words and his occasional use of shocking or vulgar imagery, he has little in common with the Futurists. His first collection, *A Twin in the Clouds,* was published in 1914. He won wide recognition after the First World War with a collection of lyrics called *My Sister Life,* written in 1917 but published only in 1922. With the publication of successive collections, he soon acquired the position of the leading younger poet of Russia. His *Spektorski* (1926) is an attempt at treatment of certain episodes of his own life. As a narrative work, it was somewhat less successful than his lyrics, as were his other narratives, *1905* (1925-26) and *Lieutenant Schmidt* (1926-27), both attempts to celebrate the revolutionary movement in Russia. Pasternak aims at a personal, lyric verse, and the revolutionary movement is a subject which seems alien to his real interests. His collection *The Second Birth* (1932) frequently employs the Caucasus and its magnificent landscapes as a setting, and these poems, like others by Pasternak, sometimes recall LERMONTOV's Caucasian poetry.

Though Pasternak's poetry is difficult and at times obscure, he has become the favorite poet of Soviet intellectuals, and there is little doubt that he is one of the leading poets of our time. The obscurity of his work, its individualism and concern for personal subjectivity have made much of his work unacceptable to orthodox Soviet critics, who attacked him for "formalism" and "alienation from the masses." Apparently driven from original creation by the hostile pressure of his critics, Pasternak turned to translation, producing excellent versions of several of Shakespeare's plays as well as selections from Armenian and Georgian poets. He took advantage of the somewhat more lenient atmosphere of the time of the Second World War to publish two new original collections: *On Early Trains* (1943) and *The Terrestrial Expanse* (1945), which show a certain simplification and greater directness by comparison with his earlier work. But in 1946 the critics launched a new attack, and since that year he has published nothing except translations.

Pasternak is a highly individualistic poet, for whom philosophical themes and the contemplation of reality are favorite subjects, along with the more conventional themes of love and nature. Nature in his poetry appears as new and strange; the poet describes her almost animistically as alive, and re-creates for us something of the elemental wonder of a primitive view of the world. But Pasternak's "primitivism" is actually part of a sophisticated but deliberately irrational approach to nature, which he depicts in strikingly rich and novel images. He is unusual as a lyric poet whose poetry tends to be prosaic in its great use of synecdoche and metonymic imagery, of part-whole and object-symbol relations. His metaphors and similes are especially remarkable in their freshness, and he is not in the least afraid to use images of objects which are of a technical nature, or are prosaic or even vulgar. Thus, he compares the guilt of a lover to a skin infection, or the color and feel of fresh air to a bundle of wash taken home from a hospital. Images of sound are particularly striking in his poetry, as when he speaks of the "clatter of winter" or the "rumble of grief."

Pasternak's prose is an extension of his poetry, with the same prosaic quality and the same unexpectedness of imagery. In 1925 he published his only collection of stories, including a long narrative, *The Childhood of Luvers*. The story is virtually plotless, full of reminiscences which Pasternak "objectivizes"; a young girl's reactions to the world about her seem to become part of that very world. Another story is *Air Ways* (1925), set against the background of the 1917 Revolution, depicting in a fragmentary and quite unsentimental manner a father's inability to save his illegitimate son, arrested for taking part in a counter-revolutionary conspiracy. But the story as such is less important than its imagery. *Safe Conduct* (1931) is an autobiographical account of the poet's youth and early spiritual development.

Pasternak has been compared to a number of modern poets, including Eliot, Hopkins and Rilke. More than they, however, he is a writer whose subject is a new manner of perception, a manner far more important than what is perceived or what is believed. It is the fresh way of perceiving reality which is original in his work. During the 1920's Pasternak had considerable influence on a number of young Soviet poets, including TIKHONOV, Bagritski (see Dzyubin) and SELVINSKI. But his influence has largely waned with the attacks on his work by Soviet critics.

Paustovski, Konstantin Georgievich (1892-), Soviet novelist and story writer. He published his first story as early as 1911, but did not become a professional writer until 1925. His stories are remarkable for their lyric feeling and treatment of landscape and nature. He often depicts nature as transformed by Soviet construction, as in his short novel, *Birth of a Sea* (1952), about the Volga-Don Canal. He has also written historical and biographical tales, such as *Lieutenant Lermontov* (1941), and a story about Pushkin called *Our Contemporaries* (1949).

Pavlenko, Pyotr Andreyevich (1899-1951), Soviet novelist. He entered literature early in the 1920's, joining the PEREVAL group. His early tales, such as *The Desert* (1932) and *Journey to Turkmenistan* (1932), depict the First Five-year Plan in Central Asia. *The Barricades* (1932) is a historical novel about the Paris Commune of 1871. *In the East* (1937) called attention to the Japanese threat and emphasized the need to fortify and develop the Siberian Far East.

After World War II Pavlenko published a novel, *Happiness* (1947), which, though very weak, brought him high official recognition. Its hero, a wounded colonel, Voropayev, is discharged from the army at the end of the war and settles in the Crimea to recover his shattered health. Here he plays a leading role in the task of war reconstruction. He also serves as an interpreter at the Yalta Conference, and is finally favored by a personal interview with Stalin himself. The Yalta Conference gives the author an opportunity to indulge in many anti-British and anti-American observations. The novel was one of the first examples of post-war anti-Westernism in Soviet literature. It also led in the post-war cult of deification of Stalin. *Happiness* is typical of recent Soviet fiction not only in its ideology, but also in its sentimental optimism and almost total absence of realistic psychological portrayal.

Pavlov, Nikolay Filippovich (1805-64), a mid-nineteenth century writer of tales, husband of the poetess Karolina Pavlova. His collection, *Three Tales* (1835), embodied a strong implicit protest against serfdom and the regime of Nicholas I. The most memorable of the tales, *The Name Day*, tells of the tragic career of a talented musician who had been a serf. Passed by the censor, the *Three Tales* created a sensation, and the censorship refused to permit further editions to be published. Pavlov's *New Tales* (1839) were less successful, and he virtually abandoned literature.

Pavlova, Karolina Karlovna (1807-93), a Russian poetess of German descent. In her youth she translated a number of contemporary Russian poets, including PUSHKIN and BARATYNSKI, into German. The wife of a minor novelist, NIKOLAY PAVLOV, she and her husband conducted a popular literary salon in Moscow. Her poetry, which had little success in her lifetime, consists of melancholy and elegiac reflections and meditations. Technically her work is of high quality, with a great diversity of rhymes and rhythms.

Pecherski, Andrey. See Melnikov, P. I.

Peresvetov, Ivan, a publicist writer who came to the Muscovite court around 1538, during the reign of IVAN THE TERRIBLE. He was active as a writer during the 1540's, when he produced a number of political tracts and petitions to the tsar. Peresvetov advocated strengthening the power of the tsar at the expense of the nobility, systematizing and enlarging the army and the civil service and making these responsible directly and solely to the tsar. His ideal model is the Turkish state, while he points to the end of the Byzantine Empire as a warning of the anarchy to which a strong nobility may lead. Probably he was led to fear the power of the nobility by his earlier service in the constitutional monarchies of Poland, Bohemia and Hungary, while his conception of an autocratic sovereign may show the influence of Western European ideas. Peresvetov's writings anticipate the later reforms of Ivan the Terrible, and probably influenced them.

Pereval ("The Pass"), a group of writers formed in 1923, and led by the critic Alexander VORONSKI. PRISHVIN and Klychkov (see Leshenkov) were older writers who joined the organization; among the younger members were Pyotr PAVLENKO, Ivan Katayev, Boris Guber, Andrey Platonov and N. Zarubin. They published in Voronski's journal, *Red Virgin Soil*. Like Voronski, they opposed the concept of enforced "proletarian" literature (see October). In 1932 the group was dissolved when all literary organizations were forcibly merged in a single Union of Soviet Writers.

Pereverzev, V. G. See Criticism, Soviet.

Perovski, Alexey Alexeyevich (1787-1836), an early romantic novelist, who wrote under the pseudonym of Antoni Pogorelski. His stories, published in the collection, *The Double, or My Evenings in the Ukraine* (1828), are fantastic tales, imitations and even adaptations of the stories of the German writer Hoffmann. His novel, *The Convent Girl* (1830-33), is a humorous treatment of the life of the Ukrainian gentry.

Perventsev, Arkadi Alexeyevich (1905-), Soviet novelist. His early novels, such as *Kochubey* (1937), depict the Civil War. *Guard Your Honor in Youth* (1948) describes the formation of a young man's character against the background of Soviet history: the Civil War, collectivization and the Second World War.

Peshkov, Alexey Maximovich (1868-1936), a leading writer of the late nineteenth and twentieth centuries, who wrote under the pen-name of Maxim Gorki ("bitter," "unhappy"). He was born at Nizhni Novgorod (since renamed Gorki), the child of an upholsterer. His parents died when he was very young, and he was brought up by his grandparents, of whom he produced unforgettable portraits in his *Childhood* (1913-14). His grandfather, who owned a dyeing establishment, soon went bankrupt and became mentally deranged. He treated the child cruelly, but the grandmother was kind and sympathetic. At the age of eight Gorki was compelled to earn his own living, and at nine to go out into the world. He travelled over Russia, toiling at painful and hard, if varied work; at different times he was employed as a servant, a scullery boy on a Volga steamer, in a bakery, and at different odd jobs; at times he simply tramped about. He had only a few months of formal schooling, and his attempts to get higher education were unsuccessful. He read voraciously in an effort to educate himself. In Kazan he met radical students, and helped to distribute propaganda for the POPULISTS. Disillusioned with his hard life at this early period, he made an attempt to commit suicide.

During his wanderings Gorki had begun to write, and in 1892 he published his first story, *Makar Chudra,* in a local paper. He continued to write and to publish in provincial newspapers. In 1895 he was discovered by the writer KOROLENKO, who published his tale *Chelkash* in *Russian Wealth.* Gorki was at once a success; overnight he became the most popular writer in Russia, eclipsing even Chekhov. He came to Petersburg, where he joined the Social Democratic (Marxist) Party. He devoted much of his tremendous literary income to the revolutionary cause, and also founded a publishing house, called *Znanie* ("knowledge"), for realist writers. KUPRIN, BUNIN and ANDREYEV were the most famous of those who were published by *Znanie.*

Gorki's radical sympathies soon made him the subject of police repression. In 1901 the Marxist journal *Life* was suppressed for publishing his *Song of the Stormy Petrel,* obviously intended by the poet as a portent of the coming revolution. He was arrested, but was soon released on account of developing tuberculosis, and allowed to go to the Crimea. In 1902 he was elected honorary member of the Russian Academy of Sciences, but the government annulled the election. He took an active part in the REVOLU-TION of 1905, and was again arrested for participating in street demonstrations and for his printed attacks on the government. World-wide public opinion forced the government to release him (his works had already been widely translated), and he went abroad to collect funds for the revolutionary movement. He came first to the United States, where a great reception had been pre-pared. But it soon became known that he was not married to the woman travelling with him (under Russian law it was impossible for him to divorce his wife), and public opinion quickly turned against him. He was evicted from his hotel, and Mark Twain and W. D. Howells refused to attend a banquet in his honor. Deeply hurt, Gorki retaliated by publishing a series of stories about New York called *The City of the Yellow Devil* (1906), a collection which still serves as a source of anti-American clichés in Soviet writing.

Returning to Europe, Gorki settled in Capri. During this period his writing lost a good deal of its freshness and vitality, while his close co-operation with the Bolsheviks cost him much of his popu-larity with Russian intellectuals.

In 1913, taking advantage of the government's offer of political amnesty, Gorki returned to Russia. At first he greeted the REVO-LUTION of October, 1917, with enthusiasm. But, shocked by the excesses of the Bolsheviks, he now began to act with considerable independence, trying through his prestige to preserve a freer air in literature and to protect and encourage younger writers. During the Civil War he literally saved many writers from starvation, found them work, and helped to publish their writings. His breach with the Bolshevik leaders, LENIN and TROTSKI, became more and more open, and in 1921 he returned to Capri, ostensibly for his health, but actually at Lenin's request.

In 1928 Gorki returned to the Soviet Union. Confronted with the achievements of the First Five-year Plan, he now announced his enthusiastic acceptance of the Soviet regime. As the "grand old man" of Soviet literature, he exercised great influence. He was instrumental in 1932 in developing the doctrine of SOCIALIST REALISM, which he undoubtedly intended as a fruitful esthetic conception, and not as the strait-jacket which it subsequently became. In 1934 he was chosen president of the newly organized Union of Soviet Writers. Through all this period he continued to publish new works. He is relatively unique as a Russian writer who wrote both before and after the 1917 Revolution and is almost equally important in both periods.

In 1936 Gorki suddenly died while undergoing medical treatment. His doctors were accused of poisoning him, and were tried and convicted. During the purge trials of 1937-38, Yagoda, former chief of the secret police, confessed to having ordered Gorki's execution as part of an anti-Stalinist, "Trotskyite" plot. But the true story of Gorki's death is still a mystery.

Gorki is relatively unique as a great writer of proletarian origin who wrote proletarian literature (actually he was of middle-class origin, but his family background gave him little start in life, and he grew up as a proletarian). In addition, he had almost no formal education, a distinction quite unique among Russian writers. Certain of his serious deficiencies as a writer are undoubtedly connected with this lack of schooling. His style is often ponderous, crude and heavy. He delights in endless philosophical conversations which are hardly literary and have little intrinsic interest. His philosophy, though well-intentioned and humanistic, is often little more than vague theorizing about the essential goodness of man. His revolutionary socialism was of the same order, and the early Marxist critics were doubtless right to accuse him of showing a hyper-emotional, undisciplined Marxism. Other defects of his writing include complete lack of a sense of humor, and the fault common to many realists of employing masses of realistic detail for the sake of sheer weight. His longer works suffer from an episodic quality and defective organization. As a realist Gorki may be compared in many of these respects to the American writer, Theodore Dreiser.

On the other hand, much of Gorki's work is redeemed by a tremendous personal vitality, most apparent in his treatment of character. Gorki's literary personages, whether fictional or actual persons, are accurately and strikingly portrayed. He had a flair for catching slight details which revealed intuitively the essence of a character. His best books, including his autobiographical works and reminiscences, are original and vivid portrait galleries.

Gorki's earlier stories exemplify an original romantic realism of his own creation. They portray members of the lower classes, often tramps and criminals, but also men of heroic power and essential idealism, in whom Gorki sees future leaders of the revolution. The story *Chelkash* (1895) is typical of this tendency. Chelkash is a gay, swashbuckling smuggler whose powerful and generous spirit contrasts with that of the greedy, cowardly peasant whom he forces to follow him. This flair for idealizing the lowest elements of society is typical of Gorki's entire romantic conception of revolution.

After 1895 Gorki lost much of his romantic idealism, and went over to a gloomy, unrelieved naturalism. *"Former" People* (1897; in English translation, "Creatures That Once Were Men)," is a collection of portraits of social derelicts who can never rise again. The stories of this period are depressing, sometimes almost to pointlessness. An exception, however, is the lyrical *Twenty-six Men and a Girl* (1899), which tells of a group of bakers, confined underground at their work like prisoners, and their love for a young girl who comes every day to buy bread from them. A soldier notices the girl and bets the bakers that he will seduce her. They pray that she will refuse them, for she is the only thing in life which they love and in which they can believe. But the soldier succeeds and, when she appears again, they drive her away with shouts and curses. The story has a moving poetry of pathos and idealism, and an expressive conciseness of manner which make it Gorki's masterpiece.

Between 1899 and 1910 Gorki produced a series of novels. All of them are in a sense failures, spoiled by long, pointless philosophical conversations and an eternal "quest" for a spiritual understanding which the hero seems too ignorant or insensitive to acquire. *Foma Gordeyev* (1899), the first of these, is also the best, though even it reads at times like a parody of itself. The characters of Foma and his father, a strong-willed patriarch who founds a family fortune, are vivid, stark portrayals, and Foma's rootlessness and his disaffection for the life around him and for the world of business which he is called upon to enter are powerfully depicted. *The Mother* (1907) demands a special word as a propaganda novel about the revolutionary movement, and the only revolutionary novel which Gorki wrote. Though Soviet critics now praise it as the first great example of SOCIALIST REALISM, it is diffuse, poorly organized and tedious. The best thing in it is the description of the mother's change from a frightened, brutish animal to a warm, tender human being, a transformation motivated by the respect which the revolutionaries, led by her son, pay her, and by her growing faith in the revolutionary cause which she serves. But, like Gorki himself, the mother is a purely emotional revolutionary; she is "bribed" by her feelings into siding with the revolutionary cause, which she never really comprehends. In another of these novels, *A Confession* (1908), Gorki developed a strange religion of the masses, who become higher than God in that they themselves "create" God. This religion of *bogostroitelstvo* ("God-creation"), as it was called, was a popular Marxist heresy of the times, held by those who, like Gorki, wanted to give socialism more of the emotional character of a religion.

In the same period Gorki wrote a number of plays. They are naturalistic representations of life, which Gorki treated—unsuccessfully—using the form of CHEKHOV's new lyric "drama of inaction." The most famous of them, *On the Bottom* (1902; English translation as "The Lower Depths"), won international fame for its sensational setting: a flop-house inhabited by a motley group of derelicts. Its philosophical theme is more interesting than usual: the conflict between a thief, who relies on his own strength, and an old pilgrim, who supplies each of the unredeemables with some romantic delusion designed to help him go on living. The conflict is never resolved in the play: Gorki obviously admires the strength of the thief, but also sympathizes with the humane and tolerant love of the old pilgrim, Luka, though later he rejected Luka's philosophy.

Beginning in 1913, Gorki published three volumes of autobiographical works: *Childhood* (1913-14), *In the World* (1915-16), and *My Universities* (1923), as well as a volume of *Reminiscences* (1924-31) of Russian writers, including Lev TOLSTOY, CHEKHOV, BLOK and ANDREYEV. The autobiographical works are actually great galleries of vivid and unforgettable characters Gorki had met in life. The reminiscences about Russian writers are equally vivid; particularly memorable are the hints of egoistic feeling which Gorki detected in Tolstoy in the latter's role of the teacher of a new ethical religion.

In his last period Gorki returned to writing novels and plays. In *The Artamanovs' Business* (1925) he chronicles the decay of a merchant family, founded by a strong-willed and rapacious ex-serf, who is succeeded by his worthless sons and foppish grandsons. A similar theme is treated in an unfinished dramatic trilogy, of which two plays (*Yegor Bulychov and Others*, 1932; *Dostigayev and Others*, 1933) were written. Finally there is the immense, unfinished novel cycle, *The Life of Klim Samgin*, of which four novels appeared between 1927 and 1936. It attempts to give a synthetic portrait of the life of the Russian intelligentsia from 1870 to 1924, with its ideological degeneration and decay. As in most of Gorki's work, there are powerful characters and gripping scenes, but the whole is uneven and episodic.

Gorki's early Soviet critics observed that, except for *The Mother*, he had produced no really positive revolutionary work, and that even this novel was colored by his undisciplined emotionalism. Even in his Soviet period he preferred to describe the decline of the bourgeoisie rather than the rise of the proletariat, and critics accused him of unconscious sympathy with the prerevolutionary bourgeoisie. It is obvious, at least, that Gorki was never a disciplined Communist. If at present he is canonized by the Soviets as the greatest Russian writer since Pushkin, this means that the Soviets have forgiven him such sins, even forgotten them. The reason for this is undoubtedly his great popularity with the reading public, as well as his stature as a writer. Except for BLOK (whose acceptance of the Revolution was short-lived and even more mystic and emotional than Gorki's), Gorki was the only major Russian writer who accepted the October Revolution and was on the side of the Bolsheviks from the beginning.

The ultimate significance of Gorki's work is still difficult to assess. Though he was a gifted writer with a tremendous creative capacity, he seems to have no really unique quality which would entitle him to the rank of a writer of first order. His literary influence was almost negligible in the 1920's; its revival in the 1930's was partly artificial, and emphasized his weakest aspects, such as the depiction of the revolutionary movement in *The Mother,* now proclaimed the first great novel of SOCIALIST REALISM. At the beginning of the century it may well have appeared that Gorki represented the beginning of a new literary current, of a new humanism of the proletariat. But the passage of time suggests more and more deeply that this is not so, and that Gorki is only the final chapter in the development of nineteenth-century Russian realism.

Peter the Great (Peter I, 1672-1725; reigned as tsar of Russia, 1682-1725; as emperor, 1721-25). Peter the Great has been associated with the systematic introduction of Western technical and cultural influences in Russia, but it is necessary to avoid the simplified view that he, single-handed and as an absolute monarch, converted Russia into a European state. The movement towards Europeanization was already strong among progressive Russians in the seventeenth century. Many of Peter's reforms had popular support, particularly among the rising landowning aristocracy (as distinct from the older boyar nobility) and the merchants. Peter must, however, be credited with influencing the choice of areas of European culture which were introduced during his reign. He was not greatly concerned with art or literature, and "Europeanization" in these fields progressed only a little more rapidly than under his predecessors. On the other hand, Peter was strongly interested in science and technology. He established schools and ordered the preparation and translation of text-books for these subjects. He reformed the army and the government along European lines, created a navy, founded a new capital, St. Petersburg, with a European style of architecture, and encouraged trade, commerce, mining and industry. He abolished the position of patriarch and partly secularized the administration of the Church. He also attempted to introduce Western dress and manners, and ordered his male subjects to shave off their beards. In such areas his reforms were arbitrary and superficial, and were successful only among the upper classes.

Peter's direct influence on literature was negligible, though he himself possessed a clear and vigorous style. He invited several foreign companies of actors to Russia, and his sister Natalya even wrote plays. His greatest influence on letters was a technical one: he restricted the older, more ornate Cyrillic ALPHABET to Church use and introduced a simpler style of characters (essentially like the modern Russian Alphabet) for civil use.

Peter's reforms were praised enthusiastically in the writings of FEOFAN PROKOPOVICH, Prince KANTEMIR, and others. His colorful life and activities formed the subject of works of literature by PUSHKIN, MEREZHKOVSKI, A. N. TOLSTOY, and others. PUSHKIN's *Bronze Horseman* is a brilliant apotheosis of his spirit as reformer.

Petrashevski Circle, a secret group of Russian Utopian socialists formed in 1845. The members met at the home of M. B. Butashevich-Petrashevski (hence the name) to discuss political problems and read illegal socialist literature. The group included the great novelist DOSTOYEVSKI, as well as the poet PLESHCHEYEV. In April, 1849, the members of the circle were arrested, and twenty-one of them, including Dostoyevski and Pleshcheyev, were condemned to death; a mock drama was staged in which they were led out to execution, though Nicholas I had already granted a reprieve. Ultimately they were sentenced to exile in Siberia or to service in the army. Though accused of plotting revolution, the circle was far more a discussion society than an actual conspiracy.

Petrov, Stepan Gavrilovich (1868-1941), a writer of the early twentieth century. A radical realist, his works were brought out by Gorki's publishing house, *Znanie* ("knowledge"), under the pseudonym of Skitalets ("wanderer," "rootless person"). His sketches of the life of tramps are influenced by Gorki (see Peshkov), and colored by Gorki's belief that these men constituted a vital class filled with revolutionary idealism. Many of his tales are autobiographical.

Petrov, Vasili Petrovich (1736-99), an eighteenth-century poet, the follower of LOMONOSOV. A courtier, he served as reader and translator to the Empress Catherine the Great; later as court librarian. He was a writer of dignified odes, as well as the translator of Virgil and Pope.

Petrov, Yevgeni. See Katayev, Ye. P.

Philosophy. *Introduction.* As a result of linguistic and cultural isolation, both from the traditions of classical antiquity and the civilization of Western Europe, Russia did not experience a "Renaissance" of classical learning until the second half of the eighteenth century—nearly three centuries after the European Renaissance. There was no Russian parallel to the widespread Western European use of Latin as a liturgical and learned language, affording a close link with the Greco-Roman world. The cultural roots of medieval Russia lay in Byzantium, but these roots brought little philosophic sustenance to the remote limbs of Kiev and Muscovy. OLD CHURCH SLAVONIC, rather than Greek, remained the language of liturgy and learning, and very few Greek writings (these few being chiefly theological or homiletic rather than philosophic) were translated into it. The origins of Russian philosophy, as an intellectual discipline distinct from the religious experience and theological speculations out of which it had developed, thus date from the late eighteenth century.

From that time to the present day, Russian philosophers have been primarily concerned with questions of ethics, social and political philosophy, and the philosophy of history. As contrasted with their German, French and English counterparts, they have given relatively little attention to logic, theory of knowledge, or metaphysics. Good and evil in individual and social life, the meaning and direction of historical development, the relation of national to universal culture—rather than the nature of being and knowledge, or the presuppositions of science—have been the focus of their philosophic interest. And they have tended to construe theoretical knowledge as part of a total life-activity, to be integrated into a synoptic vision of "the whole man in the whole society in the whole reality."

This characterization applies equally to such otherwise opposed groups as the "SLAVOPHILES" and "WESTERNERS," secular radicals and religious thinkers, "POPULISTS" and early Russian

Marxists. In what follows, we shall attempt to trace these dominant themes through the works of the major Russian representatives of these (and other) philosophic tendencies from the mid-eighteenth to the mid-twentieth century.

The Eighteenth Century. The earliest thinker in Russia who may appropriately be called a philosopher is Gregory Skovoroda (1722-94), a Ukrainian, who has, with considerable justice, been spoken of as "the Russian Socrates." A poet and theologian, as well as philosopher, Skovoroda travelled widely in Europe, and knew German, Latin, Greek and Hebrew. Some of his metaphysical theories are reminiscent of the views of Malebranche, although there is no evidence that he was acquainted with the latter's works. Skovoroda wrote brilliant philosophic dialogues which, unfortunately, offer serious difficulties to the modern reader, because his philosophic coinages have not been generally accepted by subsequent Russian philosophers. Criticizing pure empiricism, he developed a dualistic Platonic metaphysics with a mystical and pantheistic coloring. His theory of man, while broadly Christian, anticipated in some respects later psychological and philosophic theories of the "unconscious." Skovoroda's writings are shot through with moving poetry and striking philosophic insights, but he was not a systematic philosopher. His resemblance to his contemporary, William Blake, is more than superficial.

The Russian secular intelligentsia, during the late eighteenth century, was much influenced by French rationalism, skepticism, and deism—especially through the works of Voltaire—and by freemasonry, chiefly from German sources. These Western influences followed naturally in the wake of PETER THE GREAT's forced "Europeanization" of Russian life and thought. Diderot's visit to the court of Catherine II in 1773-74 offers a concrete symbol of the penetration into Russian intellectual circles of the ideas and attitudes of the French Enlightenment. Many eighteenth-century Russian followers of the French *philosophes* defended the theory of "natural law" and "natural rights," although, after the outbreak of the French Revolution, such "alien and subversive" teachings were regarded with suspicion, and certain professors were dismissed from University positions for defending them. Russian theorists of natural law included: V. N. TATISHCHEV (1686-1750), an erudite historian, the first Russian to sketch a utilitarian ethical theory; the anti-clerical Prince M. M. Shcherbatov (1733-90), who defended "natural religion"; and the brilliant humanist A. N. RADISHCHEV (1749-1802), whose *Journey from Petersburg to Moscow* (1790) was to become a model of social criticism for later Russian radicals. Its publication resulted in a sentence of death for Radishchev, later commuted to ten years' exile. In this respect, too, Radishchev set a precedent for subsequent radical thinkers, almost all of whom spent a considerable portion of their adult lives in Siberian isolation or in St. Petersburg prisons. Radishchev studied philosophy in Leipzig, coming under the influence of Leibniz, Herder, Helvetius, Locke and Priestley; he wrote on epistemological and metaphysical questions (espousing a radical realism), but was concerned chiefly with ethics and social philosophy.

Several outstanding eighteenth-century Russian scholars and scientists produced works on philosophic themes, among them the physicist and chemist M. V. LOMONOSOV (ca. 1711-65) and the historian N. M. KARAMZIN (1766-1826).

The Nineteenth Century. The nineteenth century in Russia was marked by a shift from French to German intellectual, especially philosophic, influences. After an initial enthusiasm for Schelling's nature-philosophy and esthetic theory, Russian intellectuals turned toward Kant and Fichte. Kant's critical writings were forbidden by the censorship as subversive of religion and morals, but they were widely circulated in manuscript translations among university and theology students. *The Critique of Pure Reason* was not finally published in Russian until 1867. Fichte was quite influential during the 1820's and 1830's, but he was read largely in the original German. The only Russian translation dating from this period is Mikhail BAKUNIN's version of *The Vocation of the Scholar* (1811), which appeared in Belinski's journal *The Telescope* in 1835. Hegel, of course, was the dominant influence; his chief impact upon Russian thought dates from the late 1830's, but his philosophic presence continued to dominate Russian intellectuals—not merely professional philosophers—for many years.

The chief Russian Schellingians were D. M. VELLANSKI (1774-1847); D. V. VENEVITINOV (1805-27), a gifted poet and philosopher who died very young and left few writings; and Prince

V. F. ODOYEVSKI (1803-69). Odoyevski, who later turned from Schelling's nature-philosophy to the working out of a philosophical anthropology and philosophy of history, was one of the first Russian thinkers to formulate the idea, and ideal, of "organic wholeness"—a fusion of the cognitive and non-cognitive aspects of human nature—which was to be a central tenet of the SLAVO-PHILES. Odoyevski suggested, in a moment of prophetic insight, that it might soon be possible "to produce matter from non-material energy," and to transmute one substance into another. He was the first Russian to offer a systematic critique of Western culture. The West, he insisted, cannot achieve a full or harmonious development until it finds its own Peter the Great to "infuse it with the fresh and powerful saps of the Slavic East." This theme, too, was taken up and developed by the Russian SLAVOPHILES.

The Emphasis on Distinctively Russian (or Slavic) Values. The group of thinkers known as "SLAVOPHILES," who emerged as a dominant force in Russian intellectual life during the 1840's, is often represented as politically conservative and religiously Orthodox, being contrasted in these respects with the anti-clerical and politically radical (or, at the least, liberal) "WESTERNERS." Such generalizations, however, are misleading. Obvious exceptions may be cited. For example, P. Ya. CHAADAYEV (ca. 1793-1856), who was—in his early works at any rate—an outspoken critic of Russia and warm admirer of the West, was at the same time a deeply religious and politically conservative thinker. On the other hand, Mikhail BAKUNIN (1814-76), for many years an enthusiastic pan-Slavist, ended as a radical anarchist, atheist, and revolutionary nihilist. For a majority of the Westerners, to be sure —for BELINSKI, HERZEN, CHERNYSHEVSKI and DOBRO-LYUBOV—and a majority of the Slavophiles—I. KIREYEVSKI, KHOMYAKOV, SAMARIN and K. AKSAKOV—the traditional distinction holds.

Chaadayev, who was influenced by Schelling (they met in Germany in 1825), as well as by Kant and Hegel, developed a philosophy of history reminiscent in many respects of St. Augustine's, and a philosophical anthropology which repudiated "fragmented individualism," asserting the "collective nature of human consciousness."

A. S. KHOMYAKOV (1804-60) was a brilliant dialectician, but he wrote comparatively little. He is best known for his doctrine of *sobornost* ("organic togetherness") and his emphasis on the integral wholeness of human nature—doctrines which were taken over and developed by later Russian religious philosophers. Khomyakov was sharply critical of philosophic rationalism (especially Hegelianism) and he identified it, rather confusingly, with "cultural rationalism"—which he felt to be dangerously dominant in Western Christian (i.e., Roman Catholic) civilization. His emphasis on "total reason" and the communal nature of the act of knowing, together with his critique of epistemological idealism, were all echoed by the other Slavophiles.

I. V. KIREYEVSKI (1806-56), a leading member of this group, followed Khomyakov in defending epistemological "ontologism" —the doctrine that knowing is only a part and function in man's integral activity in the world, an event in the total life-process.

In philosophy of history and culture, all of the Slavophiles were, in greater or less degree, critical of the historical development of Western Europe since the Middle Ages, seeing Russia as a redeemer of world civilization who would overcome the reigning evils of the West—variously identified as (fragmented) "individualism," (cold, bloodless) "rationalism," and (coarse) "materialism." An instructive instance of this large-scale cultural generalization is provided by Khomyakov's doctrine of freedom and unity. In his view, the Roman Catholic Church represents unity without freedom, and the Protestant sects represent freedom without unity; only the Russian Orthodox Church provides a synthesis of unity-in-freedom or freedom-in-unity, which assigns each of these conflicting elements its proper place.

The Turn to the West. The ideological competitors of the Slavophiles, known as "WESTERNERS" or "Westernizers" *(zapadniki)*, exhibit a universal passion for Hegel, usually following upon a brief infatuation with Schelling and Fichte, and giving way in turn to a more stable union with Feuerbach and the Hegelian Left. Feuerbach's *The Nature of Christianity* (1841) exerted an enormous influence upon radical Russian intellectuals during the 1840's and 1850's, though it did not appear in Russian translation (because of the censorship) until 1906.

V. G. BELINSKI (1811-48), a brilliant literary critic and essayist, reacted strongly (in the early 1840's) against the impersonalism of Hegel's absolute idealism—as did A. I. HERZEN (1812-70)—repudiating the Hegelian doctrine that the individual is only a partial manifestation, a means or instrument for the self-realization of Absolute Spirit. "The fate of the individual person," he wrote, "is more important than the fate of the whole world . . . including Hegel's *Allgemeinheit*." Like Herzen, Belinski turned toward Utopian socialism as a defense of the individual, a guarantee to all men of the right to normal life and development. Herzen later moved from his early political radicalism toward a moderate liberal reformism. In philosophy of history, he turned from his early Hegelian rationalism and determinism toward a "philosophy of contingency," stressing what he called the "whirlwind of chances" in nature and life, and the "tousled improvisation" of history. In his later years, disillusioned by what he had witnessed in Western Europe after 1848, Herzen came to regard the Russian village commune as the hope of the future. In this, he anticipated a central doctrine of the later "POPULISTS."

Both Belinski and Herzen, though they are often referred to as "materialists" (especially by Soviet writers), were not in fact philosophic materialists, but empiricists or positivists.

M. A. BAKUNIN (1814-76), after a brief flirtation with Fichte, became a convinced and dogmatic Hegelian; he was the first to exploit the Hegelian dialectic in a systematic way (in his essay *Reaction in Germany*, 1842) as a theoretical justification for violent political revolution. But Bakunin soon repudiated Hegel, turning from theoretical philosophy to political activity, and (in middle life) embracing atheism, materialism and anarchist socialism. He is associated, along with S. Nechayev (1847-82), with the first detailed formulation (in 1869) of "revolutionary Machiavellianism"—the doctrine that the "good" end of revolution justifies beforehand any means which is necessary to its realization.

Radical Nihilism. Among the later Westerners were N. G. CHERNYSHEVSKI (1828-89) and his follower N. A. DOBROLYUBOV (1836-61), both philosophic materialists and atheists, and leaders of the radical NIHILISTS of the 1860's. (Both, incidentally, were sons of Russian Orthodox priests.) Under the influence of Feuerbach, Comte, Fourier and John Stuart Mill, they developed a utilitarian doctrine of "rational egoism" as the foundation of morality. Like the earlier Westerners, Chernyshevski and Dobrolyubov stressed the "natural" rights of the individual person and the need for radical social, economic and political change to effect the individual's emancipation. Chernyshevski made influential contributions to esthetics and literary criticism; Dobrolyubov was a talented literary critic, but not a theorist. Chernyshevski's social and political views, especially his emphasis on the Russian village commune as a reservoir of socialism, and his doctrine that Russia could avoid the evils of industrial capitalism by moving directly from primitive to advanced socialism, were taken over by the Populists during the 1870's and 1880's.

Certain of Chernyshevski's views were further developed by D. I. PISAREV (1840-68), who left substantial works in literary criticism and social philosophy upon his untimely death at the age of twenty-eight. However, Pisarev modified Chernyshevski's utilitarianism by introducing the principle of "economy of intellectual energies." In Russia, he held, where "intellectual capital" was negligible, energy could not be spared for idle luxuries— "art for art's sake," "speculative philosophy," "recondite science." Indeed, he anticipated Lev TOLSTOY's moralistic-utilitarian view of art and science; both, he held, should be related directly to the "living needs" of men; they should not be abstruse or unintelligible, but practically important and universally accessible. Poets, he declared, should answer the call of militant nihilism and become "Titans, shaking the mountains of age-old evil"; otherwise they are as useless as "insects burrowing in flower-dust."

Pisarev laid great stress on the emancipation of the individual from the restraints of mob opinion, superstition, ignorance, and even moral norms and ideals! He was one of the first, along with P. L. LAVROV, to give currency to the expression "critically thinking individual."

Russian "Populism." The "POPULISTS" *(narodniki,* from the Russian word *narod,* "people, nation"), especially P. L. LAVROV (1823-1900) and N. K. MIKHAYLOVSKI (1842-1904), developed further the social and historical views of Belinski, Herzen and Chernyshevski—stressing the uniqueness of the village commune, Russia's "special path" to socialism, and the debt which the intellectuals owed the people. Both were critical of the philosophic foundations of Marxism, as these were being defended during the 1890's by G. V. PLEKHANOV (1857-1918) and V. I. LENIN (1870-1924). In opposition to the Marxists' "objective method" of studying history and society, they developed a "subjective method." "Observation of social phenomena," Mikhaylovski held, "necessarily involves moral evaluation." The Populists stressed the role of individual volition and subjective goals in social development. They employed ethical criteria in evaluating the historical progress of various peoples, defending "freedom" and "individuality" as absolute ethical values. But at the same time they accepted sociological relativism, emulated the methods of the natural sciences, and endorsed Comte's positivistic critique of speculative metaphysics. The resulting position, which has been called "semi-positivism," is an inconsistent combination of philosophic positivism with a very unpositivistic ethical idealism.

Lavrov laid central stress on ethics; in this respect he may be compared with Lev TOLSTOY, whose "panmoralism" ended in a "tyranny of ethics" over all other departments of life and thought —art, science, religion, politics, etc. To be sure, he did not go as far in this direction as did Tolstoy. Lavrov regarded the problem of free will as insoluble, but he insisted that man's "sense of freedom" is real and causally efficacious; anticipating Vaihinger's "philosophy of as-if," he declared that man sets goals for himself "as though" he were free, and Lavrov defended this as legitimate and necessary.

MIKHAYLOVSKI, developing the views set forth in the 1860's by a gifted young biologist, N. D. Nozhin (1841-66), criticized excessive specialization and division of labor as destructive of the wholeness of the individual person. Mikhaylovski conceived of history as moving from an "objectively anthropocentric" stage to an "excentric" stage (now coming to a close), and toward a "subjectively anthropocentric" stage, in which human needs, ideals and aspirations would be frankly placed at the center of the cosmos.

Two minor "semi-positivists" were K. D. KAVELIN (1818-85) —who was tutored by Belinski as a young man, and wrote lively memoirs of the latter—and M. I. KAREYEV (1850-1931). Both Kavelin and Kareyev, like Lavrov, attempted to provide a "scientific grounding for morality." Kareyev wrote important studies in the philosophy of history, including detailed and penetrating criticisms of Hegel. Kavelin left interesting works in psychology and practical ethics.

Nineteenth-Century Russian Religious Philosophy. Among the outstanding religiously-oriented thinkers of the late nineteenth century we note K. N. LEONTIEV (1831-91)—often called the "Russian Nietzsche" because of his esthetic "amoralism" and biting critique of "philistinism," "shopkeeper morality," and egalitarian values—and V. V. ROZANOV (1856-1919), famed for his theological heresies and his "metaphysics of sex." Both men were brilliant stylists and both strongly influenced Nikolay BERDYAYEV (1874-1948), the best-known, though not the most important, of contemporary Russian religious philosophers.

Vladimir SOLOVYOV (1853-1900), probably the most celebrated and certainly the most influential of nineteenth-century Russian religious philosophers, turned—under the influence of Spinoza, his "first philosophic love"—from positivism and atheism toward a mystically-colored metaphysics of "positive total-unity." From Schelling Solovyov took the concept of a "world-soul," the doctrine of intellectual intuition, and the notion of a "second Absolute," or "Absolute in process of becoming," as well as a Platonic esthetics. His system has been called "the most full-sounding chord in the history of philosophy," and it is certainly a grandiose, if not always successful, attempt at an "organic synthesis of religion, philosophy and science in the interests of the integral life," to use Solovyov's own words. Solovyov wrote penetrating criticisms of positivism and "abstract rationalism" (Hegel), as well as a pointed critique of TOLSTOY's doctrine of non-resistance to evil. He also wrote extensively on historical and social problems, and he left much brilliant literary criticism, as well as some first-class poetry and charming light verse.

Almost all of the major Russian religious thinkers of the twentieth century were directly influenced by Solovyov: among others, the Princes S. and Ye. Trubetskoy, D. S. MEREZHKOVSKI (1865-1941), BERDYAYEV, S. L. FRANK (1877-1950) and S. N. BULGAKOV (1871-1944). Most of these men, together with N. O. LOSSKY (1870-   ), who elaborated Solovyov's doctrine of "intellectual intuition" into an intuitivistic theory of knowledge, spent their later years in exile in Western Europe and America. Of these, the most philosophically significant is S. L. Frank.

Anarchist Socialism. Early Russian Marxism. Prince P. A. KROPOTKIN (1842-1921) was influenced by Guyau and BAKUNIN; he is best known for his anarchist socialism (including an unrelenting attack upon law and the state) and his critique of Darwinism. Kropotkin stressed the role of co-operation and mutual aid, as opposed to mutual conflict, in the evolutionary process. In fact, Kropotkin was only the most celebrated of a long line of Russian thinkers, beginning with Nozhin, and including CHERNYSHEVSKI, N. Ya. DANILEVSKI (1822-85), N. N. STRAKHOV (1828-95), MIKHAYLOVSKI and B. N. Chicherin (1828-1903), who criticized Darwin on this score. Kropotkin also developed a Darwinian ethical theory, based on the alleged survival-value for social aggregates of co-operative behavior patterns and "social instincts." A similar theory was developed at about the same time, although independently, by Karl Kautsky.

Marxism became a widely influential intellectual movement in Russia in the late 1880's and early 1890's. The Russian Marxists almost immediately split into at least three separate and opposed philosophic groupings. The most productive of these "deviations," philosophically speaking, was represented by A. A. BOGDANOV (1873-1928), A. V. LUNACHARSKI (1873-1933), V. A. Bazarov (1874-   ) and S. A. Volski (1880-   ). These thinkers—and Maxim Gorki was associated with them for a time—felt that Marxism as a theory of history and social change was essentially sound, but lacked an adequate ethical theory and had no real theory of knowledge. They were all literary artists of some competence—especially Lunacharski and Gorki—and they felt uncomfortable in the impersonal system of Marxian historical materialism, which reduced the individual to a "point of intersection of social relationships." In effect, they were repeating the earlier revolt of HERZEN and BELINSKI against the "impersonalism" or "anti-individualism" of Hegel's philosophy. These Russian writers turned to Nietzsche for a morality which rejected duty and obligation and stressed individual freedom, spontaneous impulse, the free artistic creation of values and ideals. Several of them did important work in naturalistic ethics and value theory, including esthetics, under this Nietzschean-Marxist inspiration.

For a theory of knowledge to supplement Marxism, they turned to Mach and Avenarius. The socially-oriented "empiriomonism" developed by Bogdanov and Bazarov (in the early 1900's) bears striking resemblances to the socially-oriented pragmatism later expounded by John Dewey.

A second group of "deviationists" saw similar deficiencies in Marxism, but turned to Kant for an epistemology and ethical theory with which to make good the lack. The most important members of this group were BERDYAYEV, BULGAKOV and P. B. STRUVE (1870-1944); all of these men later abandoned Marxism and turned to an idealistic and religiously-oriented philosophy, within the general framework of Russian Orthodoxy. Bulgakov became a priest in 1918 and subsequently devoted himself to theological writing.

The "orthodox" Marxist position was defended by PLEKHANOV, L. I. Akselrod (1868-1946) and A. M. Kollontai (1872-1952)—the last two being outstanding women philosophers among the Russian Marxists—and, of course, by LENIN. But "deviations" became apparent even within this group: Plekhanov developed an epistemological theory of "hieroglyphs" which Lenin criticized as a concession to Kantianism. Lenin himself defended a very un-Marxian doctrine of "absolute and objective truth." He also "deviated" in his philosophy of history from Marxian determinism toward an acceptance of human freedom and volition as factors shaping historical events. Lenin laid great stress on the Hegelian dialectic, and, like Bakunin, focused attention on the *conflict* rather than the *unity* of opposites—in particular, the destruction of thesis by antithesis (e.g., the bougeoisie by the proletariat). Lenin also followed Bakunin in his violent anti-clericalism, and his assertion of atheism as the religion of the proletariat. Like Bakunin, he held that the disjunction "idealism or materialism" is both exclusive and exhaustive. It was the attempt of the Russian "Machians" (BOGDANOV, *et al.*) to assert a third (positivist) position, neither idealism nor materialism, which evoked the onslaught of Lenin's ill-tempered and dogmatic *Materialism and Empiriocriticism* (1909).

Philosophy in the Soviet Union. After the Bolshevik Revolution the tension between the two heterogeneous components of Russian Marxism—classical materialism and Hegelian dialectic—led to a lively philosophic dispute between the "Mechanists," headed by L. I. Akselrod, who emphasized the materialism and neglected the dialectic, and the "Menshevizing Idealists" (as they were later called by STALIN), headed by A. M. Deborin (1881-   ), who laid almost exclusive emphasis upon the dialectic. This struggle culminated in 1930 with the official repudiation of "Mechanism," followed a year later by the official repudiation of "Deborinism." The new "orthodox" position established in 1931 was an attempt to balance the two elements. It also marked the effective termination of relatively free philosophic discussion in the Soviet Union; all subsequent philosophic disputes have been settled "from above," e.g., by ZHDANOV in 1947, and STALIN in 1950. One of the most interesting shifts of philosophic position has occurred with respect to formal logic, which, until 1947, was banned from Soviet schools and universities as a "bourgeois," static, and hence distorting representation of the flux, movement and "internal contradictions" of things. Its place was taken by "materialistic dialectic." In the academic year 1946-47, by a decree of the Central Committee of the Communist Party, formal logic was introduced into schools and universities as a compulsory subject of study. A certain amount of training in formal logic, it had been discovered, was needed to make Soviet citizens "think straight" about practical and political problems; the relevant philosophic arguments were quickly reversed, and formal logic was praised as vigorously as it had been attacked a short time before.

Soviet "philosophy" has long since lost any semblance of intellectual independence, becoming increasingly subordinated to practical and political demands. This "politicalization" of Soviet thought may be traced in detail through ethical theory, logic, esthetics, theory of knowledge, and even philosophy of history. We need hardly add that the reasons for the "ideological triumphs" of Soviet Marxism-Leninism are to be sought largely outside the realm of philosophic persuasion.

The period since the death of STALIN has been marked by several shake-ups of the editorial boards and administrative staffs concerned with teaching, research and publication in philosophy. There has been an increased frankness in acknowledging the deplorable state of graduate study, publication and teaching in the subject. But the only significant doctrinal changes appear to amount to a return from "deviations" of the Stalinist period to a more rigidly orthodox Marxism-Leninism. This is evident in the present de-emphasis of teaching and writing on formal logic and in a renewed stress upon historical determinism—the unilateral causal efficacy of the economic "base" *vis-à-vis* the ideological "superstructure." The only sign of increased intellectual freedom appears in the discussion and even publication of certain foreign non-Marxist histories of philosophy. But this is a dubious straw in the wind. It is too early to say whether this marks the beginning of a general loosening of the doctrinal strait-jacket of Soviet Marxism-Leninism.

George L. Kline

Pilnyak, Boris. See Vogau, B. A.

Pisarev, Alexander Ivanovich (1803-28), an early nineteenth-century writer of stage vaudevilles, including some of the best Russian works in this form.

Pisarev, Dmitri Ivanovich (1840-68), a political thinker and critic of the 1860's. A member of the gentry, he was the leader of the Russian NIHILISTS, as the radicals of the 1860's were nicknamed. Arrested in 1862 for printing radical propaganda, he spent the next four years in prison. There he wrote most of his critical and theoretical articles. He died from drowning in 1868.

Pisarev carried the utilitarianism of CHERNYSHEVSKI to its logical extremes. For him the test of practical utility is the one which all social institutions, such as the family, state and Church, must pass; otherwise they are worthless. Materialistic science he deified; education and the dissemination of scientific knowledge were the only hopes of Russia. He completely rejected the power of authority in art, morality or politics. Art itself was suspect for him, and he asserted that a good pair of boots was worth more than a tragedy by Shakespeare. Poetry he scorned as a dying art, and he did much to injure, for a time, the reputation of PUSHKIN. Pisarev's criticism of Pushkin as a poet who did not possess sufficient social conscience was quite logical in terms of his theories, and was helpful, at least, in demolishing exaggerated notions concerning Pushkin's social significance. Pisarev did admit the need for novels and dramas with a social purpose, and enthusiastically greeted TURGENEV's novel, *Fathers and Children* (1862), the hero of which, Bazarov, he accepted as the literary prototype of the new man, practical, hard-headed and scientific. (See Philosophy.)

Pisemski, Alexey Feofilaktovich (1820-81), a leading Russian novelist and playwright of the mid-nineteenth century. Pisemski came of an impoverished noble family. He graduated from the University of Moscow and entered the civil service, remaining there, with several interruptions, until 1872. In the 1850's he served for a time on the staff of the conservative journal, *The Muscovite*, which published his early work.

Pisemski is a realistic novelist of Russian life, whose work describes a variety of social classes. His realism is actually closer to naturalism, for he depicts all his characters—except the peasants —as mean, evil and petty. His pessimism and anti-idealism, even cynicism, set him sharply off from other realists of the time, for the most part liberals or radicals. He satirized the radicals in his novel, *Troubled Seas* (1863), and thus earned their undying hatred. He stands, together with the playwright OSTROVSKI, almost alone among the realists of the day in his relative indifference to current political and social issues. Unlike most of the Russian realists, he preferred involved plots, and the narrative interest in his work is strong. Though he was a master of peasant dialogue, his style suffers from a general lack of craftsmanship and polish.

Pisemski's first novel, *Boyarshchina* (published 1858), depicts the decaying provincial gentry and the lot of a sensitive, unhappily married woman ruined by a love affair. The collection entitled *Sketches of Peasant Life* (1856) presents a sympathetic though objective picture of the peasants, sharply at variance with the condescending sympathy and philanthropic tone of most stories of the times concerned with their way of life. Pisemski's peasants are shrewd, strong and self-reliant. *A Thousand Souls* (1858) was his most popular novel. Its hero, Kalinovich, is a talented and ambitious climber who fails as a writer, but makes his fortune by marrying a cripple, a wealthy heiress, the owner of a thousand "souls" (i.e., serfs). Ostensibly acting from noble motives, though in fact from egoistic ambition, he rises to the position of provincial governor, but, in his ruthless drive to prosecute dishonesty, he exceeds legal bounds, and is forced to retire from the service. Disillusioned in both career and marriage, he seeks consolation in an affair with an old love.

Pisemski's later novels are of lesser importance. *In the Whirlpool* (1871) is an attack on feminist emancipation. *The Burghers* (1877) is the portrayal of an idealistic SUPERFLUOUS MAN surrounded by a society which is greedy and corrupt. He was also a talented playwright, and his tragedy, *A Bitter Lot* (1859), is one of the masterpieces of the Russian drama. In it a weak but idealistic landowner seduces the wife of one of his serfs. Her husband, a strong-willed, prosperous peasant, returns home to learn of the affair; a curious conflict ensues: the husband, though serf to the landowner, is the master of his wife. In the end he kills the lovers' illegitimate child and gives himself up to the police.

Pisemski's later plays were less successful. They include historical melodramas of the eighteenth century, as well as satires on the greedy capitalist expansion of the 1860's and 1870's.

Plavilshchikov, Pyotr Alexeyevich (1760-1812), an actor and playwright, the follower of SUMAROKOV. Plavilshchikov's two most famous plays are his comedies, *The Landless Peasant* (1790) and *The Shop Assistant* (1804), noted for their early treatment of merchants and peasants on the stage.

Plekhanov, Georgi Valentinovich (1857-1918), a Russian philosopher and theoretician of Marxism. At first a member of the POPULISTS, Plekhanov went over to Marxism after his emigration from Russia in 1880. In 1883 he took part in the formation of the Emancipation of Labor, the nucleus of the future Russian Social Democratic (Marxist) Party. When the split between the Bolshevik and Menshevik wings of the Social Democrats occurred in 1903, Plekhanov at first sided with the Bolsheviks, later with the Mensheviks; subsequently he remained independent of both. As a theoretician of Russian Marxist Socialism he was the principal rival of LENIN. Plekhanov rejected the October REVOLUTION of 1917, when the Bolsheviks seized power, instead advocating continued collaboration among the socialist and liberal democratic parties and continuation of the war.

As a philosopher, Plekhanov attempted to unify the traditions of French and Marxist materialism. He demonstrates the superiority of Marxist socialism in its use of the dialectical method, its ability to deal with questions of growth and development, its recognition of the dependence of man's psychic world on economic relations. He follows Spinoza and Marx in finding true human freedom in the knowledge of historical necessity.

Plekhanov's most original contribution to Marxism was his attempt to formulate a Marxist theory of literature and art. Though his esthetics are in the main Marxist, the range of his speculations is very broad, and does not always confine itself to a rigid Marxist pattern. Following the lead of Marx, he declares that art and literature are ideological in nature, and are conditioned by the development of society. Man's esthetic sense is not absolute or autonomous, but is influenced by his biological nature and place in society, as well as by considerations of a practical order, such as the material value of objects.

Art and literature develop as society develops, are conditioned by the class struggle and reflect that struggle in ideological form. Plekhanov makes it clear, however, that art is a complex activity, and by no means a simple or direct reflection of the class struggle alone. And he later rejects the notion that one should judge art exclusively according to political convictions, instead tending more and more to distinguish the socio-political, tendentious value of literature from its purely artistic qualities. Thus his esthetic theory is broader and less rigid than "orthodox" Marxist-Leninist doctrine.

Plekhanov's influence on Soviet literary theory and criticism was strong during the 1920's. Part of his importance was due to the fact that Marx and LENIN had written very little about literature. In the early 1930's, however, Soviet critics joined in a severe attack on Plekhanov and his followers. He was accused of making too sharp a dichotomy between the purely socio-political and the esthetic values of literary works, and consequently of failing to recognize the necessity for the expression of "party spirit" (see *Partiynost*) in literature, a doctrine which Soviet critics have developed from LENIN. Failing to accept this requirement, Plekhanov remained too "objective," i.e., too neutral for them.

Pleshcheyev, Alexey Nikolayevich (1825-93), a minor poet of the mid-nineteenth century. Like DOSTOYEVSKI, a member of the PETRASHEVSKI CIRCLE, Pleshcheyev was arrested in 1849 and sentenced to serve in the army ranks. He was permitted to return to private life in 1856.

Pleshcheyev was a realist poet of civic tendency, whose poetry embodies social ideals. His verse, though well intentioned and full of noble sentiments, is flat and conventional. His translations, particularly of Heine, were more successful.

Pletnyov, Pyotr Alexandrovich (1792-1865), a poet, critic and professor of Russian literature at St. Petersburg University, from 1840 to 1861 its rector. During the 1820's Pletnyov was the close friend and literary agent of PUSHKIN, and after the latter's death he took over the editorship of the literary journal, *The Contemporary*. A poet of sentimental elegies, Pletnyov's poetry shows little originality.

Pnin, Ivan Petrovich (1773-1805), a poet and publicist of the beginning of the nineteenth century. Pnin was a follower of RADISH-CHEV in his treatment of themes of social protest.

Pogodin, Mikhail Petrovich (1800-75), a historian, publisher and writer of the mid-nineteenth century, professor of history at the University of Moscow. His journal, *The Muscovite* (1841-56), defended the official ideology of "Orthodoxy, Autocracy and Nationalism" which characterized the reign of Nicholas I. He was also close to the party of the SLAVOPHILES. His publishing activities made him an important figure in Russian literary circles, though his conservativism subjected him to frequent attacks by the liberals and radicals. His tales, published in the 1820's and 1830's, are significant for their early realistic depiction of the life of the lower classes.

Pogodin, Nikolay. See Stukalov.

Pogorelski, Anton. See Perovski, A. A.

Polevoy, Boris. See Kampov, B. N.

Polevoy, Nikolay Alexeyevich (1796-1846), a journalist, playwright, historian and critic of the early nineteenth century. The son of a merchant, Polevoy was self-educated. His journal, *The Moscow Telegraph* (1825-34), did much to encourage the development of ROMANTICISM in Russia. A liberal, his *History of the Russian People* (1829-33) was directed against the monarchist views of KARAMZIN. A critical review of a patriotic historical play by KUKOLNIK brought the closing of Polevoy's journal in 1834, and he was forced to come to terms with the reactionary opposition. His later work is more conservative.

Polezhayev, Alexander Ivanovich (1805-38), a poet of the 1820's and 1830's. He was the natural son of a member of the gentry. His riotous and dissolute life as a student at the University of Moscow is reflected in his burlesque poem, *Sashka* (1825), in part a parody of PUSHKIN's *Eugene Onegin*. The poem's liberalism and atheism, as well as its obscenity, brought it to the attention of Nicholas I, who sentenced Polezhayev to serve in the ranks of the army. He deserted, but was captured and sent to serve in the Caucasus. He sank into moral degradation and became an alcoholic, but distinguished himself by his heroism. He finally won an officer's commission, which, however, arrived only after his death in 1838 from tuberculosis.

Influenced by Byron, Polezhayev's poetry is largely concerned with themes of revolt, despair and doom. He is given to diffuseness and grandiloquence, but he developed a unique style of short, staccato lines which is striking and effective. His best-known poems, *The Song of the Shipwrecked Sailor* (1828) and *The Song of the Captive Iroquois* (1828), depict man's emotions in the face of death. Some of his poetry is revolutionary, and he is an important predecessor of NEKRASOV.

Polonski, Yakov Petrovich (1819-98), a poet of the mid-nineteenth century and a representative of the so-called PARNASSIAN POETS. His verse was delicate and transcendent in manner, and he may be considered a late echo of the "Golden Age" of Russian poetry of the early nineteenth century. He is one of the few Parnassians to express genuine emotions as well as striking images. The theme of love is predominant in his work; he also has poems on classical themes, and at times even strikes a religious note. His long poem, *The Grasshopper Musician* (1859), is a humorous and charming tale in salon style. A member of the party of the WESTERNERS, his many civic poems on social and political problems, close to those of NEKRASOV, were less successful.

Polotski, Simeon (1629-80; real name: Simeon Petrovski-Sitnianovich), a monk and graduate of the Kiev Academy who had lived in the West Russian city of Polotsk (hence his appellative, Polotski), and who came to Moscow in 1663. Here he served as a teacher and, subsequently, as court poet and tutor to the children of Tsar Alexey Mikhailovich.

Simeon Polotski brought to Muscovite Russia new literary forms already cultivated in Southwest Russia, where they had developed under Polish influence. The first is the syllabic system of versification (see Prosody), in which he wrote several volumes of rather awkward poetry, including panegyric and didactic verse: odes, satires, anecdotes, occasional verse, etc. His long panegyric poem, *The Russian Eagle*, compares Russia with ancient Greece, to Russia's advantage. It is full of classical references, another innovation in Muscovite Russian literature.

Simeon Polotski also brought the school drama to Moscow, and to him are attributed two verse plays on Nebuchadnezzar and on the Prodigal Son, both published in 1678-79.

Simeon Polotski was a talented litterateur rather than a great writer. He stood for rational progress and reform, and for Western enlightenment, though he was careful to condition his literary innovations to the ruling moral and religious temper of seventeenth-century Russia.

Pomyalovski, Nikolay Gerasimovich (1835-63), a realistic novelist of the early 1860's. His first novel, *Bourgeois Happiness* (1861), and its sequel, *Molotov* (1861), depict a strong-willed young man, practical and unromantic, who seeks to make a place for himself in the world. These novels are the first large-scale works in nineteenth-century Russian literature in which the hero is a plebeian, a *raznochinets* (see *Raznochintsy*). More famous are Pomyalovski's *Seminary Sketches* (1862-63), which reflect the author's own experiences in a theological seminary; these are realistic descriptions of the brutality and horror of seminary life of the period. Pomyalovski's early death from alcoholism at the age of twenty-eight ended the career of one of Russia's most promising realistic novelists.

Popov, Alexander Serafimovich (1863-1949), a novelist of the early twentieth century. A radical and a realist, his early works were brought out by Gorki's publishing house, *Znanie* ("knowledge") under the writer's patronymic, A. Serafimovich. After the Revolution of 1917 he joined the Bolsheviks and succeeded the poet Bryusov as head of the censorship for the Russian Soviet Federative Socialist Republic. His novel, *The Iron Stream* (1924), depicts the struggle of Red and White Cossacks in the Caucasus during the Civil War. The people appear as the true hero of the novel, and it was much praised by Soviet critics in its day for the "correctness" of the author's Marxist view of history.

Popov, Mikhail Ivanovich (died 1790). An actor, later a government official, Popov wrote plays, songs, epigrams and other poetry. His interest in folklore led him to imitate folk songs, and he assisted CHULKOV with the latter's collection of Russian folk songs. Popov's *Brief Description of Ancient Slavic Mythology* (1768) is for the most part the product of his own imagination, but it was much used as an authority by writers of the late eighteenth century.

Popular literature. See Folk literature.

Populists (*narodniki*), adherents of a radical political movement of the 1870's, 1880's and 1890's. The Populists developed their political, social and economic program on the basis of the teachings of HERZEN, LAVROV and, to some extent, BAKUNIN, while their chief theoretician was N. K. MIKHAYLOVSKI. To a large extent RAZNOCHINTSY (déclassés) by social origin, the Populists were Utopian Socialists. They regarded Russia as an essentially agricultural country which would never become highly industrialized. Hence, unlike the later Marxist Socialists, they considered the peasantry the active social class which would supply the motive force in revolution. To an extent, however, they were interested in the lower classes in general, and even in the petty bourgeoisie. The apathy of the Russian people subsequently contributed to widespread disillusion among the Populists.

The REFORMS of Alexander II, including the liberation of the serfs, did not satisfy the Populists. They envisaged Russia as an agrarian socialist country in which existing peasant communal institutions would be converted into producing units; in this, along with their idealization of the peasantry and its way of life they inherited views which, in the preceding generation, were characteristic of the SLAVOPHILES. They regarded propaganda and education as necessary steps in enlightening the people and inculcating political consciousness. In an attempt to proselytize, many Populists took work among the people. This movement reached its climax in the summer of 1874, when thousands of them went to the country to spread propaganda among the peasantry. As members of the intelligentsia, they were regarded by the people with suspicion and hostility, and many of them were turned over to the police. Hundreds were arrested and sentenced to prison or exile. This disastrous and ironic end of the movement "to the people" is described by TURGENEV in his novel, *Virgin Soil* (1877).

Failing to achieve their ends thus, the Populists tried other methods. A society known as *Land and Freedom,* organized in 1876, formed a systematic underground network and encouraged strikes and rioting. In 1879 extremists from this group organized a terroristic society, *The Will of the People,* which publicly condemned Alexander II to death and sought to assassinate him and other high officials. The government, frightened, determined to make concessions and introduce a limited constitutional and parliamentary form of government. But in 1881, after several unsuccessful attempts on his life, Alexander II was assassinated, and the promised reforms were immediately retracted by his successor, Alexander III.

Their terroristic activities discredited the Populists with most of the Russian people. While extremists continued a policy of terrorism, the moderate Populists became disillusioned, and the movement lost much of its force. This disillusionment is reflected in the writings of such Populists as GLEB USPENSKI and A. Osipovich (see Novodvorski). At the end of the century the remaining Populists were attracted by more modern and systematic revolutionary socialist doctrines. Some of them joined the underground Social Democratic (Marxist) Party, formed in 1898; this was the party of LENIN, PLEKHANOV and TROTSKI. Others were attracted to the Socialist Revolutionaries, founded in 1902. A non-Marxist agrarian socialist party, the S.R.'s, as they were known, were more properly the heirs of the Populists, and their membership was at first much larger than that of the S.D.'s.

A number of writers belonged to the Populists. These include GLEB USPENSKI, ZASODIMSKI and ZLATOVRATSKI. Their writings contained documentary treatment of peasant customs and life, combined with a strong tendency to idealize the peasant, and particularly the communal aspects of village life. GLEB USPENSKI was almost alone as a writer with Populist sympathies who did not hesitate to depict the backwardness and even the vices of the peasantry.

Poputchik ("fellow traveller"). See Trotski; Literature, Soviet.

Pososhkov, Ivan Tikhonovich (ca. 1652-1726), an economist and publicist of the time of PETER THE GREAT. His chief work, *The Book of Poverty and Wealth* (1724), advocated the introduction of the mercantile system in Russia. In 1725 he was arrested and imprisoned; he died a few months later. It is uncertain whether his arrest was caused by political or personal reasons.

Potapenko, Ignati Nikolayevich (1856-1929), a humorist of Ukrainian origin, who wrote during the late nineteenth and early twentieth century. His many novels and stories are filled with a light humor and a superficial optimism which made him extremely popular with the middle class around the turn of the century.

Premudry, Yepifanii. See Yepifanii Premudry.

Pre-Romanticism, the name given to the first phase of the movement of ROMANTICISM in European literature of the late eighteenth and early nineteenth century. It represents an early wave of revolt against the restrictions of eighteenth-century CLASSICISM. The principal characteristics of Pre-Romanticism are a greater freedom in expression of personal feelings, a new interest in landscape, the cultivation of medieval, chivalric themes as well as themes of the supernatural, and the melancholy mood of "graveyard" poetry. Interest in the folk, leading to written imitations and adaptations of folk songs and tales, is another important characteristic of Pre-Romanticism. The movement paralleled that of SENTIMENTALISM; to a large extent, in fact, it was identical with it. Besides KARAMZIN and his school (generally referred to in the history of Russian literature as sentimentalists), the leading Russian pre-romanticist was ZHUKOVSKI. PUSHKIN and most of the poets of his age may also be described as pre-romanticists, in that they did not break completely with Classicism.

Pridvorov, Yefim Alexandrovich (1883-1945), a popular poet of the twentieth century, who wrote under the pseudonym of Demian Bedny ("the poor"). A Bolshevik, he became almost an official Soviet "poet laureate" after 1917. He wrote popular journalistic and propaganda verse in the form of fables, jingles and satirical parodies. His verse is crude, but direct and effective. His libretto for a comic opera, *The Bogatyrs* ("Heroes of Antiquity"; 1936), burlesqued the Russian epic folk tradition (see *Byliny*) and spoke lightly of the introduction of Christianity in Russia. Bedny was sharply rebuked, an about-face in official cultural policy which marked the beginnings of a new nationalistic trend in the evaluation of older culture and literature.

Printing, Introduction of. Printing was introduced into Muscovite Russia from the West in 1553 (or 1563) by Ivan Fyodorov. The first book printed was the *Acts of the Apostles* (Moscow, 1564). Opposition of Church officials (including copyists) forced Fyodorov to leave Moscow, and printing was not re-introduced until 1568, after which it developed slowly. The first books were almost all of a religious character; this continued until the times of PETER THE GREAT, when secular literature began to appear on a large scale.

Prishvin, Mikhail Mikhaylovich (1873-1954), a twentieth-century prose writer. Trained as an agronomist, Prishvin was also a hunter and a naturalist by avocation. His many stories specialize in descriptions of birds, animals and landscape. He spent some time collecting folklore in the far north of Russia. His first successful book, *In the Land of Unfrightened Birds* (1905), describes animal life in the northern country. Prishvin came to prominence as a writer only in the Soviet period, however, with the publication of a long novel, *Kashchey's Chain* (1923-28), based on his own childhood. Kashchey, the enchanter of Russian folk tales, is a figure symbolic of evil, and his chain represents the moral conventions and prejudices from which the hero fights to free himself. A lyricist, Prishvin is a writer far from the beaten track in Soviet literature, but he is an outstanding story teller.

Prokofiev, Alexander Andreyevich (1900-), Soviet poet. He entered literature under the influence of MAYAKOVSKI, much of whose crudity and bombast he at first imitated. His patriotic poem *Russia*, for which he received a Stalin Prize in 1944, brought him wide recognition. His best work, however, is strongly lyrical, and concerns themes such as love and village life.

Prokopovich, Feofan. See Feofan Prokopovich.

Proletarian Literature. See Literature, Soviet; Criticism, Soviet; Proletkult; October.

Proletarian Writers. See October; RAPP; Criticism, Soviet.

Proletkult, abbreviated name of the Proletarian Cultural and Educational Organizations, founded in September, 1917. These organizations aimed at the systematic development of a new

literature created by and for members of the proletariat. Proletkult organizations were active in establishing studios for the training of writers and in publication of new work. The leading writers
who came out of the Proletkult were the so-called SMITHY
POETS, who seceded from the Proletkult in 1920.

The chief patrons and theoreticians of the new proletarian culture were the Bolshevik leaders BOGDANOV and LUNACHAR-
SKI. Bogdanov recognized that proletarian culture should serve
the needs of Party and State, but insisted that it should develop
independent of both. This antagonized Party leaders, including
LENIN, and in 1920 the Proletkult was put under the control of
the Commissariat of Education; in 1923 it was abolished entirely.
In general its cultural contribution was small.

Prosody. Russian written literature produced no poetry until the
seventeenth century, though poetic prose was known. FOLK
SONGS have existed throughout Russian history, and these show
the use of a tonic prosody, in which there is a fixed number of
stressed syllables to the line, but a free number of unstressed
syllables. This produces a relatively free line of varying lengths,
though there is often a tendency toward a more regular rhythmic
pattern in any given song, particularly in better variants. Cadences have generally the same metrical pattern throughout an
entire song, and masculine cadences are avoided.

Beginning early in the seventeenth century, the folk system of
versification was used in several works of written literature, including the *Songs Recorded for Richard James,* set down for a
member of an English diplomatic mission, and the *Tale of Misery
and Ill Fortune* (see Literature). The James *Songs* may be actual
folk songs. About the same time a more bookish style of verse
appeared, particularly in historical works dealing with the so-
called "Time of the Troubles," the first two decades of the seventeenth century. These verses bear no ascertainable rhythmic principle, save the use of couplet rhymes; probably they were read as
isochronic. The source of this free verse is not entirely clear, but
in all likelihood it was suggested by the model of Polish poetry,
coming into Russia by way of the southwestern provinces, at that
time ruled by Poland. The only point in which these verses resemble Polish ones, however, is in their use of couplet rhymes.

Feminine rhymes are not obligatory, as they were in Polish verse of the period.

In the middle of the seventeenth century, the strict Polish syllabic type of versification was introduced into Russian literature, where it endured well over half a century. Lines had a fixed number of syllables (eleven or thirteen), with a regularly placed caesura. The ultimate source of this verse was the French Alexandrine, modified to suit the character of the Polish language. Each half of the line ended with a feminine cadence, since all Polish words have their stress on the penultimate syllable. This rule of feminine cadences was arbitrarily preserved in Ukrainian and Russian poetry, in spite of the fact that these languages, unlike Polish, do not have fixed stress and permit any sort of cadence. Except for the cadences, the position of stresses in the line was of no importance in syllabic verse. This type of verse was brought to Muscovite Russia by SIMEON POLOTSKI in the 1660's, and persisted until the metrical reforms of TREDIAKOV-SKI and LOMONOSOV in the 1730's. It has been customary to criticize syllabic poetry as artificial and unsuited to the character of the Russian language, though prosodic rules are usually artificial. If read sympathetically, Russian syllabic verse will produce a definitely poetic effect. It limited possibilities for expression by its arbitrary feminine cadences, of course, and this is presumably the reason for its ultimate rejection.

In the 1730's TREDIAKOVSKI and LOMONOSOV introduced the modern syllabo-tonic system, with its regular alternation of stressed and unstressed syllables. This is the same system which is used in modern English and German verse, and it has persisted in Russian to the present day. An important distinction between Russian verse and English or German is that Russian words do not have secondary stresses. Indeed, Lomonosov originally held that every poetic stress ought to be a linguistic stress; in iambic or trochaic verse this would have prevented the use of words longer than three syllables. He ultimately withdrew this restriction, however, and thus made possible the great rhythmic flexibility and variety of modern Russian verse. As a result, each stress indicated by the metrical pattern need not actually be realized in every metrical foot, and the variation of poetically "stressed" but linguistically unstressed syllables from line to line gives a subtle variation to rhythms which might otherwise seem too regular.

The influence of folk poetry on modern Russian written poetry has produced a kind of free verse, called the *dolnik,* used by SUMAROKOV, PUSHKIN and a number of the latter's contemporaries; more recently by BLOK, MAYAKOVSKI and many others. The *dolnik* is a line with a basic pattern of repeated stresses, but with a certain variation in the number of unstressed syllables. MAYAKOVSKI developed this form into a completely free verse style of his own. Free verse also entered Russian poetry with the Symbolists, who imported it from France (see Symbolism). It has never been as popular in Russian literature as in the West. Present-day Soviet verse tends formally to be conservative and to adhere to traditional rhythms.

Blank verse, introduced early in the nineteenth century, was used by PUSHKIN in his historical drama, *Boris Godunov* (1825), and later in poetic dramas by OSTROVSKI, A. K. TOLSTOY and others. The form does not seem so naturally expressive in Russian as in English; in any case, Russian literature lacks a great body of blank verse drama.

The Russian language is rich in rhymes, and permits rhymes of two, three or even more syllables with ease. This fact helps to make Russian poetry difficult to translate into English, which is relatively poorer in rhymes. Modern Russian poets, such as MAYAKOVSKI and PASTERNAK, have made extremely subtle experiments in complex rhymes, often extending over several words, as well as in mixing assonances and true rhymes. Other euphonic effects, such as internal rhyme and alliteration, are roughly comparable in their use to English poetry.

Prutkov, Kozma, a fictitious pen-name used by A. K. TOLSTOY and the Brothers ZHEMCHUZHNIKOV for the nonsense poetry and other humorous writing which they published from 1851, with some breaks, until 1884, when Prutkov's "collected works" appeared. They gave their fictitious poet a biography, and even painted his portrait. Prutkov is a self-satisfied and platitudinous clerk serving in the government Assay Office (a hit at the poet BENEDIKTOV, who served in the Ministry of Finance) who devotes his leisure moments to the Muses. His "works" include poems, plays, fables and anecdotes, much of which is sheer nonsense, though there is some keen parody of contemporary poetry. Most famous are his amusing and occasionally penetrating proverbs, such as, "If you want to be happy, be it," or "Only in the service of the state can one find truth." The figure of Prutkov itself is a powerful satiric thrust at the officiousness and complacency of the Russian bureaucratic world. Kozma Prutkov has become one of the foremost classics of Russian humor.

Pseudo-Classicism. See Classicism.

Pushkin, Alexander Sergeyevich (1799-1837), Russia's greatest poet. On his father's side he was descended from an old aristocratic family. His paternal uncle, V. L. PUSHKIN, was a minor poet of the day. His great-grandfather on his mother's side was Gannibal, "the Negro of Peter the Great," a protégé of that emperor who had been presented to him by the Sultan of Turkey. Pushkin was proud both of his aristocratic descent and of his Negro blood; he depicted one of his paternal ancestors in his historical play, *Boris Godunov,* while he wrote the beginnings of a novel about the famous Gannibal. Educated at first by French tutors, Pushkin was sent in 1811 to the new lycée at Tsarskoye Selo, established for a selected group of children of aristocratic parentage. There he began to write Russian verse (he may already have written some French poetry at home), and was first noticed by the aging poet DERZHAVIN on his visit to the lycée. Pushkin's school companions remained among his closest friends, and he wrote a number of fine occasional poems for graduation anniversaries. The school was an excellent one for the period in Russia, and Pushkin's interests led him far beyond his courses, particularly in the study of French literature. While in school he met many of the followers of KARAMZIN, and joined their literary society, ARZAMAS, to which his uncle also belonged. Thus he became acquainted with ZHUKOVSKI and other prominent poets of the day.

On graduation in 1817, Pushkin took the sinecure in the civil service customary for a young aristocrat of the time, and plunged into the whirl of a gay social life. An ardent liberal, he composed and circulated several political epigrams and other poems of a revolutionary spirit which came to the attention of the police. Exiled from Petersburg in 1820, he was transferred in the civil service to Southern Russia. The same year he published his first

major work, the poetic fairy tale, *Ruslan and Lyudmila.* In the
south he wrote a number of important poems, and began what is
perhaps his greatest work, the novel in verse *Eugene Onegin.*
He engaged in several love affairs during this period, and jealousy
inspired by one of them resulted in his fresh exile to his mother's
estate of Mikhaylovskoye, near Pskov. The official pretext for his
exile was a letter intercepted by the police in which he expressed
atheistic sentiments.

Pushkin's exile may have prevented him from taking part in
the Decembrist Uprising of 1825 (see Decembrist Movement).
Some of his close friends, including the poet KÜCHELBECKER,
were Decembrists, and his own political attitudes made him sympathetic to their revolutionary aims. Arrested by the police for
suspected complicity in the uprising, Pushkin was brought to St.
Petersburg in 1826 and pardoned by the Emperor Nicholas I,
who promised to serve as his personal protector. The tsar's favor
turned out to be of dubious value, however, and the poet was
subjected to even closer control by the police and the censorship.
His political attitudes after 1825 are difficult to evaluate; on one
hand he made a show of being reconciled to the regime of
Nicholas; on the other he demonstrated his sympathy with the
Decembrists by addressing an unpublished poem to them in exile.
Probably he felt that the uprising had been premature, and that
Russia would necessarily continue to be ruled by an autocracy.
His dislike for the reactionary regime of Nicholas I was manifested in his repeated pleas to travel abroad, all of which were
denied. In 1831 he married a beautiful young girl, Natalya Gon-
charova, to whom he was passionately devoted. She was cold
and frivolous, however, and incapable of sharing his intellectual
interests. So that Natalya could be invited to court, the tsar made
Pushkin a gentleman of the chamber, an honor usually given to
lesser nobility, and deeply resented by the poet.

After 1830 Pushkin lost favor in the eyes of the reading public.
The taste for poetry disappeared; with the rise of a new generation of readers, particularly among the provincial gentry, the
lower ranks of the civil service and the rising middle classes, a
demand for prose fiction was created. Pushkin himself began to
write prose, and even devoted himself to historical study, but was
unable to recapture public favor. His literary reputation was

secure, but he was regarded more as a respected classic than a living force. In 1836 he was finally permitted, after repeated requests, to found a literary journal, *The Contemporary*, but it was doomed to have little success.

Offended by the attentions paid to his wife by Baron Georges d'Anthès, a Frenchman in Russian service, Pushkin challenged him to a duel. Pushkin was mortally wounded, and died two days later, on January 29, 1837. To avoid a public demonstration, the tsar ordered his body to be transported secretly to Mikhaylovskoye, where it was interred. The poet's death caused a great scandal, however, and there were rumors that d'Anthès had acted as an *agent provocateur* for the government. Though they are unsubstantiated, Nicholas' government was scarcely blameless, for the police knew that the challenge had been issued. The young writer LERMONTOV first came to public attention by circulating a poem, *The Death of a Poet*, in which he blamed the government for the responsibility for Pushkin's death.

Pushkin's personality was somewhat contradictory. In his youth he was inclined to frivolity and a light-hearted atheism, which resulted in his blasphemous mock-epic *The Gavriliada* (1821). But these attitudes were largely confined to his early work. His essential seriousness is shown by such undertakings as his *History of the Pugachov Rebellion* (1834), as well as a projected historical work on Peter the Great. Though he wrote lighter verse, the major part of his poetry is deeply serious, and his mature work reflects a keen preoccupation with ethical and spiritual problems which helped to set the tone for so much of nineteenth-century Russian literature. His critical comments on Russian and Western literatures show him to have been one of the most penetrating Russian critics of all times.

Pushkin's poetry depends for its effect on an absolute naturalness of statement. It is by no means lacking in melodiousness, imagery, or in verbal effects, but it is the qualities of concision and ease of manner which make it great. For this reason it is difficult to translate into other languages, in which it often sounds flat and uninspired. This is why non-Russians are slow to recognize Pushkin's rightful claim to be regarded as a poet of first rank. This naturalness of manner was Pushkin's unique gift. His style is based on the new elegant, courtly language of KARAM-

ZIN and his followers. In Pushkin's hands this language became stronger and less effeminate; it retained its grace and polish, but gained in vigor and ease. Part of the difference is Pushkin's frequent use of colloquial and folk elements of speech. But it is a mistake to think of his poetry as perfectly "colloquial" in style. It always remains poetic language, a unique creation, yet because it seems completely natural and logical in its own right, it often gives the impression of easy colloquial speech. Part of its effect of naturalness may also be due to Pushkin's stylistic influence on the writers of the nineteenth century; his language appears so natural in retrospect because it has become a part of the tradition of the literary language as such. But no Russian poet of a later age has been able to duplicate the ease and conciseness of Pushkin's style.

Pushkin's career may be divided roughly into four stages. From 1814 to 1821 is his youthful period, in which his verse is technically brilliant, cold and unsentimental. He had not yet found subjects entirely congenial to his talents. The principal influences on his work, besides the Russian poets ZHUKOVSKI and BATYUSHKOV, were the French poets Parny, Voltaire and André Chénier. The French poets were responsible for the classical concision and clarity of his style, which always remained with him. In this period he wrote Anacreontic poetry, epistles and elegies, all of which genres had been typical of the generation which preceded him. The culminating work of the early period is his *Ruslan and Lyudmila* (1820), a long poetic fairy tale based in part on a seventeenth-century Russian popular narrative. The work is light and ironic, excellent in craftsmanship, but it lacks any real purpose.

Pushkin's second period extends from 1820 to 1823. It is characterized by the strong influence of Byron, whose work supplied Pushkin with the subject matter which he had previously lacked, and brought a new, highly romantic outlook on life. The antithesis between the ennui, coldness and social alienation of the self-centered Byronic hero, and the healthy, vigorous, passionate life of primitive, exotic peoples became Pushkin's favorite subject in this period. He developed a predilection, which he retained throughout life, for the new form of the Byronic narrative poem, more flexible and personal than the outdated epic or verse romance. The works of this period are the richest in imagery and sound effects; Pushkin's later poetry is more sparing in their use.

The principal Byronic work is *The Prisoner of the Caucasus* (1820-21; published 1822), the story of a Russian nobleman who is taken prisoner by Circassians, but escapes with the help of a young native girl who loves him. His cold egoism prevents him from returning her love, and she kills herself. *The Fountain of Bakhchisaray* (1822; published 1824) is a resplendent picture of Oriental life in the palace of the khans of the Crimean Tartars, in Pushkin's day a ruin. These poems, though still imitative, were fantastically popular, at the expense of some of Pushkin's later and better work.

 The third stage, extending roughly from 1823 to 1830, saw the perfecting of the mature poet, who by its end had completely overcome the influence of Byron. *Eugene Onegin* (1823-31), Pushkin's great novel in verse, was written during this period. The hero, Eugene, is reminiscent of Childe Harold, and even travels abroad, like Byron's hero, to cure his disaffected spirit. This essentially good-hearted and sensitive, but bored, indolent and spoiled young man served as a prototype for a long series of ineffectual Russian heroes, traditionally known as SUPERFLUOUS MEN. But to this Byronic figure Pushkin opposed a more original and positive heroine, Tatyana, a sentimental young country girl with a strong character and a profound spirit; at first rejected by Eugene, she attains the position of a great lady in society, and in turn rejects him when he is finally captivated by her beauty and position, not out of revenge or lack of love, but from a deep moral conviction that the love he offers her is wrong; his infatuation with a woman in society is not the sort of love which she seeks. Her character, too, was of great influence in later Russian literature, particularly on the heroines of TURGENEV. The plot is far from being the whole work, and the poem is full of enchanting pictures of nature, witty and ironic asides by the poet, and a whole gallery of brilliantly drawn figures. Though in a romantic genre and concerned with a romantic subject, the spirit of the poem is hardly romantic; the wit is classical, while the character portrayal and the ethical problems introduced are closer to realism. The remarkably intricate rhyme scheme, maintained throughout the poem, testifies to the poet's technical brilliance.

The Gypsies (1824; published 1827) also shows Pushkin breaking free from the influence of Byron. The characters and the exotic atmosphere are Byronic, but the poem closes on a resolution in which the rights of society are valued above the anarchic freedom claimed by the Byronic hero. *Poltava* (1829) is on a historical subject, the victory of Peter the Great over Charles XII of Sweden, to which Pushkin added the romantic theme of the love story of the Cossack traitor Mazeppa. The poem is an imperfect combination of a national epic with a romantic narrative, but the battle scenes are magnificently treated.

In 1825 Pushkin wrote his blank-verse historical drama, *Boris Godunov* (published 1831). In it he attempted to create a Russian equivalent to the Shakespearean chronicle plays. The subject, taken from the early seventeenth-century Time of the Troubles, was highly dramatic, but the play is hardly stageworthy, with its two heroes and many short scenes, and has survived in the theater only in the operatic version by Musorgski.

Pushkin's later plays, the so-called "Little Tragedies," written mostly in 1830, are superior to *Boris,* though they are closet dramas, and were not intended for the stage. They are portrayals of character and dramatizations of ethical problems. Perhaps the finest is *Mozart and Salieri,* in which, as in the popular legend, the composer Salieri poisons Mozart from envy of his genius. The poem raises the problem of the justice of the unequal distribution of human talents. *The Stone Guest* is a variation of the Don Juan theme, in which the hero is treated as a self-deluded romantic. *The Covetous Knight* is a consummate picture of the vice of avarice. The poem is mysteriously described as "scenes from a tragicomedy by Chenstone"; apparently Pushkin had in mind the eighteenth-century English poet William Shenstone, but the latter's work contains no such play. *The Feast during the Plague* is a translation of a scene from John Wilson's *City of the Plague,* but the Russian version is more intense and powerful. The macabre passion with which the characters revel in a time of plague proves that Pushkin was no stranger to the darker sides and the destructive spirit in human life.

After 1830, Pushkin's poetry tended to become even freer of

ornament, more restrained and severe. The greatest work of this period, *The Bronze Horseman* (written 1833; published posthumously in 1841) shows a gain in intensity and dramatic power at the expense of decorative appeal. Indeed, it rivals *Eugene Onegin* in its claim to being considered Pushkin's masterpiece. It opposes the creative energy of society, personified in Peter the Great, to the individual's claim to happiness, on which society must necessarily trample in its relentless progress. Peter built his new capital, St. Petersburg, at a frightful cost in human life, in a region subject to inundations, so that it might look out on Europe. The poem describes the flood of 1824; though Peter has been dead almost a century, his spirit is incarnate in a great bronze equestrian statue. The flood drowns the sweetheart of a poor clerk, Yevgeni, who goes mad and fancies that the statue has come to life and is galloping after him. The sympathetic portrayal of Yevgeni's suffering is opposed to the grand apotheosis of the creative spirit of Peter; the two conflicting human goals are left unresolved. The figure of Yevgeni was of first importance for nineteenth-century Russian literature, and the little man, often a petty clerk, crushed by society, occurs frequently in works by GOGOL and DOSTOYEVSKI.

The final period also includes Pushkin's fairy tales in verse (1831-34). Though they suggest the manner of folk poetry, they are far from literal imitations of Russian popular songs or tales, even, for the most part, of their language and style. Pushkin has gone abroad for several of his subjects; that of the *Tale of the Fisherman and the Fish* is taken from Grimm's collection, while the plot of the *Golden Cockerel* is from Washington Irving's *Tale of the Arabian Astrologer*. But Pushkin has made all these tales Russian and popular in spirit. Light, gay, at times ironic, they are the Russian masterpieces in this genre. The *Songs of the Western Slavs* (1832) are also attempts to adapt folklore themes, but Pushkin was unaware that the originals which he had adapted, by Mérimée, were actually of spurious origin, and not translations as Mérimée had asserted. Last of all must be mentioned *Angelo* (1833), a successful adaptation in concentrated form of Shakespeare's *Measure for Measure*.

Pushkin's lyric poetry is considerable in volume, on a par with his narrative works. Love, and particularly the nostalgia of bygone love, is his favorite theme; poems on nature are fewer. Other subjects are friendship, personal freedom, his own spiritual life, and poems on political personages and events, most of which could not pass the censor. A note of melancholy pessimism pervades many of them. Several discuss the role of the poet, whom Pushkin sees as isolated, unhappy, no better than other men, but distinguished by a divine gift and mission. *The Prophet* (1826) is one of the most remarkable lyrics; it is a vision of the agonies of spiritual rebirth through which the creative genius must pass.

Pushkin turned to prose fiction after 1830, in an attempt to adapt his work to the tastes of the reading public. His prose resembles his poetry in being natural, rational and concise to the point of bareness. It is dry, completely without ornament or affectation. Voltaire's prose was his acknowledged model. The manner of Pushkin's prose, which disappointed his romantic contemporaries, has been little imitated in Russian literature, but its content was destined to have greater influence. He is the first Russian to write prose which is as fresh and absorbing today as it was when it was written.

Pushkin's first attempt at fiction was a historical novel about his ancestor, Gannibal, *The Negro of Peter the Great*. Begun in 1828, it remained unfinished. It is memorable for its portrayal of Peter, a favorite subject of Pushkin's.

In 1830 Pushkin wrote his five *Tales of Belkin,* which he published the following year as the work of a country squire, Ivan Petrovich Belkin. For the most part narrative anecdotes, one of them, *The Station Master,* was destined to be of great influence for its humane and sympathetic portrayal of the tragedy of a little man. The figure of Belkin also appears in the uncompleted and posthumous *History of Goryukhino Manor,* a parody of historical writing and a satire directed against serfdom and the Russian social order.

Pushkin's best-known story, *The Queen of Spades* (1834), is a fantastic melodrama of the supernatural. But its manner is as tense and compact as that of the other tales. The hero, Hermann, is a monomaniac who sacrifices love and his own sanity to greed. The other characters are excellently done, particularly the long-suffering young protégée and her tyrannical old mistress, prototypes of personages who appear in the novels of DOSTOYEVSKI.

Pushkin's only completed novel, *The Captain's Daughter* (1836), is a historical narrative in the manner of Scott, though it is far more condensed than any novel by Scott. It concerns the Pugachov Uprising of the eighteenth century, a subject which Pushkin had also treated in his *History of the Pugachov Rebellion* (1834). The movement interested Pushkin as a popular revolution growing out of the Russian social system, and he treated it as sympathetically as the censor would permit. The novel contains a number of memorable portraits, particularly that of a garrison captain, a humble professional soldier quite undistinguished as a person, who becomes a hero, however, in time of war. This type reappears in LERMONTOV's *A Hero of Our Times* and in TOLSTOY's *War and Peace*. Pushkin's uncompleted novel, *Dubrovski* (written 1832-33), is the story of a nobleman defrauded of his property who turns highwayman. Primarily a tale of adventure, it contains some pointed criticism of Russian social injustice.

Pushkin's letters and his literary criticism show the same qualities which characterize his poetry and fiction: clarity, simplicity and wit. Though written in a direct, colloquial style, they have great polish and elegance. His criticism is among the most discerning in Russian literature; it is only to be regretted that, living at the beginning of the great age of Russian literature, he had few outstanding writers to criticize.

The history of critical appreciation of Pushkin in Russia is practically synonymous with that of Russian literary CRITICISM. The civic critic BELINSKI praised his work for its naturalistic truth and progressive spirit, but largely overlooked his more poetic qualities. In the 1860's Pushkin's fame suffered a temporary eclipse with the radical critics, especially PISAREV, who criticized him, unjustly and anachronistically, for lack of social consciousness. Such writers as TURGENEV, DOSTOYEVSKI, and GRIGORIEV succeeded, however, in restoring him to his true position, though they did not always understand him. Today Pushkin's place is unquestionable as the greatest Russian poet—Russians would say their greatest writer—and Soviet readers and Russian émigrés hold him in equal esteem. Regrettably, the Soviet cult of Pushkin, following BELINSKI's criticism, is based on a partly distorted understanding of his true significance; following the doctrine of SOCIALIST REALISM, Soviet critics have overemphasized the realistic and revolutionary sides of his creation. In order to maintain his originality, they have also denied the importance of Western influences in his work, though there is a considerable amount of truth in DOSTOYEVSKI's assertion that Pushkin's greatness depended on his unique blending of elements of Western and Russian culture.

Pushkin's influence on subsequent Russian literature and culture is greater than that of any other Russian writer. LERMONTOV, GOGOL, TURGENEV, DOSTOYEVSKI and TOLSTOY are only the greatest Russian writers who have used parts of his legacy. If the specific character of his poetry has been less influential, this is because it is at the same time inimitable and a part of the cultural heritage of every educated Russian. His poetic narratives and prose tales have also served as a great body of subjects for arts such as the opera and ballet, including Glinka's *Ruslan and Lyudmila,* Musorgski's *Boris Godunov,* Tchaikovski's *Queen of Spades* and *Eugene Onegin,* Rimski-Korsakov's *Golden Cockerel* and *Tale of the Tsar Saltan,* Stravinski's *Mavra* and many others. Even folk literature has taken over a part of his work, as in the folk play *The Boat,* which contains a long monologue adapted from his Byronic poem, *The Robber Brothers* (1821).

Pushkin Pleiad, the name given to a group of young poets who were contemporaries and friends of PUSHKIN, and who shared to an extent his poetic outlook. The group had little unity as such, however, and each of its members had his own original creative personality. The Pleiad included VYAZEMSKI, DAVYDOV, DELVIG, YAZYKOV, VENEVITINOV and BARATYNSKI.

Pushkin, Vasili Lvovich (1767-1830), a minor poet of the school of KARAMZIN, the uncle of A. S. PUSHKIN. His work consisted for the most part of trifles: witty epigrams, Anacreontic and salon poetry.

R

R., K. See Romanov, K. K.

Radishchev, Alexander Nikolayevich (1749-1802), a leading eighteenth-century liberal writer. Of noble birth, Radishchev was sent
in 1766 to the University of Leipzig to be educated. Here he came
under the influence of French revolutionary philosophers, particularly Rousseau, Helvetius and the Abbé Raynal. Another
philosophical influence was that of Leibniz. Returning to Russia
in 1771, he entered on a career in the civil service. In 1790 he
founded a private press, and issued anonymously his *Journey
from Petersburg to Moscow,* an attack on Russian autocracy and
serfdom. Though the censor had passed the book, the Empress
Catherine ordered the writer to be arrested and the copies of the
work destroyed. He was condemned to death, but the sentence
was lightened to ten years of exile in Siberia. Emperor Paul pardoned him in 1796, and in 1801 Alexander I appointed him a
member of a legislative commission. Broken by exile and inclined
to melancholy, Radishchev committed suicide the following year.
. The *Journey from Petersburg to Moscow* is Radishchev's most
significant work. Modeled in plan on Sterne's *Sentimental Journey,*
it also shows the influence of the writings of Raynal and other
French philosophers of the Enlightenment. The book describes an
imaginary trip, on which the author meets persons of various
classes. Terrible examples of social injustice are described, including the cruelty of landowners to their serfs. The author finds
serfdom the chief root of the social evil; the serfs should be freed
and given the land which they till. The empress is hoodwinked
by those about her, the author feels, and he envisages Russia as a
constitutional monarchy.

Though the book has real feeling, its purely literary merit is
not great. It is inferior to Radishchev's poetic works, which in-

clude odes, elegies, fables and narrative poems. His ode entitled *Liberty* (written around 1783) is even more revolutionary than his *Journey*. He successfully introduced certain Greek meters into Russian poetry.

Though his *Journey* could not be republished in Russia for almost a century, Radishchev remained famous, and was celebrated by later revolutionaries as a forerunner. The Decembrists, in particular, were influenced by his ideas (see Decembrist Movement).

RAPP, abbreviated name of the Russian Association of Proletarian Writers. First organized in 1925 as VAPP (All-Russian Association of Proletarian Writers), it was reorganized in 1928 as RAPP. The leaders of RAPP, including the critic AVERBAKH, insisted that literature should express the ideological needs of the proletariat (see October). In 1929 they won control over literature, using their power to insure that writers serve the specific needs of the First Five-year Plan. This meant a virtual ban on writing which was not concerned with the Plan itself. The control of RAPP ultimately proved too rigid and inflexible, and in 1932, with the development of the new doctrine of SOCIALIST REALISM, RAPP was dissolved and replaced by the new UNION OF SOVIET WRITERS. (See Criticism, Soviet; Literature, Soviet.)

Raznochintsy, a term used to denote a part of the middle-class intelligentsia of the middle and end of the nineteenth century. The word literally means "persons of various classes," and denoted those who did not continue in the class and profession of their fathers, whether noblemen, merchants, priests or peasants, but who obtained an education and pursued an intellectual career. Thus they lost, in a sense, their class status. Their demands for economic and political recognition from Russian society and the government went unrecognized, and as a consequence they tended to radicalism. The civic critics, BELINSKI, CHERNYSHEVSKI and DOBROLYUBOV, belonged to the *raznochintsy*, and served as leaders for other members of this "classless party." PISEMSKI, POMYALOVSKI and IVAN NIKITIN are noteworthy examples of creative writers who were *raznochintsy*.

Realism, the dominant trend in Russian literature from about 1845 to 1890, and again from the 1920's to the present day. During the intervening period, 1890-1920, realism was partially eclipsed by more advanced movements, especially in poetry (SYMBOLISM, ACMEISM, FUTURISM, etc.), but remained the most popular and widely practiced literary style in prose fiction, if not the most original.

Unlike ROMANTICISM, which had been strongly influenced by the West, Russian Realism was largely an indigenous, original development, one which requires its own characteristic national definition. Though George Sand and, to a lesser extent, Balzac and Dickens were important foreign influences, their contribution to the Russian realistic movement was temporary, and determinitive largely for the beginnings onl. To a great extent, indeed, the movement of Russian Realism "just grew"; it was spontaneous to a remarkable degree, and largely unsupported by critical precepts or manifestoes.

Russian Realism is characterized by a stronger ethical tendency than Western Realism, one in accord with the teachings of the so-called "civic" critics (see Criticism), who largely dominated Russian criticism during the middle of the nineteenth century; along with this ethical trend went an active concern for social problems and (tacitly, in view of the CENSORSHIP) political problems. Correspondingly, many Russian realists were perhaps less "objective," less detached than were the members of the French school. Lev TOLSTOY, perhaps the great master of European Realism, is notoriously lacking in this quality of detachment. Nor did Russian Realism display a uniform trend in its use of descriptive detail and "photographic" realism; TOLSTOY, for example, largely abandoned these techniques as superfluous in his last period. Most of the Russian realists are preoccupied with the "here and now," with problems of contemporary Russian society, but in some of the greatest works, such as the novels of DOSTOYEVSKI and in TOLSTOY's *War and Peace,* we find a striving towards a universality of theme unlimited by time or place.

It remains to ask, then, what is the common denominator of Russian Realism as a literary movement? Obviously it does not lie merely in a desire to tell the truth about life, for this is the goal of all literary movements. Yet truthfulness to life, as demanded by the critic BELINSKI, was, perhaps, the major premise of Russian Realism. Living on the threshold of ROMANTICISM and Realism, Belinski by no means intended to exclude works of the

Romantic school from this definition. Yet his influence encouraged the development of Realism as such; fidelity to life and a concern for ethical and social problems, also demanded by him, were the common denominators of Russian Realism. The latter trend resulted in a critical realism, which exposed the backwardness of Russian society and the difficulties lying in the way of progress and reform. Many of the Russian realists are pessimistic concerning the present, but have a vague, almost irrational optimism for the future. This is particularly true of the later realists, CHEKHOV and Gorki (see Peshkov).

From the standpoint of literary evolution, Russian Realism may be defined as a revolt against ROMANTICISM, and in this revolt we see its dynamic logic. True, we find gradual blends of the two schools, as in the works of TURGENEV, which combine realistic treatment of contemporary social problems with romanticized, lyricized portrayals of love and nature. A common theme of this earlier, "lyrical" realism is that of childhood reminiscence, in which romantic nostalgia for the past colors what might otherwise be realistic portrayal. AKSAKOV's *Childhood of Bagrov the Grandson* (1858) and GONCHAROV's *Oblomov* (1859) have this quality. Nostalgia for childhood on the estate and idealization of the patriarchal system of serf ownership are shown in these works, as well as to some extent in the novels of TURGENEV; it is characteristic that all these writers grew up on the estate but later left it.

Besides the gradual blending represented by "lyrical realism," we also find sudden and violent breaks with Romanticism, and in particular with romanticist esthetics, as in the work of GONCHAROV or the young Lev TOLSTOY. Both these writers reject the "poetic" style of Russian romantic prose, for which they substitute a flatter, dryer style, one which is simple, neutral, and often little more than adequate to the writer's purpose. Tolstoy's reminiscences differ sharply from others of the period in their complete lack of idealization of childhood. His early works also seek to destroy the glamor of the romantic hero, for whom Tolstoy substitutes the average man; lyricism of treatment the young Tolstoy replaces with systematic, rationalized analysis.

Another sharp break in literary esthetics is the introduction of the everyday, the commonplace and the ugly into literature.

GOGOL helped to initiate this trend, but in his hands such materials served for a grotesque caricature which is hardly realistic. It is important to note, however, that Gogol passed for a realist in his own day, chiefly because he ignored the taboo on the depiction of lower-class and vulgar personages in literature. Gogol's lesser contemporaries, such as POGODIN, DAHL, PAVLOV and V. A. SOLLOGUB, also members of the so-called "natural school," as it was called according to the terminology of BELINSKI, likewise ignored this taboo and created a literature of tales and sketches in which characters drawn from the lower classes figured prominently, and in which could be seen the first manifestations of that "philanthropic" tendency which became so important in the 1840's and 1850's. This sentimental trend reached its height in TURGENEV's *Sportsman's Sketches* (1852) and in the tales of GRIGOROVICH; it survived in the 1860's and 1870's in some novels and tales of peasant life written by the radical novelists, especially the POPULISTS. But the dominant trend of the 1860's was against sentimentality, and even against lyricism; ugliness, horror and irony proved stronger weapons in the radical writers' hands than pathos. This new, more prosaic trend was partly a consequence of a new utilitarianism in ethics, an attitude first described in GONCHAROV's *Common Story* (1847); it was also influenced by the philosophical positivism of CHERNYSHEVSKI and his followers (see Nihilism).

The radical realists, such as RESHETNIKOV, LEVITOV and Gleb USPENSKI, produced terrifying descriptions of poverty and misery, and the brutality and vice of the lower classes which they attributed to economic exploitation. The result was naturalism, but no formal school as such ever emerged in Russia. Like realism, naturalism in Russian literature was to a large extent an indigenous development; writers like BOBORYKIN who were influenced by French Naturalism are exceptions. Gorki (see Peshkov) is undoubtedly the leading example of a Russian "naturalist," but, though Gorki's reputation outside Russia was largely the consequence of his powerful naturalistic descriptions of the dregs of society, he appealed to Russian readers more because of the strong note of romanticism and idealism in his work.

An important characteristic of Russian Realism was a stronger interest in the portrayal and analysis of character than in narrative or plot as such. Construction tends to be loose in Russian realistic novels. These qualities are particularly characteristic of the plays of A. N. OSTROVSKI, of the novels of GONCHAROV and SALTYKOV, and even, to an extent, of Lev TOLSTOY's *War and Peace* and *Anna Karenina*. An exception are the novels of PISEMSKI, in which there is considerable narrative interest; DOSTOYEVSKI's novels, too, are exceptions in that they are novels of melodrama and intrigue. But there can be no question that Dostoyevski's portrayal of human psychology is far more inspired than his overweighted and sometimes creaky narrative structure.

After 1880 an esthetic reaction set in, leading to the partial revival of lyricism in the form of stories of mood and atmosphere and to the eventual development of a new romantic realism. This last period, extending roughly from 1880 to 1900, is that of GARSHIN, KOROLENKO, CHEKHOV, Gorki (see Peshkov) and BUNIN.

New genres were created, while old ones were reformed by the realists. During the early period, the sketch, often of lower-class life, was popular as a form more flexible and closer to "reality" than the older tale. The principal genre at the beginning and through most of the period, however, was the novel. In the final period (after 1880), the short story became dominant, replacing even the novel in popular favor. The short story, more single in impression than the older tale and often more tightly constructed, became popular, partly as a reaction against long novels with excessive realistic description, partly because of a new esthetic interest in the formal structure of literary works, more clearly manifest in the more compact story than in the longer and more episodic novel. Another reason for the change, undoubtedly, was that writers of the 1880's and 1890's did not always possess the active social viewpoint of their predecessors; they depicted "slices of life" (GARSHIN, CHEKHOV) rather than long *romans à thèse*. In the stories of CHEKHOV, Russian Realism attained its greatest degree of objectivity and detachment of the author from his material; though Chekhov did not lack a social point of view, he rarely allowed his criticisms of contemporary society to be more than implicit.

Gorki (see Peshkov) begins a new and brief trend in Russian

Realism during the 1890's, a kind of romantic realism in which the crude, primitive strength of tramps and social outcasts is idealized as an expression of the heroic and revolutionary spirit of the people. But, though this new direction was popular for a short time, it failed to develop. The last decade of the nineteenth century and the early decades of the twentieth represent a transitional stage, in which Realism loses its monopoly over literature. The failure of the 1905 REVOLUTION helped to bring an escapist trend; writers retreated from the problems of everyday life to more private worlds of mysticism and individualist subjectivism. These trends, part of the movement known as SYMBOLISM, dominated the original writing, and especially the poetry, of the turn of the century. Symbolism and Realism are mixed in some fiction, as in the novels of Sologub (see Teternikov) and the stories and plays of ANDREYEV. In prose style a new decorative tendency appears, known as ORNAMENTALISM, combined with a strong eclecticism of manner. The prose styles of Bely (see Bugayev) and REMIZOV develop as hybrid, expressionist forms in which Realism plays only a minor role; the influence of these writers remains alive into the early Soviet period in the work of BABEL, Pilnyak (see Vogau), Vsevolod IVANOV and many others.

The Soviet period brings a return to Realism, largely under the pressure to create a new literature of contemporary social and political problems. But relative freedom of expression survived through most of the 1920's, and anti-realistic trends such as ORNAMENTALISM persisted. Only with the official "mobilization" of literature under the First Five-year Plan (1928-32) did the methods of Realism become compulsory in Soviet literature. With the end of the Plan this official preference for Realism was codified in the dogma of SOCIALIST REALISM, first proclaimed in 1932. (See Criticism, Soviet; Literature, Soviet.)

Realism, Socialist. See Socialist Realism.

Reforms of Alexander II. The so-called "Great Reforms" of Emperor Alexander II came during the 1860's and 1870's, following widespread dissatisfaction with the reactionary regime of Nicholas I and the conduct of the Crimean War of 1853-56. The accession of Alexander II, a mild liberal, to the throne in 1855 brought the promise of reforms already long overdue. The cautious and compromising character of Alexander's government delayed their execution, however, and restricted their scope.

In 1861 an edict was issued emancipating the serfs (see Serfdom). The peasants did not, however, receive their complete freedom. Ownership of the land was vested collectively in the peasant commune; the peasant could not leave the land without the permission of the communal authorities. These restrictions were undoubtedly intended to increase the power of the well-to-do peasants, who often dominated the village communes, and assist them in holding the less prosperous peasantry in check.

The peasants were saddled with a heavy debt in exchange for the land which they received. The government issued bonds for the value of those lands which were taken from the former landowners and given to the peasant communes. These bonds were to be redeemed by the peasants over a period of 49 years. Since the peasants often received so little land they could eke out only a bare subsistence, the debt served as a crushing burden which they ultimately proved unable to pay in full.

The creation of the so-called *zemstvos* in 1864 was another of Alexander's reforms. It provided the Russian people with their first modern form of representative government, if only in local administration. The *zemstvos* were district boards, elected by the landowners, peasants and townspeople, voting in separate curias. These boards were entrusted with control over the schools, medical affairs and roads. Though the taxing power of the *zemstvos* was limited, they were often able to effect considerable improvement in these fields, which earlier had been sadly neglected. A similar reform granting self-government to the cities was enacted in 1870.

The judicial reform of 1864 introduced the jury system, and organized lawyers into a bar, resulting in a marked improvement in efficiency and honesty in the conduct of court cases. The jury system was not extended, however, to the so-called *volost'* courts, established for the peasants.

The last of these reforms was the introduction of universal military service in 1874. The obligation to serve was broadened to include all classes, while the term of active service was drastically reduced, though it still remained five years.

Though these reforms removed the worst abuses of the tsarist regime, they failed to destroy the underlying causes of political and economic discontent. The peasants remained a class still partly bound to the land, and heavily in debt for the small tracts of land they received. Representative government was restricted to the towns and districts; there was no representative assembly for the whole nation, or even a constitution. Thus, in spite of reforms, the radical movement continued to grow, along with popular dissatisfaction, culminating in the REVOLUTIONS of 1905 and 1917.

Remizov, Alexey Mikhaylovich (1877-   ), a prose writer of the twentieth century. He came from a family of Moscow merchants, and grew up in relative poverty. He attended the University of Moscow, where he studied natural science, but was expelled in 1897 for membership in a radical society, and exiled to Penza, later to Vologda, provincial centers which figure in some of his tales. In 1904 he was allowed to settle in St. Petersburg. He wandered over much of Russia, made religious pilgrimages and lived in monasteries. At first he believed that the Revolution might purify Russia and bring spiritual rebirth. But he was soon disillusioned, fell ill, and in 1921 was allowed to emigrate. He settled in Paris, where he has remained, continuing to write and publish. His post-revolutionary production is even larger than his prolific earlier work.

Remizov is a curious personality, whose eccentricities frequently infect his literary work. He is an excellent student of Old Russian manuscripts, and his old-style calligraphy is florid and exquisite. As a whim he organized a mysterious Grand Federation of Apes, of which he himself is Clerk, and for which he issues beautifully written charters of membership for other Russian writers. A whimsical humorist and satirist who loves the eccentric, Remizov is also capable of warm human sympathy, especially for the little man. But his philosophy is pessimistic; life for him is grotesque and mad, and man the plaything of evil destiny. The only salvation from such a world lies in absolute self-abnegation and acceptance of fate.

Remizov's writing is so varied that it is difficult to characterize. His earlier tales and novels tend to naturalism, though even they achieve a certain symbolic significance. But much of his work consists of religious legends, fairy tales and chronicles of his own dreams. He has written tales which are almost pure grotesques. The most important common denominator in his writing seems to be an emphasis on style; it is the manner, not the matter of his works which is important. His style is a conscious attempt to produce speech which is purely and characteristically Russian, unaffected by Western influences, and rich in archaic and dialect forms and folk expressions. He even attempts to reproduce the syntax and intonation of colloquial Russian in his writing, in which he follows the lead of such writers as LESKOV and ROZANOV. But Remizov's Russian is not the popular spoken language as such; it is a deliberate and even somewhat bookish elaboration of popular elements, developed into a grotesque speech rich in proverbs, quips, allusions and folk etymologies, on many levels. He coins neologisms and revives archaisms. This emphasis on stylistic effect, even mannerism, makes Remizov, along with Bely (see Bugayev), a master of the new trend of ORNAMENTALISM, preoccupation with style as such, which developed out of SYMBOLISM and dominated Russian prose fiction from 1912 into the 1920's. Like Bely, he has almost no interest in psychological characterization. Remizov has apparently been more popular with other writers than with the reading public, and his ornamentalist tendencies influenced a large number of Soviet writers, including ZAMYATIN, Pilnyak (see Vogau), BABEL, BULGAKOV, A. N. TOLSTOY and others.

Remizov's early novels, *The Pond* (1907), *The Clock* (1908), and *Sisters of the Cross* (1910), are terrifying descriptions of the horror and squalor of middle-class life in the capitals or provincial Russian cities. In these tales man serves only as the plaything of fate. The same squalor is found in *The Story of Ivan Semyonovich Stratilatov* (1909), but here the technique is far from realistic. Stratilatov is a grotesque figure, a provincial clerk whose illicit affair with a young girl brings his final disgrace and death. *The Fifth Pestilence* (1912) depicts in extravagant and ornate style the downfall of a scrupulously honest but cold, unloving provincial magistrate who is finally cuckolded by his wife and driven to drink. Quite different and much simpler from the stylistic point of view is *On a Field Azure* (1922), a delicate portrayal of the growth and education of a young girl and her development into a Socialist Revolutionary.

The REVOLUTION of 1917 and the Civil War stimulated Remizov to write several long prose poems on the sufferings of Russia, which he attributes to Russia's Europeanization and her neglect of her true historical destiny, distinct from that of Europe. These are *The Lay on the Destruction of the Russian Land* (1918), a title taken from Old Russian literature, where it refers to the coming of the Tartars, and *Fiery Russia* (1921), which contains a remarkable eulogy to DOSTOYEVSKI. Dostoyevski has influenced Remizov very strongly, and in Dostoyevski Remizov finds the emotional essence of what is Russian: suffering and pity.

On a Field Azure and *Fiery Russia* were published abroad; Remizov's work in emigration also includes collections of legends and fairy tales, such as *Parables of St. Nicholas* (1924), *Trava-Murava* (1925) and *Zga* (1925), as well as remarkable recordings of his own dreams. Fairy tales and religious legends are favorite forms of Remizov; in them his poetic prose, grotesque imagery and whimsical imagination can reign unchecked. Some tales are full of demons, hobgoblins and fantastic animals; others are serious religious legends emphasizing ideals of sympathy, charity and humility. *Tsar Maximilian* (1918) is a retelling of a farcical folk play as a drama of symbol and religious mystery.

Reshetnikov, Fyodor Mikhaylovich (1841-71), a realistic novelist of the 1860's. His best-known novelette, *The People of Podlipnoye* (1864), depicts the Finnish peasants of the Province of Perm as brutalized and dehumanized by exploitation by their masters; this and others of his tales played an important role in arousing the nobility and middle class to a sense of social guilt. Reshetnikov's early death deprived Russia of a promising writer.

Revolution of 1825. See Decembrist Movement.

Revolution of 1905. The Revolution of 1905 resulted from long-standing and widespread dissatisfaction with the tsarist regime and its failure to grant reform. As yet Russia had no constitution or constituent assembly. The peasantry was disaffected because of the debt which it owed for the land obtained at the time of emancipation (see Reforms), because of the small size of the tracts it cultivated, and because the government had never granted it full citizenship rights. The growing industrial proletariat was dissatisfied because of low wages, long hours and terrible working conditions, and because it could not improve conditions so long as the government supported the capitalist entrepreneurs in breaking strikes.

Though political parties were illegal in Russia, a number of them were formed underground or abroad during the decade preceding 1905. The Social Democratic Party, or S.D.'s, as they were nicknamed, the party of Marxian Socialism, was organized in 1898. Its leaders were LENIN and PLEKHANOV. In 1903 it split into two groups: the Bolsheviks ("majority"), today the Communist Party, and the Mensheviks ("minority"). The Bolsheviks insisted on the necessity for violent revolution, while the Mensheviks supported peaceful methods and co-operation with the moderate parties. In 1902 a second socialist party, the Socialist Revolutionaries (S.R.'s), was organized. Followers of the older POPULISTS, they favored a platform of agrarian socialism, and supposed that the main revolutionary effort would come from the peasantry. Their party was the one most attractive to writers of the period, as well as to many other intellectuals.

The chief liberal party, the Constitutional Democrats (nicknamed "Cadets" or "Kadets" from the Russian initials of those two words), was organized in 1905. It was the party of the liberal nobility, the middle classes and of many intellectuals.

The opportunity for revolutionary action came in 1904, when the country was involved in the unpopular war with Japan, and the movement of the army to the East left the government too weak to cope with revolt. Riots took place in the army and navy, and there were uprisings among the peasantry. The massacre of several hundred people in a workers' demonstration before the Winter Palace in January, 1905, aroused popular feeling to a high pitch. Meanwhile a congress of the *Zemstvos*, or district boards, petitioned for reforms. In August, 1905, the government announced the establishment of a national assembly, a Duma, which, however, was to have advisory powers only. This failed to satisfy either the liberals or the radicals, and a general strike was called which proved amazingly successful. In October, 1905, the government issued a manifesto promising basic civil rights and the establishment of a representative Duma which would have the power to reject legislation proposed by the government. These reforms largely satisfied the liberals, but not the radicals, who wanted to carry out a full-fledged socialist revolution. The government's proposals succeeded in splitting the two groups, and by the beginning of 1906 the revolution was crushed. In firm control, the government could now ignore its earlier promises. The electoral law was changed several times to insure a rightist majority in the Duma (the first two Dumas of 1906 and 1907 had liberal and radical majorities and hence were both dissolved). Civil rights were soon withdrawn as well, and controls reappeared to hamper the press. From 1907 to 1911 the government took reprisals against the revolutionary leaders. Suspects were tried by court-martial and often executed; in a single year (1908) the number of executions reached 782. To quiet peasant dissension, the government granted agrarian reforms by administrative decree, abolishing the commune and other restrictions on peasant civil rights.

The failure of the Revolution of 1905 was undoubtedly a fatal blow to the Russian liberal movement, which lost a unique opportunity to take over leadership in political affairs at a time when the radical parties were not as strong as they proved to be in 1917.

Most Russian writers, even the Symbolists, many of whom had earlier been relatively apolitical, were enthused by the Revolution of 1905 and took active part in it. The collapse of the revolution produced widespread disillusionment, and many writers reacted by a retreat from active life and concern with social problems into mysticism, decadence, obscurantism or estheticism (see Symbolism). Another obviously escapist tendency in literature was a new interest in erotic subjects. This disillusionment proved a lasting one among most members of the older generation of writers, and very few of them greeted the Revolution of October, 1917 (see below) with the same radical enthusiasm they had shown in 1905.

Revolution of 1917. There were actually two distinct revolutions in 1917, occurring in February and in October (the latter's anniversary is today celebrated in November because of the subsequent calendar reform in the Soviet Union). The first revolution was almost bloodless; it resulted from loss of popular confidence in the government because of the scandalous conduct of the war and the breakdown of the food supply. It brought the abdication of the emperor and the formation of a provisional government, soon headed by the Socialist Revolutionary Kerenski. But the provisional government lacked real authority, and was hampered by the independent activity of the soviets, councils of members of the radical parties formed by workers and in the armed forces. Led by the Petrograd Soviet, these soviets issued decrees of their own. The unpopularity of the war with Germany, which the provisional government sought to continue, was perhaps the chief cause of its downfall, and of the success of the Bolsheviks' uprising in October. The attempt made by General Kornilov in August, 1917, to seize power led Kerenski to rely on the Bolsheviks for support, and thus cost him the favor of the moderates.

The Revolution of October, in which the Bolsheviks seized control in Petrograd and other major cities of Russia, was also relatively bloodless, but was at once followed by a bloody civil war between the Bolsheviks and the Whites. The war, which lasted three years, terminated only in November, 1920, when General Wrangel evacuated his forces from the Crimea. Even then sporadic resistance continued in some areas. At the beginning of the Civil War it appeared that the Whites had a good chance to win. The Reds were without much question unpopular with a majority of the people. The Whites were supported and supplied by the Allies; their troops, a large proportion of which were former tsarist officers, were better trained and disciplined than the Reds. At one period the Whites controlled all of Siberia and most of European Russia except the center. But centrality of position, with shorter lines of communication and a unified leadership, favored the Reds. The Whites lacked ideological unity; their forces included both moderates and die-hard tsarists. Time worked against the Whites, for the longer the Civil War continued, the more these divergent elements tended to split apart, and the more the people tended to identify the cause of peace with the victory of the Red regime. Thus, in spite of the Bolsheviks' tyranny, the nation was heartily glad when Red victory brought the end of the Civil War.

Curiously enough, the October Revolution has been the subject of comparatively few works of Russian literature. The brevity of the Revolution itself and its lack of finality (the real struggle came only with the Civil War) are no doubt responsible for this neglect. BLOK's great poem, *The Twelve,* is the major work which has the October Revolution as its subject. The first volume of A. N. TOLSTOY's *Way through Hell* gives a good picture, from the Soviet point of view, of both the February and October events.

By contrast, the Civil War has been a favorite subject, indeed, the most popular in Soviet literature of the 1920's. Pro-Communist writers attempted to emphasize its ideological side, while those who were more independent or who were actually anti-Soviet concentrated on depicting its struggle and pathos. Perhaps Russian literature never had a better natural subject, or one of greater inherent drama or poignancy. Writers who wrote novels dealing with events of the Civil War from what might be called an official point of view include FURMANOV, LIBEDINSKI, Serafimovich (see Popov), FADEYEV and later A. N. TOLSTOY. More independent, and therefore less stereotyped in their treatment of events were such novelists, story writers and playwrights as: BABEL, Pilnyak (see Vogau), Vsevolod IVANOV, Veresayev (see Smidovich), SHOLOKHOV and Mikhail BULGAKOV. MAYAKOVSKI, TIKHONOV, Akhmatova (see Gorenko), Bagritski (see Dzyubin) and SELVINSKI depicted the conflict in poetry. (See Literature, Soviet; Criticism, Soviet.)

Romanov, Grand Duke Konstantin Konstantinovich (1858-1915), a poet of the late nineteenth century who published under the initials K.R. His lyrical and dramatic poetry is entirely conventional. He also translated from English and German poetry, notably Shakespeare's *Hamlet*.

Romanov, Panteleymon Sergeyevich (1884-1938), a Soviet writer. Of aristocratic origin, he entered literature in 1917. His portrayals of the sexual problems of young people brought him notoriety. His stories, such as the well-known *Without Cherry Blossoms* (1926), or the novel *Comrade Kislyakov* (or *Three Pairs of Silk Stockings*, 1930), depict young people who regard love as a purely biological function, and in consequence practice promiscuity. Others of his stories and sketches depict the new way of Soviet life and characterize the "new" types of Soviet citizenry. One of the most popular writers of the 1920's, Romanov is little read today, and is officially under a cloud because his work is considered "decadent."

Romanticism. It is difficult to fix a beginning date for the Romantic Movement in Russia, for the influence of CLASSICISM survived far into the nineteenth century, and the work of many writers is transitional. The first decisive break with Classicism came at the end of the eighteenth century with the introduction of SENTI-

MENTALISM by KARAMZIN, who brought the new cult of sentiments and lofty feelings to Russia from the West. Initiated in prose, the new trend quickly spread to poetry, and at the beginning of the century ZHUKOVSKI's translations of early Western romanticists brought a stage which may be labelled as PRE-ROMANTICISM. Though possessing many of the characteristics of full-fledged Romanticism, such as the freer expression of feelings and a new interest in nature and the common people, Pre-Romanticism was more limited in its formal expression (the principal new form introduced was the ballad), and in its preference for a rather limited range of subjects drawn from such realms as the supernatural and the medieval. Nor did Pre-Romanticism bring the full-fledged cult of the individual, so typical of Romanticism.

The strong wave of influence of Byron and Shakespeare which came to Russia early in the 1820's may be held to mark the end of the Pre-Romantic period and the beginnings of Romanticism proper. But though the poets of the 1820's, the so-called "Golden Age" of Russian poetry, broadened the range and freedom of personal lyric expression, they continued to show a preference for classical forms, and even for a classically pure and elegant rather than a romantically freer and less rigid language. It is difficult to classify the greatest Russian poet, PUSHKIN, as a member of any movement or school; in many respects he is a romanticist, but he may also be regarded as a continuer and perfecter of the French and Russian eighteenth-century tradition of classical poetry.

Not until the 1830's is it possible to speak of a "high" Romanticism in Russian literature. Though short-lived, at least in prose, and destined to be supplanted by the end of the 1840's by the indigenous movement of REALISM, the Romantic Movement in Russia still produced a number of writers of importance. The most significant is GOGOL, the only major Russian romantic prose writer; his work, though often characterized as realistic, is too grotesque and fantastic to admit of such a description, and the movement of Russian Realism which followed in the 1850's is actually more of a reaction against his work than a continuation of it. The two major romantic poets are LERMONTOV and TYUTCHEV; the first is a Russian Byronist; the second, a metaphysical poet influenced by German philosophic idealism, the introduction of which also greatly stimulated the development of philosophic thought in Russia. Minor novelists and playwrights of the romanticist period gave preference to subjects which were fantastic or whimsical and grotesque; patriotic and historical themes were also popular. A few writers, such as PAVLOV, BUTKOV and DAHL, produced genre tales and sketches of middle and lower-class life which anticipated the movement of REALISM. Romanticist criticism had its leading exponent in BELINSKI, though his insistence on "naturalism" also helped to lay the foundations for REALISM.

Ropshin, V. See Savinkov, B. V.

Rostovski, Dimitry. See Dimitry Rostovski.

Rozanov, Mikhail Grigorievich (1888-1938), a writer of the early twentieth century who wrote under the pseudonym of N. Ognyov. His early stories, published before the Revolution, are morbid tales of death, influenced by ANDREYEV and Sologub (see Teternikov). His stories of the 1920's are less subjective and more realistic. His principal work is *The Diary of Kostya Ryabtsev* (1926-27; English translation as "The Diary of a Communist Schoolboy"), the story of a young man who lives through the Revolution and early years of the Soviet regime. Particularly sharp is the picture of school life, in which an anarchy of student rule and "progressive" methods governed after the Revolution. The book has been translated into many languages. Ognyov later wrote a sequel, *Exit Nikpetozh* (1930; English translation as "The Diary of a Communist Undergraduate").

Rozanov, Vasili Vasilievich (1856-1919), a leading Russian philosopher, writer and critic of the late nineteenth and early twentieth century. Born in a lower middle-class family, he studied history at the University of Moscow, and for many years taught history and geography in provincial schools. He began to publish in 1886, and attracted attention when he published a study on DOSTOYEVSKI in 1894, *The Legend of the Grand Inquisitor*. In 1899 he became a regular contributor to the conservative paper *New Times*, and thus obtained an adequate income from his writings. Though he was himself strongly conservative, he had radical flights, and even published under a pseudonym in the radical *Russian Word* while he was still contributing to the *New*

Times. The REVOLUTIONS of 1905 and February, 1917, won his enthusiasm, but October, 1917, soon disillusioned him. He continued to write, but, deprived of income from his work, died two years later in extreme poverty.

The keystone of Rozanov's thought is his emphasis on the biological nature of man and on sex. The sexual principle is for him a reflection of the generative and creative spirit of the universe. Though Christianity attracted him all his life, and he died a Christian, he was repelled by Christian puritanism concerning sex. For this attitude he sought to substitute a natural cult of the patriarchal family, in which the sexual act would constitute a central rite. Sex for him is that which is creative in man; it is his very soul. He declares even that man is but a "transformation of sex." Sex transcends the very boundaries of nature and unites us to God. He praises the Jewish people for its practice of sex as a form of piety, but here his attitudes were ambivalent, and his notorious anti-Semitism brought his expulsion from the Religious and Philosophical Society.

In his attitude toward history Rozanov was a pessimist: Christian civilization for him, as for Nietzsche, was "frozen"; Christianity itself too "monastic," "true but powerless." Man's true creativity functions properly in the family and in child-bearing.

Rozanov's literary reputation rests chiefly on his collections of maxims, aphorisms and brief essays, such as *Solitaria* (1912) and two volumes of *Fallen Leaves* (1913, 1915). These are remarkable experiments which violate the normal syntax of the written language and attempt to catch the intonations and cadence of actual speech. Rozanov resorts to all kinds of typographical devices to achieve this effect. These little fragments are often sharp and even cynically epigrammatic; though they lack structural discipline, they sometimes attain a powerful and complete originality of manner. Certain of them lay bare the soul of their author, with its conceit and deep-rooted contradictions. A contemporary of the Symbolist poets, Rozanov was greatly admired by such writers as MEREZHKOVSKI, BLOK and REMIZOV, though he himself remained independent of Symbolism as a literary movement.

As a literary critic, Rozanov is best known for his penetrating study of DOSTOYEVSKI. The husband of Polina Suslova, Dostoyevski's former mistress, he was able to achieve keen insights into Dostoyevski's personality. It was Rozanov who first stressed the central importance of Dostoyevski's *Notes from Underground* in his development; he also realized the absolute contradiction which Dostoyevski postulated between man's striving for happiness and his struggle to be free.

Russian Association of Proletarian Writers. See RAPP.

Russian language. See Language.

Russian literature. See Literature.

R—va, Zenaida. See Hahn, Y. A.

Ryleyev, Kondrati Fyodorovich (1795-1826), a poet and one of the principal leaders of the Decembrist Uprising of 1825 (see Decembrist Movement). A member of the petty gentry, he served as an army officer, later as secretary of the Russian-American Company, engaged in developing Alaska. From 1823 to 1825 he was co-editor of the Decembrist literary annual, *The Polar Star*. In 1826, following the failure of the Decembrist Uprising, he was hanged, along with four other leaders.

Ryleyev's literary production is small, and is largely concerned with revolution. His chief work is the narrative poem *Voynarovski* (1824-25), about the nephew of the Cossack leader Mazeppa, exiled to Siberia. The poem influenced PUSHKIN's *Poltava*. Much of Ryleyev's poetry concerned the COSSACKS, whose democratic spirit he greatly admired. His few lyrics are poems of civic virtue or calls to revolution, and among the best revolutionary poems in Russian.

Rylsky, Maxim (1895-   ), a Ukrainian Soviet poet (see Preface).

S

Sadovnikov, Dmitri Nikolayevich (1847-83), a poet and ethnographer of the second half of the nineteenth century. His poems, some on folk themes and regional subjects of the Volga country, include two songs (1881) on the seventeenth-century revolutionary leader Stenka Razin. One of these has since become a popular ballad.

Saints, Lives of. See Literature, Old Russian.

Salias de Tournemir, Countess Yelizaveta Vasilievna (1815-92), a novelist of the mid-nineteenth century, sister of the playwright SUKHOVO-KOBYLIN, and mother of the novelist, Count Ye. A. SALIAS DE TOURNEMIR. She wrote under the pseudonym of Yevgenia Tur, and is remembered for her strong feminist position and her sentimental stories and novels, often about young girls of good family.

Salias de Tournemir, Count Yevgeni Andreyevich (1841-1908), a historical novelist of the late nineteenth century, son of Countess Ye. V. SALIAS DE TOURNEMIR. His historical novels, such as *Rebels of the Pugachov Revolt* (1874), were extremely popular, but unoriginal and undistinguished.

Saltykov, Mikhail Yevgrafovich (1826-89), a leading Russian satirist of the second half of the nineteenth century. He wrote under the pen-name of N. Shchedrin, and is often referred to by the double name of Saltykov-Shchedrin. He was born in a family of provincial gentry, and was educated at the lycée at Tsarskoye Selo. He entered the civil service in 1844. In 1847-48 he published two stories, in which he called attention to the contradictions of social and economic inequality in Russian life. As a consequence he was exiled to Vyatka in northeast Russia. He was allowed to remain in the civil service, however, and in 1855 was permitted to return to the capital. In spite of his satirical attacks on officials, Saltykov rose rapidly in the service, and in 1858 was named vice-governor of a province. From 1862-1864 he served with NEKRASOV as co-editor of the radical journal, *The Contemporary,* but returned to the civil service in the latter year. In 1868 he retired for good from the service, and with Nekrasov became co-editor of the radical *Fatherland Notes,* a position which he retained until that journal's suppression in 1884. His work was tremendously popular with the radicals, and he was generally acknowledged as their literary leader after the death of Nekrasov. In spite of the topical character of much of Saltykov's writing and its journalistic style, his best work achieved a secure position among the Russian classics in his own day, and has held this ever since.

Saltykov's most characteristic form is the satirical sketch, often of character, and in a form intermediate between imaginative literature and journalism. The earlier collections, such as *Provincial Sketches* (1856-57), *Pompadours and Pompadouresses* (1868-73) and *Gentlemen of Tashkent* (1869-72), are lighter in tone than the later sketches; the principal target in the earlier works is the provincial official, with his tyranny, greed, smugness and lack of enlightenment. The later collections, including *In the Realm of Moderation and Precision* (1874-77), *The Sanctuary of Mon-Repos* (1878-79) and *Letters to an Aunt* (1881-82), are more serious and show greater moral indignation. Besides officials, they satirize the gentry and the rising bourgeoisie, with its rapacious thirst for profits. Saltykov's sketches are extremely topical, and are written in an allusive style which he himself called AESOPIC LANGUAGE. As a result, many of them have lost their appeal, and cannot be understood today without a commentary.

Somewhat apart stand Saltykov's *Fairy Tales* (1869-86), a series of political allegories, less diffuse and journalistic in style than the sketches.

Of Saltykov's satirical writings, the greatest is his longer work, *The History of a Town* (1869-70), a parody of Russian history, in which the successive governors of the town of Glupov (Fooltown) are caricatures of the Russian tsars, portrayed as cruel, barbarous and reactionary despots. The satire is also directed against the stagnation and timidity of the Russian citizens who passively tolerate such rulers.

Saltykov's masterpiece is his only real novel as such, *The Golovlyov Family* (1876-80). Not a satire, it is a gloomy, naturalistic picture of the decay of a family of provincial gentry. Brutal, greedy and rotten almost beyond belief, the whole family is literally consumed by its own viciousness and rapacity. The father and eldest son perish from drink. The next son, nicknamed Yudushka ("Little Judas") by all who know him, is a masterly portrayal, the outstanding example of the hypocrite in Russian literature. He wheedles his mother, the tyrannical matriarch of the family, into making her fortune over to him, then reduces her to the position of a poor dependent. But there is no real purpose behind this hypocrisy and avarice, and once in possession of the fortune he devotes himself to senseless lawsuits, fantastic accountings of his wealth, and to unrestrained babbling. Hypocritically muttering prayers, maxims and platitudes to himself all day long, he finally goes mad and, in a fruitless attempt to right the evil he has done, rushes out into the winter cold and freezes to death. The novel is one of almost unrelieved gloom. In it Saltykov implied that the Russian gentry, deprived of the artificial prop which had supported it before the emancipation of the serfs, would perish of its own weight.

Saltykov's last large work, *Old Times in Poshekhonie* (1887-89), is another gloomy chronicle of the life of a family of provincial gentry. It is largely autobiographical, and there are many reminiscences of the author's own childhood. Diffuse and less interesting than *The Golovlyov Family*, it is still read for its descriptions of life on the estate and for its characterization of the peasants and gentry.

Samarin, Yuri Fyodorovich (1819-76), a Russian philosopher of the mid-nineteenth century. A leading representative of the younger SLAVOPHILES, Samarin's thought was influenced by KHOMYAKOV and I. V. KIREYEVSKI. He elaborated the doctrine of communality developed by Khomyakov, according to which man must renounce his individualism and adhere to the communal order, ideally to the community of believers of the Orthodox faith. Through such a free act of self-renunciation, in Samarin's view, the individual would attain to a direct and personal relation with God.

Savinkov, Boris Viktorovich (1879-1925), a Russian radical novelist of the early twentieth century, who published under the pseudonym of V. Ropshin. A Socialist Revolutionary and terrorist, he organized several political assassinations at the beginning of the century. Under the Kerenski government he was made minister of war, but fled the country when the Bolsheviks came to power in October, 1917. He returned to the Soviet Union in 1924 and was arrested and condemned to death, later to ten years imprisonment. His mysterious death the following year was officially attributed to suicide.

Savinkov's novels are sensational, pseudo-factual accounts of his experiences as a terrorist, and show an interest in macabre psychology. They include *The Pale Horse* (1909) and *What Never Happened* (1913).

Sch—(names beginning in). For those not listed here, see under Shch—.

Scheller, Alexander Konstantinovich (1838-1900), a radical novelist of the late nineteenth century, who wrote under the pseudonym of A. Mikhaylov. A prolific writer, he specialized in portraits of the radical intelligentsia. His novels, such as *Rotting Swamps* (1864), and *When the Woods Are Cut Down the Chips Will Fly* (1871), are radical and tendentious, and suggest that youth, blocked in its struggle for reform, should devote itself to cultural and technological progress.

Schism. In the middle of the seventeenth century the Russian Church was split into two camps by the question of accuracy of the Church texts and Church ritual. These questions had plagued the Russian Church for almost two centuries. MAXIM GREK had been invited to Russia in 1518 in order to make corrections, but his work was denounced as heretical. In the 1640's a revision was carried out in accord with Greek and Ukrainian texts, more accurate than the Russian ones. When Nikon became Patriarch of the Russian Church in 1652, he introduced certain changes in the ritual according to the Greek model, such as the use of the triple hallelujah, the use of three fingers instead of two in making the sign of the cross, and others. These changes caused violent opposition, and many of the clergy, led by the Archpriest AVVAKUM, denounced the reforms as sacrilege. They opposed the innovations as foreign and Greek; the Greek books

and ritual were tainted in their eyes because of Greek subjuga-
tion by the Turks. Many of these men, known as Old Believers
(or Old Ritualists) because they continued to practise the older
ritual, were persecuted, arrested, tortured and exiled. Finally, in
1666-67, a Church council condemned the use of the older ritual;
besides imprisoning Avvakum, it also deposed, ironically enough,
his opponent Nikon, who had been too bold in asserting the
independence of the Russian Church from the state.

Although the issues at stake seem trifling, actually they reflected the far greater question of whether Russia would accept
enlightenment from abroad. Nikon's reforms were a necessary
preparation for the wholesale introduction of European influences by PETER THE GREAT. They also had the effect of
greatly weakening the authority of the official Church, for many
of the common people either followed the Old Believers or sym-
pathized with them, while members of the upper classes were led
by the conflict toward scepticism and indifference. Thus Peter
the Great was able to destroy the Patriarchate and subordinate
the Russian Church to the state.

The sect of Old Believers has continued to exist to the present
day, in spite of frequent persecutions, and has had a colorful
history. Many members of the sect prepared themselves for the
end of the world, and certain of these immolated themselves in
wholesale groups; others denounced the secular authorities as
the servants of Anti-Christ. Inability to consecrate priests, because of lack of apostolic bishops, has also dogged the sect and
complicated its history. The Old Believers were a picturesque,
if backward people, and hence served as exotic literary material,
particularly in the works of LESKOV and MELNIKOV-
PECHERSKI. The schism also opened the doors to the development of other sectarian movements, some of them pietistic, others
fanatical and extremist.

Schwarzman, Lev Isaakovich (1866-1938), a philosopher and critic
of the early twentieth century who wrote under the pseudonym
of Lev Shestov. He published a number of books on philosophy
and literature, among which were *The Good in the Doctrine of
Tolstoy and Nietzsche* (1900), *Dostoyevski and Nietzsche, the
Philosophy of Tragedy* (1901), and *The Apotheosis of Groundless-
ness* (1905; English translation as "All Things Are Possible"). He

took an anti-Bolshevik position after the Revolution of 1905 and emigrated. Settling in Paris, he continued to write, publishing *Dostoyevski-Tolstoy* (1923) and *Kierkegaard and Existential Philosophy* (1936).

At the core of Shestov's thought is a profound irrationalism and emphasis on faith. Reason and science for him are false in that they distort reality. Truth, he maintains, is "singular" and "incomprehensible." On the other hand, faith leads man to freedom. Shestov symbolizes these two extremes in the title of his final book, *Athens and Jerusalem* (1938), in which Athens stands for rational wisdom, and Jerusalem for the revelation of truth brought by faith. Shestov is a violent anti-idealist, whose writing often gives an impression of scepticism and nihilism, an impression which is misleading since faith in God, however irrational, stands at the center of his philosophy. He and others have compared his thought to that of Kierkegaard.

The style of Shestov's writing gives it considerable literary merit beyond its philosophical significance. It is clear, simple, elegant and lacking in all affection; at the same time it is concentrated and powerful.

Scythians, a group of writers and intellectuals who were led by the political thinker and historian Ivanov-Razumnik (pseudonym of R. V. Ivanov, 1878-1945). A leftist Socialist Revolutionary, he and his followers supported the Bolsheviks in the 1917 October REVOLUTION, which they interpreted mystically; they were not in agreement, however, with the Bolsheviks' Marxist aims. They stressed the essential difference between Russia and the West; Russia's history had its own character, distinct from the West, and hence the Russians were not Europeans, but "Scythians," i.e., half European, half Asiatic. They believed that the Revolution of 1917 would sweep away the harmful traditions of European influence and leave Russia free to follow her own historical path.

A number of leading writers came under the influence of the Scythians and accepted, if only temporarily, the Revolution of 1917 from the Scythian point of view. These included BLOK, Bely, (see Bugayev) and Pilnyak (see Vogau). Blok in his great poem *The Twelve* implies that the sufferings of the Revolution will bring Russia spiritual purification, a belief which he apparently soon lost. The Scythians greatly admired the peasant poetry of YESENIN and KLYUYEV, which contained an almost mystical acceptance of the Revolution as the destiny of the Russian people.

Selvinski, Ilya Lvovich (1899-   ), a Soviet poet. He began to publish in 1926 as a leading member of the group of CONSTRUCTIVISTS. A follower of MAYAKOVSKI and PASTERNAK, Selvinski employed a complex vocabulary and an involved style in his early poetry, with much use of technical terminology. He also made liberal use of new typographical devices to give his poetry a "modern" appearance as well as to convey its complex rhythmic structure. His poetry is predominantly narrative. *The Ulyalayev Story* (1927) depicts the activities of bandits and guerilla fighters in eastern Russia during the Civil War. *Pao-Pao* (1932) is a play in verse, one which it is difficult to take seriously, since it depicts the transformation of an ape into a human being. The ape, symbolizing the bourgeois world, is employed in a factory; there it learns the principles of Marxism, and, as a result, becomes human. *General Brusilov* (1943), another play, treats the Russian hero of World War I in an obvious parallel with the events of the Second World War.

Selvinski has frequently been attacked by the critics, who accuse him of eclecticism and lack of a correct socialist orientation. In 1947 he suggested the substitution of the term, "socialist symbolism," for the official SOCIALIST REALISM, a proposal which, though well intended, was scarcely so well received.

Semyonov, Sergey Alexandrovich (1893-1943), a Soviet novelist. His early novels, such as *Hunger* (1922), deal with the Civil War, the famine and disease of the times. He also described the disintegration of family ties in this period.

Senkovski, Osip Ivanovich (1800-58), a journalist, critic and humorous writer of the mid-nineteenth century, who wrote under the pseudonym of Baron Brambeus. Professor of Arabian and Turkish literature at the University of St. Petersburg, he published tales as well as scholarly articles on the peoples of the Near East. His other works include humorous tales and *feuilletons*. His reviews of contemporary writers are egregious for their cynical and contemptuous attitude. Senkovski's tasteless style had a strong, if harmful influence on the development of Russian journalistic writing, and, indeed, on standard written Russian in general.

Sentimentalism. Russian literary Sentimentalism was introduced by KARAMZIN, whose *Letters of a Russian Traveller* (1792) proclaimed the new cult of personal feeling and sensibility. Other characteristics of the new trend were a contented optimism in the goodness of nature and of man, an interest in landscape, and a pleasurable though rationally restrained sympathy and affection for others. In its exaltation of feelings Sentimentalism often flowed over into sentimentality. Sentimentalism was already a strong movement in the literature of the West; Karamzin's models were such writers as Rousseau, Sterne, Goldsmith, James Thomson, the Ossian of Macpherson, Klopstock, Gessner and Kleist. Sentimentalism opposed the dominant pseudo-classical school in Russian literature (see Classicism). It was beneficial in easing classical restraints on the free expression of personal feeling, as well as in introducing new literary genres. The tale and the verse tale now became respectable literary forms. For the most part, however, the sentimentalists cultivated those poetic forms which were classical, but which permitted greater freedom of personal expression, such as songs, fables and elegies. In the new style words began to be used for their grace and musical quality as well as their intrinsic meaning.

Besides KARAMZIN, the leading Russian sentimentalist writers were DMITRIEV, OZEROV, and in some respects RADISHCHEV. The influence of the movement also extended to ZHUKOVSKI and many other poets of the younger generation, who may also be labelled as pre-romantics (see Pre-Romanticism). The end of Russian Sentimentalism is difficult to date, for it blends with the later movement of ROMANTICISM: the year 1820, the approximate time of the introduction of important new influences from the West, those of Byron and Shakespeare, may be said to mark the beginnings of the Romantic Movement.

Serafimovich, A. See Popov, A. S.

Serapion Brothers, a group of young writers founded in 1921, including ZOSHCHENKO, TIKHONOV, FEDIN, Kaverin (see Zilberg), Vsevolod IVANOV, Nikolay NIKITIN, LUNTS, SHKLOVSKI and SLONIMSKI. They published their first almanac in 1922. Followers of ZAMYATIN, the Serapion Brothers had little in common; what united them was chiefly a desire for greater freedom and variety in literature, particularly from the compulsion to write on contemporary social themes. They took their name from a story by E. T. A. Hoffmann. *The Serapion Brothers*, about an individualist who vows to devote himself to a free, imaginative and non-conformist art. The Serapions insisted on their right to create a literature free from political ideology, a claim which conflicted with the official demand that all literature have political significance. These articles of faith were formulated and published by Lev LUNTS in 1922. The Serapions constituted the largest group of so-called "fellow travellers" in literature (see Trotski) in the 1920's, and the largest which actively sought independence from literary controls. Some of them, notably FEDIN, Kaverin and TIKHONOV, have subsequently tended to greater conformism and are today to be found in the camp of Soviet orthodoxy.

Serapion Vladimirski (died 1275), Bishop of Vladimir, the author of five sermons which have survived. His chief subject is the misfortunes of the Russian people under the Tartar Yoke, which he viewed as God's punishment for the people's sins. He also attacked current superstitions, especially the practice of trial by ordeal. His sermons are noted for their brevity and simplicity, in which they contrast with the prevailing rhetorical manner popular in Old Russia.

Serfdom. The Russian system of serfdom was legally consolidated in the middle of the seventeenth century, though a kind of peonage had already existed for many centuries. In theory serfdom originally represented a form of service indirectly contributed by the peasants to the state; the landowning nobility served the state, while the serfs served the nobility. The requirement that the nobles serve the state was abrogated, however, by CATHERINE THE GREAT's Charter to the Nobility in 1785. When, about the same time, the prohibition against selling serfs without the land they cultivated began to be ignored, the Russian serfs in fact became slaves, completely dependent on the whims of their owners. They could be punished summarily by their masters; such punishments included conscription into the army, exile, or floggings which might result in death.

The majority of the serfs worked in the fields, cultivating part of the noble's land as their own, though this was generally insufficient for anything more than a bare subsistence. Their obligations to their masters were discharged in the form of forced labor in the masters' fields *(barshchina)*, or quit-rent in money or produce *(obrok)*. The latter system was generally more favorable to the serfs.

Some serfs were taken from the land and employed as house servants. Certain of these might be trained to serve as cooks, secretaries, body-servants or companions for the landowners' children, even as actors or musicians. Some were employed as craftsmen in small shops maintained on the large estates. The master could also hire serfs out to entrepreneurs as labor for factories and mines, since such entrepreneurs, unless of noble birth, were not permitted to own serfs.

Peasants on the extensive lands belonging to the Russian Crown, including all of northern Russia, were generally better treated than the peasants of the private landowners, though they, too, might undergo the unenviable fate of being hired out to capitalists or conscripted into the army.

With the development of Russian liberal thought in the second half of the eighteenth century, widespread sentiment arose for bringing an end to or at least restricting the institution of serfdom. CATHERINE THE GREAT came to the throne in 1762 with such intentions, but soon realized that the majority of nobility, the ruling class in Russia, was opposed to any change; in the end her reign only strengthened the rights of the nobility over their serfs. Alexander I (1801-25) had similar intentions; the Napoleonic Wars, which impoverished many of the landowners, together with Alexander's growing conservatism, put an end to such plans. The increasing indebtedness of the nobility, whose estates were often mortgaged many times over, made liberation, or even the introduction of progressive methods of agriculture, more difficult. The serfs were liberated only in 1861, and then only on a basis highly unfavorable to them (see Reforms).

Although the tsarist CENSORSHIP made open sympathy for the plight of the serfs well-nigh impossible, Russian writers were far from blind to the evil, central in the whole reactionary tsarist system. Certain liberal writers of the late eighteenth-century, such as RADISHCHEV and NOVIKOV, who opposed serfdom and despotism, were subjected to imprisonment and exile. Writers of the nineteenth century tended to be more cautious, and often veiled their attacks. Even so, the mere depiction of peasant life might lead to difficulties with the censorship or the police. Liberal noblemen occasionally freed their serfs or tried to alleviate their lot by introducing more progressive methods. Lack of appreciation for the peasants' problems and lack of sympathetic understanding between peasants and their masters usually condemned such experiments to failure. TURGENEV's *Fathers and Children* and TOLSTOY's *Morning of a Landowner* depict the fate of such well-intentioned reforms.

Sergeyev-Tsenski, Sergey Nikolayevich (1876-   ), a novelist of the twentieth century. He began writing before the Revolution of 1917, but his reputation as a novelist has grown steadily during the Soviet period. His early work shows an exuberance and a highly mannered style, with a love of dialect and slang which places him close to the writers of ORNAMENTALISM. His early subjects are morbid ones, such as death, crime, fate and the depiction of idiocy and insanity.

After 1914 Sergeyev-Tsenski ceased to publish for some years, reappearing only in 1923 with a novel, *Valya*. His writing of the Soviet period shows less ornamentalism of manner and morbidity of subject; these qualities are replaced by a growing optimism and an interest in the depiction of the psychology of the normal. The principal subject of his Soviet novels are wars for the national defense, portrayed to show the heroic courage of the Russian people. *The Ordeal of Sevastopol* (1937-38) is a vast synthetic picture of the Crimean War of 1854-55, reminiscent in scope of Lev TOLSTOY's *War and Peace*. It devotes much attention to the diplomatic intrigues in the West which led up to the war. Sergeyev-Tsenski also has written a trilogy of novels about the First World War: *Brusilov's Breakthrough* (1943), *The Guns Are Rolled Out* (1944), and *The Guns Have Spoken* (1945). With several earlier novels these constitute part of an uncompleted epic of contemporary Russian life, given the collective title of *Transfiguration*. The three war novels are unusual in that they ignore the customary Soviet attitude of disparagement toward the First World War as an "imperialistic" conflict, and describe it rather as a heroic struggle of resistance waged by the Russian people.

Published during World War II, to which these novels obviously allude, they were at first well received, but Soviet critics soon began to attack them for their "objectivity," i.e., their failure to follow a national and party line.

Severyanin, Igor. See Lotarev, I. V.

Seyfullina, Lydia Nikolayevna (1889-   ), a novelist of the 1920's. She was a public school teacher in Siberia; her first story appeared in 1921 in a local newspaper. Her novelette, *Mulch* (1923), describes the spiritual transformation of a good-for-nothing peasant under the impact of the Revolution. Her play, *Virineya* (1924), similarly portrays the spiritual emancipation of peasant women by the Revolution. Seyfullina shows an ability to observe details from real life, but her realism is essentially crude and undigested.

Shaginyan, Marietta Sergeyevna (1888-   ), a poet and novelist of the twentieth century. She entered literature before the Revolution of 1917 as a minor poet of the Symbolist Movement. After the Revolution she gave up poetry completely for prose fiction. In the mid-1920's she published several detective thrillers *(Laurie Lane, the Metal Worker,* 1925; *Mess Mend, or the Yankees in Petrograd,* 1926) under the pen-name of "Jim Dollar," supposedly an American worker in Russia. These tales give a grotesque picture of the collapse of capitalist society under the world revolution. Their unique combination of sensationalism and Soviet propaganda, though popular with the public, was not encouraged officially. More recently Shaginyan has published *The Hydroelectric Station* (1931), a novel of the First Five-year Plan describing electrification in Armenia, and *The Ulyanov Family* (1938), about the family background of Lenin.

Shakhovskoy, Prince Alexander Alexandrovich (1777-1846), a playwright and stage director of the early nineteenth century, author of some fifty-two plays. He was a literary conservative, and some of his comedies, such as *A Lesson for Coquettes, or the Lipetsk Spa* (1815), were attacks on the new sentimental and romantic movement of KARAMZIN and ZHUKOVSKI.

Shchedrin, N. See Saltykov.

Shcheglov. See Leontiev, I. L.

Shcherbina, Nikolay Fyodorovich (1821-69), a poet of the mid-nineteenth century, a member of the so-called PARNASSIAN POETS. A Greek by descent on his mother's side, Shcherbina specialized in intimate and vivid pictures of the world of classical antiquity and the pagan spirit. These were contained in his *Greek Poems* (1849), and in two volumes of *Poems* (1857).

Sheller, A. K. See Scheller.

Shenshin. See Fet, A. A.

Shershenevich, Vadim Gabrielevich (1893-   ), a poet of the early twentieth century. He began as a Futurist (see Futurism), writing poems which sounded much like parodies of those of the Ego-Futurist Igor Severyanin (see Lotarev). Later he passed over to the newer school of IMAGINISM, founded in 1919, of which he became the leading theoretician. Subsequently he became a dramatist, adapting novels by Upton Sinclair for the stage.

Shestov, Lev. See Schwarzman, L. I.

Shevchenko, Taras (1814-61), the greatest Ukrainian poet (see Preface).

Shevyryov, Stepan Petrovich (1806-64), a literary historian and publicist, professor of literature at Moscow University. A member of the conservative wing of the SLAVOPHILES, he is important as a critic and historian of Russian literature.

Shishkov, Admiral Alexander Semyonovich (1754-1841), a writer and literary theoretician, from 1824 to 1828 Minister of Education. Shishkov was the leader of the "Slavonic" party, organized from 1811 to 1816 as the Society of the Lovers of the Russian Word. In his *Discussion of the Old and New Style of the Russian Language* (1803), Shishkov erroneously identified the Russian LANGUAGE with OLD CHURCH SLAVONIC, the language of the Russian Church and of much of earlier Russian literature. He proposed that new terms be coined from Slavonic roots, rather than borrowed from the languages of the West. Though their programs were in fact not completely different, Shishkov was sharply opposed to the linguistic and stylistic innovations of KARAMZIN and his followers. The examples of new Slavonic formations proposed by Shishkov struck his contemporaries as ridiculous, and the Karamzinians formed a society, ARZAMAS, for the purpose of parodying his activity. Though Shishkov was an amateur philologist, there was much that was sound in his theories, particularly in his desire to preserve a hierarchy of stylistic levels (see Lomonosov), and in his interest in FOLK LITERATURE as a source for the language and imagery of written literature. Although a number of poets of the day, notably DERZHAVIN, KRYLOV, GRIBOYEDOV and KÜCHEL-BECKER belonged to Shishkov's party, time decided against him and for the reforms of Karamzin.

Shishkov, Vyacheslav Yakovlevich (1873-1945), Soviet novelist. His best-known novel, *Pugachov* (1943-44), is a colorful portrayal of the eighteenth-century Cossack and peasant uprising. Shishkov also wrote novels about contemporary life in Siberia.

Shklovski, Viktor Borisovich (1893-   ), a literary theoretician, critic and writer of the twentieth century. A master of witty paradox, his ideas are brilliantly stated if not always convincing. He was one of the founders of OPOYAZ (Society for the Study of Poetic Language), the nucleus of the so-called Formalist Movement (see Criticism). He developed a theory of literature as "device," according to which literature presents reality in distorted and unusual contexts and perspectives. He likens the use of literary devices for making reality appear strange to the effect of colored glasses on our perception of landscape: the glasses distort but also arouse curiosity and interest in the otherwise monotonous landscape, which through them appears totally new and different.

Shklovski's literary theories had considerable influence on Russian writers of the 1920's, particularly on ZAMYATIN, OLE-SHA and Kaverin (see Zilberg). These writers are fond of "making strange," and of toying with the narrative so that the reader is made aware of the presence of the artist behind the work and the deliberate play of his devices. Shklovski himself took these techniques in part from Laurence Sterne, and employed them in his autobiography, called *A Sentimental Journey* (1923).

Shmelyov, Ivan Sergeyevich (1875-1950), a writer of the twentieth century. He left Russia after the Revolution of 1917, and has been a leading writer among the emigration. His tales and novels are predominantly realistic, but show extreme sensitivity and occasional symbolist overtones. *The Man from a Restaurant* (1912) is a humanitarian novel about a waiter, a little man, and his family troubles. *The Sun of the Dead* (1923), published abroad, describes the Bolshevik terror of the Civil War. *The Inexhaustible Cup* (1924) is the poetic tale of the painting of a wonder-working icon.

Sholokhov, Mikhail Alexandrovich (1905-   ), a leading Soviet novelist. Of mixed Cossack and peasant origin, he grew up among the Cossacks of the Don, and has made himself a regional novelist of their way of life. He was involved in the Civil War, though it is not certain whether he actually took part in fighting or not. Early in the 1920's he joined the Communist Party, serving in various minor clerical and technical capacities. He published his first book, the collection *Tales of the Don,* in 1925, followed the next year by *The Azure Steppe.* Both volumes deal with Cossack life during the Civil War and the early 1920's. In 1926 he began work on his masterpiece, *The Quiet Don* (1928-40) (English translation as "The Silent Don"), a long epic novel which was completed only some fourteen years later. He was compelled to interrupt it, however, while he worked on a Five-year Plan novel, *Virgin Soil Upturned* (1931; also known in English translation as "Seeds of Tomorrow"). His *Quiet Don* brought him tremendous popularity, and the work is the best-selling novel in the Soviet Union, where over 6,000,000 copies have been sold to date; it has been translated into around forty different languages in the U.S.S.R., as well as in over thirty countries abroad. In this country it was also a best-seller at the time of its appearance.

During World War II Sholokhov published some excerpts from an epic novel on the war entitled *They Fought for Their Country.* Great predictions were made for this novel in the Soviet press, but the author never completed it.

There is little doubt that Sholokhov's *Quiet Don* is the outstanding historical novel in Soviet literature, as well as the finest novel on the Civil War, and that its popularity with the reading public is to a large extent justified. Still, one must dispute the position of foremost Soviet writer given to Sholokhov by many critics in the Soviet Union and abroad. Sholokhov's work has, it is true, great objectivity and a broad grasp of the sweep of events. But it has certain defects, such as loose construction and incomplete character analysis. It is hardly so original in its treatment of the Civil War as are, say, the stories of BABEL.

The Quiet Don describes the life of the Don Cossacks during the First World War and the Civil War. The hero, Gregor Melekhov, a young Cossack, distinguishes himself in the World War; at the same time he is converted to Bolshevism. But, coming home after the war, he discovers that his family and friends advocate independence for the Cossack people. Gregor goes over to their side and joins the Whites. In the end, as the White cause becomes more and more hopeless, he fights simply out of despair, because it is wartime and there is nothing else to do; at the end of the war he fights for the Reds, too. He is a tragic figure, a born leader with a strong sense of justice who is deceived by the times in which he lives and the fact, which the novel clearly implies, in its objectivity, that the choice between the two sides is one of pragmatic logic rather than abstract justice. In the end Gregor is spiritually bankrupt; it is clear that as a former White he will be treated harshly, and it is not certain why he chooses to live or for what.

Sholokhov maintains an almost complete objectivity in the novel. The portrayal of Gregor is sympathetic; opposed to him is that of a heroic, if not entirely likable Red, Ivan Bunchuk. The novel was subjected to considerable attack by Soviet critics during the late 1920's and 1930's, but popular favor proved effective in its support, and today it is universally accepted as a classic. Its ideological difficulties may be bridged for Soviet critics by a simple piece of sleight-of-hand: Bunchuk becomes the novel's hero, and not Melekhov.

Sholokhov makes extensive use of certain of the methods of TOLSTOY's *War and Peace,* especially in his technique of shifting the scene from one group of characters to another. The novel's panoramic sweep of events and large number of characters justify comparison with Tolstoy's work. There are chapters which deal with historical events as such, and, indeed, these are considerably more objective than their parallels in Tolstoy's novel. Unlike Tolstoy, Sholokhov refrains from philosophizing about history.

Sholokhov's Five-year Plan novel, *Virgin Soil Upturned* (1931), fared better at the hands of the critics, who have proclaimed it one of the classics of SOCIALIST REALISM. It lacks much of the objectivity of *The Quiet Don,* however, and apparently it was an unwelcome interruption in Sholokhov's work on the larger novel; once the First Five-year Plan was over, he returned to *The Quiet Don* and left *Virgin Soil Upturned* uncompleted, though recently he has begun to publish a second volume.

The book describes the process of collectivization of the peasantry carried out during the First Five-year Plan. Though Sholokhov is not so objective here, the novel does give an excellent picture of the obstacles in the way of collectivization and the tragedies experienced by many peasants sent into exile or forced to join collective farms against their will.

Sholokhov has had considerable influence in Soviet literature. Along with FADEYEV, he introduced the methods of Tolstoyan realism to Soviet writers, methods which have become standard both in many of the historical novels of the 1930's and the war novels of the 1940's.

Shvartsman. See Schwarzman.

Sibiryak. See Mamin, D. N.

Simonov, Konstantin Mikhaylovich (1915-   ), Soviet poet, novelist and playwright. He was graduated from the Literary Institute of the Union of Soviet Writers in 1938. His earlier verse is mostly love poetry, of an unusually intimate character, but it also contains some poems on patriotic themes, such as his *Suvorov* (1939), in honor of the great Russian general. During World War II Simonov became the most popular Soviet lyric poet with such sentimental but effective war poems as *Wait for Me* and *Do You Remember the Roads of Smolensk?*

During the war Simonov was a newspaper correspondent. His novel, *Days and Nights* (1944), was perhaps the most popular Russian work of fiction on the war. It is an accurate picture of war, largely free from propaganda and with a good understanding of the psychology of men under fire. But it is spoiled by its conventional love story, and it must be said that it was considerably overrated at the time of its appearance. A new war novel, *Comrades in Arms* (1952), describes the undeclared war with Japan in Mongolia in 1939.

Simonov's plays are the weakest part of his work. *Russian People* (1942) is a war play which celebrates the heroism of average civilians in wartime. *The Russian Question* (1947) is an anti-American play, in which a liberal journalist is shown as selling out to the reactionary American press and consenting to write lies about the Soviet Union.

Simonov has also written film scenarios. Since the war his principal activity has been in journalism, and he has been editor of *The Literary Gazette.*

Sirin, Vladimir. See Nabokov, V. V.

Skavronski, A. See Danilevski, G. P.

Skaz, a Russian word designating a narrative told by a fictitious narrator, rather than by the author directly. The use of *skaz* narration creates the possibility of using speech forms which are more original and vivid than the style of ordinary narrative told from the author's point of view. Its use also creates the possibility of characterizing the fictitious narrator through speech peculiarities, such as dialect pronunciation or use of sub-standard expressions. These possibilities were exploited to the utmost by LESKOV, whose tales, most of which are told in *skaz*, abound in slang expressions, mispronunciations, invented words, etc. In the early part of the twentieth century the *skaz* manner was much used as a form of ORNAMENTALISM, and Leskov's influence was strong on such writers as REMIZOV, BABEL, ZOSHCHENKO and others.

Skazka. See Folk tales.

Skitalets. See Petrov, S. G.

Skobelev, Alexander Sergeyevich (1886-1923), a story writer of the early twentieth century who published under the pseudonym of Alexander Neverov. Of peasant origin, his tales were in the tradition of those of the nineteenth-century radical POPULISTS, and described the exploitation of the peasantry by other classes. After the Revolution he depicted the struggle between the poorer peasants and the *kulaks.* His best story, *Tashkent, the City of Bread* (1923), tells of a village boy's search for food during the famine of the early 1920's.

Skovoroda, Gregory. See Philosophy.

Slavonic. See Old Church Slavonic language.

Slavophiles, the members of a Russian intellectual movement which flourished in the 1840's, 1850's and 1860's. They held that Russia's strength lay in her indigenous cultural roots and in her adherence to tradition. They idealized her autocratic form of government, Orthodox religion, and patriarchal organization of peasant society. In the village commune, a form of peasant self-government (the significance of which they greatly exaggerated), the Slavophiles saw a warranty of true democracy and a bulwark against the possibility of a peasant revolution. They attacked Western Europe for its rationalism, materialism and for its form of parliamentary democracy, which they criticized, with some reason, as dominated by capitalist interests. In absolutism they saw the best guarantee

that the state would benefit all social classes. Anti-rationalists
and romantic idealists, they believed that the Russian Orthodox
Church and Russia's culture were infused with true spirituality
and deep feeling, rather than the materialism which, in their
view, dominated all phases of life in the West, even the supposedly spiritual. They were not opposed, however, to the introduction of Western technological progress, and conceded that
Russia would profit from the use of machine techniques in
agriculture and industry. But they were profoundly at variance
with the democratic and socialistic philosophy of the Russian
WESTERNERS, with whom they broke sharply in 1845.

As their name denotes, the Slavophiles were interested in the
non-Russian Slavic peoples, and their cultures. They advocated
the establishment of closer cultural relations among the Slavs, and
at times even looked forward to political union of all Slavs under
Russia. But they had no definite program for this; the Catholicism
of the Western Slavs was an ideological barrier which they could
not surmount. Russian domination of most of Poland also posed
an insoluble obstacle for them to Slavic unity.

Much of the intellectual energy of the Slavophiles was devoted
to the study of Russian ethnographical materials and Russian
antiquities. Some of the most important collections of Russian
folk songs were produced by Slavophile scholars, such as P. V.
Kireyevski and A. F. Gilferding. In the high evaluation which
they gave to Old Russian culture and Russian folk art, the Slavophiles were closer to the truth than such WESTERNERS as
BELINSKI, who underestimated Russia's older indigenous culture.

Although the Slavophiles accepted all three parts of the official
slogan, "Orthodoxy, Autocracy and Nationalism," they were
deeply opposed to the official policies of the government of Nicholas I, which persecuted them with almost the same severity with
which it treated the more radical Westerners. The Slavophiles
favored a continuation of the existing social organization of peasant life, but demanded that the serfs be liberated. They stood for
autocracy, but insisted that it be tempered by the force of public
opinion. Their Pan-Slavist attitudes were also in conflict with the
official attitude of legitimism, and the Russian government pre-

ferred to help maintain the Austro-Hungarian Empire rather than encourage the liberation of the other Slavic peoples.

Unorganized, the Slavophiles devoted much of their energies to journalism, though KHOMYAKOV, I. V. KIREYEVSKI and Y. F. SAMARIN, three of their leaders, were also outstanding as philosophers. Other leaders of the group were the brothers K. S. and I. S. AKSAKOV. A number of creative writers, such as YAZYKOV, TYUTCHEV, S. T. AKSAKOV and DAHL, were close to the Slavophiles.

In the 1860's the Slavophile groups fell apart. The liberation of the serfs and other REFORMS of the 1860's brought a partial fulfillment of their demands, while a number of their original leaders, such as Khomyakov and I. V. Kireyevski, were already dead. But the views of Slavophilism have remained alive even in the present century, influencing the platform of the Socialist Revolutionary Party as well as the so-called "SCYTHIANS." Slavophile tendencies can even be detected in the political program which Stalin opposed to Leninism.

Sleptsov, Vasili Alexeyevich (1836-78), a radical novelist of the 1860's. His chief subject is peasant life and its degradation. His use of peasant dialogue is faithful and at times highly amusing. *Hard Times* (1865), a short novel, is a satire on the liberals of the 1860's. As a radical writer, Sleptsov was satirized, in turn, by LESKOV in his anti-nihilist novel, *No Way Out*.

Slonimski, Mikhail Leonidovich (1897-   ), a Soviet writer. He was one of the initial group of members of the SERAPION BROTHERS in the early 1920's. His first stories, with their preference for grotesque fantasy, show the strong influence of ZAMYATIN, but he gradually changed over to psychological realism. His story, *Emery's Machine* (1923), attempts to depict an ideal Communist, whom Slonimski views, rather ambivalently, as a dreamer living in the future. His first novel, *The Lavrovs* (1926), portrays an intellectual who cannot find his place in Soviet society. Its sequel, *Foma Kleshnyov* (1931), shifts its focus to the portrayal of an ideal Communist, but is less successful. The earlier *Sredni Prospect* (1928) is a novel of intrigue and crime in the corrupt times of the New Economic Policy. The title refers to an actual street in Leningrad, but also has symbolic meaning ("The Middle Way"). *First Years* (1949) is a revision of *The Lavrovs* with an

attempt to correct the ideological "errors" of that work by shifting the emphasis from the "bourgeois" Revolution of February,
1917, to the Bolshevik Revolution in October of that year.

Slovo o polku Igoreve. See *Igor Tale.*

Sluchevski, Konstantin Konstantinovich (1837-1904), a poet of the
second half of the nineteenth century. A "pure" poet, Sluchevski's
early poetic endeavors of the 1850's and 1860's met with hostility
from the radical CIVIC CRITICS, and he deserted literature,
publishing again only in 1876. His poetry is metaphysical and his
prevailing mood personal and deeply pessimistic. Sluchevski is
perhaps the greatest Russian poet of the 1870's and 1880's,
but the period saw the low water mark in the development of
Russian verse, and his ideas are more striking than his verse is
eloquent.

Smidovich, Vikenti Vikentievich (1867-1945), a novelist of the end
of the nineteenth and the twentieth centuries, who published
under the pseudonym of Veresayev. As a radical, he belonged to
the group of writers who published with Gorki's press, *Znanie*
("knowledge"). He was a doctor, and his journal, *The Notebook
of a Physician* (1901), achieved great popularity as a record of
the life and trials of a medical man. His early stories are descriptions of the ideological development of the Russian radical intelligentsia. A Menshevik, Veresayev was appalled by the horror
of the Civil War, about which he wrote a novel called *In a Blind
Alley* (1923; English translation as "The Deadlock"), probably the
most impartial picture published of the conflict between the Reds
and the Whites. It chronicles the unceasing terror of successive
Red and White occupations of a city in Southern Russia, and the
refusal of an idealistic young girl, Katya, to accept either side.
Veresayev later became reconciled to the Soviet regime and was
restored to favor; his *In a Blind Alley* has since been forgotten,
and was omitted from the recent Soviet edition of his collected
works.

Smithy Poets, a group of proletarian poets of Moscow who seceded
in 1920 from the PROLETKULT; they included Vladimir KIRIL-
LOV, Vasili KAZIN, Alexey Gastev, Mikhail Gerasimov and
others. These young poets penned ecstatic hymns of praise to the
Revolution of 1917, to industrialization and the machine, and to
the working class. They favored free verse forms, which, in view

of the inadequacy of their poetic training, could hardly be distinguished from prose. From FUTURISM they inherited a tendency to crudity and modernity in their style and subjects. From SYMBOLISM they took certain cosmic images which they used to achieve grandiloquent effects and to celebrate the splendors of collectivism and industrialization. Parallel to the Moscow group of Smithy Poets were the Petersburg Cosmists.

Smolyatich, Kliment. See Kliment Smolyatich.

Sobol, Andrey Mikhaylovich (1888-1926), a twentieth-century story writer. A radical revolutionary, he was arrested after the Revolution of 1905 and sentenced to Siberian imprisonment, but escaped and fled the country; in 1915 he returned illegally and published his first novel, *Dust*, under the changed name of Andrey Sobol (his real first name was Yuli). Apparently disillusioned by the Revolution, he committed suicide in 1926. He is a realist who analyzes strange and abnormal personalities, and who was much influenced by DOSTOYEVSKI. The stories of his collection, *Wreckage* (1923), are psychological studies of those disappointed in the Revolution, whether they were Reds or Whites; other stories are characterizations of fantastic or grotesque personages, sometimes ending in suicide.

Social Democrats. See Lenin; Plekhanov; Revolution.

Socialist Realism, the name given to the doctrine current in Soviet art and literature since 1932, to a considerable degree obligatory for writers and artists in the Soviet Union today. Socialist Realism demands that art must be true to life, yet must depict some aspect of man's struggle toward socialist progress and a better life, regardless of the historical period depicted. For Soviet critics there is no contradiction in this insistence on both fidelity to life and progressive tendency, since for them the true meaning of life is expressed in human progress toward communism, and not in what they consider isolated facts of a negative character. Works of art must breathe a spirit of hope and optimism, at least for a better future. Their heroes must be positive in action, and capable of leadership. In literary practice the doctrine has brought the practical exclusion of other artistic techniques in favor of a superficial, photographic realism, and has resulted in the use of stereotyped black and write characters and in a frequently shallow sentimentalism. Similar effects have been experienced in the drama and film, while painting has been restricted to a narrow academic realism. Music, as a non-representational art, has been less affected, but an emphasis on the national and folk traditions, with a virtual taboo on "high-brow" and experimental music, has similarly been restrictive to free creation. (See Criticism, Soviet; *Ideynost, Partiynost, Narodnost.*)

Socialist Revolutionaries. See Populists; Revolution.

"Sociology, Vulgar." See Criticism, Soviet.

Sokhanskaya, Nadezhda Stepanovna (1825-84), a Russian writer of the mid-nineteenth century, who wrote under the pseudonym of Kokhanovskaya. A Slavophile (see Slavophiles), her tales idealize the life of the provincial gentry of her native province of Kharkov. Like the novels of S. T. AKSAKOV, her contemporary, much of her work is drawn from her personal reminiscences, though it is more romantic in spirit than Aksakov's.

Sollogub, Count Vladimir Alexandrovich (1814-82), a playwright and writer of tales of the mid-nineteenth century. Sollogub's stories are notable as early manifestations of realism; the most popular is his *Tarantas* (1845), a satirical description of a journey from Moscow to Kazan. The story contains much realistic description of provincial life, as well as a satire on the SLAVOPHILES. His plays include several vaudevilles.

Sologub, F. See Teternikov, F. K.

Solovyov, Vladimir Sergeyevich (1853-1900), a leading Russian philosopher, mystic and poet of the end of the nineteenth century. The son of S. M. Soloyov, a distinguished Russian historian, he grew up in a pious upper middle-class family. At the age of nine he experienced the first of three mystic visions of Sophia, the incarnation of Divine Wisdom, a being destined to play a significant role in his thought. He later described these visions in his long poem, *Three Meetings.* At the age of thirteen he became sceptical and materialistic, but later while a student at Moscow University he underwent a spiritual crisis which culminated in a deep and permanent faith. Completing the Faculty of History and Philosophy, he studied for a year at the Moscow Theological Academy and then became a lecturer at Moscow University. He made a trip to London in 1875 to do research at the British Museum, and from there, apparently summoned by Sophia, set out on a mysterious journey to Egypt; on the Egyptian desert he experienced his second mystic vision. Returning to Russia, he resumed his duties as a university lecturer. He made a public speech in 1881 in which he called on Alexander III to forgive the assassins of his father, Alexander II. As a result he was forced to resign from the university and to refrain from making public statements. The rest of his life he devoted to his writings.

Solovyov's religious thought is often complex and contradictory, and one critic has described him as the most enigmatic personality in all of Russian letters. He is, all the same, the greatest system builder (if not the most consistent) among Russian philosophers. Popularly viewed as a great "Orthodox" philosopher (with certain pro-Catholic leanings), he actually attempts the systematic unification of Christian theology with the tradition of German absolute idealism and with his own mystical experiences and study of the cabala. The result is a philosophy which is hardly Christian in the traditional sense, and which tends towards pantheism.

Solovyov's metaphysics begin with the postulation of the Absolute, the One who contains all things, including the cosmos. Following Schelling, he distinguishes a "first" and "second" Absolute; the second is the "Absolute in process of becoming," which gives rise to the world as such. The latter is imperfect, not because of any difference in its essence, but rather because of the separateness, conflict and disorder in which it finds itself. These deficiencies are the consequences of chaos, a principle contained in the Absolute Deity, which God wills into existence because of his love, and to which he gives freedom to develop. Solovyov's intuition of the dark nature of chaos and its role in the universe he owes in part to the poet TYUTCHEV; it finds vivid illustration in Solovyov's poetry. But the universe, though separated from God, strives to return to unity with Him. Human history is directed toward such a reunion, already achieved in the person of Christ. Solovyov's drive towards a metaphysics of "total unity" leads him to postulate a unified world-soul, though it, like the Absolute itself, tends toward the duality of divine principle and created being. He first identifies this world-soul, the collective spirit mediating between God and the plurality of living beings in the world, with Sophia, the Divine Wisdom. But later he distinguishes the two, and Sophia becomes the "universal substance" of God as well as the "rationale and end of creation." Sophia is the principle of unification and harmony of the fragmented universe, which will ultimately be revealed as the "Kingdom of God." For Solovyov, Sophia is a real and divine person, whom he thinks of as the "Eternal Feminine," and even as the "Mother of God," whose cult in Christianity he considers an intuition of the nature of Divine Wisdom. Though the concept of Sophia was perhaps not at the core of Solovyov's philosophy, it became central both for philosophers who followed him, such as FLORENSKI and S. N. BULGAKOV, and for the Symbolist poets, particularly BLOK. In Blok's early poetry Sophia, represented as a lovely maiden, is the mysterious principle of divine harmony in the universe.

Mankind, too, is for Solovyov a whole, a single "organism," contained in the world-soul. Solovyov's philosophy of man also emphasizes his drive for unity in his doctrine of androgynism: sensual love in man is a striving to create a "true human being" neither masculine nor feminine, but a union of both. Sexual love gives man an intuition, even a realization of Absolute Unity.

Solovyov opposed the Russian nationalistic and Pan-Slavic tendencies in the thought of those earlier Russian religious philosophers who had belonged to the SLAVOPHILES, and thus helped to lead Russian religious thought back to universalism. Like CHAADAYEV, he was critical of the Byzantine tradition in Russian culture. In formulating the idea of a universal Church, he tended towards Roman Catholicism. He dreamed of a theocratic universal state in which the absolute political power of the tsar would be joined with the religious authoritarianism of Rome. His pro-Catholic leanings brought him into opposition with the Russian Church, and several of his books, such as *La Russie et l'église universelle* (1889), which appeared in French, could not be published in Russia during his lifetime. But in the 1890's he abandoned his notion of a universal theocracy and moderated his pro-Catholic enthusiasm.

Solovyov's poetry is almost as important as his philosophy. His poetic manner, influenced by FET and TYUTCHEV, was highly personal, with intense mystical feeling. His subjects, such as the visions of Sophia, the eternal feminine, the cult of beauty, and the love lyrics addressed by him to Lake Saima, are mystical and philosophical. Though Solovyov parodied the early Symbolists, such as BALMONT and BRYUSOV, his own poetry was the chief precursor of Russian SYMBOLISM. His conception of Sophia, treated erotically, as well as his mysticism and his preoccupation with symbols, which were for him reality itself—all this served to inspire the later Symbolists, particularly Blok and Bely (see Bugayev). His most famous poem, *Three Meetings,* combines fervent mystical love and faith with an unexpected playful irreverence. Much of Solovyov's verse is humorous, even nonsense poetry as well as parody; his irony also was not without influence on the Symbolists. His letters are extremely witty, and he delights in puns and nonsensical allusions.

Solovyov's outstanding prose work, from a literary point of view, is his polemical *Three Conversations* (1900), a brilliant series of philosophical conversations on the necessity to find a synthesis of the modern conception of progress and active Christianity. In it he criticizes Lev TOLSTOY's doctrine of non-resistance to evil. *The History of Antichrist,* a curious supplement to the *Conversations,* is an apocalyptic vision of the coming of Antichrist, which Solovyov regarded as imminent, already presaged by the rise of Japan and China and the emergence of a "Yellow Peril." Solovyov seems to have believed quite literally in an Antichrist, after whose reign the Second Coming of Christ would redeem the world.

Solovyov, Vsevolod Sergeyevich (1849-1903), a historical novelist of the late nineteenth century, brother of the philosopher Vladimir SOLOVYOV. His novels, such as *Tsar-Devitsa* (1878) and *Exile* (1885), were extremely popular in his day, but lack either originality or profundity.

Songs, folk. See Folk songs.

Soviet Criticism. See Criticism, Soviet.

Soviet Literature. See Literature, Soviet.

Soviet Writers, Union of. See Union.

Stalin, Iosif Visarionovich (political pseudonym of I. V. Dzhugashvili, 1879-1953), a Soviet political leader. Of Georgian nationality, he attended theological seminary at Tiflis, where he joined the Social Democratic (Marxist) Party. In 1899 he was expelled from the seminary for radical activity. He became a professional revolutionary, and spent most of his life before 1917 in the underground. Five times he was arrested by the tsarist police and five times he escaped. In 1912 he founded *Pravda,* later the official newspaper of the Communist Party. Exiled to Siberia in 1913, he returned to Petrograd in 1917 and, after the October Revolution, was made Soviet people's commissar for nationalities. In 1922 he was elected general secretary of the Communist Party, a position which gave him great power in his struggle with TROTSKI. When Trotski was removed from power in 1925, and in 1927 expelled from the Party, along with Zinoviev and Kamenev, Stalin was left as unchallenged leader both of the Party and of the Soviet government. In general Stalin's policies represented a repudiation of Marxist internationalism and a determination to build a strong conservative socialist order in one country—the Soviet Union. The theoretical communist goal of the Soviet regime was abandoned indefinitely under his leadership, which thus constituted a shift to the right in Soviet policies.

Soviet scholars have been at great pains to demonstrate Stalin's influence in the field of literature, though his interest in belles-lettres and his contribution to Soviet literary theory were almost negligible. On rare occasions he was responsible for a literary evaluation or criticism, such as his statement that MAYAKOVSKI was the greatest Soviet poet; it is hard to know whether such judgments represent his own opinions or not. His dictum that proletarian culture should be national in form, socialist in content, has been taken as one of the primary principles in the theory of SOCIALIST REALISM, but it is difficult to see what, exactly, it implies. To Stalin is also attributed the much-quoted if rather banal observation that "Writers are engineers of men's minds."

Stalin's personal intervention in the linguistic controversy of 1950 acted to free the science of linguistics from the domination of fantastic and dogmatic theories. His pronouncements (whether original or not) in effect removed language from the area of the class struggle and made it the common property of all classes of a given nation; the same distinction, realized for literature, might well have permitted literature to develop outside the narrow bounds of the dogma of SOCIALIST REALISM. But, though the linguistic controversy was followed by greater freedom in literary criticism, and in particular by a return to the study of problems of stylistics, no new freedom resulted for writers. Only with the death of Stalin in 1953 has there been some easing of controls in

literature, and in particular the beginnings of interest in the treatment of realistic psychology. In 1956 efforts were begun by responsible Soviet circles to discredit him completely.

Stanislavski, Konstantin. See Drama and Theater.

Stankevich, Nikolay Vladimirovich (1813-40), a philosopher of the
1830's. Though not himself a writer, he exercised great influence
on Russian thought through the philosophical circle which he
founded. He was active in introducing German idealist philosophy in Russia, and in stimulating the development of a Russian
romantic idealism, characteristic for the 1840's. His influence was
important for the Russian WESTERNERS, including BELINSKI
and GRANOVSKI.

Stanyukovich, Konstantin Mikhaylovich (1843-1903), a novelist of
the late nineteenth century and adherent of the POPULISTS.
His tendentious social novels are forgotten, but he is remembered
for his series of entertaining *Sea Stories,* published in the late
1880's and 1890's, unique as pictures of Russian naval life.

Stefanyk, Vasil (1871-1936), a leading Galician Ukrainian writer
(see Preface).

Stepnyak, S. See Kravchinski, S. M.

Strakhov, Nikolay Nikolayevich (1828-96), a publicist, thinker and
critic of the second half of the nineteenth century. He was co-
editor of DOSTOYEVSKI's journal, *Time* (1861-63), and was the
close friend and correspondent of TOLSTOY. A follower of
APOLLON GRIGORIEV, Strakhov defended those elements of
Russian culture which were traditional and indigenous against
the influence of the West, which he described in his major work,
The Struggle with the West in Russian Literature (1882), as
"nihilistic" and harmful for Russia. Like DANILEVSKI, whose
disciple he was, Strakhov was an enemy of the Darwinian theory
of evolution, and struggled for some thirty years to refute it.

Struve, Pyotr Berngardovich (1870-1944), a Russian economist and
political philosopher of the late nineteenth and early twentieth
century. Struve began as a Marxist philosopher, attacking the
POPULISTS for their emphasis on agriculture in the Russian
economy, and concluding that Russia would follow the same path
of industrialization as Western Europe. But he soon became critical of Marxism and called for a reappraisal of Marx's theories and
a modification in the direction of greater liberalism. Going abroad,

Struve founded the journal *Liberation,* around which the nucleus of the later Constitutional Democratic (Cadet) Party, the leading moderate liberal party in Russia, grew up. Returning to Russia in 1905, Struve became a leader of the liberal movement, editor of the journal *Russian Thought* and an important contributor to *Signposts* (1909), a collection of essays which criticized the Russian intelligentsia, and especially the radicals, as anti-religious and anti-nationalist. After 1917 Struve joined the Whites; on the collapse of the White forces he emigrated, publishing anti-Bolshevik journals in Paris and Prague. He was the outstanding political thinker among the Russian émigrés.

Stukalov, Nikolay Fyodorovich (1900-), a leading Soviet playwright who writes under the pseudonym of Nikolay Pogodin. His play *Tempo* (1930) is a Five-year Plan drama about the necessity for speed in the construction of a Stalingrad tractor factory. Workers who seek to delay tempos are finally won over, partly by the sympathetic interest of an American engineer. *Poem about an Axe* (1931) describes the discovery of a stainless steel for use in axes. *Snow* (1932) shows the transformation of delinquents into good Soviet citizens after their exposure to the cold and snow of the Caucasus Mountains. *The Aristocrats* (1934) was the author's most successful play. It depicts the regeneration of criminals, prostitutes and *kulaks* (well-to-do peasants) in a forced labor camp in North Russia; they are employed in the construction of the Baltic-White Sea Canal. This subject is treated with considerable humor. In *Man with a Gun* (1937) and *The Kremlin Chimes* (1941), Pogodin attempted to present a sympathetic and popular portrait of Lenin.

During the war Pogodin wrote *The Boatwomen* (1943), about the courageous women who ran the ferry at Stalingrad while the city was under siege. A recent play, *When the Spears Are Broken* (1953), attacks conservativism in Soviet science.

Sukhovo-Kobylin, Alexander Vasilievich (1817-1903), a leading playwright of the second half of the nineteenth century. A wealthy nobleman, he was interested in German philosophy, and translated Hegel into Russian. His work for the stage, comprising three comedies, he considered of lesser importance. In 1850 he was arrested, accused of the murder of his French mistress. The case dragged on for some seven years before he was finally acquitted. For a time he was in prison, where he wrote his first play. His dealings with the world of judicial officials inspired in him a profound hatred for bureaucracy which he expressed in his latter two plays.

Sukhovo-Kobylin's three plays form a dramatic trilogy, in which certain of the characters appear in several plays. *Krechinski's Wedding* (1855) is a light comedy of intrigue, in the French manner. The play contrasts the clever adventurer, Krechinski, with the old-fashioned and stupid family of provincial gentry into which he almost succeeds in marrying. It is one of the most popular comedies in the Russian repertory.

The last two plays are more pessimistic, and depict the incompetence, greed and dishonesty of the world of officials. *The Affair* (1869) tells how an honest landowner is exploited and robbed by rapacious officials into whose hands he falls. The final play, *The Death of Tarelkin* (1869), is the gloomiest of the three, though the author ironically described it as a "comedy-joke." The play has, indeed, elements of the style of vaudeville and buffonade, and of a grotesque hyperbole and caricature, which Sukhovo-Kobylin learned in part from GOGOL, and which is as often macabre as amusing. The play depicts the ironic fate of an official who pretends to be dead in order to swindle his superior and escape his creditors. Like Gogol's *Inspector-General, The Death of Tarelkin* contains not a single positive character.

Sumarokov, Alexander Petrovich (1718-77), one of the leading Russian writers of the eighteenth century. Of noble descent, Sumarokov was educated at the Cadet School in Petersburg, where he began to write verses according to the models of contemporary French poetry and of TREDIAKOVSKI. His first tragedy, *Khorev* (1747), was acted by the cadets, and made his reputation. In 1756 he was named director of the first permanent Russian court theater (see Theater). For this theater he wrote eight more tragedies, twelve comedies, and two operas. He was also active as a journalist, and is sometimes described as the first Russian professional writer. His position was insecure, however, and he frequently complained of lack of official and public support, and of excessive censorship. A supporter of the new empress, CATHERINE THE GREAT (1762-96), he early lost favor with her because of his liberalism. In 1769 he retired to live in Moscow, where, neglected, he died an inveterate drunkard.

Sumarokov is most famous for his plays, which, however, seem imitative and crudely rhetorical today. Many of his subjects are taken from Russian history or legend, but there is little that is "Russian" about them. The tragedies are modelled on Racine and Shakespeare; the comedies on Molière. He first introduced the classical unities into Russian drama. His tragedies are unusual in that most of them have happy endings; this is true even of his adaptation of Shakespeare's *Hamlet* (1748). More alive are his comedies, for the looser classical standards of comedy allowed him to introduce real Russian characters and colloquial speech.

Sumarokov cultivated most of the classical genres (see Classicism) except the serious ode. He wrote comic odes, fables, satires, idyls, elegies, songs, madrigals, etc.; his vanity was pleased when others referred to him as the Russian "Racine," "Molière," or "La Fontaine." His fables are frequently witty attacks on government officials; one, the *Chorus to a Perverse World* (written 1762) is a bold attack on serfdom. Best, probably, are his lyrics, many of which, though conventional, are still effective. Sumarokov was undoubtedly the most gifted Russian innovator in poetic rhythm of the entire eighteenth century. Besides a freer, folk-like verse, he introduced complex classical meters, such as Sapphic verse.

Sumarokov somewhat modified the arbitrary three styles of LOMONOSOV, avoiding especially the high style. In his criticism he opposed the sentimental drama and novel which were developing in his day.

In the nineteenth century Sumarokov lost favor, and was regarded as an untalented hack. Today it is clear, however, that he not only deserves a high place in the history of Russian literature as an innovator, but that his work represents a substantial advance in naturalness and stylistic purity over the writers who preceded him.

Superfluous man (Russian *lishni chelovek),* the name given to an important character type recurrent in nineteenth-century Russian literature. The term denotes a hero who is sensitive to social and ethical problems, but who fails to act, partly because of personal weakness, partly because of political and social restraints on his freedom of action. The term "superfluous" was first used in this sense by PUSHKIN to describe his hero, Eugene Onegin, and was popularized by TURGENEV in the title of his story, *The Diary of a Superfluous Man* (1850). But it was the critic DOBROLYUBOV who first realized the social as well as literary significance of the type.

The first important example of this type of character is PUSHKIN'S Onegin (*Eugene Onegin*, 1823-31). Conceived in the likeness of Byron's Childe Harold as a wealthy, spoiled young aristocrat who is bored by the society about him, Onegin is nevertheless a typical product of reactionary Russian social conditions of the period, which provided little opportunity for a sensitive and intelligent young nobleman to devote himself to a constructive career. A second prototype of the superfluous man is GRIBOYE-DOV's Chatski (*Woe from Wit*, 1825), influenced by Molière's *Le Misanthrope*. Chatski is more idealistic than Onegin; he reacts more strongly when he discovers the stupidity and purposelessness of the society around him. But in the end he does no more than withdraw from society.

A third example, influenced by Pushkin's Onegin as well as directly by Byron, is LERMONTOV's Pechorin (*A Hero of Our Times*, 1840). Pechorin is the Byronic type conceived as so alienated from society that he becomes a danger to it. Pechorin revenges himself on those whom he meets by hostility, contempt, deceit and even violence.

With the advent of Russian literary REALISM, the superfluous man lost much of his romantic Byronism, and developed a more clearly political significance, though writers were still forced by the CENSORSHIP to veil their meanings. The problem of the superfluous man now centered more clearly about the failure of the Russian liberal intelligentsia to bring about reforms. The answer is found partly in the personality of the Russian liberal, partly in the reactionary conditions of Russian life. This type appears in most of the novels of TURGENEV; the most striking example is his Rudin (*Rudin*, 1856). Trained in German idealistic philosophy, Rudin dreams of bringing enlightenment and reform to Russia. In the end, however, his project for widening a river (obviously a symbol used to veil political activity which the censor would not have permitted Turgenev to describe) fails because of insufficient technical skill and lack of faith in himself. In the end Rudin dies uselessly, if bravely, on the barricades of Paris in 1848.

The most penetrating example of the type, perhaps, is the character of GONCHAROV's Oblomov (*Oblomov*, 1859). Oblomov is a young idealist who cannot reconcile his career in the reactionary and dishonest government service with his utopian dreams of happiness; he loses interest in friendship and love because of similar conflicts. In the end he ceases to act, and spends most of his time in bed. Goncharov traces his lack of will power back to his childhood on an estate, where he was fondled and petted by his family, and prevented by a horde of servants from doing anything for himself. In this almost Oriental system of upbringing Goncharov discovers the root of the Russian liberal nobility's inaction. In the novels of Turgenev and Goncharov the radical critics CHERNYSHEVSKI and DOBROLYUBOV found proofs that the Russian nobility was incapable of leading any reform movement.

After Goncharov the type continued, but more as a kind of literary cliché than a fresh sociological discovery. The work of DOSTOYEVSKI and TOLSTOY contains examples of superfluous men (e.g., Count Vronski in Tolstoy's *Anna Karenina)*, but these writers were chiefly interested in other problems of character. CHEKHOV, in his stories and plays, presents us with many examples of the type; in the fin-de-siècle mood of his period, with its enfeebled aristocracy and disillusioned and disaffected intelligentsia, the superfluous man acquired a new social setting.

The superfluous man is found in the literature of the 1920's, in which he is portrayed as an intellectual who has difficulty in adapting himself to the new conditions of Soviet life. But after the introduction of the artistic doctrine of SOCIALIST REALISM in 1932, the superfluous man disappeared as a hero in literature, since Soviet writers are now required to create positive heroes.

The heroines opposed to the superfluous men are surprising contrasts in their strength, resoluteness and ability to act. Especially striking are Tatyana in PUSHKIN's *Eugene Onegin* and Natalya in TURGENEV's *Rudin*. It is difficult to say to what extent this strong feminine type reflects the reality of nineteenth-century Russian life, and to what extent it is merely a typical literary opposition.

Surkov, Alexey Alexandrovich (1899-), Soviet poet. He began to publish poetry in 1930, but came to prominence only during World War II, when he produced many war poems. Surkov's war poetry is stern, heroic and unsentimental, and calls for ruthless revenge against the invader. His recent collection, *Peace for the World* (1950), attacks Western "warmongers."

Suvorin, Alexey Sergeyevich (1834-1912), a conservative publisher, journalist and playwright of the end of the nineteenth and early twentieth century. He is best remembered as CHEKHOV's publisher, and the recipient of some of Chekhov's finest letters on literature.

Symbolism, the leading movement in Russian literature, especially in poetry, from about 1894 to 1910. Its beginning as a conscious (and highly self-conscious) movement may be found in the publication in 1894 of the almanac called *Russian Symbolists*, containing poems by Valeri BRYUSOV and other poets. But Russian Symbolism had many diverse sources and beginnings.

In its day Symbolism was a modernist, avant-garde movement which had its parallel in many other Russian arts of the period, particularly in painting, music and the ballet. In common with these Symbolism had an estheticist conception of art for art's sake, an interest in the mysterious and exotic, and an impressionism of manner and technique. Like the French poet Verlaine, the Russian symbolists tended to liken poetry to music, and Russian poetry reached a new height of musicality during this period.

Though Russian Symbolism differs in character from its French prototype, still it was French Symbolism which influenced the formation of a Russian symbolist "school" as such, and which gave the Russian symbolists certain new technical means and an expanded poetic vocabulary. MEREZHKOVSKI, BALMONT and BRYUSOV were especially influenced by the French Parnassian and Symbolist poets, with the result that their poetry, in spite of its external brilliance, sometimes falls short of being characteristically Russian in tone.

Besides French Symbolism, there were important indigenous roots. LERMONTOV, DOSTOYEVSKI, TYUTCHEV, FET and GRIGORIEV were older writers whose influence was felt. But the most important precursor of Russian Symbolism was the philosopher-poet Vladimir SOLOVYOV, whose mystical worship of Sophia, the incarnation of Divine Wisdom, was taken over by BLOK, Bely (see Bugayev) and others. The themes and the technique of Solovyov's verse, with its ecstatic quality, were also influential. Most significant: Soloyov's poetry is the first contemporary embodiment of the Symbolist philosophical belief that the world is a system of symbols which express the existence of inexpressible, abstract metaphysical realities. In this sense Russian symbolism was more philosophical in content than French Symbolism, and more closely associated with mystical religion.

Nor were the Sophiological conceptions of Solovyov the only religious current of influence during the Symbolist Movement. MEREZHKOVSKI, his wife Zinaida HIPPIUS, and Minski (see Vilenkin) were active in the foundation of the Religious and Philosophical Society, and sought to stimulate religious enthusiasm among the intelligentsia. Vyacheslav IVANOV and his circle were interested in the creation of new religious myths in literature. Both Merezhkovski and Ivanov sought to formulate a religious and philosophical synthesis of Greek classical and Christian ideas.

Not all the symbolists, however, were concerned with religious ideas. Poets like BRYUSOV were primarily estheticists, interested in finding word symbols which could be used connotatively or evocatively on many levels of significance. In the poetry of BALMONT words are used largely for sound effect, and sense may even be sacrificed to sound. On the other hand, Fyodor Sologub (see Teternikov) employed symbols to expound a personal philosophy which is a kind of inverted religion, a cult of Satanism and Manichean dualism.

The members of the first generation of Russian symbolists were called "decadents" by the public of the day. They included MEREZHKOVSKI, Minski (see Vilenkin), BALMONT, BRYUSOV, HIPPIUS and Sologub (see Teternikov). Only with the younger generation, with Vyacheslav IVANOV, and especially BLOK and Bely (see Bugayev), was the term "symbolist" employed; later it was applied to the entire movement, not with complete accuracy, however, since not all poets of the movement made systematic use of symbols.

Besides making their verse more musical, the symbolists enriched the technique of poetry in other ways. Free verse was introduced from France, but the French type of *vers libre* had limited success in Russian poetry. More effective were freer patterns of verse developed from older verse forms, and particularly the characteristically Russian folk-inspired form, the *dolnik*, with its irregular number of syllables (see Prosody). It was re-introduced into serious poetry by HIPPIUS, and was later much used by BLOK.

In prose the symbolists were less successful, and never actually found the proper form for a great prose literature. The novels of MEREZHKOVSKI suffer from the schematic quality of their ideas. More successful are the tales of BRYUSOV, full of the erotic, fantastic and the morbid. A special place is occupied by the fairy tales and fables of Sologub (see Teternikov), which have a certain philosophic significance. Richer artistically, though less perfect, are Sologub's novels, which represent unsuccessful combinations of realist and symbolist styles. ANDREYEV's later works, particularly his plays, are popularizations of Symbolism, quite lacking in profundity. The prose works of Bely (see Bugayev) and REMIZOV, with their complex style and variety of compositional and semantic levels, are actually closer to Expressionism than to Symbolism.

Bohemianism and a flight to escape from normal, active social life were important traits of Symbolism. The symbolists were little concerned with political ideas as such. True, the REVOLUTION of 1905 did find many of them on the side of the socialist radicals. But the failure of the revolutionary movement in 1905 disillusioned them, and most of them gave up politics for good, to cultivate new mystical interests or to escape into eroticism or personal fantasy. BLOK and Bely (see Bugayev) continued, however, as radicals, but their eventual acceptance of the Bolshevik Revolution of 1917 was attained from highly personal and mystical reasons.

T

Tairov, Alexander. See Drama and Theater.

Tales, folk. See Folk Tales.

Tartar Yoke, Literature of the. See Literature, Old Russian.

Tatishchev, Vasili Nikitich (1686-1750), author of the first modern *History of Russia,* in which he consolidated scattered materials found in the Russian CHRONICLES and foreign sources dealing with Russia. In scholarship his work is comparable to the best European histories of the day.

Teffi. See Buchinskaya, N. A.

Teleshov, Nikolay Dmitrievich (1867-1945), a writer of the end of the nineteenth and early twentieth century. He published with Gorki's press, *Znanie* ("knowledge"), and in 1898 helped to organize a literary circle which included Gorki (see Peshkov), BUNIN, Serafimovich (see Popov) and others. A radical writer, Teleshov wrote sketches and stories of peasant life and of the life of exiles in Siberia. After the Revolution of 1917 he remained in the Soviet Union, and published his reminiscences of such writers as CHEKHOV, Gorki and ANDREYEV.

Terpigorev, Sergey Nikolayevich (1841-95), a rural novelist of the late nineteenth century, who wrote under the pen-name of Sergey Atava. His best-known novel, *Impoverishment* (1880), portrays the breakdown of the landowning class.

Teternikov, Fyodor Kuzmich (1863-1927), a leading symbolist, who wrote under the pseudonym of Fyodor Sologub. The son of a shoemaker and a domestic servant, he was educated at a teachers' college and became a high-school teacher, later a district inspector of schools, a career which he found tedious and hateful. He published his first volumes—both of prose and of verse—only in 1896, after he had been writing for a number of years. The popular success of his novel, *The Little Demon* (1907), enabled him to retire from teaching and devote himself entirely to literature. He was hostile to the Bolsheviks, but his attempts to secure permission to emigrate failed, and he remained in the Soviet Union until his death. He published nothing after 1922.

Sologub's thought is decadent; with him escapism is elevated to the level of a philosophy. His view of the world is dualistic and Manichean. The real world, created by God, is evil and ugly. Nothing can make this world better; man's only escape is to retreat into a world of dreams and illusions which he can create for himself in imagination and art. Thus only can he escape from the real world of vulgarity and banality to a private world of unity, harmony and peace. To symbolize this duality Sologub invokes the image of the fair Dulcinea in *Don Quixote,* who turns out in his play, *The Victory of Death,* to be the evil and graceless Aldonsa; just so real life, which we make the object of our ideals and attempt to improve, is unworthy of us. Sologub goes on to a kind of Satanism: the world of beauty and harmony is the creation of Satan, not God. Night and death are aspects of this Satanic realm of beauty and eternal peace, while the world of the day and of the sun, the "flaming dragon," is evil.

Along with Sologub's Manicheanism goes a perverse sensuality. Beauty for him is the essence of the inner spiritual world of imagination, which is our only salvation. But beauty is also the object of sensual desire, which leads us away from peace and death and back into life. Sologub's dual attitude toward desire doubtless proceeds in part from his own abnormalities: his work shows a sexual fixation directed toward children as well as a foot fetish (images of naked feet continually recur in his work). One could forgive him such eccentricities, which are not in the slightest degree corrupting, save that they often mar the power of his work.

Sologub's poetry is the highest achievement of symbolist verse before BLOK. His form is conventional, his diction classically pure and restrained, and his symbols exotic but used with precision and freedom from obscurity. It is the content of his poetry, rather than its form, which is so original and disturbing.

Sologub's verse is more balanced and classic than his prose, but it is the latter which has made his fame. His first novel, *Bad Dreams* (1896), is autobiographical, based on his life as a school teacher, gloomy, morbid and pessimistic. His greatest novel, *The Little Demon* (1907), is memorable for its portrayal of a Russian provincial town, with its vulgarity, banality and petty malice—in the novel a symbol of Sologub's real world of evil. The name of the central character, Peredonov, became proverbial in Russian to denote paranoid evil: spite, hypocrisy, malice and envy. A sadistic schoolmaster, he visits his pupils in the evenings to try to discover some pretext for beating them, befouls the walls of his apartment to spite his landlady, and steals from his own cook to find an excuse for abusing her. In the end his evil compulsions drive him mad, and he becomes the victim of a persecution complex. Pursued by a demon, a small, furry animal, the *Nedotykomka* ("unpierceable"), the symbol of his own evil, he goes mad, commits arson and murder, and is shut up in an asylum.

Opposed to the gloom of Peredonov's world is the world of the young and beautiful schoolboy, Sasha, a symbol of the world of joy and happiness. But the figure of Sasha is also introduced to gratify the writer's sensuality: the perverse Lyudmila dresses him in girls' clothing and induces him to impersonate a woman in a beauty contest; Sasha wins the contest but is almost killed by the envious women of the town. Thus the author points to the corruptibility of beauty through sensuality and contact with the world of real life. The Sasha-Lyudmila episode, though intended as a contrast to the evil of Peredonov's life, is a failure. Even more unsuccessful were the visions which Sologub elaborates in his later, more fantastic trilogy, *The Created Legend* (1908-12). In the first part the tension between realism and the author's fantasies is too strong; it is difficult to imagine the enchanter Trirodov, Sologub's Prospero-like hero, against the background of reactionary Russia in 1905. The last two parts of the work have a fantastic setting in fictitious islands in the Mediterranean.

Sologub's many stories concern themes similar to the novels. Some are fantastic fairy tales; others are more realistic and gloomy. A special place is occupied by his witty and ironic fables, some of which have great philosophical subtlety.

Sologub wrote several plays, the best of which is *Vanka the Steward and the Page Jean*, based on a well-known Russian folk ballad about a servant who becomes the lover of a princess. Sologub's play is arranged in two series of parallel scenes, which describe the affair as it might have taken place in medieval France, under the code of chivalry, and in Old Russia. The point of the play is the contrast of Russian crudeness and lack of culture with French refinement and superficial politeness.

Theater. See Drama and Theater.

Theophan Prokopovich. See Feofan Prokopovich.

Tikhonov, Nikolay Semyonovich (1896-   ), a Soviet poet and novelist. He fought in both the World War and on the Red side in the Civil War. War, with its pathos, violence and heroism, became the favorite subject of his poetry and prose. In 1921 he joined the SERAPION BROTHERS, and his first collection of poems, *The Horde*, appeared in 1922. Tikhonov's poetry shows the strong influence of the Acmeist poets (see Acmeism) in his preference for substantives and for clear, precise, concrete imagery.

In later poems, such as those of the collection, *The Quest for a Hero* (1924), Tikhonov develops an obscure style in which he uses modernist stylistic devices, invented expressions and complex rhymes characteristic of the Futurist poets (see Futurism), especially of KHLEBNIKOV and PASTERNAK. But this was a passing phase in his work. He also develops a new ballad form for the narration of tales of Soviet contemporary life.

Tikhonov's collection, *The Shade of a Friend*, published in 1936, contains his impressions and reflections of Europe on the eve of the Second World War. His poems which appeared during the war, as well as his *Leningrad Tales* (1943), depict the defense of Leningrad as observed by the writer himself, in the city during the siege. His recent collection, entitled *At the Second World Peace Conference* (1951), attacks Western "warmongers."

Tikhonov's prose is less concrete and more fantastic than his clear, sharply visual, almost realistic poetry. War and its threat to civilization is again the chief subject, as in the novel called *War* (1931). Others of his tales are more romantic, picturesque and fantastic, as are those set in the Caucasus.

In 1946 Tikhonov was removed from his post of President of the Union of Soviet Writers, which he had held since 1944. This demotion, a part of the ZHDANOV purges, does not seem to have been intended as an attack either on his writing or on himself; rather one must suppose that it was designed to emphasize the new, stricter policy in literature.

Tobilevich, Ivan (1845-1907), a leading Ukrainian actor and playwright (see Preface).

Tolstoy, Count Alexey Konstantinovich (1817-75), a leading poet, playwright and novelist of the mid-nineteenth century. Of noble birth, he was a distant cousin of LEV TOLSTOY. The childhood friend of the future Emperor Alexander II, he might have made a brilliant career at court, where he served as aide-de-camp and later master of the hunt to Alexander. But he was independent of spirit and more liberal than the emperor, and freely expressed in his writings his dissatisfaction with tsarist absolutism. He idealized early Russian history as a time of relative freedom; the Muscovite period, in his opinion, had corrupted Russia's indigenous spirit of liberty.

Tolstoy entered literature in 1841 with a fantastic horror story, *The Vampire*. In 1850 he and his three cousins, the Brothers ZHEMCHUZHNIKOV, began to publish nonsense poetry, first anonymously, and after 1854 under the collective pseudonym of KOZMA PRUTKOV. The "writings" of this fictitious author are classics of Russian humor, satire and parody (see Prutkov). In 1850 Tolstoy also began to publish lyric poetry under his own name. His lyrics are extremely varied, and include pictures of nature, charming love poems, poems as serious as his majestic paraphrase of St. John Damascene's prayer for the dead (1858), light humorous verse, and keen and witty satires on bureaucracy and tyranny. His poetry excels in its joy, vitality and love of life, in the harmony of its optimistic vision. Though some of his love lyrics tend to lapse into sentimentality, and though his poetic technique, like that of his contemporaries, is not always perfect, Tolstoy is still one of the very few poets of his day who wrote successfully in a grand style and possessed complete mastery of the language. Many of his poems have been set to music; indeed, he is close to being the most prolific Russian writer of verses which have inspired art songs.

A special place in Tolstoy's work is occupied by his many ballads. Some are free adaptations of subjects taken from the Russian epic folk songs (see *Byliny*); in these he emphasized the free and independent spirit of the epic folk heroes, the legendary *bogatyrs*, as contrasted to the tyrannical despotism of the sovereign. Others, such as his *Vasili Shibanov* (1858) and *Prince Mik-*

haylo Repnin, idealize the heroic actions of figures in Russian history. Still others, such as *The Dream of Popov* (1874), ridicule the bureaucracy and political opportunism of contemporary times. Tolstoy's comic *History of the Russian State* (1868) is a brilliant satire on tsarist absolutism and the constant search to establish tyrannical "order," evoking the poet's ironic refrain of "Still order did not come." Besides the ballads Tolstoy has several long narrative poems, such as *The Portrait* (1874), the romantic and partly humorous tale of the love of a young poet for the portrait of a beautiful lady.

Tolstoy also published a historical novel, *The Silver Prince* (1863). In the style of Scott, it contrasts the nobility and freedom of spirit of its hero, an idealistic and chivalrous nobleman, to the tyranny and sadistic cruelty of Tsar Ivan the Terrible. In spite of its simplified treatment of history, it is an absorbing narrative, and has been a favorite historical novel with younger readers.

Tolstoy wrote three historical dramas in blank verse, which form a trilogy dealing with the troubled times following the reign of Ivan the Terrible: *The Death of Ivan the Terrible* (1866), *Tsar Fyodor Ioannovich* (1868), and *Tsar Boris* (1870). Though hardly worthy of comparison with Shakespeare's chronicle plays, their ultimate model, they are intelligent and sensitive works, probably the best Russian dramas in the genre. In stageworthiness they far surpass PUSHKIN'S *Boris Godunov,* their Russian prototype. Most striking in them is the treatment of character, and in the hero of the second play, Tsar Fyodor, saintly but too weak to rule, Tolstoy has created a character of universal significance.

Tolstoy, Alexey Nikolayevich (1883-1945), a leading Soviet writer. An aristocrat by birth, he inherited the title of count, and was a distant relative of Lev TOLSTOY. He studied engineering at the St. Petersburg Technological Institute. His admiration for symbolist poetry inspired him to write, and he began with both prose and poetry, publishing a collection of lyrics in 1907. He later destroyed the collection himself. During the First World War he served as a war correspondent. Although he had belonged to the Social Democratic (Marxist) Party in 1905, he opposed the Bolsheviks in 1917, and served on the propaganda staff of Denikin's White Army. He emigrated in 1919, going to Paris and then to Berlin. In 1923 he returned to the Soviet Union; his reasons for this change of heart seem to have been somewhat opportunistic. In the Soviet Union Tolstoy was hailed as a leading writer, though he had to bear the attacks of other writers and critics suspicious of his aristocratic origin. His books were tremendously popular, however; with Sholokhov he was probably the most widely read novelist of the late 1930's and the early 1940's. He enjoyed a huge income, much of which he spent in extravagant living; his way of life continued to resemble that of an aristocrat even under the Soviets.

As a writer Tolstoy possessed great talents, but no great intellectual depth. His style, with its purity and clarity, is excellent, and he is a good narrator, a rare quality among Russian writers, with a vivid feeling for life and a lively enjoyment of it. But his characters sometimes lack clarity, and he fails whenever he attempts to employ ideological themes.

Tolstoy's early stories, such as those of the collection *Eccentrics* (1910), depict the decay of the life of the provincial gentry. His landowners are debauched idlers and cranks; they are colorful, vigorous and full of life.

Abroad Tolstoy wrote a vivid narrative based on his own boyhood, *Nikita's Childhood* (1921). There, in 1921, he also completed the first volume of his most important novel, *Way Through Hell* (English translation as "Road to Calvary"), in which he sought to depict Russian life during the World War, Revolution and Civil War. This first volume of the work, with its description of Russian intellectual life and the wild atmosphere of decadent experimentalism in art during the war period, particularly in FUTURISM, is the most entertaining and successful of the three.

Returning to the Soviet Union, Tolstoy had difficulty in adjusting himself to the requirements of Soviet literature, and his first novels are awkward attempts to conform to new demands; at the same time they attempt a sensational style. Thus, *Aelita* (1924) is a scientific fantasy in which a Soviet expedition flies to Mars and undertakes to start a social revolution there. Several other fantastic romances followed. *Engineer Garin's Hyperboloid* (1925-26; English translation as "The Death Box") is a frightening picture of a totalitarian order which the inventor of a death ray seeks to organize and force upon human society.

Tolstoy's masterpiece, the trilogy *Way Through Hell*, was

completed in 1941. The novel attempts to give a broad picture of the historical events of the Revolution and Civil War, and their effect on a group of intellectuals, who at first oppose the Reds, but gradually come to understand and accept the "people's" cause. Tolstoy revised the first volume to disguise its originally pro-White ideology. Even in altered form it remains superior to the latter two volumes, which are by comparison somewhat languid and devitalized. Yet the work has a broad sweep and panoply of characters which give it an important place in Soviet literature.

The unfinished *Peter I* (1929-45) also has claims to be regarded as Tolstoy's masterpiece. Though Peter is the central figure of the work, the author also presents a broad picture of Russia at the time of Europeanization. The novel is based on detailed research, and gives a reasonably objective picture of Peter, though there is a certain over-idealization of the emperor which anticipates the Soviet cult of the mid-1930's.

Bread (1938) is a purely propaganda novel about the Red defense of Tsaritsyn against the Whites during the Civil War. It attempts to glorify Stalin's role in the civil conflict and expose the "treachery" of Trotski.

Tolstoy's two dramas, *Ivan the Terrible (The Eagle and His Mate,* 1942; *The Difficult Years,* 1943), attempt the rehabilitation of Ivan who, like Peter, came into favor with Soviet historians during the 1930's. Tolstoy minimizes Ivan's cruelty as incidental to his struggle to unite and strengthen the Russian land. Again the work is based on extensive documentation, but there is less objectivity than in *Peter I.*

Tolstoy, Count Lev (Leo) Nikolayevich (1828-1910), an outstanding nineteenth-century novelist. Born the child of a well-to-do aristocratic family, he spent his first years on the family estate of Yasnaya Polyana ("Clear Meadow"), about a hundred miles south of Moscow. His upbringing was typical of the children of the landowning aristocracy. He was educated by foreign tutors, and cultivated a taste for such pastimes as riding, hunting, dancing and playing cards. His rank gave him a certain hauteur characteristic of his class. He always disliked the middle classes; it was far easier for him, a country gentleman, to admire the peasantry.

Tolstoy's mother died when he was barely two years old; his father when he was nine. He was brought up by other members of the family, finally going to live with his Aunt Tatyana. She spoiled him, and he tells us that she even encouraged him as a young man to cultivate a liaison with a woman in society in order to develop his character. Tolstoy was a man of strong sensual inclinations, and was not slow in following her advice. His sexual transgressions cost him severe remorse, however, and in his diary he continually reproached himself for these and other weaknesses. He kept the diary, following the model of Benjamin Franklin, chiefly in order to record such lapses and his repeated and constantly broken resolutions to do better.

In 1844 Tolstoy entered the University of Kazan, at first in the Faculty of Oriental Languages, later in Law. He left in 1847 without taking a degree, since the family was dividing its estates and he was impatient to begin life as a country gentleman.

On his estate of Yasnaya Polyana, Tolstoy attempted to improve conditions for his serfs, and devised a plan for them to buy their freedom on favorable terms. Rumors of the impending emancipation (see Reforms) were rife, however, and the peasants, who hoped (vainly, as it subsequently proved) to get the land for nothing, refused his offer. Tolstoy later chronicled the story of this failure in his tale, *A Landowner's Morning* (1856).

Tolstoy's active nature was soon bored with life on the estate, and in 1851 he followed his brother Nikolay to the Caucasus, where the Russians were engaged in a seemingly endless war with the mountain tribesmen. Here Tolstoy entered the army and obtained a commission. He enjoyed the active life, which included riding, hunting and some sporadic fighting. Partly to satisfy his need to be profitably occupied, he turned to writing (he had already made several brief attempts to write while on the estate). He completed his first story, *Childhood*, in 1852, and sent it to NEKRASOV, who brought it out in his journal *The Contemporary* over the initials L.T. In spite of the fact that Tolstoy's rather dry realism was sharply in contrast to the romanticism of the day, it had a great success, and there was much speculation concerning the unknown author's identity.

In 1854 Tolstoy was transferred to the Danube Front, and later the same year, at his own request, to Sevastopol. The Crimean War had broken out, and Sevastopol was subjected to a heavy siege by the Allies. The city put up a stiff resistance, which lasted the better part of a year. Tolstoy himself remained through the whole siege, during which he took part in some of the most severe fighting. His *Sevastopol Sketches* (1855-56) praise the heroic resistance of the Russian troops, particularly of the rank and file soldiers. In these stories Tolstoy's later views on war are already clearly implicit; the false courage of braggart officers is ridiculed, while the romantic glamor surrounding war in the popular imagination is also debunked; this was part of Tolstoy's general attack on ROMANTICISM, both as a literary style and an outlook on life.

In 1855, after the fall of Sevastopol, Tolstoy was transferred from the Crimea (though not, apparently, by intervention of Emperor Alexander II, as legend would have it). He went to St. Petersburg, where he was enthusiastically received as a leading writer. But he did not care much for the literary world, and was soon back at Yasnaya Polyana.

In 1857 and 1860-61 Tolstoy visited Western Europe, partly for the purpose of studying educational methods and philanthropic institutions there. On the second journey he witnessed the death of his elder brother, Nikolay, who died from tuberculosis. The sight of his death, coming after days of agony, produced a tremendous impression on Tolstoy, and inspired the terrifying portrayals of death in *War and Peace, Anna Karenina* and *The Death of Ivan Ilyich.* Indeed, Tolstoy's thought moves in terms of the two poles of life (biological drive) and death; he attempts to escape from his biological urges, which torment him with guilt, by renouncing them; at the same time he seeks to accept death as the inevitable end of life. But both phases of the struggle—to renounce life and to accept death—are carried on at tremendous cost, and Tolstoy never quite succeeds in winning either. It is the intensity of the conflict which makes him great as a man, and not the sublimation of his instincts in his final ethical system.

Returning from his second journey abroad, Tolstoy founded a school for peasant children at Yasnaya Polyana. He allowed the pupils and their parents to select the subjects of instruction; at the same time he eliminated examinations and the whole system of rewards and punishments. His ideas were an interesting anticipation of the methods of modern progressive education. The school was successful, chiefly, perhaps, because of Tolstoy's natural ability as a leader. He published a journal, called *Yasnaya Polyana*, on his experiences with the school, and wrote a number of reading texts for his pupils which are masterpieces of simplicity and directness.

Tolstoy's work with the school was interrupted by his marriage, in 1862, to Sophia Behrs, a young lady of aristocratic family. At first their marriage was a happy one. It inspired the description of the family life of Kitty and Levin in *Anna Karenina*. Tolstoy had strict views on the duties of a wife: she must manage the household as well as nurse and rear her children, neither of which was customary for upper-class Russian women of the period. Sophia bore him thirteen children, besides which she helped with his literary work, copying the manuscript of *War and Peace* some five times.

Gradually certain stresses developed in their relationship. Tolstoy became more and more preoccupied with moral questions as he moved toward the time of his so-called "conversion." Ultimately he was brought to the conclusion that sexual intercourse could be justified only for the purpose of procreation; his consequent neglect of his wife widened the growing breach between them. The story of their last years together is a complex and tormented one.

From 1863 to 1869 Tolstoy worked on *War and Peace;* from 1873 to 1876, on *Anna Karenina*. He had reached the pinnacle of his genius. But artistic success brought little satisfaction. More and more preoccupied with the necessity for finding a meaning in life, and with the fear of death, Tolstoy entered a period of gloomy scepticism, which lasted from about 1875 to 1879. At times he considered killing himself. But eventually, in his new ethical creed, he was able to find a way out. In 1878-79 he wrote his *Confession,* in which he describes how he came to his conversion; he revised it in 1882. The work was published in Switzerland but not in Russia, where the Church censor prevented its appearance. Preoccupied with the need to propound his new ethical and religious ideas, Tolstoy virtually forsook artistic literature between 1878 and 1885. During this period he wrote A *Criticism of Dogmatic Theology,* A *Union and Translation of the Four Gospels,* and *What I Believe,* none of which could be published in Russia at the time. Meanwhile he rejected almost all his earlier writings as worthless; they had been written, he believed, without comprehension of the meaning of life. But in 1886 he returned to fiction with the publication of his great story, *The Death of Ivan Ilyich*.

Tolstoy's moral beliefs attracted world-wide interest, and Yasnaya Polyana became a virtual place of pilgrimage for travellers from all over the world. Tolstoyan circles were founded everywhere, and his influence as a teacher became extremely strong. As a young man Gandhi read his work, and Gandhi's doctrine of non-violent resistance is in part an adaptation of Tolstoy's principle of non-resistance to evil.

In accord with his theories, Tolstoy renounced the rights to his books, though he allowed the Countess to retain the Russian rights, necessary to the support of their large family. The royalties from his novel *Resurrection* (1899) Tolstoy devoted to support the migration of the Dukhobors to Canada. This strange Russian sect had attracted his attention because of its pacifist beliefs.

Tolstoy believed that every man should do physical work and should, ideally, make himself economically self-sufficient. After his conversion he often worked in the fields or at such trades as cobbling. He sometimes (but not always) wore peasant clothes, such as the Russian shirt, renamed *tolstovka* in his honor.

In later life Tolstoy devoted much attention to problems of philanthropy. In January, 1882, he undertook a study of slum conditions in Moscow; the experience was almost more than he could bear. In 1891-92 he took an active part in organizing famine relief in the stricken area a hundred miles southeast of Yasnaya Polyana. His ideas extended even to the subject of diet, and he fed the peasants a much more varied diet than that to which they were accustomed.

In October, 1910, Tolstoy suddenly resolved to leave Yasnaya Polyana. He believed that he had no moral right to enjoy the protection of his estate and its wealth. His mind was perhaps weakened by senility. He left on November 10, 1910 (new style), with his daughter, Alexandra, the only member of his family who accepted his teachings during his lifetime. On the way he developed an inflammation of the lungs, and on November 22 he died in the house of the station-master of Astapovo, apparently of nervous exhaustion. His death brought thousands to Astapovo and to his funeral at Yasnaya Polyana. No Christian prayers were said for his repose, however, for in 1901 he had been excommunicated for his open opposition to the organized Church.

Tolstoy's character was in many respects complex and contradictory. He was a man whose proud nature and strong sensuality were sharply at variance with an exceptionally keen sense of moral responsibility. This strong ethical sense appears in him at a very early age; indeed, it is almost his only systematic point of view on life. Its leading trait is a search for the usefulness of everything; life itself for Tolstoy must have its rational purpose, without which death would be too terrible to contemplate. As a young man Tolstoy accepted a kind of pantheism, and came to believe that death is a natural phenomenon which man ought to accept as a normal part of life. He never entirely outgrew this conception, but later adds to it a more positive and definite moral understanding of life. He despises in himself the sins of indolence, purposelessness, and self-indulgence, which seems to him a waste of time and energy. Sexual intercourse itself he could accept only on the condition that it had its biological purpose, that of procreation. As he grew older, Tolstoy drew further away from a conception of a "natural," good life; for him life in its biological aspects tends to be evil, and the critic of his views might almost say that he would reject life in order to propitiate his own fear of death.

Tolstoy's first writings may best be understood as attempts to break sharply with literary ROMANTICISM and to create a sense of real life as it exists. To this end he employs a great deal of specific, almost photographic detail. This detail seems not so much to depict objects and persons as to create the illusion of depth and reality, to imply that things are described with encyclopedic thoroughness. This use of specific detail is continued through *Anna Karenina* (1875-77); only after his spiritual conversion did Tolstoy abandon it as an unnecessary "mannerism" of the realistic style. In his early work he also strikes a prosaic tone, free of lyricism as well as sentimentality. His favorite technique is that of analysis, an analysis which is motivated by a drive to discover a moral *raison d'être* in life, as well as by a belief —one which recalls the philosophers of the Enlightenment—in the power of rational analysis. Tolstoy constantly seeks to re-assert the force of reason in life, and his final ethical system represents the triumph of rationalism; the good he identifies with a way of life which is rational. But though he could make such an identification for *that which ought to be,* he could not do the same for *that which is,* and his philosophy of history ends with the admission that human history is too complex to submit to any analysis.

In his break with Romanticism Tolstoy goes back to the eighteenth century for his sources. One of these is Laurence Sterne, particularly in *Childhood,* which employs the techniques of toying with the narrative so favored by Sterne. Another source is Rousseau, whose glorification of the natural man colored Tolstoy's whole philosophy of "living naturally," a principle which is at the basis of his ethical ideas both before and after his "conversion." The cult of the natural man is a romantic survival, almost the only one, in Tolstoy's writing.

The three short novels, *Childhood* (1852), *Boyhood* (1854) and *Youth* (1857), constitute a trilogy which is largely autobiographical, though Tolstoy did alter names and a few factual details. They are closer to reminiscences, in fact, than to fiction. In spite of a certain sentimentality (which Tolstoy very early lost), the best of the three is *Childhood,* with its unforgettable gallery of characters, such as the children's weak-willed father or their eccentric German tutor. In *Boyhood* and *Youth* the element of moral analysis is stronger; the chief subject is the exposure of the selfishness and moral hypocrisy of children, for whom Tolstoy has no sentimental regard whatsoever.

The theme of war appears in the two sketches, *The Raid* (1853) and *The Wood-Felling* (1855), based to a large extent on Tolstoy's experiences in the Caucasus, and continues in the *Sevastopol Sketches* (1855-56). Here Tolstoy shows most clearly his opposition to Romanticism. In the popular romantic novels of BESTU-ZHEV war was depicted as glamorous and heroic. Courage was the noblest virtue of the romantic hero, who performed prodigies of daring. Tolstoy undertook to expose the falsehood of such a view of war. Instead of the hyperbole of the romanticists he employs understatement; instead of poetry prosaic language; instead of a single hero he presents a number of characters, none of whom is central. His officers are motivated not by true courage but by a narcissist desire to be regarded as heroic. True courage consists, as Tolstoy realizes, not in the complete absence of fear, but in the realization that fear in war is natural and in the ability to cope with it.

Perhaps the sharpest break made by Tolstoy with Romanticism was in the use of narrative plots. For the unlikely coincidences and exaggerations of the romantic novel, Tolstoy substitutes a narrative form which is almost plotless. The events which occur are those of everyday life. Nothing is artificial or elaborated; indeed, Tolstoy chooses the commonest, most elemental incidents of daily life to build on. Much of his material he draws from his own life or the life of those about him. This type of construction Tolstoy employed until his conversion; his later work tends to be richer in the use of plot.

Family Happiness (1859) is his first attempt at a conventional novel, one strongly influenced by English fiction of the period. It is the story of his love affair with Valeria Vladimirovna Arseneva, a young lady whom he for a time considered marrying. The work is a curious attempt to prove that if the two had married, they would have been unhappy. In general it, along with others of his tales of this period, is decidedly inferior both to what came before and to what followed.

With the stories, *Three Deaths* (1859), and *Kholstomer, the Story of a Horse* (1861; English translation as "Yardstick"), Tolstoy first shows his typical preoccupation with the meaning of life and death. Both stories are satirical; their satire proceeds from the author's failure to accept the habitual and conventional human viewpoint and scale of values. In the first story he achieves satire by presenting death as an arbitrary and unsentimentalized fact of life, no more sacred than any other. The best death, he implies, is found by the creature which lives in closest harmony with the natural order. In *Kholstomer* satire is achieved by examining human life through the eyes of a horse; man comes out badly by comparison, for his life appears unnatural and silly by contrast to the natural existence of the animal. These two tales exemplify the pantheistic phase through which Tolstoy was passing at the time; man for him becomes first of all a creature of the natural order whose life can be good only as it is lived in close touch with that order. The same viewpoint colors his novel,

The Cossacks (1863), which includes details and incidents drawn from his service in the Caucasus.

War and Peace (1865-69) is universally acknowledged to be Tolstoy's masterpiece. Criticism breaks down in an attempt to analyze this vast work, which is so rich and re-creates, to such an extent, the actual feeling of life. The novel has the form of life itself, and its principal events are the elemental events of life: birth, maturing, marriage, childbirth, aging and death; war and peace. It is both a family chronicle, presenting the histories of several families over a period of about a generation, and a historical novel, describing the Russian campaign against Napoleon and the French. Formally it is perhaps the first great example (and ultimately the greatest) of the "open-end" novel, or *roman fleuve*, in which the stream of life itself creates the form of the novel, and in which the beginning and end points in the narrative are almost arbitrary.

The characters in *War and Peace* have all the complexity of living beings, and hence it is not easy to give any succinct definition of their meaning. But they do tend to a certain universal significance as well. Pierre Bezukhov is an average man, attempting, like Tolstoy himself, to discern the good in life; his search is a long and bungling one, and in the end he finds the solution where he had continually overlooked it—in the process of living itself. It is the peasant Platon Karatayev who teaches Pierre the lessons of simplicity and naturalness, that the good is that which is least artificial and elaborated. Learning this, Pierre becomes much less a professional philanthropist, but much more a positively good man. Prince Andrey, too, seeks the good in life, but is ultimately alienated from life by his own profound hauteur and lofty intellect. The only lesson he learns, perhaps, is that of death, the Tolstoyan faith that death itself is a natural part of life. Natasha and Nikolay Rostov are typical, healthy children who are growing up: relatively thoughtless as children, maturity turns them into good parents and home-makers. As such they are excellent animals, and, though Tolstoy of course approves of their natural, intuitive way of life, we can hardly help but detect a painful note in the picture of Natasha, the lovely instinctual young girl, transformed into the slovenly wife and mother. Similarly, Nikolay, who is able, without hypocrisy or dishonesty, to fall in love with the plain, frustrated Princess Marya as a means of recouping the family fortunes, changes, apparently for the worse. Yet, in spite of this almost vegetative decay which Tolstoy's ideal of life on the manor may seem to present, *War and Peace* does have significance as a rare example of a great novel which is life-asserting and optimistic; it seems to exist to show us a happy life as it can be achieved, and this without any falsification of life's premises.

War and Peace contains a great many historical and philosophical chapters which present Tolstoy's views on war and history. War Tolstoy sees as a kind of unpredictable chaos, which can never be planned or organized, since it involves a great number of human beings with independent motivations of their own. Strategy and tactics break down just because they cannot cope with the human element. What wins battles, in Tolstoy's opinion, is morale, which cannot be controlled or even predicted. From this anarchic view of war Tolstoy goes on to develop his philosophy of human history. Here, too, we are dealing with a tremendous number of individual beings; unless we can understand the causes of the actions of every individual who takes part in history, Tolstoy argues, we can never understand history as such. Dissatisfied with anything less than a full and completely rational account of history, Tolstoy rejects any compromise and declares his complete agnosticism.

War and Peace was followed by *Anna Karenina* (1875-77), Tolstoy's most popular novel. It has much of the breadth and scope of *War and Peace*. Contrary to popular impression, Tolstoy does not attempt to show in this novel that Anna is punished because of her sin of adultery (other characters in the novel commit this sin and go unpunished); rather she is destroyed because she is unable to cope with the social and psychological consequences of her adulterous relation with Vronski. The book is magnificent as the psychological study of the degeneration of a woman who loves and who fears compulsively that her lover will desert her.

The adulterous love of Anna and Vronski, culminating in Anna's suicide, is contrasted to the conjugal love match of Kitty and Levin, based on Tolstoy's own experiences in marriage. But, as in *War and Peace*, Tolstoy's picture of ideal life on the estate may seem a bit boring, and perhaps not even entirely edifying.

The end of *Anna Karenina* depicts, in Levin's conflicts and his search for the meaning of life, the spiritual crisis through which Tolstoy himself was passing, and which came to a head in the years 1878-79. His *Confession*, written in these years, records in a concentrated and highly expressive form the experiences of this religious conflict. In the *Confession* Tolstoy describes his successive disillusionment with a life of pleasure, with conventional religion, and with science and philosophy. None of these provided him with any answer to his quest for the meaning of life. In all his searches he had looked to the upper classes to provide an answer; the true solution, he finally discovered, he tells us, by observing the life of the peasants. He noted that they did not fear death, which they regarded as the natural and inevitable consequence of life, and thus he decided that their life itself must be good and natural. (Apparently it did not occur to him that the peasants might not fear death because their life was so hard.) In their toil, indeed, as well as their generous and co-operative spirit, he found the key to their happiness.

In his idealization of peasant life Tolstoy was not, of course, blind to the faults of the peasantry. He could depict these in truly horrifying form, as in his drama, *The Power of Darkness* (1888). What he seems rather to idealize is the peasant way of life and its institutions. To a large extent he regarded the vices of the peasantry as due to the corrupting influence of civilization.

In his conversion Tolstoy accepted a strongly modified form of Christianity, centered about the teachings of Christ. But the dogmas of Christianity, including that of Christ's divinity, he could not accept; he sought to make religion rationalistic and, in ruling out all that was irrational, reduced religion to little more than an ethical system. For him there is no future life, and God himself is not a personal spirit. Nor does he know any principle for the expiation of sin or guilt; the Tolstoyan who sins can only resolve to do better. Tolstoy builds his ethical system around five prohibitions, which for him are central in the teaching of Christ: (1) do not resist evil; (2) do not be angry; (3) remain true to one woman, and avoid sexual desire as much as possible; (4) do not take oaths; and (5) love your neighbor, and do not judge your fellow man in anything. In arguing the first and last of these prohibitions, Tolstoy pushes the ideal relation among individuals to anarchic extremes; man has no right, in his opinion, to form any conclusions concerning the motives or actions of his fellows, or the moral consequences of these actions. Hence he is never justified in judging his fellows or in doing violence to them. Even preventive and punitive violence are wrong for Tolstoy; for him one evil never justifies another, and there is no such thing as "greater" or "lesser" evil. This principle Tolstoy carries out in his whole conception of society. Government is wrong for him, for it is based on the premise of force. All organizations, even the Church, are wrong, for they acquire power and hence work injustice. Modern civilization is wrong, for, predicated on the division of labor, it brings the exploitation of the fruits of the labor of some men by their fellows. Tolstoy was a critic of modern society rather than a utopian systematist, and hence it is unfair to judge him by what might be called his "ideal" society. Still, it is plain that he would favor a social order which would be agrarian and extremely primitive. Implicit in his thought is a firm belief in the moral benefit of physical labor. Each man would produce at least the greater part of his own needs by the sweat of his brow; other necessities might perhaps be satisfied by the free co-operation or the generosity of individuals, rather than by any formal system of social organization. There would be no private property, for its existence would imply inequality among men. Tolstoy's ideal economic order would be a primitive agrarian communism, differing radically from Marxian socialism in the absence of any formal division of labor.

For some years after his conversion Tolstoy refrained from writing fiction almost entirely. His energies were devoted to the systematic formulation of the principles of his new ethical system. He was especially preoccupied with Biblical scholarship, which he applied in an attempt to separate the essential ethical teachings of the Scriptures from the false dogma which he felt had grown up around them. To this end, he even made a special study of Hebrew. In 1881-82 he prepared his own *Union and Translation of the Four Gospels*. He also published many moral tracts, and on occasion even undertook to challenge the tyrannical authority of the tsarist regime. His *I Cannot Be Silent* (1908) is a protest against the use of martial law to condemn summarily those convicted of taking part in the REVOLUTION of 1905. Because of his world-wide fame, the tsarist government refrained from taking direct action against Tolstoy himself. But certain of his writings, published abroad or underground, were officially banned, and severe punishments, including exile to Siberia, could be meted out to those possessing them.

After his conversion Tolstoy assumed a new attitude toward art. He condemned his earlier writings, which he now regarded as harmful, since, in his opinion, they were written from motives of vanity and in ignorance of the truth. Art, in his later view, ought to be infused with a spirit which is morally uplifting. This does not mean that art must necessarily be didactic; rather it should not corrupt, and should inspire by its tone if not through any specific teaching. Indeed, Tolstoy himself wrote many works after his conversion which are free from didactic elements. In the name of this principle Tolstoy does, however, severely condemn sensuality in art.

The second general requirement which Tolstoy demands from art is that it be simple enough for most men to comprehend. Here Tolstoy found himself in a dilemma; an intelligent man himself, he was quite capable of appreciating works of art which were beyond the comprehension of the average person. But consistency compelled him to place higher value, for example, on Russian folk songs than the music of Mozart or Beethoven. After his conversion Tolstoy wrote many simple tales for the people, often employing characters and motifs taken from folk tales.

The Death of Ivan Ilyich (1886) was the first great work of literature which Tolstoy produced after his conversion, and his greatest tale. It depicts death and the whole process of dying, the result of a mysterious fatal disease. Dying brings Ivan Ilyich, who is a kind of Everyman, to a realization of the spiritual bankruptcy of his life and, finally, to the Tolstoyan view of death as an inevitable fact of life which he can only accept. One may see a certain irony in the fact that Ivan Ilyich accepts the very universe which blindly strikes him down, but Tolstoy scarcely intended such an irony.

Of Tolstoy's popular and didactic tales, many are minor classics.

What Men Live By (1881) is based on a Russian folk legend; it tells how an angel is banished from heaven and sent down to earth to learn that, though hatred is almost universal among men, it is love by which men live. The earlier story, *God Sees the Truth, But Waits* (1872), is the tale of a man unjustly imprisoned for a murder he has not committed; his undeserved punishment teaches him humility. *How Much Land Does a Man Need?* (1886) is an ironic commentary on material greed. A man runs all day in order to encompass as much land as possible and acquire it for himself; as the sun sets he falls dead from exhaustion. "Six feet of land was all that he needed," is the story's pointed ending. *Alyosha Gorshok* (1905) is the beautiful tale of a simple man who is happy in his complete naiveté and self-abnegation.

Tolstoy's two novels of this period, *The Kreutzer Sonata* (1890) and *Resurrection* (1899), are far less perfect; both are spoiled by tendentiousness. In the first he seeks to demonstrate that physical desire without spiritual love leads to jealousy. The story relates how a husband murders his wife after surprising her with her lover. But the conclusion does not seem the inevitable result of the premises; Tolstoy seems mistaken in his identification of sexual desire and jealousy. In *Resurrection* we see the almost complete breakdown of the novel form under the didactic load which Tolstoy piles on it, as he intrudes again and again into the narrative to inveigh against the judicial and penal systems in modern society. No doubt he is right in his criticism; he presents, however, no real alternative. The story shows the moral regeneration of a nobleman, Nekhlyudov, who has seduced a young girl named Katya; later she becomes a prostitute, and Nekhlyudov, faced with the realization that his seduction of the girl has caused her downfall, resolves to marry her. She is convicted for a crime of which she is innocent, and Nekhlyudov follows her to Siberia to share her life there. Eventually she is redeemed by his love, but, herself in love with another, does not marry him.

Of Tolstoy's plays, the most famous is *The Power of Darkness*, a classic of the naturalistic drama. Banned for many years from the Russian stage, it was first produced in Paris in 1888. It describes the moral degeneration of a young peasant involved in an adulterous affair, who is led by his passion to commit terrible crimes. Tolstoy returns here to his favorite theme of the corrupting power of evil, a theme made explicit in the Russian proverb which serves as the play's subtitle: "If a claw is caught, the bird is lost." The play also gives a positive portrait of an honest, hard-working peasant. His profession (that of cesspool cleaner) and his very limited intellect make him seem ridiculous, though by these qualities Tolstoy meant only to exemplify his humility.

The Fruits of Enlightenment (1891) is a light comedy which pokes fun at the fads and excesses of fashionable society. The aristocracy develops a craze for spiritualism, while the hard-headed peasants manipulate séances for their own profit. More serious is *The Living Corpse,* published posthumously, the story of a man who destroys himself in debauchery. To free his wife, who wishes to marry another, he pretends to be dead; when the police finally discover that he is still alive he kills himself. Again we see a profoundly disturbing picture of the corrupting power of evil, one which it is hard to reconcile with Tolstoy's faith in the good and its reasonableness. But in this play Tolstoy also demonstrates a real sympathy for human weakness which is rare in his work. (See Drama and Theater.)

The resolution of this inconsistency seems to come in the posthumous tale, *The False Coupon.* The first half of the story shows how the evil of a slight initial action grows and spreads until it corrupts a large group of people, and finally leads to violence and murder. But the most sinful of the evildoers repents, and his good example in turn influences all the others who have been involved in the tangled web of evil to reform. The story is quite unrealistic, but it is deeply moving, and displays a profound faith in the ultimate power of the good to triumph over evil.

Tolstoy returns to the sexual theme in two posthumously published stories, *The Devil* and *Father Sergey.* In the first a landowner establishes a liaison with a peasant woman while his wife is pregnant. Later he is unable to break off the liaison and, tormented, at last commits a terrible crime: in one version he kills the girl; in another, himself. *Father Sergey* contains an unusually frank treatment of sex, but the real theme of the work is the hypocritical pride of a recluse, who lives in self-satisfied isolation.

The short novel *Hadji Murad* is the last of these posthumous works, and shows a surprising return to the idealization of the primitive so typical of the young Tolstoy. The Hadji, a Mohammedan religious leader fighting the Russians in the Caucasus, goes over to them when his authority is wrongfully usurped by one of his countrymen. But he soon discovers that the Russians are dishonest and corrupt, and in the end he escapes to rejoin his countrymen, who kill him.

Tolstoy's greatness no doubt depends ultimately on his stature as an artist, rather than his position as an ethical thinker and leader. Still, we must not overlook the fact that a deep interest in moral problems is implicit in almost everything which he wrote. It is to a large extent his drive to analyze character and morality which constitutes the motivating force behind his realism. He could interest himself in and successfully depict the apparently petty details and the most elemental facts of everyday reality just because, as a moralist, he was concerned for them in a sense profoundly moral.

In its earlier phase this realism is rooted in the use of extensive detail, which, so to speak, "documents" the presentation, creating the illusion of reality. This is Tolstoy's external approach to events and characters, in which he is very scrupulous in maintaining a consistently realistic, almost photographic point of view. Thus, in *War and Peace,* no matter what he is describing, he is careful to have an observer present, and to show the reader only what this observer is himself able to perceive. But Tolstoy also has an internal, intuitive approach to his characters, and it is this which gives them their ultimate reality and their depth. If Natasha Rostova is the most appealing character in *War and Peace,* it is because Tolstoy actually feels her charm and lightness, because he understands the mental state of a young girl growing up.

After his conversion, Tolstoy abandoned much of his earlier epic manner and use of external, photographic detail. His style became more concise, and he limited the narrative strictly to that which was essential. At the same time he sometimes began to use conventional plots of a kind almost unknown in his earlier work. Yet we can hardly call this second period much inferior to the first. True, it produced no *War and Peace,* but the first period lacks anything so profoundly moving as *The Death of Ivan Ilyich, Alyosha Gorshok,* or *The False Coupon.* Even the didacticism of Tolstoy's final manner did not destroy his acute artistic sense.

As a writer Tolstoy is perhaps the most significant of nineteenth-century "epic" novelists, and has had an influence on the *roman fleuve* comparable only to that of Dostoyevski on the psychological novel. Such writers as Galsworthy, Thomas Mann, and Jules Romains owe much to him. Similarly, in Soviet literature the manner of the Tolstoyan realistic novel, with its great number of characters, external point of view and introduction of historical materials (as in *War and Peace*) has been influential. The Civil War novels of such writers as FADEYEV and SHOLOKHOV, and indeed the Soviet historical novel generally, has shown the strong effect of Tolstoy's work.

Tournemir. See Salias de Tournemir.

Trediakovski, Vasili Kirillovich (1703-69), a leading writer and literary theoretician of the eighteenth century. The son of a poor peasant of Astrakhan, Trediakovski ran away from home to Moscow in 1723, where he studied at the Slavo-Greek-Latin Academy. From 1725 to 1730 he studied abroad at the Hague and in Paris. Here he became acquainted with contemporary French poetry, even writing French verses himself. In 1773 he was made Secretary of the Russian Academy of Sciences; one of his duties was to compose solemn odes, panegyrics and orations for public ceremonies. He was constantly humiliated by the nobles of the court, who were contemptuous of his humble origin. Polemic disputes with LOMONOSOV and SUMAROKOV also made his position an unhappy one. Retiring in 1759, he died in poverty and oblivion.

Trediakovski sought to establish working rules for the newborn Russian Pseudo-Classical literature (see Classicism). In his *New and Brief Method for the Composition of Russian Verses* (1735), he advocated the replacement of syllabic verse by the modern syllabotonic system (see Prosody); his reform was incomplete, however, in that it was applied only to poems with long lines; for short lines Trediakovski preferred the existing syllabic prosody. He introduced the hexameter into Russian, and employed it in his translation of Fénélon's *Télémaque* (1766). In his *View on the Origin of Poetry and Verse* (1752) and other writings, he introduced Russian readers to the classical theory and practice of art. As a literary historian and philologist, Trediakovski did much to lay the foundations for the scholarly study of Russian antiquities.

Trediakovski wrote odes, songs, madrigals, a verse tragedy, and other poetry. His original work and his translations are both mediocre, especially in style. He mixes words of diverse linguistic origin with little or no feeling for their stylistic value. He was not entirely responsible for this and other weaknesses in his poetry, however, since the rapid change in language and literary taste of the times made achievement extremely difficult.

Trenyov, Konstantin Andreyevich (1884-1945), a twentieth-century writer. His early stories, influenced by Gorki (see Peshkov), are of little significance. He is remembered chiefly for his play, *Lyubov Yarovaya* (1926), about the heroism of a village schoolmistress, a Bolshevik married to a White officer. It has been one of the most popular Soviet plays. Trenyov wrote several other dramas about the October Revolution and the Civil War, as well as on historical subjects.

Tretiakov, Sergey Mikhaylovich (1892-   ), a Soviet poet and playwright. After the Revolution Tretiakov entered poetry as an advocate of FUTURISM, and became one of the leading theoreticians and critics of LEF. His best-known work is his play, *Roar, China!* (1926), in which he attacks Western imperialism. He disappeared from literature at the end of the 1930's.

Trotski, Leon (pseudonym of Lev Davidovich Bronstein; 1879-1940), a Russian revolutionary leader. He joined the revolutionary movement in 1896, and subsequently spent most of his life in Siberian exile or abroad. After 1903 he wavered for many years between the Bolshevik and Menshevik wings of the Social Democratic (Marxist) Party, before finally throwing his lot in with the Bolsheviks. In 1917 Trotski became People's Commissar for Foreign Affairs under the new Soviet government. He developed a theory of permanent revolution, according to which the Russian Revolution would be followed by revolutions in other countries; the Soviet Union's primary duty was to aid in such uprisings. This was the main theoretical difference between Trotski and STALIN, who drove him from power in 1925; in 1927 he was expelled from the Party, and the following year exiled to Turkestan. In 1929 he was banished from the U.S.S.R. He finally settled in Mexico, where he was assassinated in 1940 under mysterious circumstances; presumably his assassin was a Stalinist agent.

Trotski's book, *Literature and Revolution* (1923), is directed against the possibility of creating a new and distinct proletarian literature, an idea which Trotski demolishes with characteristic scorn and striking sarcasm. The proletariat, in his view, must devote its efforts to the cause of world revolution, and will have no energy to devote to culture as such; moreover, it will not exist as a class for long, in any event, since under Communism it will be replaced by a classless society. Thus Trotski opposed the attempts of BOGDANOV, LUNACHARSKI and other Soviet theorists to create a proletarian literature (see Criticism, Soviet). Like LENIN, Trotski recognized the importance of preserving the pre-revolutionary cultural legacy as a basis for new cultural progress, something which the "proletarians" would not admit.

In the same book Trotski coined the term "fellow traveller" *(poputchik)* to designate those writers of the 1920's who, though they were in general sympathy with the aims of the REVOLU-TION, could not grasp its purely *communist* aims, and who were not willing to accept the party line in all respects. The phrase became an extremely popular one to denote the many writers of the 1920's who were not communists.

Trus, Pavlyuk (1904-29), a Belo-Russian Soviet poet (see Preface).

Tsvetayeva, Marina Ivanovna (1892-1941), a twentieth-century poet. She left the Soviet Union in 1922, and became one of the leading writers of the emigration. In 1939 she and her husband returned to the U.S.S.R., where Tsvetayeva committed suicide two years later. Her return to Soviet Russia failed to bring official Soviet acceptance of her work. Tsvetayeva had already published and won recognition by the time of the Revolution, but she is essentially an émigré writer. Her poetry is spontaneous, inpetuous, full of passion and fire. Her typical verse is a short, highly rhythmic staccato line, which occasionally serves for a cryptic, telegraphic style. She specialized in unusual and intricate rhymes and complex sound effects. Much of her poetry has folk inspiration; one of her finest narratives, *Tsar-Devitsa* (1922), is a retelling in verse of the popular fairy tale about a maiden tsar. Other volumes are *Mileposts* (1922), *Poems to Blok* (1922) and another fairy tale in verse, *A Fine Fellow* (1924).

Tsyganov, Nikolay Grigoryevich (1797-1831), a minor poet of the early nineteenth century. The son of a serf, he followed a career as an itinerant actor. He wrote sentimental romances in a pseudo-folk style. Many of them struck a truly popular note, and are still sung today.

Tuptalo, Dimitri. See Dimitri Rostovski.

Tur, Yevgenia. See Salias de Tournemir, Countess Ye. V.

Turgenev, Ivan Sergeyevich (1818-83), a leading Russian novelist and playwright of the nineteenth century. He was the child of landowning gentry of the province of Oryol. His mother, a wealthy heiress, ruled the household as a petty tyrant. Though fond of her son, she treated him with great severity, even cruelty. He revenged himself by making her the model for the unsympathetic women of his novels and stories.

In 1833 Turgenev entered the University of Moscow, a year later transferring to the University of St. Petersburg. While a student he began to write poetry, and first published some verses in 1838. On graduation he went to Berlin to study philosophy at the university there. In Berlin he met BAKUNIN, STANKEVICH and GRANOVSKI, Russian liberal and radical political thinkers. Already a liberal and an enthusiast for Western European culture and political institutions, Turgenev joined their circle. He also met the great radical thinker, HERZEN, and the two were friends for many years. Turgenev remained a Westerner in his orientation all his life (see Westerners), though he was not blind to the distinctions between Russian and European life, and always retained a strong sense of nostalgia for the old way of life, comfortable if scarcely progressive, on the Russian estates.

Turgenev returned to Russia in 1841, and entered the civil service. But after two years he left the service and devoted himself entirely to literature. This, together with his infatuation for the well-known singer, Pauline Viardot-Garcia, displeased his mother, and an open break between the mother and son came in 1845. She refused to support him, and he was forced to live entirely on his slender literary income until her death in 1850, when he came into his inheritance. Meanwhile he had gone abroad again in 1847, following Mme. Viardot. His love for her lasted all his life, and was one of the reasons, together with his acknowledged preference for the West, for his repeated trips abroad. The precise nature of his relations with Mme. Viardot is not clear; she and her husband tolerated his attentions to her, but the relationship, which was largely, if not entirely, Platonic, seems to have cost him pain and humiliation.

Meanwhile Turgenev had given up poetry for prose. In 1847 he published the first of the stories which were subsequently to be collected in his *Sportsman's Sketches* (1852). These sketches, for the most part sympathetic treatments of the life of the peasants, made his reputation, and he was greeted as one of Russia's leading writers. But official circles did not regard him so favorably. An enthusiastic obituary article on GOGOL, written in 1852 and published in defiance of censorship regulations, resulted in his arrest and exile to his estate for eighteen months.

The 1850's saw Turgenev at the height of his popularity, and the chief representative of the liberal point of view in Russian literature. His novels *Rudin* (1856), *A Nest of Gentlefolk* (1859) and *On the Eve* (1860) were accepted as faithful portrayals of the unsolved conflicts in Russian life and of the character of the Russian liberal, with his weaknesses and limitations. With Turgenev's discreet and veiled, yet objective treatment of social questions, he was able to find favor with most groups in Russian society. While abroad, he maintained close relations with such radicals as HERZEN and BAKUNIN, but his friends at home also numbered members of the more conservative-minded SLAVO-PHILES, such as K. S. AKSAKOV. A liberal by his deepest convictions, Turgenev could still sympathize with radicalism, but not accept it; he could also be sympathetic toward more conservative attitudes, so long as they were essentially idealistic. He himself placed his hopes for Russia's future in the promulgation of reforms, particularly in the liberation of the serfs, the introduction of civil rights, and the opening of schools. More radical reforms seemed premature to him, and he was not certain, for example, of the value of universal suffrage.

The appearance of a new generation of radical youth in the 1860's constituted a threat to Turgenev's popularity and influence. In his novel, *Fathers and Children* (1862), he attempted to portray this new radical generation, practical, materialistic, with a blind faith in science and education, but in nothing else. Their lack of faith in tradition and authority led him to apply the name of

NIHILIST, already known but little used, to the radicals of the 1860's. The word has been used ever since to describe the Russian radicals of this period. But Turgenev offended both the conservatives and the radicals with his portrayal of his nihilist hero, Bazarov; the former found his treatment too sympathetic; the latter, too hostile, though PISAREV and his followers did accept the name of nihilist for themselves, and hailed Bazarov as their ideal of the new man.

Wounded by this unfavorable reception, Turgenev spent more and more time abroad, in Germany and in Paris. He even thought for a time of abandoning literature completely, and announced such an intention in a prose poem entitled *Enough* (1865), in which he expressed the increasingly pessimistic cast of his thought, influenced by Schopenhauer.

Turgenev's last two novels, *Smoke* (1867) and *Virgin Soil* (1877), proved unable to recapture his former favor with the public. The latter, especially, was criticized for its lack of grasp on the reality of life in Russia, which Turgenev scarcely knew any longer at first hand. But, though his later work was sharply criticized, Turgenev never lost the position of a classic, whose popularity even increased before his death. More and more disillusioned, however, he expressed his pessimism and fear of death in a new series of philosophical prose poems and in several stories of the supernatural.

Turgenev's early poetry includes a long narrative, *Parasha* (1843), to a considerable extent an imitation of PUSHKIN's *Eugene Onegin*. Though it was well received, Turgenev soon gave up writing poetry for prose. But the poetic and lyric impulse, as well as the influence of the Golden Age poets, and especially Pushkin, was always strong in his work.

Turgenev's earliest tales, with their Byronic heroes and plots, were influenced by LERMONTOV. But he soon found a more personal and original form in his sketches of peasant life, the first of which, *Khor and Kalinych*, was published in 1847. The entire collection, entitled *A Sportsman's Sketches* (or, more literally, *Notes of a Hunter*), appeared in 1852. It describes the author's chance meetings with serfs while hunting in his native district. Turgenev describes the peasants as intelligent, imaginative and humane, with a dignified and purposeful way of life.

The few landowners who appear are cruel or vulgar. Though his purpose in writing the *Sketches* was to inspire sympathy for the peasants and help win their liberation, he does not go out of his way to present horrifying examples of the way serfs were treated. Thus, though its purpose is the same, his book is quite different in tone as well as artistic quality from *Uncle Tom's Cabin*, to which it has often been compared. He seeks rather to win admiration for the peasantry by showing their essential human worth. The book created a sensation, and is said to have influenced the future emperor Alexander II in his decision to liberate the serfs. Told in a rich, pure and graceful lyric style with a wealth of imagery, the *Sketches* have little plot, and are portraits rather than tales.

One of the *Sketches*, *A Hamlet of the Shchigrov District*, is on a theme more reminiscent of DOSTOYEVSKI, the fate of an intelligent and sensitive landowner who nourishes a boundless ambition, but who fails to win the respect of those about him, and finally degenerates into a kind of buffoon in order to win attention from others. A similar theme is treated in the independent tale, *The Diary of a Superfluous Man* (1850), which popularized the name "SUPERFLUOUS MAN" as a designation for this type of idealistic but inactive hero, of which so many examples can be found in nineteenth-century Russian literature. In these two tales Turgenev reacted against German idealist philosophy, so influential in Russian thought of the times, as too abstract and cloudy; he especially opposed the revolutionary attitudes of the left-wing Hegelians, among others of his old friends, BAKUNIN and HERZEN. Other notable portraits of superfluous men are given in the stories *Faust* (1856) and *Asya* (1858), and the type reappears in Turgenev's novels.

In his stories, *The Inn* (1852) and *Mumu* (1852), Turgenev continued the series of sympathetic portraits of serf life; *Mumu* is his most famous tale, one of the most pathetic in all Russian literature. It is the story of a deaf-mute serf who loses the only human being who loves him, a young peasant girl, when she is made to marry a drunkard so as to serve as a "steadying influence" on him. He then begins to keep a dog, but is forced to kill it when its barking prevents the mistress from sleeping.

Several of Turgenev's finest tales, such as *Asya* (1858), *First*

Love (1860) and *Spring Freshets* (1872), portray young people in love, a subject which he treats with special tenderness and insight. His love stories invariably end unhappily, usually with the desertion of the girl by her lover, who leaves her for an older and more experienced, if less pure woman.

Turgenev wrote a number of dramatic works early in his career, the most successful of which was *A Month in the Country* (1850), a lyrical drama concerned with this theme of the rivalry of a young girl and a mature woman for a young man's love. In its construction, with its lyrical mood and relative absence of action, the work is notable as a forerunner of the plays of CHEKHOV.

Turgenev's first novel, *Rudin* (1856), is the portrait of an enthusiastic liberal, a man of high ideals who lacks the will to put his principles into action. His eloquence has a striking effect on all around him, and wins him the love of a pure and courageous young girl, Natalya. But he is too weak and ineffectual to risk his fate with her, and gives her up. His Utopian schemes turn out disastrously, and in the end he dies heroically, if uselessly, on the barricades of Paris in 1848. Rudin is a noteworthy example of the long tradition of SUPERFLUOUS MEN in Russian literature, and perhaps the finest portrayal of the frustrated and disillusioned liberals of the 1840's in literature. His real-life prototype was supposedly BAKUNIN, though their fates, of course, were very different.

Rudin was followed by *A Nest of Gentlefolk* (1859). Here again we see a vacillating hero, Lavretski, and a courageous and self-sacrificing heroine, Liza. Lavretski believes his wife, Varvara, to be dead, and plans to marry Liza; his wife has in fact deserted him, but reappears when she learns of his coming marriage. Their happiness blighted, Liza goes into a convent to devote herself to humanity, while Lavretski is forced to effect a reconciliation with his wife and settle down to a life of cultivating the soil. The book contains a striking picture of the older, more rigid and self-contained way of life of Muscovite Russia, followed by the old aunt, and sharply contrasted with the Europeanized and modern existence of the younger generation.

On the Eve (1860) is considerably less successful than the novels which preceded it. It contains a portrayal of a radical leader capable of action, Insarov, but Turgenev makes his hero a Bulgarian, as if he did not believe in the possibility of an effectual Russian radical. Insarov is scarcely believable, in any event. He dies before he can return to Bulgaria to work for his country's liberation.

Fathers and Children (1862) is Turgenev's greatest novel. For the first time he creates a strong-willed and believable radical hero, Bazarov, to whom he gives the nickname of "nihilist" (see Nihilists). Bazarov, like the younger radicals of the 1860's, opposes all tradition and authority, and believes in nothing save materialistic science. His manners are frank, even crude, but in spite of everything he is heroic and likeable, and his strength and will of action contrast him strongly with the other characters of the book. He is opposed to two brothers, older landowners, who are shocked by his talk of breaking with the past and of destroying tradition to build Russian life anew. He easily defeats them in argument, but his conflict with one brother, Pavel, a nobleman with aristocratic tastes, puts him in the position of fighting a duel, and thus forces him into complying with the very tradition of which he is so contemptuous. His unrequited love for a noblewoman, Odintsova, destroys his faith in himself and in his revolutionary principles; he had not believed in love, which for him had been nothing more than a biological drive, but now he finds his spirit broken by it. He loses his faith in the Russian masses as well, and in the end, deprived of will for life and action, dies of an infection which he has contracted. With his death Turgenev seems to symbolize the fact that, even though the revolutionary youth of Russia may have the will to bring about a revolution and change society, conditions in Russia are not yet ripe for such violent change. Besides the theme of social revolt, Turgenev has employed the classic theme of "fathers and children" in his novel. Arkadi, Bazarov's friend and follower, is the eternal type of young man who rebels against his parents and is a radical in his youth, but who soon settles down to follow in the way of his fathers.

Though Turgenev's depiction of Bazarov shows his admiration for the strong-mindedness and idealism of the young radical generation, still he was far from completely sympathetic with it.

The other radicals in the book are mere caricatures. Bazarov dies without real followers.

Turgenev's next novel, *Smoke* (1867), was less successful. It contains one of his finest love stories, but the love narrative is unsuccessfully intertwined with a treatment of the Slavophile-Westerner controversy (see Slavophiles, Westerners), and there are long diatribes on political and social questions. The intellectual protagonist of the novel, Potugin, maintains that Russia has so far acquired only superficialities from the West, and needs to learn much more. Russian intellectual life is, on its present level, mere smoke—the significance of the book's title.

Virgin Soil (1877), Turgenev's final novel, is the weakest of all. It describes the events of the famous summer of 1874, when thousands of radical POPULISTS went out to the people in an effort to inspire them to revolt. Turgenev chronicles the disastrous failure of their campaign and the destruction of the movement. The book was much criticized as too far removed from the reality of events; in spite of this, it must be said that Turgenev understood the unpreparedness of the movement and the causes for its failure. Purely fantastic, however, is the character of Solomin, a factory manager who develops his personal formula for revolution: patient waiting and work to establish schools for the masses.

In his final period Turgenev produced a number of new tales and stories. One of the best of these, the novelette *A Lear of the Steppes* (1870), is a retelling of the Shakespearean story in a Russian setting. Tragic and powerful in mood, the change of locale is entirely convincing. There are also a number of stories of the fantastic and the supernatural, the most famous of which, *Klara Milich* (1883), concerns spiritualism. These are much inferior to Turgenev's realistic work. Also less successful is Turgenev's final collection, his *Poems in Prose* (1879-83), originally entitled *Senilia*. Sometimes mere mood pictures, sometimes brief narratives or fables, they concern such pessimistic subjects as death, fate and human futility.

Turgenev's writings, and especially his novels, are a profound commentary on the problems of Russian society in the mid-nineteenth century, and especially on the development of the liberal and radical movements. He took over the personality type of the SUPERFLUOUS MAN, sensitive, intelligent, but incapable of action, as found in the work of earlier Russian writers, and particularly in PUSHKIN's *Eugene Onegin;* in this character type, as well as in the reactionary and restricting conditions of Russian society, Turgenev saw the reason for the failure of the nineteenth-century liberal and radical movements to bring political and social change. Forced by the censorship to veil his true meaning, Turgenev's pictures of radicalism are often enigmatic. Thus, in *Fathers and Children* we hear only the vague phrase, "Bazarov's cause," as a description of his life's work and purpose. Judging by Bazarov's nature as well as by Turgenev's private comments on his hero, this cause is obviously a revolutionary one, but whether a political or a purely social revolution is intended, we cannot be certain. In any event, the author is sceptical of the success of any Russian revolutionary movement: Rudin is a talker who cannot act; Insarov, a Bulgarian and not a Russian; Bazarov dies, spiritually bankrupt and without successors. The whole meaning of Turgenev's novels as political commentaries seems to be that liberal reform, though long overdue in Russia, will come all too slowly because of the inertia of Russian society, while a revolution in Russia is out of the question.

Though valued by his contemporaries, Turgenev's treatment of social and political problems is perhaps the most dated aspect of his work. Today his writings are remembered and read chiefly for their more universal qualities. His greatest gift, perhaps, is that of psychological intuition. It enabled him to understand mentalities as diverse as those of radical leaders, serfs, and young girls in love, and to depict their most subtle states of mind with keen and sympathetic appreciation. It is true, of course, that his treatment of character is somewhat conventional and old-fashioned in its psychology. But Turgenev was not so much interested in psychological analysis as in presenting character as a finished product, as it affects others, and as others react to it. In his work the force of a given personality is to a large extent conveyed by the use of mood and atmosphere. Among Turgenev's most successful characters are his heroines. Unlike his ineffectual heroes, they are strong, even passionate, as well as idealistic and entirely feminine. He is at his best in depicting the lyric mood of young girls in love. His heroines are capable of almost infinite devotion and self-sacrifice.

Turgenev's second great gift is for a highly lyrical style, almost poetic in its grace and delicacy. He is most lyric in his treatment of love and nature. His predominant mood is itself lyrical, a melancholy pessimism and passive resignation with which his characters submit to their fate. Another mood typical of his work is the nostalgia of life on the estate, a contented, almost vegetative existence which constitutes a powerful ideal of life opposed to the social idealism of his heroes.

Turgenev is perhaps the least modern in spirit of the great Russian writers. He avoids those sides of life which might shock or distress his readers. His manner, consciously artistic, has sometimes been accused of being "arty." His style, with all its refinement, grace and ease, lacks color or vigor. But it would be unfair to criticize him for not being what he did not want to be. If he is the most Victorian of Russian novelists, he is also the most perfectly balanced, the most impersonal and objective, and the most conscious of the formal and technical demands of art. His influence on later Russian, as well as Western writers, has been tremendous. A whole tradition in Russian lyric prose stems from his work, the greatest representatives of which are CHEKHOV and BUNIN. Abroad, his influence was strong on such writers as Henry James, whom he knew personally. He has influenced no less a contemporary writer than the American Ernest Hemingway. In France he became the leading representative of Russian letters, as well as the close friend of Mérimée and Flaubert. He himself, indeed, was the first Russian writer to win fame in the West, and it was largely through his intermediacy that the West first came to a knowledge of nineteenth-century Russian literature.

Turovski, Kirill. See Kirill Turovski.

Tvardovski, Alexander Trifonovich (1910-   ), Soviet poet. He began to publish in 1930, and achieved fame with a long narrative poem, *The Land of Muravia*, which appeared in 1936. It tells the story of a peasant who resists collectivization, setting out instead to find the legendary paradise of Muravia, where he will enjoy complete freedom. Finally realizing that no such land exists, he joins a collective farm. The poem is obviously influenced by NEKRASOV's *Who Can Be Happy in Russia?*

During the war Tvardovski published another humorous narrative poem, *Vasili Tyorkin* (1941-45). His hero is a happy-go-lucky soldier whose good humor and gaiety are curtailed only by his grim duty as a defender of his homeland.

Tychyna, Pavlo (1891-   ), a leading Ukrainian Soviet poet (see Preface).

Tynyanov, Yuri Nikolayevich (1894-1943), a Soviet novelist, literary historian and theoretician. Tynyanov was a leading member of the Russian Formalists (see Criticism). His novels are scholarly re-creations of the biographies of literary personages; they show considerable success in the treatment of psychology as well as a tendency towards experimentalism in style. First of them was *Kukhlya* (1925), about the quixotic poet, Wilhelm KÜCHEL-BECKER, exiled a hundred years earlier to Siberia for his part in the DECEMBRIST MOVEMENT. *The Death of Vazir-Mukhtar* (1927; English translation as "Death and Diplomacy in Persia") describes the brutal death of GRIBOYEDOV (Vazir-Mukhtar was Griboyedov's Persian title as Russian ambassador to Persia) at the hands of a mob in Teheran. *Pushkin* (1936-38) is more direct and realistic, but it lacks the psychological freshness of the first novel as well as the stylistic intricacy of the second. Tynyanov's success in the genre of the biographical novel helped to make it popular, and a number of such novels appeared at the end of the 1920's and during the 1930's.

Tyutchev, Fyodor Ivanovich (1803-73), one of Russia's greatest poets. The son of an ancient noble family, he was educated at the University of Moscow. Entering the diplomatic service in 1822, he was sent to Munich. He remained in Germany and Italy some twenty-two years. He was married twice, both times to Bavarian women. He corresponded with Schelling and Heine, and was the first to translate the latter's poetry into Russian. Though Tyutchev began to write poetry very early, he preserved his anonymity, and for many years his work was unknown. He published some of his best poems in Pushkin's *Contemporary* in 1836 and 1837 over the initials F.T., but they aroused no attention, and for some years he almost gave up poetry. In 1839 he was dismissed from the diplomatic service for leaving his post in Turin without permission. Remaining abroad several years longer, he returned to Russia in 1844 and received a position in the censorship, which he kept until his death.

In 1850 Tyutchev's work was suddenly discovered by the poet

NEKRASOV, who revealed his identity. Four years later the first collection of his work was published by TURGENEV. Though his popularity was never great during his lifetime, he was acknowledged as a leading writer by the literati of his day. His painful love affair with his daughter's governess inspired some poignant love poetry; her death in 1864 plunged him into despair. He remained active in literature, however, until his death.

Tyutchev's poetic production is small and entirely lyric, consisting of about 300 short poems. He is the only major Russian poet of the nineteenth century who largely ignored the influence of ZHUKOVSKI and PUSHKIN; his poetry, though romanticist in mood, has its roots in the great eighteenth-century poets, LOMONOSOV and DERZHAVIN, particularly in their mighty odes to nature. Much of Tyutchev's poetry concerns nature; some of his poems are mere landscape pictures, but the greatest reveal a profoundly philosophic consciousness, and he is the leading Russian metaphysical poet. His view of nature, influenced by Schelling and German romantic idealism, is pantheistic and dualistic—Manichean in its opposition of two worlds, Cosmos and Chaos. Cosmos—the world of life, order and beauty—is but an island precariously situated in the great ocean of Chaos, or nothingness, which for Tyutchev is the only ultimate reality, and which itself animates the Cosmos. The two worlds, manifested as pairs of opposites such as light and darkness, good and evil, or love and death, are constantly passing into each other. All things are therefore transitory. Man's existence as an individual is an illusion; he lives in an isolated prison of his own being. He cannot even communicate with his fellows, for "an uttered thought is but a lie," as Tyutchev says in a famous line of his poem, *Silentium!* (1833).

Tyutchev's nature lyrics are metaphorical expressions of this great cosmic drama of dualism. Favorite themes are night and day *(A Vision,* 1829; *Holy Night,* 1849); shade and light *(Twilight,* written early in the 1830's); dream and waking *(As the Ocean Embraces the Globe of Earth,* 1836; *Dream on the Sea,* 1836). Many of his poems are rich in the imagery of vision and sound, full of movement and power. Others are more striking in their solemn, declamatory style, reminiscent of the eighteenth-century ode. His love poetry is poignant and direct, full of tenderness and compassion for the mistress of his old age, who incurred disgrace because of her love for him.

The language of Tyutchev's poetry is archaic. He uses the vocabulary of Russian eighteenth-century poetry, but with a metrical freedom and an inventiveness which are romantic rather than classical. His prose writings, including political tracts and letters, are in French, which he spoke fluently; he also has a few French poems of lesser significance.

Tyutchev's political poetry, written late in life, is inferior to his other work, though at times it is notable for its wit and invective. In politics he was a conservative nationalist with tendencies towards Slavophilism (see Slavophiles). Russia, he hoped, would unite the Slavs and dominate Eastern Europe. In autocracy he found the best warranty of political stability, though he still feared the spread of the Western revolutionary movement to Russia.

The general decline of Russian poetry in the second half of the nineteenth century resulted in the partial eclipse of Tyutchev's reputation. At the end of the century he was rediscovered, however, by the Symbolists. They found a kindred spirit in this metaphysical poet who preached cosmic duality and the isolation of the individual. Since then he has remained without question one of the greatest Russian poets, second, perhaps, only to Pushkin.

U

Ukrainian literature. See Preface.

Ukrainka, Lesya, pseudonym of L. Kosach (1871-1913), a leading Ukrainian writer (see Preface).

Ulyanov, V. I. See Lenin.

Union of Soviet Writers. By decree of the Central Committee of the Communist Party dated April 23, 1932, all existing literary organizations were dissolved, and a single Union of Soviet Writers formed. Thus the domination of RAPP and AVERBAKH came to an end. But the creation of a single union by the Party hardly made for greater freedom in literature; in fact, the very creation of the union (to which all professional writers have, in practice, to belong) reflected the fact that dissident elements had already been eliminated and it was now possible to enforce a uniform literary policy.

With the creation of the Union, the newly formulated doctrine of SOCIALIST REALISM could be brought forward as a uniform artistic dogma which writers were obliged to follow. At its writers' congresses and in its newspaper, *The Literary Gazette,* the Union undertook to propagate this doctrine and to insure adherence to it by its members. The strictest control available to the Union is that of expulsion, which implies the exclusion of the writer from the literary profession. Expulsion was employed in 1946 in the cases of ZOSHCHENKO and Akhmatova (see Gorenko). Undoubtedly the implicit threat of expulsion is itself adequate to prevent deviation on the part of the members.

On the other hand, the Union has had a beneficial effect in fixing favorable working conditions for Soviet writers, who are among the most highly paid persons in the Soviet Union, and in making literature a respected profession.

Uspenski, Gleb Ivanovich (1843-1902), a leading realist writer of the second half of the nineteenth century. He combined a career in journalism with writing; his unique form is the sketch of peasant life, almost ethnographic in its details, as in his collection, *Power of the Soil* (1882). Originally an adherent of the POPULISTS, Uspenski refrained from idealizing the peasantry in typically Populist spirit; in his later work he showed his disillusionment with Populism, which he regarded as inadequate in its attempt to solve the problems of peasant life through education. In the early 1890's Uspenski's personality underwent a traumatic split, and he spent the last ten years of his life in an asylum.

Uspenski's first book, *Manners of Rasteryayeva Street* (1866), is a collection of sketches of slum life in the suburbs of his native city of Tula. Crushed by toil and poverty, the people can escape their hard life only through drunkenness; for drink they will steal or pawn their last possessions. The later collection, *Power of the Soil* (1882), shows Uspenski's subsequent disillusion with Populism; he concentrates his attention on the hardships of peasant life, the greed of the well-to-do peasantry, the ignorance and vices of the peasants. Uspenski still believed in the peasant spirit and its eventual power to bring something better, but he pointed out to the Russian reading public, which scarcely knew the peasants, that they were only potentially able to rise, but in fact had not risen and had no social or economic premises for doing so.

Uspenski's style is not without humor, and his dialogue is an accurate reproduction of peasant speech. But his writing lacks organization, and is often journalistic and topical. Though he remains an important figure in the history of Russian literature, he is almost unread today.

Uspenski, Nikolay Vasilievich (1837-89), a realist and satirist of the second half of the nineteenth century, the cousin of Gleb USPENSKI. His witty sketches, published in the 1860's, describe the ignorance and backwardness of Russian peasant and provincial life, which, unlike most of the radical writers of the times, Uspenski refused to idealize. His sketches are noted for their humor and the accuracy of their use of peasant dialogue. Failing to gain popularity as a writer, he became a tramp and finally committed suicide.

V

Vagner. See Wagner.

Vakhtangov, Yevgeni. See Drama and Theater.

VAPP. See RAPP.

Vellanski, Daniil Mikhaylovich (1774-1847), a philosopher and professor of botany. He attempted to reform Russian science in the spirit of Schelling's nature philosophy and transcendental idealism. For Vellanski, empirical knowledge is inadequate; the task of science consists not in the empirical study of individual objects, but in the search for the general organic unity of nature and life.

Veltman, A. F. See Weltmann.

Venevitinov, Dmitri Vladimirovich (1805-27), a poet of the 1820's, a distant relative and friend of PUSHKIN. His premature death at the age of twenty-two robbed Russia of one of her most promising young poets. A follower of the idealist philosophy of Schelling, he was one of the leaders of the society of the so-called *lyubomudry* ("wisdom-lovers" or philosophers), founded in the 1820's. His poetic production is very small. For the most part philosophical, his poems concern such themes as friendship, love, and the role of poetry in life.

Verbitskaya, Anastasia Alexeyevna (1861-1928), a novelist of the early twentieth century. Her novels, including her five-volume *Keys to Happiness* (1909-13), were popular for their erotic themes and their emphasis on woman's right to happiness in love.

Veresayev, Vikenti. See Smidovich, V. V.

Versification. See Prosody.

Vesyoly, Artyom. See Kochkurov, N. I.

Vilenkin, Nikolay Mikhaylovich (1855-1937), a poet of the late nineteenth and early twentieth century, who wrote under the pseudonym of Minski. He began to publish in the 1870's with

idealistic "civic" poems. His idealism shows an impotence close
to that of GARSHIN and NADSON, his more popular contemporaries. In the 1880's Minski passed from civic poetry to mysticism and estheticism. He cultivated a philosophy of "meonism"
(non-being), which combined the ideas of Nietzsche with oriental
mysticism; he conceives of non-being as the Absolute, in contrast
to our world of being. One of the founders of the Religious and
Philosophical Society, along with MEREZHKOVSKI, he was thus
a precursor of the Symbolists (see Symbolism). He took part in
the 1905 REVOLUTION as a radical journalist (actually he served
as a "front" for the Bolshevik newspaper, *The New Life*). For
this he was subsequently arrested; later he left Russia and spent
the rest of his life abroad.

Virta, Nikolay Yevgenievich (1906-   ), a Soviet novelist and playwright. His first novel, *Solitude* (1935), dealt with the Antonov
peasant uprising of 1920 in Central Russia. Virta later dramatized
the story under the title of *The Land* (1937). A sequel, *Lawful-
ness* (1936), describes a new anti-Soviet movement which is shown
as springing up from the ruins of the Antonov movement. This
conspiracy is later crushed in the purges of the 1930's, and the
book is one of the first indictments of "Trotskyism" in fiction.

Virta's post-war play, *Our Daily Bread* (1947), gives a realistic
picture of collective farm life after World War II, with the
struggle to eliminate "survivals" of bourgeois attitudes among the
Soviet people. *The Conspiracy of the Condemned* (1948) is an
anti-American play depicting the machinations of American warmongers in post-war Czechoslovakia.

In spring, 1952, Virta was involved in a controversy over the
question of conflict in Soviet drama. He advocated a "conflictless" drama as the best solution for the practical difficulties which
beset Soviet playwrights, who frequently had their plays rejected
by overcautious theatrical officials. Since Marxist theoreticians
had announced that the elimination of class distinctions in the
Soviet Union had brought an end to all class contradictions,
theater managers feared to stage plays which admitted the survival of real elements of social conflict. Hence Virta advised playwrights to cultivate the "conflictless" play, in which the only
dramatic conflict would be one between the "good" and the
"better." His article was a bold piece of invective against spineless

theater directors, but its effect rebounded, and he himself came
in for the heaviest criticism. In spite of this attack on Virta, how
ever, many playwrights have continued to produce what are in
effect dramas without conflict.

Vishnevski, Vsevolod Vitalievich (1900-51), Soviet novelist and playwright. He served on the Red side in the Civil War, and his plays
are for the most part depictions of the war. The most recent of
these, *The Unforgettable 1919* (1949), is full of adulation for the
role played by Stalin. Vishnevski has also written film scenarios.

Vladimir Monomakh (died 1125), Grand Prince of Kiev, 1113-25,
renowned for his untiring efforts to make peace among the Russian princes and to unite them against the nomad Polovcians,
who were encroaching on the Russian lands from the steppes to
the southwest. Vladimir is famous as the author of a *Testament*
or *Instruction*, written for his children. It expresses a piety,
humility, devotion and standard of morality remarkable for a lay-
man of the times. It also testifies to a relatively high level of culture in Old Russia. The *Testament* is preserved in the *Laurentian
Chronicle* of 1377.

Vladimirski, Serapion. See Serapion Vladimirski.

Vogau, Boris Andreyevich (1894-1937?), a novelist and story writer
of the 1920's and 1930's, who published under the pseudonym of
Boris Pilnyak. His first important story appeared in print in 1915,
and he soon rose to the position of a leading Soviet writer. Though
he accepted the Revolution, his reasons for this attitude were
largely unorthodox, and as time went on his work brought more
and more criticism. His *The Tale of the Unextinguished Moon*
(1927), resulted in sharp official disapproval and confiscation of
the journal in which it appeared. The story dealt with the death
of the Civil War hero, General Frunze, on the operating table;
in Pilnyak's tale he is murdered by a physician who takes his
orders from a mysterious Communist leader with an appearance
obviously suggesting that of Stalin. From this time on Pilnyak's
career became increasingly difficult. His novelette, *Mahogany*,
was published in Berlin in 1929 in spite of the fact that it had
been refused publication in Russia, a misstep which brought
Pilnyak's expulsion from the All-Russian Union of Soviet Writers.
His Five-year Plan novel, *The Volga Flows into the Caspian Sea*
(1930), failed to redeem him in official eyes. In 1937 he disap-

peared, and is reliably reported to have been arrested and shot.

Pilnyak first attracted wide attention with his novel, *The Bare Year* (1922). It deals with the year 1918-19, portrayed in a series of rather fragmentary episodes. The manner of this novel is deliberately modern, with its variety of new stylistic and experimental typographical devices, deriving from the ORNAMENTALISM of Bely (see Bugayev) and REMIZOV. The descriptions are naturalistic, and human life is portrayed as degenerating during the Civil War to a purely animal level. But this elemental, primitive vigor and passion are the sources of Pilnyak's delight in the Revolution; in passion and feeling he sees the mark of the true, "Asiatic" character of the Russian people, which asserts itself in defiance of the superficial rationalism of Western ideas. Pilnyak consistently refuses to accept the orthodox Communist emphasis on reason and logic. In his view of the Revolution he is a follower of the SCYTHIANS. His later novelette, *Mahogany* (1929), suggested that its author longed for a return to the time of the Revolution as an era of frank, honest feeling morally superior to the era of the 1920's and the New Economic Policy. Pilnyak incorporated the materials of *Mahogany* into his Five-year Plan novel, *The Volga Flows into the Caspian Sea* (1930), a fantastic account of a huge hydroelectric project which never existed. His hyperbolic descriptions suggested that he regarded the whole plan as gratuitous and out of all proportion. *O.K.* (1931), his final novel, gives impressions of his visit to the United States.

Pilnyak was hardly a great writer; both his ideas and his style derive to a large extent from Bely. His work often lacks taste and restraint. His experimentalism was typical of the time of conflict in which he lived, but it has hardly remained significant for later epochs. He deserves credit, however, as one of the most independent of Soviet writers and one of the most courageous in his opposition to the official line.

Voloshin, Maximilian Alexandrovich (1877-1932), a symbolist poet. He translated from French, including Verhaeren and Paul Claudel. His poetry is highly sensual and pictorial, with a rich, opulent imagery. His most significant collections are his *Mute Demons* (1919) and *Poems of the Terror* (1924), in both of which he reflects upon the 1918 Revolution, which he interprets mystically. He abhors the Revolution, but must forgive Russia that which he believes is her destiny. Thus, in spite of personal antipathy and fear of the Revolution, he accepted it, and remained in the Soviet Union. Many of his outspoken poems on the Revolution could not be published, and after 1925 he was entirely silent.

Volynski, A. See Flexer, A. L.

Voronski, Alexander Konstantinovich (1884-1937?), a leading Marxist critic of the 1920's. He opposed attempts to create a new and distinct "proletarian" literature as lacking in spontaneity. Voronski favored a policy of moderate toleration in literature, designed to encourage intellectuals to come over to the Bolshevik side. He founded and from 1921 to 1927 edited the Soviet periodical, *Red Virgin Soil*, in which many so-called "fellow travellers" (see Trotski) published. He also supported the PEREVAL writers. His policy of moderation was temporarily victorious in the mid-1920's, but in 1927, with the emergence of RAPP, it gave way to a stricter policy of literary regimentation. Voronski was arrested and exiled to Siberia. In 1930 he was permitted to return, but in 1937 he disappeared for good.

Vyazemski, Prince Pyotr Andreyevich (1792-1878), a poet and critic of the early nineteenth century, the close friend of PUSHKIN. Though he belonged to the group of romanticist poets of the 1820's, and was their journalistic leader, his own poetry is primarily impersonal and classical. He wrote occasional verse, epigrams, madrigals and epistles, for the most part light and Epicurean in outlook. His correspondence with Pushkin includes some of the finest and wittiest of Russian letters. Vyazemski far outlived the poets who were his contemporaries; living to see the death of his own popularity, he became an embittered and isolated figure.

W

Wagner, Nikolay Petrovich (1829-1907), a zoologist and children's writer. His *Fairy Tales of Kot Murlyka* (1872) are charming idealistic fantasies which have been republished many times, and are popular with adults as well as children.

Weltmann, Alexander Fomich (1800-70), a Russian novelist and poet of the mid-nineteenth century. His writings are characterized by their whimsical humor and grotesque fantasy of invention. *The Wanderer* (1831-32) is influenced by Sterne; like Sterne, Weltmann delights in playing with the narrative, in punning, digressing and chatting with the reader. *Adventures Drawn from the Sea of Life* (1848-63) is a cycle of novels which anticipate DOSTOYEVSKI in their grotesque melodrama and tendency to obliterate the borderline between realistic and fantastic personality traits. Almost forgotten since his own day, Weltmann deserves greater popularity. He is important as a predecessor of DOSTOYEVSKI and LESKOV.

Westerners, the members of a Russian intellectual movement which took form around 1840, and which sharply opposed the official ideology of the regime of Nicholas I, as well as that of the Russian SLAVOPHILES. Though both the Westerners and the Slavophiles had roots in German idealist philosophy, and both were animated by a romanticizing, liberalist spirit, the two groups split sharply into opposing camps around 1845 over the question of Russia's relation to the West. The Westerners contended that Russia was an integral part of European civilization, though her cultural progress had been delayed by the Tartar Yoke. Her present task was to catch up with the West. She must not only assimilate European technological advances, but also the fruits of Western culture and the progressive forms of government and social organization developed by Western political thought. Some of the Westerners, such as GRANOVSKI, would have been satisfied by the introduction of limited, constitutional monarchy, but the most eloquent leaders, such as BELINSKI and HERZEN, inclined towards Utopian Socialism. Herzen's later views, however, represent a synthesis of Slavophile and Westernist ideas in the form of agrarian socialism. Under the reactionary regime of Nicholas I, the Westerners could not express their ideas openly, and their complete formulation came only with Herzen's emigration to the West.

In imaginative literature moderate Westernism was represented by TURGENEV, whose novel, *Smoke* (1867), portrays the Slavophile-Westerner controversy from the point of view of the Westerners. Other Westernist writers were DRUZHININ and the poets OGARYOV and POLONSKI. Like Slavophilism, Westernism has continued to influence Russian political thinking to the present day, and the Communist Party itself has manifested a split between the two views. Lenin and Trotski, as internationalists, showed Westernizing tendencies, while Stalinism, with its concentration on the task of building socialism in Russia and its communistic agrarian program, has been closer to Slavophilism.

Wogau. See Vogau.

Writers, Union of Soviet. See Union.

Y

Ya., P. See Yakubovich, P. F.

Yakubovich, Pyotr Filipovich (1860-1911), a revolutionary writer of the late nineteenth and early twentieth century. He belonged to the radical terrorist wing of the POPULISTS, the People's Will. He spent three years in prison and eight years in Siberia, and was later forced to publish under pseudonyms: he signed his poetry "P. Ya.," and his prose "Melshin," "Grinevich," or "Ramshev." His principal work is a remarkable collection of sketches of prison life, *In the World of Outcasts* (1895-99). His "civic" poetry, though popular with the radical youth of the turn of the century, was very weak.

Yanovsky, Yury (1902-54), a Ukrainian Soviet writer (see Preface).

Yasinski, Yeronim Yeronimovich (1850-1931), a writer of the late nineteenth and early twentieth centuries, who published under the pseudonym of Maxim Belinski. Influenced by the French naturalists, Yasinski believed in art for art's sake; he was one of the first Russian realists to treat sexual subjects freely. In 1917 he was one of the very few writers to join the Bolsheviks immediately after the October Revolution.

Yavorski, Stefan (1658-1722), a leading churchman and writer of the age of PETER THE GREAT, of Ukrainian origin. He took part in Peter's reorganization of the Russian Church, but opposed the virtually complete subordination of Church to state which Peter enforced, though his opposition was seldom open. He wrote panegyrics, including some in honor of Peter, elegies, sermons and polemic works.

Yazykov, Nikolay Mikhaylovich (1803-46), a Russian poet and contemporary of PUSHKIN. A descendent of a noble family, he attended the University of Dorpat; at the same time he began to write poetry. On leaving the university he retired to his estate to write and to collect folk songs. He became an extreme chauvinist, and in the 1840's joined the camp of the SLAVOPHILES.

Yazykov's early poetry is exuberantly Anacreontic, in praise of wine and the joy of life. Its dazzling use of language and compelling rhythms caused Pushkin to describe it by the word, "Intoxication!" The same qualities are manifest in Yazykov's poems on nature, such as his brilliant *Waterfall* (1828). His later Slavophile poetry is weak but some of his later elegies retain brilliance of language, while acquiring a human significance which his earlier poetry had lacked.

During later life Yazykov lost popularity with the younger generation because of excessive nationalism and a poverty of ideas, but his work has enjoyed a revival in our century.

Yeleonski, S. See Milovski, S. N.

Yepifanii Premudry ("the very wise"), a monk and writer of the end of the fourteenth and beginning of the fifteenth century, the author of lives of the Russian saints Stefan of Perm and Sergey of Radonezh, both of whom he had known. Yepifanii is one of the first Russian writers to follow the literary tendencies introduced under the so-called Second South Slavic Influence (see Literature). Following these new trends, he created a complex, highly rhetorical style, bristling with invented words and endless lists of synonyms.

Yershov, Pyotr Pavlovich (1815-69), a minor poet of the mid-nineteenth century. He is remembered exclusively for his popular fairy tale in verse, *The Hunchback Horse* (1834), a reworking of themes taken from a number of Russian folk tales.

Yesenin, Sergey Alexandrovich (1895-1925), a leading poet of the early twentieth century. The son of a peasant family of Ryazan Province, he came to Moscow as a youth, and there studied at a free university while he worked as a proof-reader. BLOK, Bely (see Bugayev) and KLYUYEV were his poetic teachers and models. Yesenin welcomed the 1917 Revolution, which, he believed, would bring a new and better life for the peasantry. But his hopes for the Revolution were soon disillusioned, and he began to hate Bolshevik industrialization and proletarianization of the village, which he remembered nostalgically from his boyhood as "wooden Russia." Disaffected, he joined the Moscow circle of Imaginist poets in 1919 (see Imaginism), took part in their rowdy café life and made the vogue of tavern "hooliganism" a household word in Russia. In 1922 he married the dancer Isadora Duncan and went abroad with her. Their brief marriage was a turbulent one, and scandalous reports were circulated concerning his brutal treatment of his wife. They separated the following year and he returned to Russia, where he married again, this time to a granddaughter of Lev TOLSTOY. But he could not find himself again. He suffered a mental collapse, and in December, 1925, he cut his wrists, wrote a farewell poem in his own blood, and hanged himself.

Much of Yesenin's poetry is pretentious and affected. Such are the poems in which he greets the Revolution, as well as his blasphemous anti-religious poetry. His best verse is simple and commonplace in subject, with a powerful nostalgia of feeling and an unparalleled melodiousness. The country landscape, the joys of village life, work and holidays are among his subjects. Though sentimental, his poetry succeeds because its mood is infectious and because of the musicality of his verse. With Yesenin's growing disillusionment, his joy in the country turns to sadness and anger; he does not recognize the village, so changed under the Revolution and the Soviet regime. He feels he has lost his homeland, and can no longer reconcile himself to his rowdy life in Moscow, which he describes in such poems as *Tavern Moscow* (1924) and *Confession of a Hooligan* (1924). Yesenin's "tavern" poetry, though it reflects a pose, shows remarkable honesty and even keen self-analysis. His weird narrative, *The Black Man* (1925), describes a dialogue with a man in black who enumerates his sins; in the end the black stranger turns out to be himself.

Yesenin's "hooliganism" was in vogue and much imitated in the Soviet Union during the mid-1920's, when the Revolution failed to live up to popular expectation. Because of the poet's rowdy life, his ultimate rejection of the Revolution, and his suicide, considered a "bourgeois" act, the Party found it necessary to combat his influence. He was described officially as a *kulak* (well-to-do peasant) poet, and for a long time his works were not reprinted and his very name made almost taboo. But he remained fantastically popular for his sweet, simple and touching lyrics, and there is little doubt that he is the most widely read Russian poet of the twentieth century, both in the Soviet Union and among the émigrés.

Yushkevich, Semyon Solomonovich (1868-1927), an early twentieth-century writer. Born in a Jewish family of Odessa, he depicted the life of the Jewish middle class in the cities and contrasted it to the pathetic poverty of the poorer Jews. He emigrated in 1917.

Z

Zadonshchina, a Russian prose poem, probably from the early fifteenth century, describing the defeat of the Tartars by the Russians, led by Prince Dmitri Donskoy, in 1380. The title of the work refers to the scene of the battle, fought on Kulikovo Plain south of the upper Don. The work was written by a priest of Ryazan named Sofonii.

The *Zadonshchina* employs many phrases and poetic devices taken from the *IGOR TALE*, as well as a large part of that work's narrative plan. Although this borrowing is for the most part organic, and the *Zadonshchina* is on a high artistic level, it is fair to say that it is a derivative work. The fact that both works describe campaigns against Eastern nomads helps to account for Sofonii's use of *Igor* as a model. The *Zadonshchina* is an answer to the prophetic gloom of *Igor;* it shows the Russian people again in the ascendancy over the pagan nomads.

Sceptics of the authenticity of the *Igor Tale,* such as André Mazon, have supposed that the *Zadonshchina* is actually the original work, and that *Igor* is an imitation. But it seems clear that certain motifs common to both are more in place in *Igor,* and therefore original in it.

Zagoskin, Mikhail Nikolayevich (1789-1852), a Russian historical novelist and writer of comedies. His *Yuri Miloslavski* (1829), a historical novel in the manner of Scott, deals with the end of the Polish occupation of Moscow in 1612. The novel is crude and unhistorical, but full of action and patriotic feeling. It was tremendously popular, and helped to create a vogue for the historical novel in Russia.

Zaitsev. See Zaytsev.

Zamyatin, Yevgeni Ivanovich (1884-1937), a novelist and story writer of the twentieth century. In his youth he belonged to the

Social Democratic (Marxist) Party, and was arrested and sent into exile for a time, but was later pardoned. By profession he was a naval engineer, and in this capacity he was sent to England during the First World War. His tale, *The Islanders* (1922), is a satire on the British cult of respectability. He had already published his first story in 1908, but only after the 1917 Revolution, when he returned to Russia, did he become an important writer. He helped to inspire and train the SERAPION BROTHERS, a movement formed among younger writers of the early 1920's who opposed Communist regimentation and were seeking to create a literature of greater variety and independence. Though he had formerly been a Social Democrat himself, Zamyatin now opposed the Bolsheviks and declared that true writers are "madmen, hermits, heretics, dreamers, rebels or sceptics, not . . . government officials." In his novel *We* (1924) a leading character states his belief in eternal non-conformism and "infinite" revolution. This novel is a criticism of totalitarianism, and obviously hits at the Soviet regime. Although Zamyatin never attempted to publish *We* in the Soviet Union, he did allow it to appear abroad in French, English and Czech translations. The appearance of an unauthorized Russian version in Prague brought his censure by the Soviet Writers' Union, and severe denunciation in the Soviet press. In 1931 he was suddenly allowed to leave the Soviet Union, evidently because Gorki had interceded for him. He settled in France, continuing to write until his death.

Zamyatin's fiction is influenced by GOGOL, LESKOV and REMIZOV in its fantasy and great variety of stylistic effects. In manner it is highly ornate, a leading example of the stylistic ORNAMENTALISM so popular early in the 1920's. The subjects are grotesque pictures of life which are almost tangential to reality, but still express much of the pathos and horror of life under the Soviet regime. His stories of the Revolution, such as *A Tale about What Is Most Important* (1923) and *X* (1927), are constructed on a complex range of artistic levels, with much toying with the plot on the part of the author. This interference suggests the artificiality and futility of the Revolution itself. *X* is a marvellously funny tale about a church deacon turned Bolshevik who becomes infatuated with a woman named Martha, and for her deserts the gospel of Marxism for that of "Marthism." *The*

Fires of St. Dominic (1923) uses the background of the Spanish Inquisition to suggest the Soviet Cheka, the secret police, and its terror.

Zamyatin's novel *We* (1924) is his most significant work from an ideological point of view, though it is by no means so successful artistically as many of his shorter tales. It describes a regimented, collectivist state of the twenty-sixth century, obviously intended to suggest the Soviet regime, with its goal of a technocratic social order. Individualism has almost completely disappeared in this "Utopia." The citizens have no names, but are known only by number. Love has been eliminated, and even sexual activities are restricted to prescribed occasions by a system of pink ration tickets. Otherwise the citizens, or "numbers," as they are called, have lost all privacy, and even live in transparent dwellings. But the tendency to individualism has not been uprooted completely; two citizens commit the crime of falling in love and conspire to lead a revolution. Their revolt is thwarted, however, and the state moves to prevent further revolutions by extirpating the last root of unhappiness, the faculty of imagination, which the citizens lose by submitting to a simple X-ray operation. Zamyatin's *We* possibly influenced Aldous Huxley's *Brave New World,* and quite certainly George Orwell's *1984.*

In emigration Zamyatin published the first part of a novel about Attila, called *The Whip of God,* a subject which clearly alluded to the Soviet Revolution.

Zaretski, Mikhas (1901-?), a leading Belo-Russian writer (see Preface).

Zasodimski, Pavel Vladimirovich (1843-1912), a radical novelist of the late nineteenth century and adherent of the POPULISTS. His tales and novels, many of which were published under the collective title of *Tales from the Life of the Poor,* give an idealized and sentimental picture of the peasantry and depict their exploitation by other classes.

Zaumny yazyk. See Futurism; Khlebnikov; Kruchonykh.

Zaytsev, Boris Konstantinovich (1881-   ), a novelist and story writer of the twentieth century. He left Russia in 1922 and has since been one of the leading writers of the emigration.

Zaytsev's early stories and novels are in the tradition of TURGENEV's novels of manor life, and he has even published a study of Turgenev (1932). His work shows a nostalgic, idealized mood, lyrical atmosphere and delicate sensitivity of manner. Extreme subjectivism characterizes his style, particularly of his stories. His novel, *The Golden Pattern* (1925), portrays the fate of a family of intelligentsia, who, with their distaste for work, become "superfluous." *Anna* (1929) is a tragic love story of the time of the 1917 Revolution, while *The House in Passy* (1935) portrays the life of Russian émigrés in Paris. *Gleb's Journey* (1935) is an autobiographical account of Zaytsev's boyhood on the estate.

Zemstvos. See Reforms.

Zhdanov, Andrey Alexandrovich (1896-1948), Soviet political leader. A secretary of the Central Committee of the Communist Party, he led the post-war purge of the Soviet cultural world which virtually paralyzed Soviet literature from 1946 to 1953. In a resolution passed by the Central Committee in August, 1946, Zhdanov demanded the purge of the Leningrad journals *Zvezda* and *Leningrad,* together with the exclusion of the writers ZOSHCHENKO and Akhmatova (see Gorenko) from the UNION OF SOVIET WRITERS, demands to which the Union promptly acceded. The significance of Zhdanov's purge went far beyond its immediate targets, however; in effect it laid down a new policy in Soviet literature which was as narrow and restrictive as any followed at any time during the Soviet regime. Zoshchenko and Akhmatova were presumably little more than examples designed to give Zhdanov's words their desired weight.

In the resolution Zhdanov demanded that Soviet writers stop imitating, even venerating the West. Thus he announced that policy of narrow, self-satisfied insularity which has so distorted Soviet thought since the Second World War. He also demanded that Soviet writers adhere to the principle of PARTIYNOST, or "party spirit," in their work, that is, that they follow closely the line in literature as laid down for them by the Party.

Zhdanov's resolution began an anti-Western campaign in all fields of Soviet thought and culture. Along with literature and art, philosophy and the biological sciences were hard hit. Literary scholars were bitterly attacked for calling attention to foreign influences in the work of such Russian writers as Pushkin or Lermontov. The effectiveness of these attacks may be judged by the fact that they were almost inevitably followed by public "confessions" of guilt on the part of those attacked.

The death of Zhdanov in 1948 did nothing to mitigate the rigor of the new spirit, and only with the death of STALIN in 1953 was it possible to see a certain relaxation following the "Zhdanov era."

Zhemchuzhnikov, Alexey Mikhaylovich (1821-1908), a minor Russian poet of the mid-nineteenth century. Together with his two brothers and his cousin, A. K. TOLSTOY, Zhemchuzhnikov wrote nonsense poetry and other humorous works, which the group published under the collective pseudonym of KOZMA PRUTKOV. In his later poetry Zhemchuzhnikov concentrated more on social and civic themes, treated from a liberal point of view. He sharply criticized the generation of the 1880's for its abandonment of the reform spirit.

Zhukovski, Vasili Andreyevich (1783-1852), a leading pre-romantic poet and translator of the early nineteenth century. The natural son of a nobleman of the Bunin family, Zhukovski was educated in Moscow, where he came under the influence of Masonic circles and the literary movement of SENTIMENTALISM. He entered literature in 1797, and in 1802 published his famous translation of Gray's *Elegy,* a work which became at least as significant in Russian poetry as it had been in English. He served in the militia during the Napoleonic Invasion of 1812. In 1818 he was made tutor to the son of Nicholas I, the future Alexander II, on whom he had a liberal and humanizing influence. Respected by the court, Zhukovski often interceded to save young liberal writers, such as PUSHKIN, from official persecution. In 1841 he retired from court life, settling in Germany, where he was on friendly terms with such prominent writers as Goethe and Tieck. His last years were marked by strong mystical and quietist leanings.

Though Zhukovski was primarily a translator, he is a major Russian writer and, after PUSHKIN, the most important poet of the early nineteenth century, the "Golden Age" of Russian poetry. His translations from German and English poetry introduced the new current of PRE-ROMANTICISM to Russia. Many of them are actually superior to their originals. The poets whom he translated were for the most part his contemporaries, and include Gray, James Thomson, Southey, Scott, Moore, Byron, Uhland, Bürger,

Schiller and Goethe. His two adaptations of Bürger's *Lenore*, called *Lyudmila* (1808) and *Svetlana* (1812), created a vogue for the melodramatic ballad of the supernatural in Russia. His early translations show a preference for gloomy subjects and scenes, for "graveyard" themes, the supernatural, the medieval, and the whole panoply of the romantic ballad and the Gothic novel. But he also translated poetry of a more intimate, meditative and contemplative character, sweetly melancholy and resigned.

Zhukovski's original production is slim in extent, but on a par with his translations, and in the same mood. It is highly personal and subjective. Among his poems there are a number of stylized imitations of folk songs and folk ballads.

Zhukovski's poetic style is serene and eminently musical. Following the stylistic reforms of KARAMZIN, he created the vocabulary of Russian romantic poetry, elegant, refined, yet expressive and natural. His subject matter, style and diction were of major influence on the whole generation of poets who followed him, including PUSHKIN. Also influential was his choice of meters and genres, and he introduced blank verse (unrhymed iambic pentameter) into Russian poetry.

Until the 1820's Zhukovski was the acknowledged leader of Russian poetry; with the rise of PUSHKIN and the poets of the so-called "PUSHKIN PLEIAD," his reputation faded, and he lived to see himself forgotten even by his romanticist followers. At the same time his own style and tastes changed. His poetry became less soft and mellifluous, more severe and classical in manner. In his later period he made translations of the *Odyssey* (1848-49), in hexameters, and of the Persian epic *Rustem and Sohrab* (1848). Though made from German versions, they are both of high quality.

Zilberg, Veniamin Alexandrovich (1902-   ), a Soviet novelist who publishes under the pseudonym of Veniamin Kaverin. He studied Oriental languages and literature at the University of Petrograd. He began writing very early, and first published in 1921; the same year he joined the group of young writers known as the SERAPION BROTHERS.

Kaverin's novels and stories of the 1920's show the strong influence of the theories of Viktor SHKLOVSKI and the Formalists (see Criticism). Kaverin delights particularly in the Sterneian device of toying with the narrative in an arbitrary manner, so favored by Shklovski. His early work also shows a preference for subjects of fantasy and adventure, with little interest in social or political problems of the day. Such is his tale, *The End of a Gang* (1926), a picture of the Leningrad underground during the period of the New Economic Policy. His novel, *The Ruffian, or Evenings on Vasili Island* (1928), portrays the literary world in Leningrad and parodies the polemics carried on by Shklovski and the Formalists.

Perhaps Kaverin's most original novel is his *Artist Unknown* (1931; English translations as "The Unknown Artist"). It upholds the dignity of the individual and his sense of ethical responsibility as essential social values which threaten to disappear with the development of Soviet collectivist society. The hero of the novel, an individualistic painter named Arkhimedov, loses everything in life, but leaves a great picture, a masterpiece, though it survives only as an anonymous work.

In the 1930's Kaverin gave up much of the originality of his former manner and, in conformity with the new doctrine of SOCIALIST REALISM, went over to a more conservative psychological realism. His long novel, *The Fulfillment of Desires* (1934-35; English translation as "The Larger View"), deals with the theme of the intellectual's adjustment to Soviet society. *Two Captains* (1940-45) is a novel primarily for children, about the adventures of a boy who later becomes a famous explorer.

Zlatovratski, Nikolay Nikolayevich (1845-1911), a radical novelist of the late nineteenth century and adherent of the POPULISTS. His novels idealize and sentimentalize the peasantry as the future hope of Russia. His chief novel, *The Foundations* (1878-83), depicts the struggle between the democratic commune and the *Kulaks,* or well-to-do peasants. Important are his memoirs of the reform epoch of the 1860's, entitled *How It Happened* (1911).

Zoshchenko, Mikhail Mikhaylovich (1895-   ), a Soviet humorist and satirist, one of the leading Soviet writers. Of aristocratic descent, he came from the Ukraine. He studied law at the University of Petersburg, but did not graduate. During the World War he served as an officer in the Russian army, and in 1918 volunteered for service with the Reds. After the Civil War he joined the newly founded group of SERAPION BROTHERS in 1921, and the same year began to publish.

Zoshchenko's first stories concern the World War and the Civil War, and his earliest style was the prevailing ornamentalist manner of the early 1920's (see Ornamentalism). Gradually he began to combine his ornamental style, which became more and more slangy in manner, with comic and satirical subjects. By the mid-1920's he had achieved a unique and perfect story form, in which the narrative is told in a curious, disjointed fashion by a badly educated, "new" Soviet citizen; the vulgarity of his thoughts, dreams and desires fully accords with the vulgarity of the speech, sometimes sub-standard, sometimes ridiculously hyper-correct, which the author puts in his mouth. As a humorist Zoshchenko was strongly influenced by GOGOL and, as with his great predecessor, a favorite subject of his is the banal, petty and philistine in life. Other influences on his work include LESKOV and CHEKHOV. Zoshchenko's satire continually deals, on a highly specific level, with the conflicts in Soviet life between the ideal and the real, in which, in spite of all hopes and promises, reforms remain purely theoretical and the level of human existence is hardly raised. The hero of these tales may be a member of the theoretically defunct, but in fact vigorously surviving middle class, or he may be a petty official, with a bourgeois craving for creature comforts, social prestige and quick promotion. Sometimes the target is a Party member himself, with all the cultural traits of the parvenu, often with the same "bourgeois" longing for personal preferment and self-satisfied comfort.

The large number of humorous sketches and tales which Zoshchenko published in the 1920's include the collections called *Tales* (1923), *Esteemed Citizens* (1926; a second volume was published in 1940), *What the Nightingale Sang* (1927), *Nervous People* (1927), and a collection of *feuilletons*, *Trifles of Life* (1927). Extremely popular with the reading public (during the 1920's Zoshchenko was perhaps the most widely read of all Soviet writers), these and other collections went through countless editions. The every-day character, even frequent vulgarity of Zoshchenko's subjects, along with his hilarious humor endeared him to many readers who otherwise were strangers to good literature. On the other hand, his satire can be serious and even profound when it takes as its target the smugness of the new order. Zoshchenko clearly implies that the Soviet system has failed to create a new culture of its own which is anything more than a caricature. Though none of his stories is a direct attack on the Soviet system as such, the total of his work seems to constitute a powerful indictment of the narrow-mindedness, insularity and vulgarity of Soviet life and the Communist ideal. Certainly Zoshchenko has been critical of specific Soviet weaknesses: the housing shortage, for example, or the largely theoretical character of many "reforms," such as the drive to liquidate illiteracy. His treatment of everyday problems makes him one of the best Soviet writers—as well as one of the most enjoyable—to read for an actual picture of the character of Soviet life.

For a time Zoshchenko's satire could be tolerated by the Communist Party, which itself opposed the survival of the bourgeois mentality criticized by him. But by the 1930's the Party line in literature had become much stricter, and the official attitude was one of relative self-satisfaction with Soviet progress; satire was no longer welcome. Zoshchenko's manner gradually became paler and less biting. First, however, he succeeded in publishing a novel called *Restored Youth* (1933), the story of an aged professor who succeeds in reviving his lost youth. He marries a young girl who soon deserts him; the shock paralyzes him, and in the end he is forced to give up his pursuit of the girl. Zoshchenko employs a great deal of pseudo-scientific talk about biological problems which was actually taken seriously by Soviet critics as an attempt to unite science and literature! One suspects that Zoshchenko was ridiculing the Soviet emphasis on science and technology as means for the complete transformation of life.

In *Before Sunrise* (1943), Zoshchenko sought to break away from the stultifying tendentiousness which Soviet critics were attempting to force upon him. The tale deals with his own life and failure to find personal happiness. Such a theme was considered anti-social and even "amoral," and a storm of criticism broke immediately after the appearance of the first two serial installments. The magazine then discontinued the tale.

Finally, in 1946, came Zoshchenko's complete fall from grace, and his expulsion from the Union of Soviet Writers, demanded by Andrey ZHDANOV, a secretary of the Central Committee of the Communist Party. The apparent cause for Zoshchenko's expulsion was the story, *Adventures of a Monkey* (1946), a not very original

tale poking fun at the artificialities of human life as seen by comparison with the natural existence of a monkey. Coming at the
end of the war, the story may have offended the sensibilities of
some Soviet readers, though there is no evidence that the author
intended his satire to apply to Soviet citizens alone. More likely
the Party required a scapegoat to dramatize its new, more rigid
line, and Zoshchenko, along with Akhmatova (see Gorenko), was
chosen to fill the part because of his whole career of non-conformism.

Zoshchenko's expulsion from the Writers' Union meant the possibility of a total end to his literary career. By 1950 he had again
begun to publish, however, and produced several short pieces of
satirical journalism on officially approved themes. At the present
writing it is very doubtful whether he will ever achieve anything
like his former independence or importance.